Robert Schumann
AND THE Piano Concerto

Robert Schumann

AND THE Piano Concerto

Claudia Macdonald

Routledge
Taylor & Francis Group

NEW YORK AND LONDON

Published in 2005 by
Routledge
Taylor & Francis Group
270 Madison Avenue
New York, NY 10016

Published in Great Britain by
Routledge
Taylor & Francis Group
2 Park Square
Milton Park, Abingdon
Oxon OX14 4RN

Printed in the United States of America on acid-free paper
10 9 8 7 6 5 4 3 2 1

International Standard Book Number-10: 0-415-97247-7 (Hardcover)
International Standard Book Number-13: 978-0-415-97247-5 (Hardcover)
Library of Congress Card Number 2005013606

Library of Congress Cataloging-in-Publication Data

Macdonald, Claudia.
  Robert Schumann and the piano concerto / Claudia Macdonald.
      p. cm.
  Includes bibliographical references and index.
  ISBN 0-415-97247-7 (hardback : alk. paper)
  1. Schumann, Robert, 1810-1856--Criticism and interpretation. 2. Concerto. 3. Piano music--History and criticism. I. Title.

ML410.S4M19 2005
784.2'62'092--dc22   2005013606

Taylor & Francis Group
is the Academic Division of T&F Informa plc.

Visit the Taylor & Francis Web site at
http://www.taylorandfrancis.com

and the Routledge Web site at
http://www.routledge-ny.com

Ivánnak

Contents

Acknowledgments ix

Introduction xi

1 Amateur and Virtuoso Musician 1

2 The Virtuoso Concerto 13

3 First Concerto Expositions and Their Models 37

4 First Romantic Piece 51

5 Beethoven and Mozart Reception 73

6 Critical Observer: The Old Form I 91

7 Critical Observer: The Old Form II 111

8 Critical Observer: New Forms I 135

9 Critical Observer: New Forms II 169

10 *Concertsatz* in D Minor 197

11 *Phantasie* 223

12 *Concertstücke* 247

13 Team Programs 273

Epilogue 297

Notes 307

Works Cited 335

Index 345

Acknowledgments

I am presenting to the patient reader the culmination of twenty years' work to which many colleagues and friends have contributed: Philip Gossett, who, as my dissertation advisor, helped launch and support the project in its earliest stages; Robert L. Marshall, who held my hand through all its stages; Jon W. Finson and Nancy Reich, whose belief in the worth of my endeavors was unfailing; Russell Stinson, who read and kindly commented on Chapter 10; and John Daverio, whose buoyant response to every one of my enterprises is sadly missed.

Many German institutions graciously accommodated me on numerous visits: the Heinrich-Heine-Institut Düsseldorf; Robert-Schumann-Forschungsstelle Düsseldorf; Universitäts- und Landesbibliothek Bonn; Staatsbibliothek zu Berlin—Preußischer Kulturbesitz, Musikabteilung mit Mendelssohn-Archiv; Robert-Schumann-Haus Zwickau; and in Austria, the Gesellschaft der Musikfreunde Vienna. The Universitäts- und Landesbibliothek Bonn kindly granted me permission to reproduce transcriptions of portions of the Schumann music manuscript materials in their collection. Ute Bär, Gerd Nauhaus, Martin Schoppe, Bernhard R. Appel, and Matthias Wendt were always attentive hosts for whom I have much affection. At home I worked at the Boston Public Library; Harvard University Library; Brown University Library; New York Public Library; Library of Congress; University of Chicago Library; and Newberry Library. During his time as Conservatory Librarian at Oberlin College, Daniel Zager made major acquisitions to support my work; the present staff, including Deborah Campana and Kathleen Abromeit, has been equally responsive to my needs.

Many foundations for many years generously underwrote my work: the National Endowment for the Humanities; American Philosophical Society; Deutscher Akademischer Austauschdienst; American Council of Learned Societies; International Research and Exchanges Board; American Association of University Women; Fulbright Commission; and, through a Research Status Appointment, Grants-in-Aid, and Powers Travel Grants, Oberlin College. David Stull, Dean of the Oberlin College Conservatory of Music, also offered generous support.

Richard Carlin's faith in my output, his sensibleness, and blessed good cheer have been constant since our initial discussions. The patience, meticulous work, and kindness of Robert Sims and Laura Lawrie reassured me through the final stages of production. Assistance from the Manfred Bukofzer Publication Endowment Fund of the American Musicological Society defrayed the cost of the musical examples.

For long stretches friends in Germany warmly took me into their families: Karin and Hans-Rudolf Ebel, Heide Seyfarth, whom I will always remember, Ingrid and Winfried Seyfarth, Ulrike Seyfarth, Ruth and Alfred Kunt. At home, my family—Martha, Don, Jacob, and Gwendolyn Kudela, James Stapleton, Leah and Christopher Twymon—has cherished me as an author and a mother. My husband, Ivan Waldbauer, to whom this book is dedicated, read and improved it repeatedly.

Thank you. Whatever faults remain are my own entirely.

Introduction

The purpose of this study is twofold: to follow Robert Schumann's development as a composer of works for piano and orchestra and to trace the history of the genre from about 1810 to the mid-1850s as seen through his eyes. Between 1830 and 1853, a span that covers his entire career as a composer, Schumann composed five works for piano and orchestra, or rather six, if the *Phantasie* that was reworked to become the first movement of the Concerto in A Minor, Op. 54 is counted separately. His ideas about the concerto are richly documented. From 1836 to 1843 he addressed the subject in a series of critical essays. These are complemented by a plethora of observations in his letters and diaries.

The first part of the study, Chapters 1 through 4, centers on a group of concertos dating from about 1810 to 1830. It begins with an account of Schumann's personal development in the small-town environment where he took his place as a musical amateur and developed his aspiration to become a professional pianist. His ambition was bolstered by public performances of florid concertos by Johann Nepomuk Hummel and Friedrich Kalkbrenner, works whose style differs markedly from the accompanied lieder, piano four-hand duets, and chamber pieces with piano that he played in the homes of friends. Already his youthful Concerto in F major from 1830 to 1831 shows a degree of reconciliation between the two styles. It grafts his own newer, romantic leanings onto a bravura concerto of the type composed by the generation of composers active during his youth, including two whose works served as immediate models, Hummel and Henri Herz. Chapter 4 will show that such reconciliation is not unique to Schumann; it also is apparent in the two piano concertos of Chopin from 1829 to 1830 and 1830.

The second and largest part of the study, Chapters 5 through 11, is devoted primarily to Schumann's reviews of concertos, both from score and as he heard them in performance during the 1830s in Leipzig. By 1832, when it became clear to him that an injury to his finger would not heal, Schumann gave up his ambition to become a professional pianist. In 1834 he founded and for the next ten years edited the *Neue Zeitschrift für Musik,* a journal addressed to an elite readership of music professionals and educated amateurs. Its purpose was to serve as an arbiter of musical taste generally and, specifically, to support new music by the youngest generation of composers. To this end Schumann reviewed hundreds of newly published works, including some thirty recent piano concertos by Hummel, Kalkbrenner, Ferdinand Ries, John Field, Herz, Sigismund Thalberg, Ignaz Moscheles, Felix Mendelssohn, Sterndale Bennett, Clara Wieck, and many lesser lights. His criticisms show him still seeing merit in concertos that cling to an older style but also approving more modern experiments in form. The latter aroused his interest, but sympathy for the older style, stimulated by a newly acquired knowledge of Beethoven's concertos, led him to suggest a type of piece that would accommodate characteristics of both practices. This was, once again, a conscious effort to reconcile the public function of his concerted pieces with his own affinity for the more intimate style of piano works he composed throughout the 1830s.

No doubt Schumann believed this reconciliation of styles would appeal to an audience of musically educated amateurs, an audience congruent with the readership of his journal. It is evident in two of his own productions: an unfinished but nearly completed *Concertsatz* in D minor from 1839, and the *Phantasie* of 1841 that was later revised to become the first movement of the A Minor Concerto. Both works eschew virtuosic display. Both also reflect his affinity for the amateur musical culture around him, with its emphasis on home performance. The *Concertsatz* is rooted in his exposure to Bach's instrumental works and the special niche they occupied in this climate. Both it and the *Phantasie* take their cue from the very experiments Schumann observed in the genre during the 1830s, involving above all connected movements and thematic transformation across movements. Today these ideas are best known from Liszt's two concertos, which, although not published until 1857 and 1863, have sketches dating to the 1830s. Unlike Schumann's works, Liszt's concertos reflect their composer's years as a traveling performer playing before large and diverse audiences.

A final part of the study, Chapters 12, 13, and an epilogue, begins with Schumann's essay from 1843 about a group of one-movement works for piano and orchestra. Mostly he is impatient with the state of the genre. His own concerted compositions from 1845 on, the first he saw publicly performed and published, make clear his interest in a new direction: the complete A Minor Concerto, including a revised first movement and newly composed middle and final movements (1845); the *Introduction und Allegro appassionato,* Op. 92 (1849); and the *Introduction und Allegro,* Op. 134 (1853). They are realizations of ideas he developed during the 1830s, but also reflections of performance opportunities available to the pianist for whom they were composed, his wife, Clara Schumann. The A Minor Concerto became a staple of her repertory, and is still a standard today. If the other two pieces, each a one-movement work, have not fared as well, it is not because they have lesser intrinsic worth, but because they derive from conditions peculiar to musical programming of an earlier time. Yet, despite their common practical origins, the two works are contrasting in nature. Op. 92 is symphonic. In this sense it can be compared to two other concerted works by Schumann, the *Concertstück* for Four Horns, Op. 86 (1849), and Cello Concerto, Op. 129 (1850). Op. 134, like the *Phantasie* for Violin and Orchestra, Op. 131, which also was composed in 1853, is more virtuosic. At the same time, it eschews the notion, still with us today, that a concerto offers little more than entertainment. It is, in its aesthetic if not in its style or form, a direct ancestor of Brahms's First Piano Concerto (1854–58).

1

Amateur and Virtuoso Musician

The story of Robert Schumann and the piano concerto must begin very early in his life, with his growing up as a young, middle-class gentleman in a very small Saxon town. The effects of these two facts on his musical development are well known. The first explains the depth of his attachment to music cultivated by an educated class of connoisseurs; the second, the necessity of that attachment, for there was no one in the town of Zwickau (population c. 5,000) to prepare this young man of prodigious talent and impressive ability for a professional career. What has been less explored is Schumann's engagement with music intended for a wider public, his embracing of a virtuosic repertory on those occasions when he set himself apart from his fellow amateurs by venturing onto a larger stage.

This chapter will show precisely what pieces Schumann played with his fellow amateurs and what ones he chose for the public arena. The divide between the two repertories is profound, especially from a modern point of view. With his friends he played works by Haydn, Mozart, Beethoven, Weber, Schubert, and various lesser lights; for public performances he chose pieces by the current reigning virtuosos, Ignaz Moscheles, Friedrich Kalkbrenner, and Johann Nepomuk Hummel. Whereas he knew symphonies, chamber pieces, and piano works by Beethoven and Mozart, as this chapter will make abundantly clear, he did not know their piano concertos, which by the 1820s were considered old-fashioned.

Naturally, the repertory Schumann knew impacted what he composed. His earliest pieces, written to share with his friends, were modeled on works they played together, most conspicuously by Schubert.[1] After successful appearances before a large public in Zwickau and Heidelberg led him to decide on the career of a piano virtuoso, Moscheles, Kalkbrenner, and Hummel became his models. The influence of these virtuosos on Schumann's early Concerto in F Major is straightforward, and will be the subject of chapters three and four. Subsequent chapters will show that the influence continued, affecting his reception of concertos by Mozart and Beethoven as these became again widely disseminated in the 1830s; his reviews of concertos during the same decade; and his compositions for solo and orchestra of the 1840s and beyond. Although the reviews and compositions also reflect Schumann's allegiance to his roots as a gentleman lover of music, their template for the concerto derives from fashionable works of the day.

This returns us to the indelible stamp that growing up in Zwickau left on Schumann. In the first place, it meant he did not decide to turn to music as a profession until he was twenty, unusually late for a career choice of this nature. This does not mean he lagged in skills: the repertory he played attests amply to his ability, as do his accomplishments as a sightreader.[2] However, until he left Zwickau for Leipzig, the music he knew was not determined by any systematic educational program, by any group invested in special pleading for music of the past, nor by the cosmopolitan cross-currents of a large city. More than anything else the music Schumann knew, both in Zwickau and later during his first year in Leipzig and stay in Heidelberg, exemplifies the day-to-day environment of home music-making. Especially as regards the concertos that are the subject of this study, it typifies the flood of selections that were written for immediate performance rather than for all time to come.

* * *

Schumann was born in Zwickau, Saxony, on 8 June 1810, the youngest of five surviving children. Neither of his parents were trained musicians, nor did any of his siblings share his early passion for music. But his mother, Johanne Christiane, knew many songs and sang with him; his "constant singing [*vieles Singen*]" first made her and his father, Friedrich August, aware of his talent.[3] At the age of seven, the child was taken to Baccalaureus Johann Gottfried Kuntsch for private instruction on the piano. Kuntsch was organist at the *Marienkirche,* the city church where Schumann may later have sung under the direction of the cantor Karl Christian Siebeck in a choir drawn from students at the Zwickau *Lyceum.*[4] Kuntsch also organized occasional municipal concerts for the presentation of works such as Hadyn's *Creation.* By 1821, his young pupil had advanced enough to play the keyboard (probably reinforcing the instrumental parts) to accompany a performance of Friedrich Schneider's popular oratorio *Das Weltgericht* (1819) at the *Marienkirche.*[5]

In 1821 Schumann also made his first appearance, as partner in a four-hand variation set in G major by Ignaz Joseph [?] Pleyel, on one of the evening recitals at the *Gymnasium.* These were long programs that alternated musical numbers, including orchestra, chamber and solo pieces, choruses, vocal quartets and operatic selections, and recitations. Often he accompanied the choral numbers on the *Gymnasium* programs, and from 1822 to 1828 he played a string of solos calculated to show off his considerable technique to a broad public: variation sets; Carl Maria von Weber's rondo, *Aufforderung zum Tanz;* and, for his last appearance on 25 January 1828, a concerto by Friedrich Kalkbrenner in D minor.[6] Only August Vollaert played piano works of comparable difficulty on these programs.[7] Six years older than Robert and a boarder at the Schumann house from 1818 until about 1823, his accomplishments may have been a first example for the young boy who writes of the joy of performing.[8]

Other opportunities for public performances may have come with the *Gymnasium* recitals. Schumann's friend Friedrich August Piltzing recalls hearing Moscheles, Variations on *La Marche d'Alexandre* with accompaniment; Henri Herz, Variations, Op. 20; and the music to Bernhard Anselm Weber's melodrama *Gang nach dem Eisenhammer.* There also may have been a performance of the Kalkbrenner Concerto in Schneeberg.[9] But the public arena was not the only venue for Schumann's performances. At the heart of his musical activities in Zwickau was instead his daily participation in the private music-making of his school friends and other amateurs. Two homes, although by no means the only ones where Schumann's music was welcomed and even expected, were centers for this private music-making, Postmaster Johann Georg Schlegel's (an amateur pianist), and the merchant Karl Erdmann Carus's (an amateur violinist). In November 1823 Schumann was present at two quartet evenings at Schlegel's. For the second he took the piano part in Mozart's Piano Quartet in E-flat, K. 493, the strings being played by a mixture of amateurs and professionals including Carus, Karl Gottlob Meißner, the city music director (who taught Schumann flute and cello), and Siebeck.[10] Other works heard on these two occasions were by Rothe (recte Pierre Rode?) and Prince Louis Ferdinand.[11]

At Carus's house, Schumann heard quartets by Haydn and Beethoven.[12] He also accompanied the amateur singer Agnes Carus, Karl Erdmann's sister-in-law, in songs by Gottlob Wiedebein and Louis Spohr,[13] and may have performed with her or in her presence the piano reduction of B. A. Weber's melodrama *Der Gang nach dem Eisenhammer.*[14] Finally, Schumann had various partners for four-hand playing, including Susette Liebenau, wife of the commander of the infantry regiment garrisoned at Zwickau, Oberst Friedrich Christian von Liebenau, and Piltzing, son of the regimental oboist and a fellow piano student. With Frau Liebenau, Schumann played Beethoven's *Eroica* Symphony.[15] Piltzing reports playing four-hand arrangements of Haydn, Mozart, and Beethoven overtures and symphonies, and original works by Hummel, Weber, and Czerny.[16]

Often Schumann played what he later called thrilling improvisations for his hosts, or regaled them with a flashy solo piece.[17] In this way, an aspect of the works he played for the large and musically less knowledgeable public in attendance at the *Gymnasium* concerts, and at times the very works themselves, found their way into the same performance venue as the songs, chamber pieces, and piano duets shared by a more intimate and musically sophisticated circle. For the concertos, this meant a reduction to their solo parts alone. During the round of visits he made to his Zwickau friends at Christmastime 1828 Schumann played, on 22 December, a rondo by Charles Mayer at the home of his sister-in-law Emilie (the wife of his brother

Julius); concertos by Hummel (in A minor) and Kalkbrenner (the D Minor) at Schlegel's; Weber's *Aufforderung zum Tanz,* a toccata, nocturne, and variations by Mayer, Schubert waltzes, variations by Czerny, and his own improvisations at the home of Superintendent Gottlieb Lorenz (Emilie Schumann's father), whose new grand piano had just arrived.[18] The next day he was again at Schlegel's and played again the Mayer Rondo and Nocturne, the last movement of Kalkbrenner's Concerto, and a *Fantasie* on themes from Mozart's *Le nozze di Figaro,* Op. 77, by Ries.[19] Some of these are the same pieces he played on the *Gymnasium* programs (the Weber and Kalkbrenner), and others (the Ries and Hummel, at least) are their equal in technical difficulty and flashy display.

In his own home Schumann played after dinner every night for his father, then with some school friends he began to try more ambitious programs.[20] The first effort was a performance of Vincenzo Righini's Overture to *Tigrane* with Schumann filling in for any missing instruments and directing at the piano. In 1822 he set the 150th Psalm specially for his ensemble (at the piano he had to play only the bass), and began but did not complete a couple or more overtures, apparently also for his ensemble to play.[21] By 1823 he had expanded the programs to include several choral and instrumental numbers. On 7 December, the group performed (with Schumann's friend Carl Praetorius sharing the direction), in order:

> Ernst Eichner, *Sinfonie*
> Haydn, "Die Himmel erzählen die Ehre Gottes und seiner Hände" (chorus
>   and fugue from *The Creation*)
> Weber, Variations for Piano and Clarinet, Op. 33
> Conradin Kreutzer, vocal trio
> Ludwig Böhner, Piano Concerto, Op. 7
> Weber, "Die Sonn' erwacht!" (chorus from the incidental music to
>   P. A. Wolff's play *Preciosa*)
> Jan Willem Wilms, variations for flute and piano
> Heinrich Leberecht Mühling, vocal trio
> Jan Ladislav Dussek, sonata for violin and piano
> Pierre-Antoine-Dominique Della Maria, overture.[22]

It is likely that all the orchestral numbers were played with no more instruments than those listed under the opening *Sinfonie,* namely, four strings (two violins, one played by the clarinet soloist, viola, and bass), two flutes, one horn for both the first and second parts, and the supplementary (and for the Böhner Concerto, also solo) piano.[23]

In 1824 Schumann went public, advertising his concert, whose normal audience would have been only his school friends and father, with a printed program and admission fee.[24] The occasion may have been the arrival of a fine Streicher grand piano from Vienna (which Schumann put down variously to 1824 and 1826).[25] He carried over some of the numbers from 1823 (the

Eichner *Sinfonie,* Della Maria Overture, Weber Clarinet Variations, and Chorus from *Preciosa*), and added to these an overture by Georg Christoph Grosheim; andante for two glasschords, flute, oboe, and clarinet (composer unnamed); aria from Mozart's *Die Entführung aus dem Serail;* chorus from Adrien Boieldieu's *Jean de Paris;* and piano concerto by Lecour (recte Pierre Lecourt).[26] Although some of the works on these two programs cannot be identified precisely or easily found, those that are known (the Haydn and Weber choruses) or can be assumed to be similar to known works (the Boieldieu chorus, Eichner *Sinfonie,* Kreutzer trio, Wilms flute variations) are suitable for amateur ensemble. The aria from *Die Entführung* may be a more ambitious piece (the performer and exact number are unnamed), as are the Weber Clarinet Variations.

In his running commentary on the first program (he left none for the second), the Weber is the piece that excited Schumann most. He praised (with all due modesty) his own performance, "I played with seeming ease and polish," adding that his friend Piltzing played the difficult clarinet part "even more smoothly."[27] Probably Schumann's special joy at his success with the Weber was because it is the only piece on either program, including the two piano concertos (Schumann's only comment on the Böhner was "Tolerable [*Leidlich*]!"), that is truly a display piece. The others belong among a class of works that could be considered suitable more for amicable music-making among friends than a bravura exhibition for a larger public of strangers. In fact, Piltzing says the musicians did not perform in order to receive any glory but, rather, to satisfy an inner urge.[28]

The musical stimuli Schumann received in the homes of Zwickau's most prominent families through his exposure to pieces written for the educated amateur, many of which today are considered classics, reflect the refined upbringing and education he received in general.[29] His father was a successful bookseller who sent him first to the private school of Archdiakonus Dr. Gotthilf Ferdinand Döhner, then beginning in 1820, the Zwickau *Lyceum.* Latin and Greek were the primary subjects at the *Lyceum,* and Schumann became a talented translator of the classics.[30] Little time was spent on modern German literature, so together with his classmates he formed a literary society (*Litterarischer Verein*) that met thirty times from 1825 to 1828. They read primarily plays and poems by Schiller, and biographies from Karl Heinrich Jördens's six-volume *Lexikon deutscher Dichter und Prosaisten* (1806–11), but also works by Raupauch, Jean Paul, Schlegel, and Fichte, among others.[31] Already the schoolboy had collected some of his own poems into a volume titled "Allerley aus der Feder Roberts an der Mulde" (1822–25), and gathered a miscellany of poems (his own and others), dramatic fragments, album entries, aphorisms, reminiscences, translations, short biographies of composers, excerpts from Friedrich Daniel Schubart's *Ideen zu einer Ästhetik der Tonkunst,* and other articles in his "Blätter und Blümchen aus der goldenen Aue" (1823). Around this time he also wrote a number of autobiographical sketches (1825), began his dairy (1827), and sketched several dramatic and prose texts, including an autobiographical novel, "Juniusabende und Julitage" (1828).[32] He observed that, by 1827, "Poetic attempts often supplant musical ones," and wondered if he would become a poet.[33]

The dilution of Schumann's musical pursuits by his devotion to literature no doubt reflects the wide scope of his father's activities. August Schumann had written several novels, published pocket editions of German and foreign classics including works by Sir Walter Scott, Byron (in his own translation), and Bulwer Lytton, founded and edited a provincial paper, and begun a large commercial lexicon of information on Saxony.[34] Occasionally Robert was engaged in writing projects for the family business: at age twelve (1822–23) he was assigned to copy out [*abschreiben*] biographies of famous musicians for his father's portrait book, *Bildnisse der berühmteste Menschen aller Völker und Zeiten;* in 1828 he read proofs for a new edition of Egidio Forcellini's *Totius latinitatis Lexicon* that his brothers published after they inherited the family business.[35] But, for Robert, another attraction of literature may have been that, whereas as a musician he was "a youth among adults," he shared the passion for poetry with his classmates who made up the *Verein,* and with his closest friends a year or two older, Emil Flechsig, Eduard Röller, and Hermann Walther.[36] Flechsig recalls the joy of being allowed to spend Sunday afternoons in the private library Schumann's father normally kept locked.[37] Röller says that at least in school Schumann leaned more toward literature [*Schriftstellerei*] than music. He notes that Schumann shared with him plans for future philological works but never discussed with him any outward influence on his eventual decision to become a musician.[38]

If the even balance between Schumann's literary and musical pursuits reflects his education as a gentleman of the middle class who had leisure to become both an accomplished musician and writer, it also was determined by the fact that, even were he inclined to pursue a career as a professional pianist and composer, there was no available guidance nor model for this in Zwickau. Indeed, later he was to write that perhaps it was himself who served as a model.[39] According to his own account his teacher Kuntsch's playing was "only mediocre" and by 1822 or 1823 he had surpassed him and quit his lessons.[40] Thus most, if not all, of the difficult solos he played for the *Gymnasium* recitals were prepared without Kuntsch's advice.[41] Beyond that, Schumann heard no "great artists" from out of town.[42] His longing for the experience was likely the incentive for his father's plan to take him to Dresden to study under Carl Maria von Weber, the nearest musician of international repute, but the plan fell through when Weber died in June 1826, just two months before Schumann's father.

In his musical reminiscences Schumann carefully noted the names of artists he did hear or meet: a flutist, Joseph Wolfram; harpist, [first name unknown] Swoboda; organist, Ernst Köhler; and from Dresden, the cellists, Justus Johann Friedrich Dotzauer and Friedrich August Kummer; tenor, Johann Gottfried Bergmann; and organist, Václav Horak.[43] None were of widespread fame. An encounter in 1818 or 1819 with Moscheles in Carlsbad became a vivid memory, unforgettable after more than thirty years, even though Schumann apparently did not hear the artist play on this occasion but only sat in front of him at a recital by the singer Pauline Anna Milder-Hauptmann. In 1851 Schumann wrote Moscheles that for a long time he had kept as a souvenir a program Moscheles had touched. Although he was famous, the composer's modest demeanor among the guests at the resort became a symbol for the youth.[44] Later, Moscheles's *Alexander* Variations was one of his signature pieces for public performance.[45]

* * *

When Schumann left Zwickau for Leipzig in spring 1828 to enroll as a law student at the university, the nature of his sphere of private music-making was much the same as it had been in his hometown. He was a frequent guest at the home of Dr. Ernst August Carus, where he continued to accompany his wife, Agnes, in songs by Beethoven, Schubert, Spohr, Loewe, Franz Danzi, Carl Arnold, or of his own composition.[46] Four-hand playing remained a favorite pastime indulged at the home of the music publisher Heinrich Probst, and with his fellow students Johann Friedrich Täglichbeck, August Nathanael Böhner, Julius Knorr, and Christian Gottlob Glock.[47] The repertory included numerous works by Schubert, others by Czerny, Herz, Kalkbrenner, Moscheles, George Onslow, Carl Gottlieb Reissiger, Ries, and Christian Rummel, also his own polonaises and set of variations.[48] With his friends Schumann also gathered regularly to play piano trios and quartets at *Quartett-* and *Terzettabende*. They read works by Böhner, Cramer, Dussek, Kalkbrenner, Charles Philippe Lafont, Joseph Mayseder, Reißiger, and Weber; played more than one work each by Beethoven, Prince Louis Ferdinand, Mozart, Onslow, and Ries; and gave repeat performances of works by Prince Louis Ferdinand, Pixis, Ries, and Schubert (Piano Trio in E-flat Major, Op. 100).[49] The final meeting, on 28 March 1829, was celebrated with a performance of Schumann's own Piano Quartet in C Minor, Op. V, which the group had begun practicing as early as 31 January.[50] Quite naturally, the young musician continued to entertain his friends with brilliant solos, including the Kalkbrenner and Hummel concertos, but also other virtuosic pieces, sonatas, rondos, variations, polonaises, and toccatas by Czerny, Hummel, Franz Hünten, Kalkbrenner, Mayer, Moscheles, Mozart, Ries, and Weber.[51] He improvised every day, most often at home, but also for his friends.[52]

What opened up considerably for Schumann in Leipzig, a town ten times the size of Zwickau, was his exposure to professional musicians, and, as he recalled, "good music."[53] He became a regular attendee of the concerts of the Gewandhaus Orchestra where he witnessed orchestral performances of seven of Beethoven's nine symphonies, and heard numerous concertos and concertinos.[54] Unlike the chamber pieces he played in the homes of his friends, among the latter works there were very few that might be played today (violin concertos by Spohr and Rode; the Weber Concertino for

Clarinet) but, instead, a raft of pieces by composers alive at the time but now mostly forgotten, for example: Mayseder, and Johannes Wenzeslaus Kalliwoda (violin concerto, violin concertino); Bernhard Henrik Crusell (clarinet concerto); Christian Gottlieb Belcke (flute concertino); Christian Gottlieb Müller (bass trombone concertino); Friedrich August Kummer (oboe concertino); Ries (piano concerto). Their works were performed by numerous local soloists, most from the Gewandhaus Orchestra, and occasionally a more (or less) famous visiting artist, as when Kalliwoda came to town, or the fourteen-year-old Friedrich Wörlitzer played the Kalkbrenner Concerto—probably the first performance of the piece outside his own that Schumann heard.[55] At the Caruses, Schumann met the well-known piano and voice pedagogue who soon became his own teacher, Friedrich Wieck, then later, through Wieck, the director of the opera, Heinrich Marschner.[56] It was as Wieck's student that he first associated with pianists as accomplished as himself, Wieck's daughter Clara and Emilie Reichold among them.[57]

The lessons with Wieck began in August 1828. According to Schumann's later testimony, his teacher carefully coached him in technique and tone production beginning with "the C major scale."[58] He practiced etudes by Cramer and studied from Hummel's *Clavierschule*.[59] By his own assessment he was industrious in his study of the piano, and made great technical strides in his playing, although Wieck wrote Schumann's mother on 9 August 1830 that her son was a contentious pupil who regularly excused himself from lessons.[60] One of Schumann's first assignments from Wieck was Hummel's Concerto in A Minor.[61] As was already mentioned, he played the piece for his friends in Zwickau when he returned there for a Christmas vacation in late 1828. He then continued his practice on it in spring 1829 until on 21 March he tried it out at one of his quartet evenings.[62] In the meantime he also began working up Moscheles's *Alexander* Variations.[63] Lessons with Wieck and practice on both the Concerto and Variations continued through 9 April.[64] Schumann's efforts culminated in a public performance of both pieces, not in Leipzig, but Zwickau, where he probably felt more secure in his role as public performer. He returned home, then on 15 April, the day after his arrival, gave the Concerto a hearing at the home of his oldest brother, Eduard. On 23 April there was a rehearsal at Schlegel's, then on 28 April the dress rehearsal and public performance of the Concerto's first movement and of the *Alexander* Variations.[65] Schumann wrote his Leipzig friend Gisbert Rosen that an audience of 800 to 1,000 was present.[66] He was later to recall this as one of his finest hours.[67]

* * *

After the sojourn in Zwickau, Schumann left for Heidelberg, where he was to remain as a law student until fall 1830. His ostensible reason for coming to the city was to study with Karl Joseph Anton Mittermaier, a teacher of criminal law and advocate of moderate liberalism, and Anton Friedrich

Justus Thibaut, a specialist in Roman law, also scholar of early church music and founder of a choral society that met weekly at his home.[68] However, the move may have been motivated as much by a desire to be with his friend and fellow law student, Gisbert Rosen.[69] Schumann went to Thibaut as soon as he arrived in Heidelberg in late May, and later was present for at least two of his performances.[70] He even wrote his mother that he spent his "most enjoyable hours" at the Thursday evening meetings at Thibaut's, but his diary entries do not indicate that he was a regular at the gatherings.[71] To Wieck Schumann wrote that Thibaut's views on music were narrow-minded and pedantic; he mocked Thibaut's love of Handel arias, which he confided to his diary were "somewhat boring."[72] Röller recalls that whereas Schumann often spoke enthusiastically of Thibaut's musical soirées, he never expressed a desire to imitate them or work in the genres (of the *alte Kirchenmeister*) they promoted.[73]

For amateur music-making, Schumann seemed to prefer the circle of his own friends, and quickly gathered around him a group for this purpose. He played piano four-hands with Theodor Töpken, chamber music with the cellists Julius Klughist and J. August Lemke, and violinist Hermann Wolff, performing on different evenings works by Beethoven, Schubert, Spohr, and Onslow.[74] He accompanied the singer Friedrich Weber, mentioning specifically Wiedebein's lieder.[75] He was acquainted with Friedrich Joseph Hofmann, the city music director, and Christian Faulhaber, a music teacher, and was a guest in the homes of Dr. A. Wüstenfeld and the Englishman J. Mitchell where he played (and heard) solo and chamber music and improvised.[76] Töpken says Schumann excited a wide circle through his improvisation and came to be expected in certain houses.[77] He also continued to impress the Heidelberg students with his virtuosic performances, often enough, of the Hummel Concerto. Töpken, on first meeting Schumann, was astounded by the aplomb of his playing and conscious artistry in his performance of this very piece.[78] In his letter of 6 November 1829 Schumann let Wieck know that he was still practicing the concerto, and had even given a fellow student of the piece some suggestions on tone production.[79] By this time he had learned to play the first movement "calmly, with assurance, and technically without fault."[80]

Schumann also joined a *Museum,* a society for social intercourse and cultural activities whose members, primarily students, put on regular concerts of instrumental music, including symphonies by Beethoven and Haydn, but also instrumental solos, of works mostly forgotten by now, by Karl Keller (variations for flute), Rode (violin concerto), Dotzauer (rondo for cello), Kreutzer (double concerto for two violins), and Frantisek Martin Pechatschek (variations for oboe).[81] At one of these Schumann decided to appear with the *Alexander* Variations. Beginning at least as early as 26 November 1829 he spent weeks preparing for the concert that took place on 24 January 1830. The appearance, his "glory day," generated "unending applause" leaving him in high spirits, but afterward he seems to have fallen into a funk and stopped practicing.[82] On 5 March 1830 he wrote, "Short piano exercises, entirely neglected for 4 weeks," that is, since just after the January performance.[83] He may have been forced to quit after overstraining himself, even to the extent of harming his finger.[84] Diary entries from this time show him often drinking excessively.[85] But, the performance had in fact gained him a substantial reputation among all the influential people in the area.[86]

Gradually Schumann resumed practice, with sometimes good and sometimes bad results. A trip to Frankfurt to hear Nicolò Paganini perform on 11 April 1830 may have encouraged him to forge ahead. Although he had reservations about the concert, he also wrote of his rapture, and later recalled that Paganini excited him to work to extremes.[87] Around this time he also may have heard the young violin virtuoso and acclaimed student of Paganini, Heinrich Wilhelm Ernst. Röller reports that when Ernst came to Heidelberg in 1830 Schumann associated with him assiduously, and thus it was possible that the sixteen-year-old professional worked a strong and perhaps decisive influence on the law student.[88] By 3 June Schumann wrote his brother Carl that he was playing the piano daily from eight to ten o'clock every morning, and by 25 September he reported to Dr. Carus that he had practiced three to four hours every day for the last twelve weeks.[89]

The incentive for this new regimen was a plan to quit his law studies and prepare himself for a career as a professional musician. On 30 July 1830 Schumann wrote to ask his mother's approval of a step he said Thibaut, the town's most prestigious musician even if not one Schumann admired uncritically, had long recommended.[90] His idea was first to return to Wieck for lessons, then go to Vienna to study with Moscheles (who was, in fact, living in London). Within six years he intended to be the technical equal of any pianist. At Schumann's urging his mother wrote Wieck, who promised to turn Schumann into one of the world's greatest living pianists in a mere three years provided he submit to a rigorous program of piano and theory study.[91]

* * *

Schumann prepared for his turn from unusually gifted, much feted, and very skilled amateur to aspiring professional not only by his commitment to the training Wieck outlined but also by composing pieces that suited his ambitions. Three large and difficult works were begun in Heidelberg: a toccata in C major (Op. 7, published in 1834), the *Abegg* Variations (Op. 1, published in 1831), and a Concerto in F Major.[92] The *Abegg* Variations grew out of Schumann's improvisations for his friends, and as we know them today are for solo piano.[93] Early on, though, Schumann dressed up their impressive piano part with an orchestral introduction.[94] Had he completed this version no doubt it would also have had orchestral interludes, just like Moscheles's grand *Alexander* Variations that Schumann played for audiences in Zwickau and Heidelberg, or a work he did not yet know but would practice assiduously after his return to Leipzig, Chopin's Variations on *Là ci darem la mano*, Op. 2.[95] As we shall see in Chapter 3, the Concerto also follows models Schumann knew well from his performances, concertos by Hummel and Kalkbrenner.

Schumann's earliest compositions—songs, piano four-hand pieces, a piano quartet—grew out of shared music-making with a few friends. It was with these friends, and at Gewandhaus concerts, that he nurtured a love for works by composers of an earlier generation: Haydn, Mozart, Beethoven, and Schubert. When he made plans to step onto a larger stage, works by these older composers, or more particularly any concertos by Mozart or Beethoven, were not his models, even supposing that he knew their concertos which he probably did not. His first pieces addressed to a large public look instead to more recent, more brilliant pieces by still-living, highly acclaimed, and internationally admired pianists.

2

The Virtuoso Concerto

The piano concertos that Schumann knew and studied early on can be labeled, if rather loosely, virtuoso concertos. Into this category fall works by Field, Herz, Hummel, Kalkbrenner, Moscheles, Pixis, and Ries, to name only those composers whose concertos were certainly known to Schumann by 1831 when he finished the solo part of the first movement of his F Major Concerto. His most important models were Hummel's A Minor Concerto, then later Herz's A Major, but these are no more than representative examples of a larger group of works with which they share many characteristics. The overview that follows surveys these characteristics in order to establish the background against which Schumann composed his own first concerto. The discussion will be confined to first movements as that is all Schumann completed of his concerto (he began a third movement that breaks off after its thirty-third measure; no part of a second movement is extant). It will concentrate on twelve concertos, listed here, which Schumann's meticulous record keeping shows he knew.

Field	A-flat Major	composed 1811?, published 1816
Ries	E-flat Major, Op. 42	composed 1811, published 1812
	C-sharp Minor, Op. 55	composed 1812, published 1815
	C Minor, Op. 115	composed 1809, published 1823
Hummel	A Minor, Op. 85	composed 1816, published c. 1821
	B Minor, Op. 89	composed 1819, published c. 1821
Moscheles	F Major, Op. 45	published 1819
	E-flat Major, Op. 56	composed 1823
	G Minor, Op. 60	composed 1820; in some publications, Op. 58
Kalkbrenner	D Minor, Op. 61	composed 1823
Herz	A Major, Op. 34	published 1827?
Pixis	C Major, Op. 100	published 1829?[1]

At the time he was composing his F Major Concerto, the concertos of Mozart and Beethoven were of little interest to Schumann as compositional models. If he knew any at all, possibly through his contact with the Wiecks, he made no record of it.[2] Even in 1833, when he was already acquainted with some of them, he saw in Beethoven's Fifth Concerto in E-flat Major, the *Emperor,* only a fine but antiquated example from a bygone era; Beethoven's Third Concerto in C Minor he considered not worth inflicting on an audience even in that capacity.[3] Today, however, when we are so familiar with the classical concertos of Mozart and Beethoven and very little beyond these up to Schumann and Liszt, it is best and easiest to describe and assess the virtuoso concertos Schumann knew in terms of their relation to the Mozart-Beethoven legacy.[4]

The most important point of similarity is the pattern of alternating large tutti and solo sections, whereas one of the most conspicuous differences is the radically changed relationship between tutti and solo sections. Dominance of the solo sections tends to increase in the virtuoso concerto to the point at which thematic interplay between tutti and solo becomes crucially attenuated. After the first tutti, the function of the orchestra is reduced most of the time to mere accompaniment so that the shaping of the form falls largely if not entirely to the solo. The piano writing can afford to be, and usually is, highly idiomatic. It also becomes increasingly sectionalized on both small and large levels: melodic and passagework areas are clearly separated from each other; within the passagework the several figural and harmonic gestures are individualized into relatively small, discrete units. We will begin with a discussion in general terms of the construction of the tuttis and solos, also of the large-scale sectionalization of the solos in the classical and virtuoso concerto. The individualization of smaller units within passagework areas will require a more rigorously analytical approach, which will conclude the chapter.

Before beginning our discussion, we must mention two concertos of an earlier type, by Ludwig Böhner (1787–1860) and Pierre Lecourt (b. 1755), that Schumann performed in his home with a small orchestra of his friends when he was only thirteen or fourteen years old.[5] The Lecourt Concerto in C Major, Op. 1 (published 1786), is a later offshoot of a style predating even Mozart's early years. Böhner's Concerto in E-flat Major, Op. 7, although perhaps showing the influence of Beethoven's early concertos, falls, like Lecourt's, into a category of concertos that could be performed by amateurs.[6] I believe both may be disregarded as influences on the twenty-year-old Schumann's concept of the art form: unlike the virtuoso concertos he learned in his youth, in later years he seems to have shown little interest in either. No other record of the Lecourt Concerto can be found in any of his writings. Although he retained the score of the Böhner at least through 1830 or 1831 when he drew up the inventory of his musical library, in later reviews of his works Schumann characterizes Böhner as a composer from an older school whose more recent works (post c. 1825) are generally eccentric and uneven.[7]

* * *

Classical and the virtuoso concertos share an overall outline in their first movements of four tutti ritornellos framing three solo sections, the latter corresponding to the exposition, development and recapitulation of sonata form. Within this outer form all virtuoso concertos exhibit certain character-istic divergences from the Mozart–Beethoven practice, with regard to con-struction, key schemes, and thematic interrelations that tend to become greater as time goes on. It is best, therefore, to begin by summarizing the earlier practice, laying special emphasis on those features that will undergo varying degrees of changes in the hands of successor generations.

The procedure of the mature Mozart is to introduce in the opening tutti only some, not all, important themes of the movement (in this regard, the near monothematicism of the C Minor Concerto, K. 491, is exceptional). He invariably begins with the theme that also serves as the first theme of what can be considered the full sonata exposition that comes in the first solo. A transitional passage that stays with rare exception (for example, the E-flat Major Concerto, K. 449) in the tonic key leads to the next theme. Some-times, perhaps more often than not, this new theme reappears in the subse-quent solo exposition, but always in a decidedly less prominent position (in K. 449 it serves as the second member of the second theme group). When it is absent in the first solo, it is certain to surface in the later course of the movement.

Returning to the opening tutti, the new theme is followed by a closing group in the tonic key, consisting of at least two, sometimes three thematic segments with varying degrees of motivic relationship to themes heard pre-viously. Some of these, too, may or may not be present in the subsequent solo exposition, but the last short member never is. It is worth giving it the label "special tutti close," for most of the time it is used in this role in the second and fourth tuttis. A most important hallmark of Mozart's scheme is that he reserves one particularly prominent theme for the solo exposition alone. The theme used to start out the second theme group in the new key is almost always absent from the tutti (one notable exception being the A Major Concerto, K. 488). When first heard, it stands out conspicuously because of the long dominant preparation and artful reduction of the texture to a single brilliant piano line immediately preceding it.

Concerning the first solos of Mozart's piano concertos there are three important points. First, on a few occasions he introduces the sonata exposi-tion proper by a passage that may be a cadenza (for example, in the C Major Concerto, K. 467), a full-fledged theme (in the D Minor Concerto, K. 466, or the C Minor, K. 491), or some combination of the two (the C Major Con-certo, K. 503). Second, he always assigns the orchestra some significant role in the solo exposition (as he does also in the solo development). Thus, the twofold presentation of the theme that starts out the new key area is usually given once to the solo, once to the orchestra, and a similar sharing of duties occurs in other segments as well. Even in segments in which the solo dominates by virtue of the brilliance of its passagework, the role of defining thematic identity often falls to the orchestra (in K. 503, beginning at bar 130). Third, whatever themes the opening tutti and the first solo may share with one another, the brilliant solo close of the exposition is always new, even when many motivic threads (often in the orchestra) severally connect it with previously heard themes. The close features passagework but always forms a grammatical unit complete in itself, a phrase (possibly repeated) or several phrases, which are then amply and volubly extended. In other words, they are, to use William Rothstein's term, large suffixes.[8]

This last point will be taken up in greater detail in the analytical portion of this chapter. For now, it should be noted that constructing the opening tutti and the first solo with such flexibility in the use of its multifarious thematic entities is the principal source of the dramatic potential of the Mozartean concerto movement. On hearing any one of the themes, the listener cannot help but wonder where and when it will return, whether played by solo or by tutti, and in company with what other themes.

In constructing his first tutti and first solo, indeed his entire movement, Beethoven maintains all essential features of the Mozart model. This is easily seen in such details as the high profile of the orchestra within the solo sections, or the grammatical integrity of the brilliant solo close. Less immediately noticeable in Beethoven is the flexibility afforded by a multitude of different thematic entities. The principal reason is his proclivity for motivic integration. More even than Mozart during his last years, Beethoven fashions thoroughly different themes from identical motivic material (for example, the two themes in bars 1–14 and 15–28 in the first movement of the G Major Concerto). Conversely, he uses the same conspicuous musical idea to establish connections between themes of thoroughly different motivic content (the use of the mediant chord, either as such or as V of VI, in the first theme of the G Major Concerto, then in the first half of the thematic entity in bars 29–43). Procedures like these abound in Beethoven's concertos, creating *de facto* the same kind of thematic diversity and dramatic potential observed in Mozart.

In one respect, though, Beethoven's practice differs from Mozart's: in three of his five piano concertos and in the Violin Concerto he presents already in the tutti the theme Mozart usually reserves for the inauguration of the second key area in the solo exposition. To be sure, this difference by itself is of no great moment in three of these four works (the C Major and E-flat Major Piano Concertos, plus the Violin Concerto), as in them the tutti steers clear of the second key area just as in Mozart. The C Minor Concerto, however, represents a genuine departure: the secondary key of E-flat major is thoroughly established in the tutti; the theme in question begins in that key, turning back to the home tonic only in the course of a second statement. More than anything else, it is probably this Beethoven concerto that contributed to a false notion arising sometime in the nineteenth century that the classical concerto has two expositions, one by the tutti, the other by the solo.[9]

The remaining sections of the classical concerto, the second and third tuttis, the second and third solos, and the final tutti, need only a few remarks. It is important to emphasize that thematically as well as in every other respect they are organic outgrowths of the first tutti and the first solo, because this will not be so in most virtuoso concertos. The second tutti is fashioned out of one or more portions of the first tutti and usually includes the special tutti close.[10] The second solo, despite the term, is actually a dialogue between solo and orchestra, the piano playing obbligato some of the time. It develops previously exposed material and often enough gives one party the opportunity to take up themes previously reserved for the other (Mozart's C Major Concerto, K. 503, is a particularly telling example). The key scheme rarely involves any but directly related keys.

The recapitulation and the final tutti represent a dénouement in the classical concerto. Third tutti and third solo are not separated from one another; instead, orchestra and piano join forces in presenting the opening theme. This presentation is always different from those previously heard: usually the orchestra takes the lead, the solo plays obbligato at least some of the time. Thereafter, both the transition and the second group of the solo are expanded as they now bring together all materials previously exposed separately in the first tutti and the first solo. The final tutti is similar to the second as it is again fashioned out of portions of the first tutti, but it stops at the suitable point on a cadential six-four chord for the solo's cadenza *ad libitum*. After the cadenza, the conclusion of the movement usually features the tutti's special close. Just how much, or rather how little, the cadenza represents any kind of pianistic free-for-all can be judged from the cadenzas Mozart and Beethoven wrote for some of their concertos, including the one (not *ad libitum*) that Beethoven composed for his E-flat Major Concerto with an important part for the orchestra.

The twelve virtuoso concertos listed at the beginning of this chapter all differ in varying degrees from the classical model. The three most important differences show up right at the beginning, in the construction and new role of the first tutti, in the relationship between the tutti and first solo, and in the construction and impact of the solo close, called by Schumann rather characteristically the *brillante Schluß*. To a large extent, all other differences are consequences of these three. Naturally, these differences did not arise from one day to the next and they did not arise with any sort of purposeful linearity, either. As our survey will show, the lines of development are sometimes conflicting. A general statement can be made, though, namely that the youngest of the seven composers in our survey, Herz (b. 1803), and the one most closely associated with the Parisian school of piano virtuosos, composed a concerto that could stand in for our proposed model of the virtuoso concerto. In turn his concerto very much follows Kalkbrenner's (b. 1788), who was also associated with the Parisian school, as was Pixis (b. 1788). Works by older composers (Hummel, b. 1778; Field, b. 1782; Ries, b. 1784) who were removed from the Parisian orbit show more characteristics left over from the classical model. The incorporation of such characteristics by the younger Moscheles (b. 1794), who also had little to do with Paris, appears to be a deliberately conservative choice.

The first difference is that the opening tutti of the virtuoso concerto tends to become an independent unit, practically a closed form in itself, in contrast to Mozart, where its primary role is prefatory. The principal musical reason is twofold: the first tuttis of all the virtuoso concertos include the so-called second theme, and in most this theme enters in a new, thoroughly established secondary key. Only in the Moscheles E-flat Major Concerto is the second theme played in the home tonic key. After the return to the home tonic the close frequently refers back to the opening theme, creating the impression of a self-contained **ABA'** form, with the special tutti close (if there is one) serving as a codetta. The impression is all the stronger because most of these concertos contain only two memorable themes: the one at the opening, the other in the secondary key.

Second, as does the first tutti, the first solo also tends to become a unit in itself. Although its construction parallels that of the first tutti, but for the fact that it stays in the secondary key, it takes the form of a free variation or even a free fantasia for the piano alone over themes sounded in the preceding tutti. Gone is the thematic give-and-take of the Mozartean prototype. A characteristic feature in many of our sample concertos is the ever more dubious relationship between the opening themes of first tutti and first solo. The latter always have bravura elements in their free introduction, but on occasion such a free introduction can become no more than a brilliant cadenza with just a few references to the tutti's first theme or none at all.

Also, further subdivisions of the first solo tend to be more sharply separated from each other, both by texture and by strongly articulated cadences, than is the case with Mozart or Beethoven. In nearly all cases the transition contains a separate passagework area fully separated from what precedes it by a clearly articulated cadence and a change in texture. In cases in which the transition begins as a counterstatement of the first theme, there still remains a separate brilliant passagework area. The only exception is the Moscheles Concerto in F Major, in which a counterstatement of the first theme serves alone as a transition. The artful thinning down of the texture toward the end of the dominant preparation, an inheritance from the older concerto, is found in nearly all the virtuoso concertos. All the second groups repeat the pattern of thematic area followed by passagework. In the thematic area none allows the orchestra more than occasional punctuation of cadences, or a few bars or motives from the theme, always played to the solo's obbligato.

The third important difference is that both the construction and the impact of the brilliant solo close are radically changed in the virtuoso concerto as compared to its classical model. It is still a suffix to the first full cadence in the new key (as Rothstein calls this and other closes), but now it is a long string of short appendices, cadential gestures tacked onto that cadence. It is not made up of the full-fledged grammatical units expanded from within, that is to say, of so-called large suffixes that were justly named closing themes in classical concertos. As these virtuosic cadential vamps can be tacked on practically without end, can be varied, can be transposed for intriguing modulations, and can be further expanded from within, the virtuoso close tends to become ever longer, considerably longer than its classical counterpart. This very length, also the *l'art pour l'art* pianistic brilliance and the requisite compositional ingenuity, tend to transform the solo close into two things at once, the true raison d'être of the virtuoso concerto and at the same time some kind of a time-out or free-for-all.[11]

Because the construction of the brilliant close will be subject to more intensive scrutiny toward the end of this chapter, here it will only be noted that, as in the classical concerto, in the virtuoso concerto a cadence normally signals the end of the preceding thematic area and the beginning of the close, but in the virtuoso concerto the break between the two is likely to be more emphatic. In Mozart, the usual sixteenth notes of the passagework may already begin in an obbligato decoration to the preceding theme. The performer may wish to nuance the cadence of the theme by drawing it out, but no abrupt break will be heard. In Beethoven, a most eloquent example is found in the G Major Concerto, where the piano obbligato to the orchestra's presentation of the final theme of the second group (begins bar 134) runs seamlessly into the close (begins bar 157). The orchestra continues as the primary carrier of the main thematic and rhythmic motives, reaching a cadence to close alone (at bar 180, where its first inversion tonic chord also begins the special tutti close).

On rare occasions the smooth rhythmic transition from the thematic area to the close found in classical concertos survives in virtuoso concertos. In Hummel's A Minor Concerto the winds, supported by the piano which also plays sixteenth-note obbligato, carry a portion of the tune in the theme preceding the close. With the beginning of the close (bars 201–11, partially in Example 2.2), the winds start a new phrase and the piano continues the obbligato. More often in the virtuoso concerto the separation between thematic area and close is abrupt: the lyrical theme, with its *espressivo* tempo fluctuations necessitated by the free-flowing and cadenza-like pianistic embellishments, cadences immediately onto the rhythmically strict passagework of the close, creating a sense of sharp contrast. Often enough the spell of a languorous melody is broken by a vigorous tonic-dominant vamp. In Ries's C-sharp Minor Concerto the theme of the second group ends *espressivo* in eighth notes. The passagework, triplet sixteenth notes over a tonic-dominant vamp, follows immediately. In Field's A-flat Major Concerto the nocturne-like theme of the second group is repeated in the minor, *pianissimo* and *diminuendo,* then followed straight away by a *con spirito* vamp, *mezzo forte.*

As mentioned earlier, most other departures in the virtuoso concerto from its classical predecessor follow from those described above. As there is little thematic interplay between first tutti and first solo, there is little reason to have much reference in the second tutti to the first. The main function of the second tutti is to signal the end of the exposition and to lead into the key of the second solo. The special tutti close that used to bestow a certain separate identity on classical tuttis is dispensable; in many concertos, it does not reappear.

The pattern of second solos is the same in almost all virtuoso concertos: a closed, *espressivo* thematic statement usually in a remote key (for example, F-sharp major in Pixis's C Major Concerto; E-flat minor/major in Kalkbrenner's D Minor Concerto; B-flat major/minor followed directly by D-flat major in Hummel's B Minor Concerto) is often introduced by a free bravura passage and is then always followed by passagework that modulates back home. A close relationship between the *espressivo* theme and earlier materials is exceptional; mostly it ranges from the highly tenuous to the nonexistent. The passagework, too, is mostly new, with only occasional references to earlier materials, and usually with minimal orchestral participation. Modulatory routes tend to match in adventurousness those heard in the brilliant close: sequences traverse a number of keys before arriving at a retransition to the recapitulation. The only two concertos that show some variance from this model are the Field, and Moscheles E-flat Major.[12]

In the recapitulation there is no call for the kind of dénouement seen in Mozart, in part because of the very nature of the opening theme, in part because of the general paucity of themes exposed. The entire first group area is more or less drastically reduced; in two instances (Herz and Pixis), the third tutti is altogether eliminated. Similar curtailments can be observed in every other virtuoso concerto under consideration. The only thing expanded in the recapitulation is the brilliant close, which in some instances becomes an even more extravagant display than in the exposition. Whereas the closes in Ries's three concertos are near to their original exposition form, those in the other nine concertos show more variation, at least in their figuration if not their general outline. The closes of the Hummel B Minor, Kalkbrenner, and Herz concertos are fully new.

As the brilliant close cannot be surpassed, final tuttis tend to be short, with no room for a solo cadenza. They merely provide the concluding blast. Only the Moscheles G Minor Concerto incorporates a short written-out cadenza. Usually the eight to sixteen bars of a final tutti involve some reference to the opening theme; only the three Ries and the Pixis concertos incorporate the special tutti close. Its fate is perhaps emblematic of the changed concept of the genre. Its presence in all of the first tuttis of all the concertos except the Field and Moscheles F Major shows the dependence of the new model on the old. It serves in every case the very practical purpose of quieting down the orchestra in preparation for the solo entrance. At the same time, its rare recurrence in or complete elimination from subsequent tuttis shows it to be a rudiment with hardly any other function.

In the light of these summary statements, the classical concerto can be seen to have a high degree of organic unity that is lacking in its virtuoso successor. The form of Mozart's and Beethoven's first movements unfolds gradually as solo and orchestra cooperate in equal measure in answering all questions raised and fulfilling all promises made. The form of the virtuoso concerto, with its sharp divisions between and within sections, tends to become a fixed framework for display. Its virtues lie in what is displayed: grand themes of an often theatrical nature and truly brilliant virtuosity.

The virtuoso concerto as essentially a piece for piano alone with orchestral introduction is, of course, connected with the drastic reduction or complete elimination of any orchestra role in the three solo areas. Among the twelve virtuoso concertos under consideration, even in those five in which the orchestra is allowed some role (namely, in the Field, Hummel A Minor and B Minor, Ries C Minor and E-flat Major, and Moscheles E-flat Major) the role is vestigial compared to Mozart or Beethoven. One can only wonder how this situation came about. To be sure, the changing aesthetic climate of the time with a growing interest in sheer virtuosity and in an instrument that is constantly growing bigger and better may have much to do with it, as undoubtedly do the personal inclinations of the composers themselves. But the strongest reason may well be a purely practical consideration. Often enough, the touring virtuoso found himself performing in small towns in the company of an underrehearsed, semiprofessional *ad hoc* orchestra, or none at all.[13] The independent tutti may go by the board; the independent first solo may become the beginning of the concerto. Common publisher's practice provides here a hint. The options offered of purchasing a concerto's piano part alone, or with quartet parts, or with full orchestral accompaniment testify to the various performance possibilities.[14]

* * *

As mentioned earlier, construction of the passagework in the brilliant close (and sometimes elsewhere as well) is rather different in the classical and virtuoso concertos. This will be illustrated by detailed examination of the closes of three concertos, by Beethoven, Hummel, and Herz, with primary emphasis on what Rothstein calls phrase rhythm, but also with a view toward the changing concept of what constitutes pianistic virtuosity. The Beethoven example is from the C Minor Concerto, Op. 37, because this concerto resembles, at least in some respects, the virtuoso model.[15] Furthermore, its close can be taken as representative of the close as it was developed by Mozart, even if on a somewhat larger scale. Concertos by Hummel (A Minor) and Herz (A Major) were chosen because of Schumann's interest in these works as a performer and composer. Hummel's work represents an older style, closer to that of his teacher Mozart or to Beethoven, with whom he had some personal association, and will bear on the discussion in the next chapter concerning the first work Schumann completed on his F Major Concerto.[16] Herz's exemplifies the newer, Parisian school and will be discussed in connection with Schumann's later work on his concerto, to be taken up in Chapter 4.[17]

In adopting an analytical framework for the comparisons in this and subsequent chapters, I am guided by two recent studies on phrase construction, Rothstein's *Phrase Rhythm in Tonal Music,* and Ivan F. Waldbauer's "Riemann's Periodization Revisited and Revised," both from 1989. The approaches of these two historically oriented studies differ to some extent but, fortunately for our purposes, in the matter of certain basic concepts inherited from Heinrich Christoph Koch's over two-centuries-old *Introductory Essay,* there is a large area of general agreement between them. Koch distinguishes basic phrases, phrases expanded from within, and phrases extended by additions from without, the additions being either prefixes (prefaces), suffixes (appendices) or parentheses (interpolations). Rothstein redefines these by the Schenkerian conception of tonal organization and by recourse to more recent studies on rhythm and meter.[18] He rejects Hugo Riemann's assumption that all music is related to the basic eight-measure period, which he considers an unacceptable apriorism. In contrast, Waldbauer, whose study centers on Riemann's system, takes the Riemannian eight-measure assumption as his point of departure but makes a number of important revisions. All of the revisions are intended to alleviate the ill effects of Riemann's apriorisms; they make the system flexible enough to render Riemann's number-based analytical method applicable to a wide range of eighteenth- and nineteenth-century music.

Waldbauer is particularly successful exactly where the principal interest of the analyses in the present and subsequent chapters lies, on suffixes large and small. Incidentally, despite his reservations about Riemann in general, Rothstein, too, considers Riemann's original contribution to the concept of suffix of surpassing value.[19] For this reason, and for its immediate visual value, the Waldbauer-Riemann method (to be detailed later) will be used in examples featuring suffixes and similar constructions, but only rarely in other types of phrase construction. In these other types, Rothstein's thinking will be followed, but with verbal explanations obviating the need for Schenkerian charts.

In Riemann's view all music of the common practice period divides into four-measure phrases, which represent antecedent and consequent halves of an eight-measure period. Caution: the word "measure" refers to one fourth part of the phrase (or subphrase in Rothstein's terms), *not* necessarily to the notated bar. Thus, throughout the analyses in this study "measure" refers exclusively to the Riemannian subdivision, "bar" to the notational bar. Waldbauer explains the shorthand Riemann developed for his system as follows:

> [It employs] the numbers from 1 to 8 for the eight discrete values of the period. ... The numbers 8 and 4 denote, respectively, the final and medial cadences; 7 and 3 stand for the measures leading up to these; and 5–6 and 1–2 denote comparable initial pairs of measures to which the cadential pairs provide the answer. When a given period contains more or fewer measures than eight, the numbers show the precise nature of the extension or elision. Within the period they may indicate which values are extended

by elongation, which others by repetition (non-literal and sequential repetitions included), and which values are elided, either simply left out or
contracted (e. g., 4=5, 8=1, 8=5, etc.) [Rothstein's term for internal extensions is "expansion"]. Two other kinds of extension may occur as additions to a phrase or period complete in itself. They are the preface
(*Vorhang*) ["prefix"] and the appendix (*Anhang*) ["suffix"]. ... The
appendix is one or several (literal or non-literal) repetitions of a cadence
after a fully stated period or phrase, and it may include one or several
shifts to other scale degrees (*Kadenzverschiebungen*). Appendices are
denoted by repetitions of the number 8, or 8=7–8, or 8=6–7–8, even
8=5–6–7–8, etc. When Riemann finds a phrase standing by itself, that is,
one that does not form a full period with either the preceding or the following phrase, he uses the numbers from 5 to 8.[20]

The above summary needs the addition of five minor points by way of
clarification:

- First, *Kadenzverschiebung* allows appendices and strings of appendices
  to modulate. Although such "sequential repetitions" may not always
  constitute internal expansions within independent basic phrases, as
  Rothstein demonstrates, they always represent extensions, that is to
  say, additions from without, in strings of appendices.
- Second, a given appendix may appear to be a full phrase, but its dependence on the preceding unit remains. Typically, when the initial measure of such an appendix overlaps with the final of the preceding unit
  (in shorthand, 8=5–6–7–8) we have only what will be called a pseudo-
  phrase, a fully dependent unit. There are, however, degrees of such
  dependency. For instance, when an appendix begins with an overlap
  but then repeats its initial measure (in shorthand, 8=5a–5b–6–etc.) it
  acquires a degree of independence.
- Third, the size of the true measure varies in a composition, both within
  and between its constituent phrases. This affects what Waldbauer calls
  the pacing of the music, that is, the rate at which it progresses toward
  its various goals, but not its density, that is, whether a given passage
  actually moves forward, does so with various excursions, or merely
  marches in place.[21]
- Fourth, ambiguity inheres in all types of musical materials, but even
  more so in matters metrical, because of the heavy dependence of the
  latter on context. For this reason, two or even more simultaneously
  valid metric interpretations of a given passage are possible. In the
  analyses that follow the most immediately plausible interpretations
  will be given; alternatives will reserved for the few cases where they
  are relevant.
- Fifth, Waldbauer's cited summary of Riemann's shorthand does not
  refer to the type of expansion called parenthesis or interpolation. This
  is the insertion of one or more units of extraneous musical material

into another, virtually at any point within that other unit.[22] In the present chapter, one short passage in Example 2.1 can be considered an interpolation.

* * *

In the examples that follow, the numbers above the system refer to the notated bars of the movement, the numbers underneath to the true measure as identified by the Waldbauer-Riemann method. Lines underneath the notated bars indicate the length of the true measure and may show that the bar line

Example 2.1 Beethoven, Concerto in C Minor, Op. 37, first movement, solo exposition, close.

Example 2.1   (*continued*)

is in effect nullified, the true Waldbauer-Riemann measure being two or more times longer than the notated bar. Occasionally a second interpretation of the Waldbauer-Riemann measure is given underneath the first. In these cases both interpretations are enclosed in braces.

The close of Beethoven's C Minor Concerto is in three parts, bars 187–99, 199–205, and 205–27, each itself a large suffix within the entire large suffix that forms the complete close. The first part consists of a complete basic phrase in four measures, and its expanded repetition. Example 2.1 shows only the basic phrase; the expanded repetition contains an artful transition from half and quarter notes through eighth notes and eighth-note triplets to, at the point of cadential overlap with the beginning of the second part of the close (bar 199), the sixteenth notes that begin the second part of the close. The second and third parts are variants of one another. Both begin by cadential overlap indicating dependency on the preceding phrase; both acquire a degree of independence by repeating their initial measures; and both are complete phrases. The second part (bars 199–205) sequentially expands the antepenultimate only (m. 6 = bars 201–3, what Rothstein would call a three-bar hypermeasure), then compresses into the penultimate (m. 7 = bar 204) an entire I^6–ii^6–V^7 progression. The repetition in the third part (bars 205–27) expands the antepenultimate into four bars (207–10) and spreads out the harmonies of bar 204 into sixteen bars (211–26) with enough room to contain the parenthetically interpolated phrase in bars 219–22. The full *Stillstand auf der Penultima,* to use Riemann's oft-quoted term, contains three harmonies and a parenthesis. The registral coding takes the form of a threefold ascent from the lowest register to ever higher; the final trill is on the apogee and a nearly five-octave scale drops from there to the perigee of the final. The growth of the close is on its way.

The close of Hummel's Concerto in A Minor is in two parts, bars 201–19 and 219–57. It represents (as does the entire work), an intermediate stage between the close of Mozart and Beethoven's day and what it became in the 1820s. As in Beethoven's concerto, it begins with an independent phrase. As is usual in the classical concerto, too, the orchestra has a role: to the solo obbligato the clarinet plays a motive prominent at the beginning of the first tutti and the solo exposition. Example 2.2 shows only the beginning of this independent phrase; it continues at a sedate pace (two or three bars per measure), ending with a series of short suffixes alternating dominant and tonic harmonies every two bars (in bars 211–18). The second part of Hummel's close shows two newer features: (1) short suffix construction; and (2) changing musical affects, signaled by a rich variety of pianistic figurations, dynamics, and other performance markings. The short suffixes represent the lowest degree of musical density, a marching in place offset only by the many changes of pace in the surface motion, where varying degrees of headlong rush are now and then interrupted by momentary pauses.

The four-bar vamp opening the second part of the close (bars 219–22) continues at the sedate pace of the first part until bars 223–24, which manage to suggest two or even three different harmonic rhythms all at once. Viewed from what precedes them, a two-bar tonic pedal suggests a continuation of the two-bar hypermeasures. At the same time, passing motion in the inner voice of bar 223 is repeated in bar 224, seemingly creating two separate true tonic measures. Finally, because the passing motion is an emphatic I-I-IV-V progression, it introduces a one-harmony-per-beat pattern that will dominate the surface of bars 225–28.

Example 2.2 Hummel, Concerto in A Minor, first movement, solo exposition, close.

Yet a new surface pattern is introduced at bar 229. The right hand produces one figure every bar, while the left hand seems to proceed by two harmonies every bar up to the middle of bar 232. Because, however, these harmonies outline merely passing motion between two tonic chords, that is, they imply at best an overall I-V-I progression over three and one-half bars, shorter true measures are not implied. Double-bar true measures continue until a change of harmony in the middle of bar 232 creates two large 3/2 units, as shown in the example by a dotted bar line and bracketed time signatures. This rhythmic-metric play precedes the final, semi-independent

Example 2.2 (*continued*)

phrase (but still a short suffix) of the close, which leads at last to a drop to
the low register for the antepenultimate and beginning of the long penultimate measure. Along with the other changes of pace, such rhythmic play
brings to mind not the closes but the cadenzas of Mozart and Beethoven.

In Mozart and Beethoven the close represents a single affect, and this
dictates a limited number of scale and arpeggio figures and a single dynamic
gesture, normally one more or less unbroken crescendo, implied rather than
actually prescribed. In contrast, Hummel individuates every particle in
the string of his gestures through different and ever more extravagant figurations and dynamic markings, a very cavalcade of different affects. In the second part alone, the score shows the following: broken octaves and tenths,

Example 2.2   (*continued*)

mezzo forte, and scales, *con leggierezza, piano* (bars 219–22); bariolage figures of two kinds, the first with weak-beat *sforzati* (223–28); scales in double thirds with strong-beat *sforzati, piano* then *forte* (229–32); bariolage
figures of two different kinds, *forte* (233–36); arpeggios, *fortissimo* (237–38).
Finally, in the eighteen-bar-long penultimate, rising scales in thirds and
sixths, *piano* then *crescendo* (bars 239–41), and, in the highest register,
bariolage figures, chromatic scales and trills embedded in figures ranging
over five plus octaves and switching, rapid-fire, between *piano* and *forte,*

Example 2.2 (*continued*)

lead to the thirty-second-note scalar descent that concludes the close. This cavalcade of gestures and affects in Hummel's short suffixes also modifies the registral coding, again in ways that bring to mind classical cadenzas: a plethora of high points are reached, notably those in altissimo at bars 220–21, 222–23, 236-37, and 241-44, before a traversal of the keyboard from its highest note to the lowest register signals the end (bars 256–57).

Herz's Concerto in A Major exemplifies the virtuoso concerto in its full-fledged form. Its close is constructed exclusively from short suffixes; it is also, with respect to affect, fully, even jarringly separated from the *espressivo* theme that precedes it. A second, *sostenuto* statement of this theme comes to a dramatic halt on a deceptive cadence, then trails off *diminuendo, calando,* that is, until its final, tonic downbeat, which also kicks off the close with a sudden turn to *con brio, fortissimo* in bar 155, the beginning of Example 2.3. As in the second part of Hummel's close, the short suffixes that follow

Example 2.3 Herz, Concerto in A Major, Op. 34, first movement, solo exposition, close.

engage our interest through the changing particulars of their repeated returns to the tonic, in what could be called a shimmering surface of melodic, harmonic, and expressive gestures. Like Hummel's close, Herz's begins with a moderately-paced, mid-register tonic-dominant vamp that moves by double, then single bars (155–60, 161–62). From here on, however, Herz ventures gestures yet more extravagant, and yet more melodically individuated and harmonically remote than Hummel. The sequence (initiated in bar 161) that speeds the pace of the surface harmonic motion, also shifts the cadence from E major to E minor (bar 163) then F-sharp minor (bar 165); a new sequence

Example 2.3 (*continued*)

returns the cadence to E major (bars 165–67). This move away from and
return to E in bars 164–67 can be interpreted as a series of cadence shifts, or
as a full phrase of sorts. The memorable melodic profile of the two different
sequences, the changes of dynamic with each bar, then *diminuendo, ritenuto*
in bar 166 invite the performer to milk the full-phrase interpretation.

A new tonic-dominant vamp holds sway in bars 167–70. The high register, and *piano, leggiero assai* markings underscore a sense of standstill, until
a move to mid-register, a *crescendo* then *forzato* chords dramatically off-set

Example 2.3 (*continued*)

by octaves prepare a modulation to G-sharp (enharmonically written as A-flat), and another harmonic standstill, time-out over an A-flat tonic-dominant vamp. The time-out is what Tovey calls a purple patch; in its present guise, removed to the high register, *piano, delicato*, it represents a cliché of the virtuoso close. The vamp finds its way to mid-register and *forte* by bar 177, then turns to the minor mode and *piano* in bars 178–79. At bar 179 a scalar descent in the bass harmonizing a chromatic ascent in the treble leads, *molto crescendo*, to the dominant that begins in bar 181 and continues with some embellishment until the final tonic chord in bar 199 (Example 2.3 shows only up to the beginning of bar 187).

The amassing of small, individuated units in Herz's close takes the place of Beethoven's (or Mozart's) larger gestures. The astonishing variety of figurations, registers, dynamics, and harmonies play out a little drama of their own. The appeal is to a decidedly romantic imagination, and indeed it would be quite easy to imagine a program to Herz's close. Our heroine begins life in the security of the home tonic-dominant vamp (bars 155–61) from which she ventures out to conquer the world. Life turns momentarily dark (the minor tonic, *piano,* bar 163), but she garners the energy to pass her first trial (the sequential phrase, bars 164–66) and arrive at the delightful plateau of her first secure accomplishment (the *leggiero* vamp of bars 167–70). Suddenly an ominous fate threatens (bars 171–72). To her relief a way opens to a distant Elysium (the *delicato* A-flat vamp, bars 173–77). This is a pleasant, but false paradise. She must turn from it (A-flat minor, bars 178–79), to reality, where hard work will bring true rewards. An end is in sight (the dominant, bar 181); in two great leaps (embellishments of bars 185–86 and 191–92), and after a long climb up the register to an exhausting three-bar trill, she returns with laurels to a celebrated homecoming (the tonic arrival, bar 199). Placing the solo thus, that is, following a suggestion of Joseph Kerman, in the role of conquering heroine, takes the virtuoso close beyond mere idle display of pyrotechnics.[23]

* * *

In the hands of Mozart and Beethoven the concerto is a dialogue about musical ideas between two equals. As the solo is the more voluble and flexible of the partners, it is only fitting that the last statement it makes at the stage when the argument is first fully defined demonstrates the strengths of its idiom to best advantage—thus, the fireworks in the close of the solo exposition, fireworks that are necessary to advance the proceedings from one level to another, and hence their casting in the form of a statement. There is no such argument in the virtuoso concerto, no interaction between partners for the simple reason that the partners are not equal. The orchestra merely sets the stage with a long introduction and provides thereafter nothing more than, here and there, a few brief comments. The solo states the entire argument by itself, which may be considered completed at the conclusion of the last independent melodic idea, that is, at the end of the second-group theme or themes. What comes after is not one more necessary step but a reverberation or a resonance to what went on before, something expressed by the German word *Ausklang.* Its activity may be by turns exuberant and whimsical as in Hummel's Concerto, or bold and fanciful as in Herz's, but it does not move forward, it stops on level ground, hence its additive form.

This does not make the virtuoso concerto *ipso facto* inferior to the classical model, just different. Hummel, Ries, and Moscheles all hold the stage for the rest of the century and beyond;[24] Chopin's two piano concertos in the same style are admired to this day. The worst that can be said about the virtuoso concerto is that, in the abstract, it does not make maximum use of the potential of both forces at its disposal, but then in its days one of the forces may have been in distinctly short supply, and the other was becoming, from year to year, more powerful. At any rate, this is what Schumann assimilated circa 1830 and this was his point of departure even during the next two decades. He made the genre his own in his F Major Concerto, adapting it there, and in his later works, to his particular musical tastes and propensities.

3
First Concerto Expositions
and Their Models

We turn now to Schumann's first prolonged compositional effort in the concerto genre, an exposition for a Concerto in F Major that exists in two separate fair copies. The earliest of these was likely the beginning of a Concerto in F Major Schumann said he composed in Heidelberg in 1830.[1] The second is a later version, perhaps also completed in Heidelberg, but more likely composed sometime later in Leipzig, around May 1831. It is this second version that Schumann returned to repeatedly to revise and continue, until in August 1831 he could play the complete solo parts of the entire first movement of the Concerto for a group of his friends.[2] Revisions and continuations of this second version will be the subject of the next chapter. In this one we will take up the first version of the exposition, as it is found on pages 41–44 of Schumann's Third Sketchbook, and the second version of the exposition in its unrevised form, as it is found on pages 5–8 of his First Sketchbook.[3]

Overall, the piano part of each exposition is self-sufficient with only occasional indications of the orchestral part. The texture of each is thoroughly pianistic: right-hand melody, sometimes elaborately ornamented and in the high register, against left-hand bass support and middle filler, and in the passagework areas, etude-like scales, arpeggios, and trills. The models for this style were the concertos Schumann practiced (by Kalkbrenner and Hummel) or played from sight ("practically all concertos," he claimed, but presumably those in his possession by 1830–31, by Field, Ries, Moscheles, Pixis, and Herz).[4] Furthermore, the two versions have in common their opening thematic gestures and a more lyric theme that follows. However, in their transitions the two versions diverge. The first follows a structural model seen in no concerto that I know from the time. It will occupy our attention briefly, as it does raise the question, why would Schumann compose a work so different from anything he could have known in the genre? The second version will take up more of our time, as it shows Schumann carefully constructing a piece that, in its surface detail and larger structure, follows patterns he knew well.

Before embarking on a discussion of the specifics of each exposition, I would like to make two points about modeling. The first has to do with biography and can be dealt with in this and the following paragraph. To wit, at this early stage in his compositional career it was only natural that Schumann should look to other composers for examples. This is born out by his work in other genres. In every case what he composed was determined by two factors, the repertory with which he was immediately involved, and the particular opportunity that presented itself for performance. In 1821, the same year he participated in a performance of Schneider's oratorio, *Das Weltgericht,* he set the 150th Psalm then performed it with a group of his school fellows.[5] In 1823, when a permanent theater opened in Zwickau, he reported composing the beginnings of operas and overtures.[6] His early songs (1827–28) were inspired by readings of lieder with Agnes Carus; a set of polonaises for piano four-hands and a set of variations (1828) were played through with his regular four-hand partners; and a piano quartet (1829) was rehearsed and performed as part of his regular quartet evenings.[7]

Similarly, Schumann's earliest attempts at composing a concerto also are directly associated with compositions he knew and with performance opportunities available to him. A concerto in E minor was begun in 1827, the same time he was working up the Kalkbrenner D Minor Concerto to perform on the *Gymnasium* program of 25 January 1828.[8] In fall 1828 he started a concerto in E-flat major. He had fallen in with a fellow piano student, Emilie Reichold, and on 15 December they were together at Wieck's for a lesson. She may have played Ries's Concerto in E-flat Major, Op. 42, which she performed the next month (22 January 1829) with the Leipzig Gewandhaus Orchestra. The very day after the lesson Schumann was moved to begin a concerto in the same key, perhaps imagining a performance of his own with the Gewandhaus Orchestra.[9]

In sum, to use Charles Rosen's words with reference to adolescent composers, "[h]is models have largely a biographical, but not much critical, significance—he may, indeed, reject his early models by the time he reaches his majority."[10] Schumann's rejection of his early models will occupy a large part of later chapters. For now, the biographical significance of the models he chose for his earliest surviving concerto lies in his restricted choice, determined first by the consequences of a small-town upbringing, which is to say, a limited exposure to the repertory and lack of a teacher to suggest any other models, then later by a career goal (to become a professional pianist) that presupposed the composition and preparation of the type of concertos and large variations sets expected by the concertgoing public of the day.

The second point about modeling has to do with its nature. In deciding to write a concerto (or any other work, for that matter), Schumann chose what Jeffrey Kallberg calls "a frame" that affects the decisions made by the composer in writing the work and the listener in hearing the work. A kind of "generic contract" develops between composer and listener: the composer agrees to use some of the conventions, patterns, and gestures of a genre, and the listener consents to interpret some aspects of the piece in a way conditioned by this genre.[11]

Kallberg goes on to say that the contract may be signaled in a number of ways, including more commonly, by "title, meter, tempo and characteristic opening gesture." These are the most obvious and simplest ways to arouse expectation as to genre, they are also easily copied. More difficult is the delivery of the norm these opening signals promise, that is, to work within what Kallberg calls "an ordered mental space" or form that these signals invite.

As we would expect, modeling can happen on either of these genre-defining levels. That is, to borrow from Peter Burkholder, modeling can occur either through the appropriation (1) of a piece's underlying structure, or (2) of the surface details associated with that structure or with the piece's overall style.[12] The first type, appropriating a piece's structure, means following its long-range pacing and harmonic planning. It subsumes the second type, which by itself has to do only with imitating details of melody, figuration, or gesture that are considered appropriate at particular junctures of the piece or are part of general usage. Schumann came only later to the first and more sophisticated type of modeling, in the second version of his exposition and in its revisions and continuations. Subsumed under both types is the copying of specific music in what can be identified as third and fourth types of modeling, both of a more restricted nature: (3) incorporating a piece's particular melodies; and (4) imitating a composer's particular style. Types three and four may be a consequence of types one or two (and for the historian, may even help uncover the source of types one or two). They also may stand on their own as acts of homage or parody (although parody will not be the case for the young Schumann), or as a result of familiarity. For both reasons, they will come into play in our discussion of each version of the exposition.

* * *

We begin with the opening gesture and theme following it, which both the first and second versions of the exposition have in common. In the first version, this constitutes thirty bars, in the second, thirty-three. In both cases, the general plan followed in these bars, a flashy, introductory melody (dotted rhythms, *forte*) followed by a lyric melody over broken arpeggios (*piano* and *semplice*), is one Schumann could have copied from any number of concertos, by Moscheles, Hummel, or Ries, to name a few. Although I can make no claim that Schumann copied the specific music (as opposed to following the general outline) of any one concerto he knew in composing this music, I would like to point to two instances in his Concerto where the line between generic similarity and specific copying seems to blur. Whether one attributes this to Schumann's knowledge and copying of, even paying homage to, specific concertos, or to coincidence coming about through his thorough familiarity with the expected gestures of the genre, is of little moment. The point is, rather, the small difference among specific different manifestations within general expectations in the genre.

The first instance, shown in Example 3.1a, involves a comparison of the first five bars of Schumann's solo exposition with the first eight of the solo exposition of the first movement of Moscheles's Concerto in F Major, Op. 45 (1819). The two are similar with respect to their opening motives (bars 1–2), overall harmonic layout (the move from tonic to dominant and back), decorative arpeggio figuration, and general down and up registral curves, even given that Moscheles's opening is more expansive. Later, when Schumann wrote the opening tutti to his Concerto, he began it with a free

Example 3.1 Moscheles, Concerto in F Major, first movement, and Schumann, Concerto in F Major, first movement.

rhythmic augmentation of the first bar of his solo part that seems, especially because it is in the same key, to outright copy (at a quieter dynamic) the opening bar of Moscheles's tutti (see Example 3.1b).

Of course, along with this possible specific model for the first solo entrance of his Concerto, Schumann had any number of more general ones. Examples of solos that begin *forte* with wide-ranging arpeggios or scales and a dotted motive are found in Field's Concerto in A-flat Major; Kalkbrenner's in D Minor; Moscheles's in E-flat Major; and Ries's in E-flat Major. Still, although no documentary evidence exists that Schumann knew Moscheles's F Major Concerto in 1830, it would be surprising if the likeness between the two concertos were merely coincidental. Schumann's fond childhood memories of Moscheles, his public performance of Moscheles's *Alexander* Variations, and his plan to study with the composer all favor the view that it was intended as an homage to the older composer.[13] The absence of the Moscheles score from the list of those the young Schumann owned, or the fact that he first specifically mentions the F Major Concerto in writing only as late as 1836, do not contradict this supposition.[14] What is more important, though, is that beyond any conjectured tribute to Moscheles's Concerto, Schumann's opening shows his excellent grasp of what the genre calls for at this point.

The second instance is the lyric or second theme in Schumann's first group and a lyric theme in the second group of Field's A-flat Major Concerto (Example 3.2). To my ear, this is no more than a general resemblance, but I believe it may be representative of what two contemporary observers, Heinrich Dorn and Friedrich Wieck, heard in Schumann's movement (in its last extant version, which retains this melody), namely a "Field'schen Charakter."[15] Most likely their remark refers generally to what Wieck called the "Field'sche Schule" of music, with its characteristic expressiveness, in which he had trained his daughter. Still, this does not eliminate the possibility that Wieck had in mind a specific resemblance to Field's Second Concerto, a piece he had taught Clara and claimed she was ready to perform in 1831.[16] Schumann seems to refer to the work as early as summer 1829,

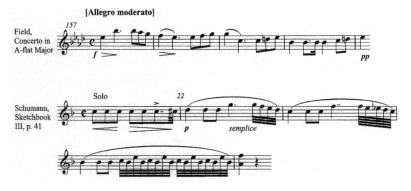

Example 3.2 Lyric themes in the first-movement solo expositions.

when he recorded improvisation based on a Field concerto, presumably the Second, which he had in his possession.[17]

Given the young Schumann's sure hand in producing a concerto whose opening thirty-odd bars easily call to mind any number of contemporary works in the genre, it is all the more surprising to see that the overall plan of the first version of his exposition is like no other he could have known. It remains in the tonic through two statements each of its first and second melodies, landing on the dominant only after some passagework and two statements of yet a third melody (which I take as marking the beginning of his second group), that is, only in its seventy-first bar (of a total 132), at the beginning of its closing passagework. Already in its sixth bar this close turns toward A minor, then, after a long stay on the dominant of A minor, suddenly reverts to the dominant of F and prepares an ending in F major, the home tonic. Schumann may have intended to draw attention to the return to F major by overlaying the arpeggios of the piano part with a few bars of melody in the orchestra (indicated by blank staves over two of the piano systems, bars 95–104), but what he has recorded is only the piano part, which continues from this point with thirty-eight bars of somewhat anonymous scales, arpeggios, and trills on or around the dominant.

Two possible examples we could look to for the same type of long passagework and abundance of melodic statements as in this exposition are Field's Second Concerto, and two concertos composed by Ries when he resided in Russia (1810–13) and came under the influence of Field (who had lived in Russia since 1803), his Op. 42 in E-flat Major (1811) and Op. 55 in C-sharp Minor (1812).[18] But even if it were Field who suggested to Schumann certain expressive melodic gestures, the nature and harmonic direction of Schumann's closing passagework hardly take their cue from Field. Although Field's close is protracted (fifty-one bars), it stays solidly in the dominant major and minor.

In Ries's Concerto in E-flat, by contrast, there is something of the harmonic whimsy of Schumann's second group. A long cadenza over the dominant of B-flat minor prepares the first theme of the second group (in B-flat minor); the cadence of the second group theme is in turn delayed some ten bars (through a diversion to the sixth degree) before the beginning of the close in B-flat major. What the cadenza and second group theme represent are not merely the brief color contrast of the parallel minor to an already established major tonic, but a long detour away from a new tonic, B-flat major, that, although not yet heard, is anticipated (inasmuch as solo expositions invariably close in a major key). We recall that Schumann may have taken more than a passing look at the Ries Concerto when his friend Emilie Reichold was practicing it in fall 1828. Still, Ries's dawdling around B-flat minor before settling onto the solid and expected close in B-flat major do not begin to approach the giddiness of Schumann's brief rush through C major and beyond to a ten-bar stretch on the dominant of A minor, then anticlimactic retreat to a big F-major close.

Why, in the face of the fact that every concerto he could have known forcefully confirms the new tonic of the second group at the end of the solo exposition, did Schumann compose a solo exposition that returns to and for thirty-eight bars confirms the tonic key of the first group? The most obvious explanation is that he was an inexperienced composer who recognized this as a misstep, rejected it, and then began anew with the intention of correcting his error. It makes sense, given that the only surviving continuation of this first version of the exposition is a separate draft of a thirty-five-bar second tutti and the first three bars of a solo development. Thereafter the version was dropped; all further rewritings and completions of the Concerto's first movement are based on the second, more conventional version of the exposition found in Sketchbook I, pages 5–8. That the first version may be a document of Schumann's difficulties in recreating the formal expectations in the genre is further suggested by a letter he wrote a year later to Hummel in which he confessed that he composed in the concerto form because it was freer and seemed easier than the sonata.[19]

To this explanation I would add only the obvious caveat: although it may be that Schumann saw his composition foundering in the first version, and therefore decided it was fruitless to continue in the direction it was headed and began anew, we cannot know for sure what he had in mind. Without belaboring the point, I would like to mention just two things. First, Schumann's usual working method at this time was to produce different versions of the same piece, any one of which may have preserved the possibility of becoming the final product.[20] This does not seem to be the case with the first version of the Concerto exposition, which never became part of a finished movement. Nonetheless, the possibility brings us to the second point, namely that in this first version Schumann may have deliberately (rather than ineptly) crafted a structure that does not conform to any agenda dictated by custom. Admittedly the evidence for this is slim, particularly given Schumann's age. I will mention only that it is not the only concerto exposition composed in 1830 that, to the dismay of some critics, remains firmly in the tonic, as those acquainted with Chopin's Concerto in E minor know.[21] If there is a point of comparison between the two expositions, I believe it is that both composers are more interested in contrasting patterns of mood and texture than in following conventional harmonic schemes.

* * *

Whereas the first version of Schumann's exposition has no overall structural model, the second one, in Sketchbook I, follows the form of most contemporary concertos. As compared to the earlier exposition in Sketchbook III, everything in the later exposition after the first two thematic statements and five bars of passagework, that is, everything after bar 37 is newly composed and conforms to a new structural plan. The main features of this new plan are precisely those expected in the solo exposition of a virtuoso concerto: transitional passagework that modulates to the key of the second group;

a theme that clearly signals the beginning of the second group; closing passagework that confirms the key of the second group.

Schumann could have copied this arrangement from any number of concertos he knew. Because many of its particulars are well-worn clichés, it is
difficult to know if any one concerto served him as a model. However, biographical evidence suggests that Hummel's Concerto in A Minor may have
been nearest to hand. We know already (see Chapter 1) that he spent months
practicing and preparing it for a performance that he considered one of his
finest. On 12 December 1830 (two months after his return to Leipzig from
Heidelberg), he first wrote his mother of a plan to study with Hummel
rather than Moscheles, his earlier choice.[22]

For over a year Schumann continued to cherish the notion of traveling to
Weimar to study with Hummel. In a letter of 20 August 1831 he proposed
the idea to the composer, enclosing for his perusal a copy of the solo exposition of the first movement of the F Major Concerto (most certainly a revision of the second version, which we will discuss in the next chapter).[23]
Likely it was at this time that he also wrote out a dedication of the Concerto
to Hummel.[24] It is not difficult to imagine that both acts of homage, the
sending of the manuscript and the putative dedication, may be reflected in
the musical content of the exposition. At any rate, the plan to study with
Hummel stuck in Schumann's mind for awhile: eight months later, on 25
April 1832, having received no reply, he again wrote Hummel, again seek-
ing to make arrangements to go to Weimar.[25] Years later, he may still have
had Hummel's Concerto in A Minor in mind when he composed his own
Concerto in the same key. The signature melody played by the winds in bars
4–7 is similar to a signature melody in the first group of Hummel's Concerto. In each second group the melody returns in C major (for Hummel's
melody, see Example 2.2, bars 201–2; Schumann's is given in Example 11.1
[motive **a**]).

Turning now to possible musical consequences of Schumann's admiration for Hummel, we begin with two clichés of the virtuoso concerto's
exposition: first, the martial gesture that, in various guises, often informs the
theme of the second group. In Schumann's exposition and in Hummel's, the
theme begins with dotted rhythms outlining notes of a C major triad (see
Example 3.3). Both composers soften the militaristic quality with a *piano*
dynamic mark (Hummel adds *dolce*), simple texture in the accompaniment
(not shown), and high-register melody. Hummel unleashes the martial mood
full force with a sudden *forte* on the final chord of his theme, a prelude to
the *risoluto,* dotted-rhythm double thirds that follow. Schumann also
pounds out a dotted rhythm with *sforzatos* in the last bars of his theme.

Although comparison of these two themes is suggestive, not least
because of their shared key, we need to note that Schumann's model for his
theme could have been more general, because, in varying degrees, the martial gesture is found in the themes of the second groups of several concertos
of the time. Kalkbrenner's Concerto in D Minor and Pixis's in C Major have

Example 3.3 First themes in the second group of the first-movement solo expositions.

near copies of Hummel's *risoluto* (Kalkbrenner writes *dolce* over his). The *risoluto* also seems to lie behind the *Moderato e cantabile* melody (in three-four time) of Moscheles's Concerto in G Minor. Even the free-floating nocturne melody in Chopin's Concerto in F Minor gives way to more regular dotted rhythms after just four bars. Of course, not all these concertos engaged Schumann as early as 1830: the Pixis he may not have known until he returned to Leipzig and heard Clara Wieck practicing it;[26] the Chopin was not even published until 1836. Nonetheless, all bear witness that in the second version of his exposition Schumann produces the expected gesture when it came to the theme of his second group.

The second cliché is the tonic-dominant vamp that signals the beginning of the closing passagework. It is found in numerous concertos of the time, including the ones shown in Examples 2.2 and 2.3 by Hummel (where a vamp begins the second part of the close) and Herz. Schumann's entire close, with two elisions, is given in Example 3.4 (note: he does not supply the final tonic chord). Because it is is C Major, as is the close of Hummel's A Minor Concerto, it is hardly surprising that the vamp beginning the second part of Hummel's close (bars 219–22) and the vamp beginning Schumann's close sound remarkably similar.

Whether he was following the example of Hummel's A Minor Concerto, or a more general model of the virtuoso concerto, Schumann produced the clichés expected in the second-group theme and the vamp signaling the start of the closing passagework with a sure hand. Both are points of stasis in the

Example 3.4 Schumann, Concerto in F Major, first movement, solo exposition, close (Sketchbook I, pp. 7–8). Editorial additions are shown in parentheses.

structure. More problematic for him proved to be areas of sustained harmony that at the same time build tension, specifically the rhythmic, dynamic, harmonic, and registral changes of the closing passagework following the vamp. This is a freer area, in which formulaic constructions do not apply. Whether Schumann turned to Hummel as a model here as well, comparison of the two closes will show that he was not yet at home in producing the varied gestures that wax and wane until the inevitable final build in the virtuoso concerto's close.

Example 3.4 (*continued*)

Beyond the vamp, the first part of Schumann's close continues with a sudden switch to E minor, *leggiero* (bars 87–88), a bizarre change of harmony, texture, and register, albeit one he must have liked, as he retained this passage in all revisions of the exposition and transposed it with only minor alterations in the recapitulation. Then begins, *piano,* a snaking ascent up a bare chromatic scale from the lowest register (bars 89–95). The climb is essentially a dominant prolongation. It ends, *crescendo,* with a circle of fifths sequence that returns the close to the tonic and high register.

Section two of Schumann's close begins with a series of two bar cadential extensions, each repeated and each returning to the tonic (bars 96–107). The distinctive melodic profile and chromatic inflection of each of these units lend them a quality that calls to mind Schumann's published later works, a matter we shall take up in Chapter 4. Although he is at ease in this mode, as was the case following the vamp of bars 81–86, he is less sure when it comes to moving from its harmonically static and independent

bar 127
repeats
bar 126

[8]

Example 3.4 (*continued*)

segments to a more sustained and climactic final gesture. Once again he
takes a bizarre harmonic turn, from the root position tonic, through a series
of six-four, seventh, and ninth chords to a six-four chord over A-flat (bars
108–10).

The nine-bar area over A-flat is mere dithering, with none of the inten-
sity of the big flat-sixth arpeggio of Hummel's close (Example 2.2, bars
237–38). Hummel's arpeggio is the climax of a series of tonic-dominant
vamps (bars 229–36) that are most frenzied in melodic energy and highest
in registral reach just at the point where, as the hypermeasures show, they
reach harmonic stagnation. The vamp breaks off with a jolt, followed by a
surprise intrusion on the second beat of bar 237, *fortissimo* and, for the first
time in the close, in the lowest register. An arpeggio sweep up and down the
keyboard leads to the kick-off of the final six-four chord, which begins a
climb back to the high register via a sequence of six-three chords. Once the
altissimo is reached (bars 242–44) there is a shallow dip in register, some
playful left-hand crossings from low to high register over the short and ever-

higher trills of the right hand, until a long trill leads up to the highest note of the keyboard, the springboard for a thirty-second-note dive to the depths and a *fortissimo* landing on the tonic.

In sum, although Hummel's close, like Schumann's, is constructed of a series of cadential extensions, and in fact begins with a chain of small units of changing figuration, dynamics, registration, and even affect, Hummel builds the final long cadential gesture of his close with a rhythmic elasticity and registral expansion that are absent in Schumann. Schumann's flat-sixth pedal continues the two-bar units begun in bar 96, and leads to a dominant trill (bars 120–28) that chugs further in units of two bars. The sequence of six-three chords (bars 122–25) is but another of these. It does not contribute to any grand sweep of the registral curve, which, although several times reaching fairly high, finds its way to the bottom of the keyboard only as an afterthought in the last bar.

* * *

By way of summary, I would like to return to the opening points about modeling and Kallberg's "generic contract." Already in the first version of his concerto exposition Schumann easily copied the most obvious gestures associated with the virtuoso concerto, its grandiose opening and the etude-like nature of its passagework close. The lack of a defining mid-point, in the form of a new theme announcing the second group, and of a climatic close in a new key no doubt doomed this version, and it was never completed. The second version does indeed find its way to a new theme in the dominant of F major. For this, as for the opening gesture Schumann had any number of models at hand, although we have noted that in each case his opening theme for the first and for the second group sounds remarkably like one in the same key, by Moscheles and by Hummel, respectively. Where we saw Schumann encountering more difficulty was in the construction of a sustained harmonic climax in the closing passagework of his exposition. Although we cannot be certain that he looked to Hummel for a model in this matter, the similarity of the vamp opening his close and one in Hummel's close is suggestive. But a comparison of his passagework to Hummel's shows Schumann's lack of finesse in building a sustained and vibrant close.

4

First Romantic Piece

The second version of the exposition that Schumann wrote for his F Major Concerto, in Sketchbook I, pages 5–8, was the basis for a series of revisions and continuations. By August 1831 these were complete to the extent that he played the solos of the entire first movement for a group of his friends, and then sent a copy of the exposition to Hummel as an example of his best work. He called the piece his first that inclined toward the romantic. As we shall see in this chapter, the revisions of the exposition left the thematic areas essentially untouched. What changed radically were the passagework areas: a complete rewriting of the close of the exposition, and, when it came to the recapitulation, as is customary in the virtuoso concerto, almost entirely new passagework for the close. This first foray into a style that Schumann heard as romantic also had a completely new model. The Hummel A Minor Concerto was laid aside in favor of Henri Herz's Concerto in A Major, Op. 34.

Schumann heard Clara Wieck perform the final movement of Herz's Concerto in August 1831, and probably heard her practicing it before that.[1] That he took more than a passing interest in the Concerto is evidenced by three different charts in his first sketchbook on pages 61, 43, and 46. Each chart compares the number of bars in the various sections of his concerto with those in Herz's A Major. At the very least the charts show that Schumann was making a section by section comparison of the length of his concerto and Herz's. Beyond that, they suggest he modeled the proportions of his concerto on those of the Herz, and we will find some evidence for this. What the charts do not directly show is that Schumann also copied both the style of and even certain music from Herz's Concerto, just as he did earlier from Hummel's. Indeed, Herz's example was instrumental in effecting the most radical alteration in Schumann's Concerto, namely, a revision of the close of the exposition that turned it from a desultory attempt to follow Hummel to the newer style of Herz.

Schumann associates the new, romantic style of his concerto with what he calls a changing cast of characters and array of ideas in his work.

We will examine the drama they play out in the recapitulation of his movement, where Schumann transmutes the virtuoso model to suit his own
expressive ends. This will bring us to another virtuoso concerto that was
composed at almost exactly the same time and with the same models in
view as Schumann's, Chopin's Concerto in F Minor. Even more than Schumann, who was his exact contemporary, Chopin subverts the very conventions of the virtuoso concerto he follows. Schumann's ecstatic review of the
F Minor Concerto when it was published in 1836 suggests that he recognized in this work a full realization of the romantic style toward which he
believed he inclined in his own earlier, abandoned concerto.

* * *

From a twenty-first-century perspective, saying that Schumann's first work
in a romantic style drew heavily on a virtuoso concerto by Herz is tanta-
mount to accusing him of sleeping with the enemy. Herz's name has come
to represent every degenerate influence that Schumann spoke forcefully and
derisively against from the early 1830s on. It stands for the whole school of
Parisian virtuosity that is chided for catering to a public demanding the
most inane displays of pianistic bravura. Schumann himself set the tone for
this present-day reductionism in a preface to the first edition of his *Gesammelte Schriften über Musik und Musiker,* published in 1854. With reference
to 1833, the time he and a group of friends decided to found the *Neue
Zeitschrift für Musik,* he writes, "One cannot say that musical conditions in
Germany at that time were very gratifying. On the stage Rossini still ruled,
while at the piano it was almost exclusively Herz and [Franz] Hünten."[2]
According to Leon Plantinga this attitude summarizes Schumann's stance in
the journal from the beginning. "The early volumes of the [*Neue Zeitschrift
für Musik*] treat the reigning virtuosi of the day with a kind of cool derision.
In the very first issue ... the reviewer remarks, 'Before Herz and [Carl]
Czerny I doff my hat—to ask that they trouble me no more.'"[3] Herz and
Czerny were two well-known and prolific writers of salon music. Hünten,
who some twenty years later became Czerny's stand-in, was a lesser figure
on the Parisian scene. In the *Zeitschrift* Schumann hardly bothered with his
music, but in his retrospective Hünten's name proved convenient for creating an enduring alliterative image.[4]

It cannot be said that Schumann was a fan of Herz's published music (he
never heard Herz play). In summer 1831, he likened Herz's *Rondo pour le
pianoforte sur un choeur favori de l'opéra Moïse de Rossini,* Op. 37, to the
kiss of a prostitute.[5] But neither was Schumann's reaction to Herz's music
categorical disdain. In 1836 he still remembered his interest in Herz's Concerto in A Major, holding it up as an example while panning Theodor
Döhler's Concerto in A Major, Op. 7.

> ... if someone works in so grand an art form, one before which the best
> in the land come with diffidence and caution, then he has to understand

just that. And that is the thing that is so irritating here. The most talented routine composers, Herz and Czerny, take pains in their larger works to deliver something of greater worth.[6]

Although the Döhler Concerto has some pleasing melodies that may have appealed to Schumann, it is also filled with long sections of hackneyed passagework, which serve to show off a fluency in playing right-hand octaves.

It is in these types of sections that Schumann had already pointed to Herz as a master, in a review from 1835 of two sonatas by Carl Loewe.

> The older I become, the more I see how, in essence, the piano is expressive on account of three things in particular—fullness of voice and harmonic change (as in Beethoven and Franz Schubert), use of pedal (as in Field), or volubility (as in Czerny and Herz). In the first class one finds the *en gros* players, in the next the fanciful, and in the third the purling ones.[7]

Purling attack was the primary aim of Schumann's practice during the summer of 1831, that is, when he was working under Friedrich Wieck's supervision in preparation for his career as a professional pianist.[8] But as the review suggests, purling has as much to do with the type of passage being played as with the quality of its presentation. In May 1831 Wieck told Schumann he played his own Concerto "too monotonously, and the passages ... too much one like the other."[9] Schumann's answer was not just to practice these areas more, but to revise them completely. For this he kept the Herz Concerto at his elbow as a model.

* * *

Herz's Concerto shadowed Schumann through every revision of his concerto movement that followed from the second fair copy of the exposition in Sketchbook I, pages 5–8, which he completed in the form discussed in Chapter 3 no later than May 1831. He recorded the course of these revisions on three charts; each refers to Herz's Concerto. The first (transcribed in Figure 4.1 with bracketed line numbers and italicized translations added for convenient reference) is found in Sketchbook I, page 61. It lists the number of bars in various sections of the movement according to an initial plan for a revision and continuation of the exposition. At the top of the chart (line 1) "H" stands for Herz; 52 for the number of bars in the first group of the solo exposition of the first movement of Herz's Concerto in A Major (the actual count is fifty-three).

According to the chart, Schumann planned to follow the thematic area of the first group (line 1) with a tutti (line 2). The absence of a bar count for either of these sections suggests that neither was finished. The thematic area is probably the one that begins in Sketchbook I, page 45, and continues onto the first bar of page 46, where it breaks off. It is followed by a verbal description (given in Figure 4.2) matching the plan of the page 61 chart shown in Figure 4.1.

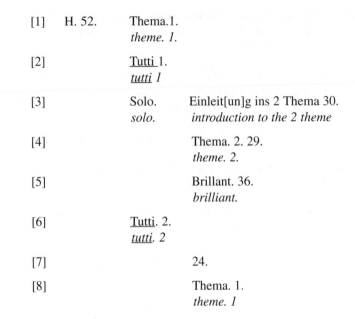

[1]	H. 52.	Thema.1.	
		theme. 1.	
[2]		<u>Tutti</u> 1.	
		<u>tutti</u> 1	
[3]		Solo.	Einleit[un]g ins 2 Thema 30.
		solo.	*introduction to the 2 theme*
[4]			Thema. 2. 29.
			theme. 2.
[5]			Brillant. 36.
			brilliant.
[6]		<u>Tutti</u>. 2.	
		<u>tutti</u>. 2	
[7]			24.
[8]			Thema. 1.
			theme. 1

Figure 4.1   Transcription of the chart in Sketchbook I, p. 61.

[1]	Skizze.	Thema 1. mit brill. Schluß.
	sketch.	*theme 1. with brilliant close.*
[2]		Tutti: I. groß.
		tutti: I. grand.
[3]		Einleit[un]g ins 2te Thema. C dur
		introduction to the 2nd theme. C major
[4]		Thema. 2. mit brill. Schluß.
		theme. 2. with brilliant close.
[5]		kl[eines]. Tutti.
		small tutti.
[6]		Bearbeitung der Thematen
[7]		mit Überleit[un]g [?] in den Anfang
		development of the themes
		with transition to the beginning

Figure 4.2   Transcription of the verbal description in Sketchbook I, p. 46.

No musical record remains of the (grand) tutti that both the chart and verbal description place after the newly revised first thematic area (lines 1 and 2 in Figures 4.1 and 4.2). The chart shows a slightly shortened solo transition area after this tutti (thirty bars as compared to thirty-eight in the exposition on pp. 5–8), but thereafter, according to the bar counts given in lines 4 and 5, indicates no change from the exposition on pages 5–8 in either the second theme area or close.

Another revision of the exposition is outlined in a small chart written at the bottom of Sketchbook I, page 43, and transcribed in Figure 4.3. Here the count of bars in the Herz movement has been expanded to include the close of the exposition (forty-four bars, line 3) and the solo development (thirty-seven bars, line 4). There is also a count of bars for the first group and close of the exposition of Ries's Concerto in C-sharp Minor, Op. 55 (fifty-five and forty-eight bars, lines 1 and 3). However, Schumann's use of Ries's Concerto seems to have been limited. He may have been attracted to individual moments of charm in the close: a languid turn from conventional figuration to a sweet melody at the half-way point, the playful interruption of a climactic build near the end. But ultimately, Ries's florid lines and conservative harmony were not a style Schumann reproduced. He never disparaged Ries, but saw the composer as part of an honored older generation (he was born in 1784). In 1836 he wrote, "Ries has written a C-sharp Minor Concerto and can quietly rest on his laurels."[10] The Concerto dates to 1815, and although Schumann admired it, he probably found it too far removed from his interests to excite his imagination.

Written above the page 43 chart, and continued onto page 44, are thirty-five bars of music. They derive from (or were perhaps a preparatory sketch for) the opening of the exposition in Sketchbook III, page 41, bars 1–35, that is, the beginning of the first fair copy of the solo exposition that was briefly discussed at the beginning of Chapter 3 and that represents the earliest layer of work on the Concerto. Nonetheless, the page 43 chart indicates that Schumann planned to return to the second fair copy of the exposition in Sketchbook I, pages 5–8. In the column labeled *Skizze,* the number of bars in the first group, sixty-two (line 1), derives from the thematic area of the first group of that exposition (thirty-two bars) plus the shortened transition recorded on the page 61 chart (thirty bars). For the thematic area of the second group (line 2), no bar count is given, indicating that it was unchanged. The close is revised, from the original thirty-six bars of the exposition on pages 5–8 to thirty-five bars (line 3; cf. Figure 4.1, line 5).

[1]	Herz: 52. *Herz:*	Ries 55 *Ries*	Sk[izze]. *sketch.*	62
[2]	Thema: *theme:*	—		—
[3]	44.	48		35
[4]	37.			

Figure 4.3 Transcription of the chart in Sketchbook I, p. 43.

The page 43 chart is a preliminary version of a large chart on p. 46 that accounts for the entire first movement of the Concerto (Figure 4.4). It tallies the number of bars in every section of the first movement of Herz's Concerto. From the time it was first laid out, the chart included a complete outline of the various sections of Schumann's concerto movement, side by side with a complete count of the number of bars in each corresponding section of Herz's Concerto. Inasmuch as the chart was a working outline, it contained at first only the number of bars in the solo exposition and development of Schumann's movement. As he revised and completed the movement these numbers were changed, and the number of bars in the different sections of the recapitulation were filled in. The chart is the final record Schumann left of his progress on the movement to near completion.

Rather than give a line-by-line explanation of each of Schumann's numbers and corrections as he recorded them on the large chart transcribed in Figure 4.4, as we have done with previous charts, we will instead summarize

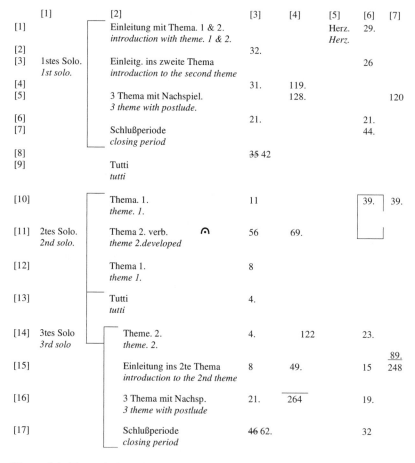

Figure 4.4 Transcription of the chart in Sketchbook I, p. 46.

our findings so far then relate them to what is written on the large chart. For a more detailed description of each line of that chart, the reader is referred to an earlier study I wrote on this subject.[11] First is the number of different versions Schumann wrote or planned to write of the beginning of the exposition. These are, the first fair copy in Sketchbook III; the second fair copy in Sketchbook I (beginning on p. 5); a revision of the opening thematic area of the second fair copy and plans for a change to the transition to include a grand tutti (Sketchbook I, pp. 45–46, and p. 61 chart); a revision of the opening thematic area of the first fair copy (Sketchbook I, pp. 43–44). This list, with its revision of the second fair copy and new plan for its continuation, then reversion to the first fair copy, supports what we already concluded about Schumann's working habits in Chapter 3, namely, that of all these possibilities he viewed none as a definitive replacement of another, but each as a valid alternative. The version he settled on in the page 46 chart (Figure 4.4, lines 2 and 4, thirty-two plus thirty-one bars) incorporates into the second fair copy of the exposition the rewriting of the opening thematic area found in Sketchbook I, pages 43–44, and revisions of the transition written into the fair copy itself.

Second, in his revisions to and continuations of the second fair copy of the exposition, Schumann made no substantial changes to its thematic areas. Through all the changes described above, the two themes of the first thematic area of the exposition remained essentially the same (see Examples 3.1a and 3.2). Also unchanged were the theme of the second group (fourteen bars long; the first eight bars are shown in Example 3.3) and what Schumann calls its *Nachspiel* or postlude (an additional fifteen bars; Schumann incorrectly gives the total of fourteen plus fifteen bars as twenty-one bars on his chart, see Figure 4.4, line 6).[12] In Chapter 3, this postlude was referred to as section one of the close of the exposition (in Example 3.4, bars 81–95). In this chapter, we will adopt Schumann's division, and use the word close to refer only to that part of the exposition he labels *Schlußperiode* (Figure 4.4, lines 7 and 8), that is, the part referred to as section two of the close in Chapter 3 (Example 3.4, bars 96–131). It is in the *Schlußperiode* that Schumann made the only radical changes to the second fair copy of the exposition, through a thorough revision involving a new style.

All newly composed music for what Schumann recorded on the large chart as the final version of his revised close of the exposition is given in Example 4.1.[13] Bars 1–12, which are not shown, are a revision, primarily a refinement of the beginning of the close as we already saw it in Example 3.4, bars 96–107. New music begins in bars 13–16 (from Sketchbook I, p. 76), then continues with bars 17–37 (Sketchbook I, p. 83, indicated on p. 76 as an insert), and bars 38–42 (a return to p. 76). In sum, beginning with its thirteenth bar, the revision eliminates everything of the original close in Sketchbook I, pages 7–8. This includes the nine-bar A-flat pedal and the twelve-bar dominant pedal that, for the most part, hover around the middle register (in Example 3.4, bars 110–18, 120–31). The twelve bars that are

Example 4.1 Schumann, Concerto in F Major, first movement, solo exposition, close (Sketchbook I, pp. 76 [bars 13–16, 38–42] and 83 [bars 17–37]). Editorial additions are shown in parentheses.

retained consist of a series of two-bar units that continually return to the tonic, C major. In fact, the first twenty-four bars of the revised close (twelve bars of old music then twelve of new) consist entirely of two-bar units, in all, six different ones, each stated then immediately repeated, usually with a register shift up or down an octave; every odd bar returns to C major, except bars 19 and 21, which are shifted to E minor. The Waldbauer-Riemann labels for the separate bars of these two-bar units are first the cadence measure 8 then the penultimate measure 7, a pace that is unvaried in bars 1–20 (Example 4.1 shows only the music from bar 13 on), including the temporary shift to E minor in bars 18–20, then continues at an accelerated rate (with further shifts to E minor) in bars 21–24. What does vary is the

Example 4.1 (*continued*)

distinctive harmonic and melodic profile of each unit. Harmonic changes occur on nearly every beat, and the harmonic progression is different for each set of two-bar pairs. In the right hand, often enough note stems clearly distinguish short melody lines from accompanimental filler, and these, too, are new for each set.

Did Schumann, who was looking so closely at the proportional relationships of the various sections of Herz's Concerto, copy any of Herz's music into his close? A look at bars 161–66 in Example 2.3 (Herz's close) is suggestive. The local harmonic movement is as restive as in much of Schumann's close, and the distinctive sound of sixteenth-note melodic sequences over an eighth-note oompah bass also finds its way into many bars of Schumann's close. In fact, bars 161–62 have the same harmonic progression as Schumann's bars 21 and 23. One is tempted to conclude that Schumann moved to E minor at this point specifically to incorporate Herz's progression at its original pitch. Be that as it may, what matters is that Schumann saw in Herz's close a way to extend his own close in a manner that satisfied his aesthetic inclinations. Like the twelve bars that he retained from his earlier close, and like the twelve, newly composed bars that follow them in his revised close, these six bars in the Herz avoid melodic and harmonic clichés that result from repeated soundings of a limited number of chords closely related to the tonic. Instead, every two-bar unit ranges through, relatively speaking, more distant harmonies underpinning less stereotypical melodic gestures. At the same time, because of their continual returns to the tonic or tonic minor (bars 161, 163, and 167) the units can be strung together indefinitely, thus obviating the construction of a longer melodic or harmonic line.

We could conclude that Schumann did not need Herz's Concerto at all, that he would have found this particular solution to his problems with the closing passagework of his Concerto on his own. Already when he wrote the exposition on pages 5–8 he conceptualized its entire *Schlußperiode,* including the amorphous nine-bar A-flat pedal and the twelve-bar dominant pedal, as a series of individual four-bar units. Over each bar of bars 96–99, 100–103, 104–107, 108–111, and 112–15 he wrote in rotating order the number 1, 2, 3, or 4, and over the first of every four bars thereafter (bars 116, 120, 124, and 128) the cue number 1 (refer to Example 3.4).[14] Still, I believe Herz's close gave Schumann a needed impetus for full-scale incorporation into his close of that certain type of low-level, repeated cadential extension which, despite his division of the entire close on pages 7–8 into four-bar units, is truly found only in its first twelve bars. I also think that the drive toward the final dominant that, in Schumann's revised close on pages 76 and 83, begins with a series of cadential shifts (repeated shifts of measure 7) was inspired by his knowledge of the Herz.

The kick-off for this drive is, first, the accelerated shifts of bars 21–24 that copy Herz's harmonic progression in his bars 161–62, then, a string of descending sixth chords in bars 25–26, which bear a remarkable resemblance to Herz's bars 159–60. Schumann brings the descending sixth chords to a halt with a series of cadential shifts, three different diminished-seventh chords covering the entire keyboard, the first two moving from low to high, the third returning from high back to low (bars 27–29). An upward climb through a segment of the circle of fifths begins in bars 30–33 (from D minor to V of E), followed in bars 34–35 by a descent back through and beyond the same segment (from E major to V of C) continue the excitement of the continual cadential shifts. Next comes a turn to the flat-sixth degree of C major in bars 36–37. Altogether, the long drive leading up to this antepenultimate, with its descent to the low register (bars 25–29), slow ascent to the high register (bars 30–33), then swift, bare, *diminuendo* descent (bars 34–35) onto the off-beat, accented A-flat seventh chord, is Schumann's own ingenious design. Yet, the design takes as its starting point the descending thirds of bars 25–26, which are so like Herz's in his bars 159–60. These descending thirds are then echoed in the ascending and converging thirds of the cadential shifts in bars 30–33. A more conventional sound begins at bars 34–35 with the descent to the flat-sixth degree and ultimate continuation of the full phrase that includes the final dominant pedal. The flat-sixth chord itself is copied from Hummel (Example 2.2, bars 237–38), and the wide reach of the dominant pedal (bars 38–42) bears some similarity to Herz (bars 193–98, not shown in Example 2.3), but, for the most part, it produces its own version of a generic climax over a dominant pedal with appropriate trills.

* * *

The version of the close of the exposition on pages 76 and 83 is the final one recorded by Schumann that is extant. It is probably the version he played on 14 August 1831 when he produced a performance of the entire first movement *sans* tuttis for his assembled friends. All reacted favorably, each singling out a favorite spot for special mention. Schumann's own summary comment was "this seems to me like the first thing written in my style that inclines toward the romantic."[15] If he gave no definition at this point as to precisely what he considered romantic characteristics, eight years later in 1839 he did write that the best young composers of his own generation were called romantic.[16] What he may have meant thereby we can surmise from what he wrote in 1835, when he assigned this same generation the task of waging war against a music dominated by technique.

> Our intention ... is simple ... to do battle with the most recent past as an inartistic one, for which only the great advancement of the mechanical has afforded some compensation—finally, to prepare and help speed the progress of a fresh poetic future.[17]

In the concerto, the place for showing off the "great advancement of the mechanical" is the precise focus of our study, namely, the close. In his own work, Schumann followed a traditional form, leaving the close in position and retaining its function as a climatic and virtuosic ending first to the exposition then to the recapitulation. At the same time, he replaced the generic formulae that make up this area in concertos by his immediate predecessors, Hummel, Ries, Kalkbrenner, and Field, with the more individual and presumably poetic sound of chains of melodic fragments. In sum, Schumann endeavored, successfully I believe, in unleashing a rapturous music in the very section of the concerto that heretofore put merely conventional gestures at a premium.

Aside from the new style of its passagework, another aspect of his movement that Schumann may have considered romantic is its modern approach to a design problem inherent in the concerto, to wit, the relationship of orchestra and solo. It was already noted in Chapter 2 that characteristically the virtuoso concerto has no orchestral interludes within its three solo sections. A further feature of special note in the Herz Concerto is its curtailing of the interaction between orchestra and solo with respect to the four tuttis that generally remain. Herz's first tutti is a full introduction (seventy-nine bars long). However, thereafter the second tutti (between the solo exposition and development, twenty-two bars long) serves little more than the utilitarian purpose of confirming the tonic of the new key E major (fifteen bars) then swiftly modulating to D minor. Its main motive must be considered a very much transformed version of the opening motive of the first tutti, if it is related at all. The third tutti is eliminated entirely. The final tutti merely reaffirms the closing A major chord while recalling briefly the opening motive of the first tutti (eight bars).

Essentially, then, Herz's movement is a piano solo with long orchestral introduction and short orchestral close. In between one relatively short tutti effects a change of mood from the rousing ending of the solo exposition in E major to the *Risoluto* then *espressivo* beginning of the development in D minor. The exaggerated separation of orchestra and solo in this scheme turned out to be a useful model for Schumann, who never did finish either the orchestral introduction to his movement nor the tutti linking the end of the solo exposition and beginning of the solo development. Ultimately, this lack of integration between the two playing forces in his movement had fatal consequences for the tutti that normally signals the opening of the recapitulation with its own first theme, as there is no easy connection between the opening theme of his first tutti and the first or second theme of his solo exposition. Schumann's solution was to eliminate the third tutti, just as Herz had.

A final aspect of Schumann's Concerto that he may have considered romantic has to do both with its new style and its modern form, namely, a certain whimsicality. When Dorn and Wieck compared the Concerto to Field, this is the very aspect that Schumann adamantly defended as entirely new.

> Dorn and Wieck want to ascribe to the Concerto a Field-like character
> that is thoroughly foreign to me. Without admitting to an idea of compar-
> ison of myself with him, Florestan expressed the opinion, in yours there
> are indeed more figures and expressive characters; he said the arrange-
> ment and form are also different.[18]

The description suggests many shifts from one musical figure or expressive
character to another. To quote Richard Petzoldt on Schumann's early works:
"In colorful alternation pictures and ideas of an extra-musical type wander
through Schumann's keyboard poems." Petzoldt considers these features
characteristically romantic and reminiscent of the *Sturm und Drang* of C. P.
E. Bach's time.[19] But for the direction they take in the development and
recapitulation of the Concerto Schumann had no model. Rather, as we shall
see, he followed his own imagination.

In another study, I have shown that the dramatic opening of Schumann's
development has much in common with Herz's and likely was modeled on
it, and that the general construction of the passagework immediately following this area also draws on Herz.[20] What is entirely Schumann's own invention is a certain sweetness in the passagework and a resultant lack of build
toward a climactic retransition and return. The solo piano plays alone, a
rocking figure in the highest register, a kind of embellished sixteenth-note
trill around the dominant, which slows to quarter notes in its final bar, then
stops completely on highest C before heading, *a tempo,* into the recapitulation. The lone high C signaling the return of the opening solo theme (cf. the
opening of the exposition, Example 3.1a), although accented, hardly
resounds with the same power as the *forte* chords of the tutti that are normal
at this point. Indeed, one could conclude that Schumann eliminated the third
tutti for the very purpose of enhancing the understatement of his return.

In the recapitulation Schumann follows the virtuoso model to the extent
that the first group is considerably reduced as compared to the exposition,
the result of shortening the transition to less than one third its original
length (nine bars vs. thirty-four). As is also common in the virtuoso concerto, he composes new music for most of the close, lengthening it as compared to the exposition by twenty bars. Of the sixty-two bars he records for
the *Schlußperiode* on the page 46 chart (Figure 4.4, line 17), only the first
eight are familiar from the exposition.[21] Fifty-four bars of newly composed
music continue the nullification of anticipated climaxes already begun at the
end of the development. Example 4.2, the last thirty-nine bars of the close,
that is, nearly two thirds of the close, shows how the typical short suffix
construction of the virtuoso close allows Schumann to undermine the very
model he is following. The entire close begins with twelve bars of the conventional V–I vamp, followed by another short suffix that is hugely
expanded by whimsical chromatic meanderings. Example 4.2 begins with
the last ten bars of this expanded short suffix. The expansion, in itself, is not
unusual. Normally it would lead through a resounding subdominant and a
long, triumphant dominant to the climactic tonic, but Schumann uses it for a

Example 4.2 Schumann, Concerto in F Major, first movement, solo recapitulation, conclusion of the close (Sketchbook I, p. 82 [bars 26–35, beat 1], and bifolium pp. 58/71 [bars 35, beat 2–bar 64]). Editorial additions are shown by diamond notes or parentheses.

quite different effect. With a German sixth (bars 26–28) leading *ritenuto* to a temporary halting point on A (V of vi, bar 29) that I believe can only be sounded by the performer with a touch of irony, he glides imperceptibly over the tonic goal (bar 31), continues the oompahing sequence through bar 32 to the German sixth and V of F (bars 33–35), reaching the tonic, *piano*,

Example 4.2 (*continued*)

in bar 36, not with a bang but a whimper, tossed off lightly and further bag-
atellized by the return of the oompah bass.

The whimsy continues with the next, nearly as hugely expanded short suffix (bars 36–48), which begins with the tonic arrival. After a descent through
two diminished-seventh chords (bars 37–38) it would seem the traditional
build toward a triumphant dominant is on its way. But once again Schumann
halts this with a further turn through what is essentially the circle of fifths
(bars 45–48), gliding over the tonic goal in bar 48 almost but not quite as
perfunctorily as before. Now, with the final I (bar 48)–IV (bar 49)–V (bars

Example 4.2   (*continued*)

50–58)–I (bars 59 ff.) progression, tradition seems to triumph at last, only to
be foiled once more by Schumann. The exultant long dominant does arrive,
but instead of leading to the bang of the tonic, it subsides from bar 53 on into
an ever so delicate *pianissimo* whimper at bar 59. The performer who might
like to pound out the last three tutti chords should resist the impulse. Schumann marked these *pizzicato*. He intended the movement to die off quietly,
I suspect precisely for the purpose of countering tradition.

* * *

When Schumann composed his Concerto he could not have known either of
Chopin's works in the genre. Although they were written at almost exactly

the same time as his own, in 1829 and 1830, the Concerto in E Minor, Op. 11 (the later-composed), was first published in 1833, the Concerto in F Minor, Op. 21 (the first-composed), in 1836. Soon afterward Schumann was moved to write the final and crowning essay of a series of eight (covering fifteen works), run from February through April 1836 in the *Neue Zeitschrift* under the title "Pianoforte: Concerte." This long essay is more a general appraisal of Chopin's historical position, present reception, and potential achievement than a critique of his two concertos *per se*. It contains high praise for the F Minor Concerto especially, taking particular note of the *Adagio* (recte *Larghetto*). More detailed description is shunned with the explanation that Chopin's music belongs to a category that should be listened to, not talked about. "Why write about Chopin?" Schumann asks. "Why force readers to boredom? Why not create first hand, play oneself, write oneself, compose oneself? For the last time, away with musical journals, this one and the rest!"[22]

Plantinga has observed that "the more Schumann likes a composition, sometimes, the less he really says about it."[23] But with the Chopin concertos it is also the case that much needs no explanation, as they follow the well-established traditions of the virtuoso concerto. John A. Meyer assumes this tradition is the only one Chopin knew.

> It is almost certain that Chopin knew none of Beethoven's concertos at the time his own were written, before he left Warsaw for Paris. The concertos he did know and admire were above all Hummel's A minor and B minor, Moscheles's G minor and Field's Second.[24]

Mutatis mutandi, the same statement could be made about the young Schumann. Indeed, the two concertos that are consistently cited as models for the first movements of Chopin's concertos, Kalkbrenner's in D Minor, Op. 61, and Hummel's in A Minor, Op. 85, are the two Schumann knew best from practice and performance.[25]

That two young composers of exactly the same age should know and esteem two of the most popular concertos of their day is no surprise. During the 1820s Hummel was admired as the greatest living pianist. His A Minor Concerto was composed for a European tour in 1816; the B Minor Concerto followed for another tour in 1819. Both were published in 1821, and thereafter were widely played and circulated, remaining popular throughout the nineteenth century.[26] Already in 1824 a biographical memoir of Hummel in the English music magazine *Harmonicon* cited the A Minor Concerto as one of his most significant compositions.[27] Kalkbrenner's Concerto in D Minor was likewise one of his most successful works, going through many editions. He composed it in 1823 for the German tour that brought him the great breakthrough of his career, the beginning of his fame as an international artist.[28]

Nevertheless, Schumann's review does not trace Chopin's concertos to a lineage running through Hummel.

> As in former times Hummel, for example, followed the voice of Mozart, in that he clothed the thoughts of the master in a more brilliant, flowing garment, so Chopin followed that of Beethoven. Or, without metaphor: as Hummel shaped the details of Mozart's style for the gratification of the virtuoso in his particular instrument, so Chopin brought the Beethovenian spirit into the concert hall.[29]

Schumann instead compares Chopin to Beethoven. We will have more to say about this in Chapter 5, when we discuss Schumann's reception of Beethoven. Here we will only note that Schumann does not say that Chopin owes any specific debt to Beethoven's concertos, but, more generally, that Beethoven "trained his spirit in boldness."[30]

Schumann does not tell us what was bold in Chopin's concertos, but another observer does. After he heard Chopin play his E Minor Concerto in 1832, Friedrich Wieck wrote:

> Completely Field-like. If I had not known whom it was by, I would have taken it for a work by Schumann; it is not to be played before a diverse audience, since the passages are new, monstrously difficult, and not brilliant in the usual manner.[31]

The Field-like characterization undoubtedly refers to the expressiveness of the thematic areas, which, in Chopin's concertos as in Field's, have a nocturne-like quality. The new, unusual, and monstrously difficult passagework can hardly be compared to Field's, which falls back on traditional formulae. Wieck can only compare it to what he has heard from Schumann.

In Chapter 6, we will look more closely at Chopin's E Minor Concerto. For the sake of comparison to Schumann's F Major Concerto, we will look now at Chopin's F Minor Concerto. Like Schumann's close, Chopin's is constructed primarily of short, repeated cadential extensions (see Example 4.3, which shows the close up to the final six-four chord). These extensions return continually to the Waldbauer-Riemann measures 7 and 8: in the original tonic C minor (bars 151–60, including a dominant prolongation in bars 156–60 that is a particularly affective flourish, an ingenious way of staying in one place); whiling away on an A-flat deceptive cadence (bars 161–70); or in accelerated shifts back from A-flat through F minor to C minor (bars 171–72).

As in Schumann's close, the series of cadential extensions in Chopin's close form a chain of linked, individual gestures, rather than a single long gesture. As in Schumann's close, too, each of the cadential extensions in Chopin's close has an individual melodic profile defined by its particular surface detail. In Schumann's close, this detail derives from the frequent changes of harmony, but in Chopin's what catches the attention are on-the-beat clashes of melody and harmony: the accented A-flat appoggiaturas in bars 152 and 154, the F or D-flat against an A-flat chord in bars 161 and

Example 4.3 Chopin, Concerto in F Minor, first movement, solo exposition, close.

163; or the clash from the juxtaposition of chords in their major then minor modes in bars 159–60. For G. W. Fink, the editor of the *Allgemeine musikalische Zeitung,* who reviewed Chopin's concertos a few months after Schumann, this is the "dark shading" found much more in the "appoggiaturas and passing tones, than in the larger chord progressions."[32] An apt description, for the dark shading lends cheery clichés of the virtuoso concerto a decidedly richer hue. In Chopin's hands, the usual spirited chug-chug of the opening vamp becomes instead a poignant, arching melody; by bar 165 the time-out for frivolity on the flat-sixth turns to a touching sequence whose off-beat accents invite the performer to linger. If Schumann heard in the virtuoso concerto he left unfinished the first in his style that "inclines toward the romantic," in the seductive surface detail of Chopin's virtuoso concerto he surely heard a romantic style in full bloom.

* * *

Example 4.3 (*continued*)

After he performed his Concerto on 14 August 1831, Schumann sent a copy to Hummel along with a letter inquiring about the possibility of studying with the composer. This suggests that he concurred with Wieck's judgment that it was his "best work" to date.[33] In the fall he wrote his family that he hoped to finish the Concerto and dedicate it to his mother.[34] He did some composing on the last movement in November, and the next summer made a note to himself to complete the piece.[35] In the meantime, he had injured his third finger, overstraining it while practicing with a mechanical device that he used in hopes of gaining greater independence of his fingers.[36] Schumann dates the injury to October 1831; by summer 1832 he was undergoing various cures.[37] Soon thereafter it became clear to him that he would not have a career as a pianist.[38] Seemingly, the worst damage was done during the time Wieck was away with Clara on a tour to Paris, from 25 September 1831 to 1 May 1832. Schumann left few diary entries for this time, but Dorn, with whom he continued his counterpoint lessons, recalled that he practiced little.[39] He did prepare *Papillons,* his opus 2, for publication. But when it came time for a private performance in May 1832 he gave over the playing to Clara Wieck.[40]

Through the decade of the 1830s, Schumann continued to compose and publish solo piano pieces. In summer 1832 he also turned to orchestral composition, writing a symphony in G Minor the first movement of which had its premiere performance in November.[41] A year later he orchestrated a concerto movement for Clara Wieck, but the orchestral part of his own concerto was never completed.[42] Indeed, he did not fully resolve the problem he faced in this regard until he completed his A Minor Concerto in 1845.

Already in 1833 Schumann knew the career of a soloist was behind him; for the time being, so was the composition of piano pieces intended for performance before a large public. Although many of the piano pieces that he did write in the 1830s are of an extraordinary difficulty (the Symphonic Etudes or *Kreisleriana,* for example) that surely derives from his own exceptional facility, Anthony Newcomb points out that they were nonetheless still of a type that truly succeeded only in private concerts for connoisseurs.[43] In 1832, when Clara performed the *Papillons* for the small gathering at Wieck's home, Schumann noted that the dances did "not seem to have gone down quite right with the public—for they looked at each other with surprise and could not grasp the rapid changes." The same observation held in 1840 when Liszt played selections from *Carnaval* for the general Leipzig public. "Many things in it will charm this or that person, but the musical moods change too quickly for them to be followed by a whole audience that does not want to be shaken up every minute."[44] For Schumann, this was the other problem that loomed large in the concerto genre: how to write virtuosic music with immediate appeal to a general audience without compromising an aesthetic vision that allows for a certain whimsy of form and demands an original style. Schumann's further writings about and compositional approaches to these complex problems in the concerto—the orchestra's role, the soloistic style, the overall form—will be primary subjects of the remainder of our study.

5

Beethoven and Mozart Reception

In January 1839, on the occasion of the publication of the first issue of the tenth volume of the *Neue Zeitschrift für Musik,* Schumann summed up the purpose of his journal since its founding nearly five years earlier in an article heralding the new year.

> While sundry views may push themselves to the fore, the promotion of German sensibilities through German art, whether it comes to pass through reference to older, important models or through privileging younger talent the most distinguished of which, to be sure, one also hears called romantic—at the present time that promotion may still be regarded as the object of our endeavor.[1]

With respect to the concerto, the next four chapters are devoted to showing what Schumann considers the best older models, and who he sees as the distinguished younger talents called romantic. In this chapter we will narrow our attention to two composers whose German art symbolizes what Schumann calls German sensibilities: Beethoven primarily, but also Mozart.

We will begin with a survey of nearly every mention Schumann makes of Beethoven or Mozart in his reviews of piano concertos from 1836 to 1840. It will show that these two giants as powerful but also vague background presences. Then we will turn to two questions. First, how Beethoven and Mozart come to be present at all in Schumann's reviews of concertos in the late 1830s when we consider that our survey of his exposure to piano concertos up to mid-1831 suggested that he heard no live performances of concertos by these composers, may not have known any from score, and ultimately showed no interest in them as models for his own composition in the genre. To answer this question we will look at the number of performances of concertos by Mozart and Beethoven in Leipzig from 1821 to 1840. As we might expect, it will show an increase in the 1830s as compared to the 1820s, which is surely related to an increased interest in Beethoven's music and older music generally in other centers of music in Europe.

Second, given Schumann's increased exposure to Beethoven's and Mozart's concertos, we will consider why, in his reviews and ultimately his compositions, these works represent more a distant, emblematic ideal than an immediate, specific influence. One answer will be found in the next four chapters: Schumann is interested in progress, and for him progress is built on what directly precedes the current product. A more encompassing answer also must take into consideration just what Schumann heard when he heard a Mozart or Beethoven concerto performed. It will show the powerful presence of the virtuoso concerto: it overshadowed Beethoven's concertos and set standards for a radical recomposing of Mozart's concertos.

We will then look at performance practice from after Mozart's death (in 1791) to circa 1820, and at changes to that practice that came with the publication of new, updated arrangements of his concertos. Advocates of each made claims for its authenticity. Those promoting the newer practice emphasized the importance of wider dissemination through new editions whose purpose was twofold: to appeal to modern tastes through an updating of the keyboard parts so as to accommodate the newest instruments and techniques, and to encourage consumers to play the concertos in their homes by offering arrangements for solo keyboard or keyboard with small ensemble. Mozart's concertos were to become at once more flashy and more intimate. Critics and audiences acclaimed Mozart's concertos in their new guise, but there was also a backlash, a call for a return to a purity supposedly contained in older editions. The result was a dual life for the concertos. They were historical relics in an old style, and at the same time newly minted bravura pieces. As we shall see, Schumann's reaction to this mixed breed was a decided nonengagement. Mozart's concertos take a place in his musical world much like Duke Bluebeard's exiled brides of Bartók's opera: although beautiful embodiments of an ideal, they remain distant and divorced both from the inner workings of their husband's mind and from the outer realities of his life.

The reception of Beethoven's concertos is not as complex. Their keyboard parts were not modernized. Yet in many other ways they followed the same path as Mozart's concertos. Publishers and arrangers pushed hard to get them into homes as chamber or solo pieces. The result was the same curious mix as in Mozart editions: the piano dominated, but within the confines of the salon. Furthermore, whatever the success of educating the public in their homes about Beethoven's concertos, in the concert hall the response was less than positive. Schumann remained distant. For him, as we shall see, the C Minor Concerto was outmoded and tiresome, at best a historical curiosity. Although he showed a higher regard for Beethoven's two later concertos, the G Major and *Emperor,* faced with the reality of the earlier style of the C Minor he beat a hasty retreat from the tedious Beethoven of the concertos to a cherished ideal, found in the masses and symphonies of the very same Beethoven.

* * *

From 1836 to 1840, Schumann reviewed twenty-four concertos; references to Beethoven or Mozart occur in eleven of these. They show Beethoven, and to a lesser extent Mozart, as a background presence in reviews of works Schumann championed and of ones he panned. They do not show him suggesting that modern composers return to specific older practices of these masters in the genre, nor that they take these practices as a basis for new developments. Concertos of a younger, although not the youngest, generation of composers serve this purpose instead—that is, as we shall see in the next chapter, works by Hummel, Ries, and Field.

For Schumann, the names of Beethoven and Mozart represent a general, although not precisely defined, standard by which to measure the excellence of a composer's achievement. Thus, Chopin is described as "following the voice of Beethoven," as bringing "the Beethovenian spirit into the concert hall," as taking "his instruction from the mightiest, from Beethoven, Schubert, and Field," and as welcoming Mozart in his later works. Schumann even puts himself on the side of Beethoven, fancying that he, too, bears "some small resemblance to Beethoven" by refusing to read the clumsy reviews of Chopin in a "petticoat journal."[2]

Spirit and attitude are measures of Chopin's and Schumann's kinship with Mozart and Beethoven, not any specifics of their art. Indeed, in a review of Wilhelm Taubert's Concerto, Schumann explicitly calls on composers not to reproduce the concertos of times past.

> But do we want concerto composers to imitate our ancestors in everything down to wig and queue, and, as a small concession to more modern requirements, to also throw in something new to boot, if it is good—and are we convinced that a genius like Mozart if born today would rather write Chopin concertos than Mozart ones.[3]

Even where Schumann holds up the concertos of Mozart and Beethoven as more concrete models, the link to the youngest generation of composers is not direct but, rather, through the mediation of another composer or teacher. Thus, when he finds in E. H. Schornstein's First Concerto a happy copy of "the beauty of form that ... is so admirable in the school of Mozart and especially in Hummel's compositions," he immediately pegs the young composer, not as an imitator of Mozart, but rather as unmistakably a student of Hummel.[4]

For Schumann, the classical concerto is part of a revered past. He recognizes Bach, Handel, Mozart, and Beethoven as gifted keyboard players, and acknowledges that with Beethoven, compositions for the instrument took "a bolder flight." Yet he sees concertos by these composers as honored, older achievements whose quality sets a fine example for the tone of a concert, rather than as models to be emulated in newer pieces.

> However, one thing we could reasonably demand from the younger composers: that as a substitute for that serious and worthy concerto form, they

might give us serious and worthy solo pieces. ... Until then, however, we
must keep seizing ... onto those admirable compositions of Mozart and
Beethoven; or ... onto one by Sebastian Bach.[5]

Even in his next suggestion in this same review, namely, that if ultimately
you want to perform something new, then choose something, "in which
the old path, namely the Beethovenian one, is taken further with skill and
success," Schumann has in mind more the emulation of the spirit, rather than
the precise arrangement of any Beethoven works.[6] Outright borrowing from
Beethoven, detected by Schumann in Herz's Third Concerto in D Minor,
Op. 87, is mocked rather than praised; an attempt by Hartknoch to imitate
Beethoven's successful use of motivic reminiscences across movements is
deemed trivial.[7]

In other words, Beethoven, the measuring rod, may also become a stick
for beating composers who cater to the commonplace. Schumann derides
Herz as a richly rewarded amuser, but at any rate an honest one who has
never compelled anyone "to love and to praise Beethoven's last quartets less."
Herz's works, Schumann decides, have their uses.

> We are convinced that he who has mastered Herz's bravura pieces can
> play a Beethoven sonata, if he understands it, that much more easily and
> freely than he would without that particular skill. ... "Everything has its
> good side, even for us Beethoven lovers."

Of course, by the conclusion of this review of Herz's Concerto in C Minor,
Op. 74, the hierarchy of greater and lesser works must, in a more serious turn
of mind, be set right.

> Should [Herz's C Minor Concerto] chance on an evening's concert to be
> given with a certain C Minor Symphony [that is, by Beethoven], then one
> begs that the selfsame be placed after the concerto.[8]

Similarly, in a review of Ferdinand Hiller's First Concerto in F Minor,
Op. 5, Schumann concludes that one should "by no means neglect to make
the acquaintance of the compositions of Hiller," but also cautions that in
order to properly judge them one should "take up right away afterward something known to be healthy, solid gold (as by Beethoven or Mendelssohn)."[9]

* * *

Beethoven's spirit loomed large over Schumann's reviews of concertos, and
not without reason. Beethoven was a presence, and Leipzig had a reputation
already in the 1820s, at least among champions of Beethoven in Berlin, as a
city that husbanded his music.[10] But, this applies first of all to performances
of his symphonies. For the years 1821–30, Alfred Dörffel's history of the
Leipzig Gewandhaus concerts reports eighty-five performances of symphonies by Beethoven (including the cycle of all nine symphonies in 1828–29,
already mentioned in Chapter 1), and, from among symphonies by Mozart,

at least thirty alone of the *Prague,* K. 504; E-flat Major, K. 543; G Minor, K. 550; and *Jupiter,* K. 551.[11] By comparison, for the same years Dörffel and other sources show only five performances of concertos by Beethoven, and two of concertos by Mozart.[12] There were no performances of concertos by either composer during the time Schumann was resident in Leipzig, from spring 1828 to spring 1829.

The few performances of concertos by Mozart or Beethoven in Leipzig during the 1820s were overwhelmed by the large number of performances of concertos by Hummel, Ries, Kalkbrenner, and Moscheles, the very concertos that Schumann knew best at the time.[13] In all, as compared to seven performances of concertos by Beethoven or Mozart from 1821 to 1830, there were twenty-nine of these selected newer concertos (see Table 5.1).[14] Some of the newer concertos were played by local performers, including Friedrich Schneider (1786–1853), organist of the Thomaskirche and musical director of the city theater; Marianne Wieck (later Bargiel, 1797–1872), wife of Friedrich Wieck; Moritz Adolph Fuhrmann (b. 1800) and Christian Friedrich Pohle (b. 1807), local music teachers; and Emilie Reichold, a student of Friedrich Wieck. More often, and in contrast to performances of Beethoven or Mozart concertos, they were played by visiting virtuosos. Aside from the composers themselves, those who performed the newer concertos were Bernhard Dotzauer (1808–34), from Dresden; Carl Eduard Hartknoch (1796–1834), a student of Hummel in Weimar; Carl Gottlieb Reissiger (1798–1859), a former resident of Leipzig where he began his music studies, but in 1824 in the employ of the King of Prussia; Louise David (later Dulcken, 1811–50) from Hamburg; Joseph Krogulski (b. c. 1816), from Warsaw; Léopoldine Blahetka (1811–87), from Vienna; Friedrich Wörtlitzer (b. c. 1814), from Berlin; Caroline Perthaler (b. 1805), from Gratz; and Caroline de Belleville (1808–80), from Vienna.

Beginning in the 1830s, the number of performances of Beethoven and Mozart concertos increased, not only in Leipzig but also in major European centers of music, Berlin, Paris, London, and Vienna. The increase came on the coattails of an upsurge of interest in the music of earlier composers generally (in Beethoven's music particularly, but also in Mozart's and Bach's), already noticeable in Berlin, Paris, and London by the mid- to late 1820s. Table 5.2 lists Beethoven and Mozart piano concertos played in Leipzig from 1831 to 1840. Out of fifteen performances, ten were by Dorn, Taubert, or Mendelssohn, all students in Berlin of Ludwig Berger, one of the most important music teachers of his time, and an esteemed interpreter of Beethoven.[15] Another performer, Ludwig Schuncke, moved to Leipzig in December 1833, and almost immediately took up residence in the home of the music patron and accomplished amateur pianist Henriette Voigt, also a student of Berger and an ardent admirer of Beethoven.[16] The conclusion that during the 1830s Berger, through his pupils who came from Berlin, was a new and prominent influence on the promotion of older works for piano and orchestra in Leipzig seems justified.

Table 5.1 Hummel, Ries, Kalkbrenner, and Moscheles Piano Concertos
Performed in Leipzig, 1821–30

Date	Concerto	Performer
26 February 1821	Hummel	Friedrich Schneider
7 April 1821	Hummel, A Minor	Hummel
18 October 1821	Ries, E-flat Major	Marianne Wieck
7 February 1822	Hummel, A Minor	————
18 October 1822	Hummel, B Minor	Bernhard Dotzauer
17 March 1823	Hummel, B Minor	Carl Eduard Hartknoch
29 January 1824	Ries, C Minor	————
14 May 1824	Hummel, A Minor	Carl Gottlieb Reissiger
18 October 1824	Moscheles, G Minor	Moscheles
23 October 1824	Moscheles, E-flat Major	Moscheles
17 November 1825	Kalkbrenner, D Minor	Moritz Adolph Fuhrmann
28 December 1825	Moscheles, G Minor	Louise David
1 April 1826	Hummel, *Les adieux*	Hummel
—April 1826	Hummel, A Minor, 1st movement	Joseph Krogulski
—April 1826	Kalkbrenner, D Minor, 1st movement	Krogulski
23 April 1826	Kalkbrenner, D Minor, 1st movement	Léopoldine Blahetka
25 April 1826	Ries, C-sharp Minor	Blahetka
25 September 1826	Moscheles, C Major, 1st movement	Moscheles
29 September 1826	Moscheles, E-flat Major	Moscheles
19 October 1826	Ries, E-flat Major	Emilie Reichold
23 November 1826	Hummel, A Minor	Christian Friedrich Pohle
30 December 1826	Ries, *Abschieds*	Ries
29 May 1828	Kalkbrenner, D Minor	Friedrich Wörlitzer
29 September 1828	Moscheles, G Minor	Reichold
20 October 1828	Kalkbrenner, E Minor	Caroline Perthaler
22 January 1829	Ries, E-flat Major	Reichold
23 November 1829	Moscheles, E-flat Major, Adagio & Rondo	Reichold
9 October 1830	Kalkbrenner	Anna Caroline de Belleville
15 October 1830	Hummel, A Minor	de Belleville

In Berlin another important Beethoven advocate was Adolph Bernhard Marx, who gave frequent expression to his fixation on Beethoven's music in the *Berliner allgemeine musikalische Zeitung,* the journal he edited from 1824 to 1830 (its entire run).[17] He called for repeated performances of Beethoven's symphonies, and also of his concertos.[18] Historian Klaus Kropfinger confirms that by the end of the 1820s, Beethoven piano concertos as well as symphonies were becoming known in Berlin. He refers to seven performances from 1829 to 1833 of four of Beethoven's concertos, and there were at least two more. Six of the nine performances were associated with special all-Beethoven concerts commemorating either the composer's birth or death, and seven were for soirées organized by Karl Möser, concertmaster of the Berlin *Hofkapelle.*[19] Similarly, when Kropfinger points to the increase of interest in Mozart's piano concertos, he cites a performance by Wenceslas Hauck in celebration of the composer's birthday, on 27 January 1830, at one of Möser's concerts.[20] Thus, although concertos by Beethoven and Mozart were being performed more frequently in Berlin, they hardly entered the mainstream of the concerto repertory. Performances of these concertos on birth and death anniversaries, sponsored by those with a reputation for special pleading, reinforced the iconic nature of Beethoven and Mozart's presence, much as we already saw it in Schumann's reviews.

Table 5.2 Beethoven and Mozart Piano Concertos Performed in Leipzig, 1831–40

Date	Concerto	Performer
24 November 1831	Mozart, D Minor	Heinrich Dorn
1 December 1831	Mozart, D Minor	Dorn
31 October 1833	Beethoven, C Minor	Wilhelm Taubert
27 January 1834	Beethoven, *Emperor*	Ludwig Schuncke
4 December 1834	Beethoven, G Major	Emil Leonhardt
11 December 1834	Beethoven, C Minor	*Demoiselle* Guschl
5 February 1835	Mozart, C Minor	Leonhardt
28 January 1836	Mozart, D Minor	Mendelssohn
3 November 1836	Beethoven, G Major	Mendelssohn
12 December 1836	Beethoven, *Emperor*	Mendelssohn
1 January 1837	Mozart, D Minor	Ignaz Tedesco
8 January 1838	Beethoven, C Minor	Mendelssohn
1 March 1838	Mozart, C Minor	Mendelssohn
2 November 1839	Beethoven, C Minor	Camilla Pleyel
30 January 1840	Mozart, two pianos	Mendelssohn Ferdinand Hiller

Aside from the influence of the Berliners Berger, Marx, and Möser in directing attention toward Beethoven and Mozart's music, there was, beginning in 1828, the enthusiastic reception of François-Antoine Habeneck's concerts of Beethoven's symphonies (the Third and Fifth) and concertos (the Violin Concerto and C Minor Piano Concerto) at the Paris Conservatory, most notably by the young Berlioz.[21] The concerts may have been the impetus for the Paris premiere of Beethoven's *Emperor* Concerto by Hiller on a program of Berlioz's music conducted by Habeneck at the Conservatory on 1 November 1829.[22] By demand Hiller repeated his performance of the *Emperor* on 23 March 1833.[23] On 18 March 1832, Mendelssohn performed Beethoven's G Major Concerto with the Conservatory Orchestra and it was dubbed a *beau succés*.[24] In private homes he also played Mozart concertos with quartet accompaniment.[25] Jeffrey Cooper notes, however, that although most of Beethoven's concertos "were sampled early" they were "slow to win fame." Mozart's piano concertos, he says, "were discovered in the 1840s."[26]

In London, public performances of Beethoven and Mozart symphonies had a continuous history at least since the formation of the Philharmonic Society of London in 1813. The Society's original intention was to exclude concertos, but these were introduced by 1819 with a performance of a Mozart concerto on 26 April by John Beale. Charles Neate, who knew Beethoven personally and acted in England as his agent, gave the English premiere of Beethoven's First Concerto on 8 May 1820.[27] In the 1820s nearly every other performance of a Mozart or Beethoven concerto on the Society's regular series was by Cipriani Potter (1792–1871), who in 1817 "was drawn to Vienna by the presence of Beethoven, whose music he had admired despite discouragement from it by his elders."[28] Another English premiere was Mendelssohn's performance of Beethoven's complete *Emperor* Concerto on 24 June 1829 at a benefit concert for the flutist Louis Drouet.[29] But it was the late 1830s before Beethoven's concertos were permanently established in the repertory of the Philharmonic Society.[30] As for Mozart's concertos, Therese Ellsworth writes, "Performances of Mozart's piano concertos took a firm hold in the concert life of London only when J. B. Cramer began to include them at his concerts," beginning in 1815 but more prominently from 1820 on.[31]

The city of Vienna came along, too. From 1820 to 1829, the only performances of Beethoven concertos reported by the correspondent for the *Allgemeine musikalische Zeitung* were by the local celebrities Léopoldine Blahetka, Carl Czerny, and Carl Maria von Bocklet. Of four performances, three were on concerts connected with Beethoven's death: a memorial concert, a concert to mark the anniversary of his death, and one to raise money for a monument over his grave.[32] Then, from 1830 to 1839, the *Zeitung*'s correspondent reported twelve performances of Beethoven concertos, some by the local artists Bocklet, Fanny Sallomon, Julius Hoffmann, and Nina Sedlak, but nearly as many by the visiting celebrities Sigismond Thalberg,

Adolf Henselt, and Franz Liszt.[33] Similarly, the correspondent reports no performances of Mozart's piano concertos during the 1820s, but one by the touring artists Ignaz Tedesco and Mozart Jr., and one by Bocklet during the 1830s.[34]

* * *

It is apparent that Beethoven's and Mozart's concertos began to be more widely heard by the mid-1820s, and took an even firmer hold in the concert repertory in the 1830s. The questions we will address now are what was the performance practice with regard to these concertos, and how did it affect their reception. We will begin with Mozart, the more complex case, then turn to Beethoven. Although we are interested most of all in the new editions of Mozart's concertos that began to be published in the 1820s, we will need to begin a little earlier, with editions of his concertos that were published soon after his death. In this way we can trace two threads that run through changing fashions in Mozart performance: claims of authenticity based on the authority of the composer, and a call for modernization for the purpose of appealing to contemporary audiences. For audiences of the 1830s each thread was readily detectable, the clash of old and new plainly audible.

Early on, the need to supply cadenzas and elaborations for the slow movements of Mozart's concertos was recognized. Eighteen cadenzas by Mozart were published by Artaria in 1801; in that same year André published cadenzas and elaborations for the slow movements of six of Mozart's concertos, by Philipp Carl Hoffmann.[35] As A. Hyatt King explains, Hoffmann's publication solved "the problem of performance caused by the bareness of [the slow movements'] melodic line[s], and by a certain monotony that results from the repeated statements of the themes ... with little or no ornamentation."[36] Although they made no claim to authenticity, King suggests that Hoffmann published the editions because he had heard Mozart play. Certainly a movement was afoot soon enough to play Mozart's concertos exactly as Mozart did. Just five years after Mozart's death, in 1796, A. E. Müller published a *Guide to the Accurate Performance of the Mozartean Piano Concertos Principally with Respect to Correct Fingering*. Its purpose, according to the author, is to present for the amateur "*all* the important and difficult passages of *all* the Mozartean concertos that are published" (although in fact it covers only five concertos, concentrating on their outer movements). In one example Müller claims, "Mozart himself used this fingering."[37]

Hand in hand with the tradition of authentic performance after the manner of Mozart came another one, namely, that Mozart's concertos are different from those coming afterward, particularly from the late 1810s on. From the examples in Müller's *Guide* we can infer that his performances, and those of his wife, Maria Catharina, were not elaborated. After hearing Madam Müller play a Mozart concerto in March 1820 one Leipzig critic concluded that the composer's concertos "seem to have been set aside by our virtuosos, perhaps because they are too easy for them."[38] Not only did this critic believe that Mozart's concertos were easier than modern, virtuosic, ones, but also that they should be performed differently. He rebuked Wolfgang Amadeus Jr., who played in Leipzig just two and one-half weeks before Madam Müller, for introducing tempo changes into a concerto by his father, even though he considered these appropriate for a concerto of the son's own composition.

> A certain idiosyncrasy of his playing occasionally hurt [the compositions] of his father. In particular, Hr. M. accelerated or retarded the tempo in the solos incessantly, and to such an extent that one would not do him an injustice, if one maintained that no three measures in a row were absolutely the same. However, just as he did it, so it was heard by many with pleasure, specifically, in those places where the composition was so arranged. That was the case with his own concerto [in C Major, Op. 14] ... but that ... those compositions like the ones of his father and especially, too, like [the aforementioned] concerto [in C Major, K. 467], ought not to be so performed, certainly requires no proof.[39]

The distinction the younger Mozart failed to make between the performance style of his concerto and one by his father suggests a change in the way Mozart Sr.'s concertos began to be brought before the public. New editions of the concertos reflect this new manner. In the early 1820s J. R. Schultz of London commissioned Hummel to arrange twelve concertos by Mozart for solo piano with optional flute, violin, and cello.[40] In 1823 Schultz also was approached by Kalkbrenner and Moscheles who had in mind a similar publication. In an appeasing letter to Hummel explaining the desirability of cutting these two composers into the deal, Schultz encourages him to "change out-dated places after your tasteful judgement." He further recommends retaining the name concerto (as opposed to sonata) and keeping the tuttis intact. "[I]t would be best if they would be complete piano pieces, with scrupulous retention of all Mozart's harmonies and melodies."[41] Moscheles added to Schultz's recommendations his own.

> Herr Schultz's project: to bring out a selection of Mozart's concertos with enriched solo, reinforcement, [especially in the] closing passagework, seems of special interest to me. If you undertake this enterprise, you cannot fail to succeed. Would you kindly just explain the following points further: 1) if in the tuttis and the obbligato parts the accompaniment ought not to be written out for the piano in small notes (as in your concerto). 2) If occasionally due to the increased brilliance, a few measures could not be added to the principal passages.[42]

The proposed changes to Mozart's concertos for these editions were twofold: first, to take them from their usual public venue and bring them into the homes of amateur pianists, to play either alone or with a few friends accompanying. Hence, the question of whether the generic name should perhaps be changed to sonata. The second change was to update the concertos, especially in the passagework areas, to accommodate them to modern tastes, which is to say, to make them more brilliant, perhaps through the addition of extra bars of passagework and certainly by increasing their compass to match that of the modern keyboard, especially in the high range. In short, to make Mozart's concertos sound more like virtuoso concertos, a distinct about-face from the Müllers' style of performance without elaborations, but one that also put in a claim for authenticity. Schultz wrote Hummel that he was eager to have the arrangements from him because "as a pupil of Mozart for several years you are initiated into the artistic secrets of the immortal one, are imbued with his spirit. And, finally, you have often heard Mozart himself perform these concertos."[43]

Hummel's arrangements of seven of Mozart's concertos were published between 1828 and 1835.[44] At near the same time, between 1825 and 1835, J. B. Cramer published arrangements of six concertos, three of which Hummel also arranged (the D Minor, C Minor, and E-flat Major, K. 482).[45] Exactly what changes these make to Mozart's piano part I have discussed in more detail in another place.[46] There is also an excellent article on the subject by David Grayson.[47] Here we will note that, generally, Hummel's and Cramer's editions reinforce the solo part, particularly in the bass which is meant to substitute for, and often transcribes exactly, the missing orchestra part. They modernize the passagework by taking it higher, making it fuller and more ornate. In the first movements, the majority, but not all of the arrangements include written-out cadenzas.[48] All undertake lavish elaborations of Mozart's slow movements.

To give the reader some idea of the extent of the changes, we can turn to the first movement of Mozart's D Minor Concerto. In this particular movement neither Hummel nor Cramer makes many changes to the themes. Most are reserved instead for the passagework. At the beginning of the close (shown in Example 5.1) the changes do not alter the underlying structure. They do, however, decorate Mozart's leaner line, fragmenting it into the many small gestures characteristic of the close of the virtuoso concerto. Mozart's exact repeat of the second bar of his phrase in the fourth, which seems to ground the beginning of the phrase through repetition, is changed in Hummel's version to an ornamented repeat, which gives more the feel of a whimsical turn away from what was just heard. In Cramer's version the disjunction between the first two and second two bars of the phrase is even greater, as he sails into the piano's highest octave in the second bar of the phrase, then comes down with a bump for the varied repeat in the third and fourth bars.

Some critics defended the modern arrangements on aesthetic grounds. When Ludwig Rellstab heard Kalkbrenner's rendition of Mozart's C Major Concerto, K. 503, in Berlin on 15 June 1833 he reported that it was "arranged with much taste and great discretion."[49] Aside from modernizing

Example 5.1 Mozart, Piano Concerto in D Minor, K. 466, first movement, solo exposition, beginning of the close, bars 143–47.

Mozart's passagework, Kalkbrenner's usual procedure in his edition of this concerto is to extend any dominant preparation by one or more bars, adding to it further arpeggios, scales, or trills. G. W. Fink, too, hailed Kalkbrenner's edition when he reviewed its publication (by Probst) in 1829. The virtuosos, Fink says, know that they will not receive applause if they do not play "the usual leaps, crowded fingerings, and monstrous double runs." Thus, "[w]e should praise the undertaking, whereby, without in any way spoiling the essence or offending taste, an acknowledged master adds only an enticing flavor, without which even the most nourishing and restorative things are generally shoved aside."[50] Furthermore, Fink says, Mozart himself embellished his concertos.

For Fink, Kalkbrenner's arrangement has aesthetic appeal, but it is also an important tool for educating the masses about music that can "excite the inner self." At least one detractor, Gottfried Weber, saw similar value in Hummel's arrangements. In a review from 1832 of Hummel's arrangement of Mozart's C Minor Concerto, Weber places himself firmly in the camp of earlier critics who set aside Mozart's concertos as requiring a different type of performance than modern ones. For Weber this style is associated with the composer not through any oral tradition handed down from those who heard him perform his concertos, but through a written one, in the case of Mozart's C Minor Concerto as embodied in André's edition, in instrumental parts, from 1800. This, according to Weber, is the work in its "ursprünglichen echten Gestalt," as opposed to Hummel's "arrangement," which Weber says is "not so much an arrangement of a Mozart Concerto reduced to a more modest accompaniment, but rather much more a Hummelian recasting of a Mozart Concerto."[51] All the same, Weber is reconciled to Hummel's dressing up of the solo "to the latest fashion's taste ... to give the player an opportunity to shine through the execution of prodigious difficulties." Like Fink, he sees the main purpose of Hummel's (or Kalkbrenner's) arrangement as the reintroduction of Mozart's concertos, which by then, he says, had disappeared from the concert repertory, into salons and private circles. From there they will find their way into the concert hall.

For the public who were to be educated by the new arrangements with their elaborations, the impression could be a strange meeting of old and new. After hearing Wenceslas Hauck (1801–34), a pupil of Hummel, play Mozart's D Minor Concerto at a concert celebrating the composer's birthday, on 27 January 1830, the correspondent for the *Allgemeine musikalische Zeitung* stated that "one must not be too particular about the mixing in of the modern style," that is, of Hummel's style in his cadenzas (which the audience applauded) alongside Mozart's. The correspondent added that what still remained for him was "the undisturbed joy of the magnificent tutti areas, likewise the sparkling instrumentation," an indication that Hauck also modernized the solo part, perhaps in a manner suggested by his teacher, or following the edition already published by Hummel in 1828.[52] In whatever manner Hauck played the Concerto, the reviewer for the *Haude- und Spenersche Zeitung* still saw it as set off from more modern fare because of its lack of bravura display. "It was extremely interesting, for once to hear finally one of Mozart's pianoforte concertos, which are still completely alien to our modern virtuosos, because there is not enough passagework in them."[53]

The two different reports of Hauck's playing of Mozart's D Minor Concerto, one emphasizing its modernity, the other its antiquity, show that when Mozart concertos were played in the modern, embellished fashion, audiences and critics heard whatever was new against a backdrop of something old. Despite their fancy new clothes, they still heard these pieces as belonging to another era. In London, *The Harmonicon* reported in 1833 that Mendelssohn performed Mozart's Concerto in D Minor with "scrupulous exactness ... without a single addition or *new reading* of his own."[54] The concerto was old, but the cadenzas, which *The Harmonicon* says were of Mendelssohn's own composition, were new. George Macfarren (b. 1813), writing in 1884, remembered it differently. He says that Mendelssohn amplified Mozart's score, and even claims some historic basis for what Mendelssohn did by linking him to a chain of amplifiers that runs backward from Cipriani Potter to Thomas Attwood to Mozart. The new (the elaborations) and the old (the grounding of these elaborations in times past) are found in one and the same style of performance.[55]

The clash of old and new perhaps seemed less jarring to Macfarren when he remembered it in 1884 than to those on the spot in the early 1830s. In the late nineteenth century, arrangements of Mozart's concertos were still being played, though changes were made with a considerably lighter touch.[56] A bit closer to the swing in fashion away from heavy embellishments is the testimony of Friedrich Wieck, written in 1852. Showing no nostalgia for yesterday's craze, he authoritatively decries it.

> It was inevitable that, as a consequence of such more brilliant and more grandly resounding tonal effect [of modern pianos], the already classic but still simpler and less demanding keyboard compositions of Handel, Mozart and Haydn should be neglected or even bowdlerized, as happened to Mozart's piano compositions at the hands of Kalkbrenner and Hummel. One played them in the modern manner, i.e., more brilliantly, more virtuosically, faster, more ardently and more emphatically, in a word, more "concert-like," thus denying these works the piety due them.[57]

Already in 1845 Clara Wieck Schumann seems to have adopted her father's view published seven years later. She condemned a performance of Mozart's D Minor Concerto in Dresden by Hiller who, she thought, "did not play with the respect such as one can demand from a good artist." The example that came to her mind was Mendelssohn, who, she says, executed works like Mozart's with "love and mastery."[58] Given what Macfarren wrote, one wonders, what did Mendelssohn play when he played Mozart?

Or, to come to the point, what did Schumann hear when he heard Mozart concertos played in Leipzig in the 1830s? And, how did he react? When he heard his theory teacher, Dorn, perform Mozart's D Minor Concerto on the occasion of the fifty-year jubilee of the Gewandhaus concerts on 24 November 1831 (and at a repeat performance, by demand, one week later), it was in Hummel's arrangement.[59] But when Mendelssohn played Mozart's D Minor

Concerto on 28 January 1836 the *Allgemeine musikalische Zeitung* reported that he shunned the current fashion for elaboration.

> Hr. Fel. Mendelssohn-Barth. performed Mozart's splendid Piano Concerto in D Minor ... with the usual confidence, discretion and power, just as the master wrote it, that is, not in an arrangement. The accompanying cadenzas, composed by himself, were related in the most natural way to the themes, especially the first one, and were artistically executed in their flow to new heights of technique. The applause was stormy.[60]

Whatever he may have played in London three years earlier, Mendelssohn played in Leipzig without noticeable elaborations. But the cadenzas, with their new heights of technique drawing forth stormy applause, tell us that, just as with the young Hauck's performance of the same concerto in Berlin six years earlier, this part of the piece was in the modern style: a single fermata, and the old style is brushed aside to run head on into the new.

We have no comments from Schumann on Mendelssohn's performance. However, almost exactly a year later when he heard Ignaz Tedesco play the same concerto on 1 January 1837, he wrote of his disappointment. The *Allgemeine musikalische Zeitung* concurred, the concerto did not please.[61] Similarly, when Emil Leonhardt, a young pianist from Dresden, played Mozart's C Minor Concerto on 5 February 1835, the *Allgemeine musikalische Zeitung* reported again that the performance seemed, for the most part, not to please.[62] Schumann left no comments about Mendelssohn's performance of the same concerto on 1 March 1838. However, the *Zeitung* reports it, like his performance of the D Minor, brought forth a storm of applause, especially after the first-movement cadenza which was "executed with ever-increasing bravura," and was "ever more attractive, more brilliant the more it went on."[63]

Whatever Schumann heard or thought of Mozart's concertos in the 1830s, by 1848 he seems to have fallen in with the fashion of a new time, or at the very least with the ideas of his father-in-law and one-time teacher Friedrich Wieck, and of his wife Clara Wieck Schumann. He took a stand against embellishment which surely embraces Mozart's concertos. In his *Musikalische Haus- und Lebensregln* he wrote, "In pieces of good composers, regard it as something abominable to change, to omit, or to apply completely new-fangled embellishments. This is the greatest insult that you can offer art."[64] Inasmuch at it applies to Mozart's concertos, this mid-century view was reached after at least two about-faces in the reception history of Mozart's concertos, each championed in its turn by critics, composers, and performers who were deeply engaged with Mozart: the Müllers, Hummel, Cramer, Gottfried Weber, and Mendelssohn. What Schumann's cool assessment seems to show instead is the very disengagement that his dearth of comments on Mozart's concertos suggests. He is content to leave out the new-fangled embellishments, to let Mozart's concertos stand alone, as isolated artworks, more distant ideals than a vital and alive presence affecting concertos of the day.

* * *

At first glance, it would seem that Beethoven's concertos were disseminated differently and received differently than Mozart's. The 1830s brought announcements of the first full-score editions, of the First Concerto by Haslinger in Vienna in 1833; of the First, Second, and Third by Dunst in Frankfurt am Main in 1834–35. Full scores of the Fourth and Fifth Concertos had to wait until 1861 and 1857, respectively.[65] But already in 1835 a reviewer for the *Allgemeine musikalische Zeitung* wrote that one of the greatest desires of both virtuosos and composers was to own Beethoven's complete concertos in full score.[66] Nothing of the kind was planned as early for Mozart's concertos. Full scores began to be published only in the 1850s: by André in Offenbach am Main, and Richault in Paris.[67]

However, just as Mozart's concertos were brought into the drawing room in the 1820s and 1830s through chamber arrangements, so, too, were Beethoven's.[68] When Xaver Gleichauf's four-hand arrangement of the *Emperor* Concerto appeared around 1839 the reviewer for the *Allgemeine musikalische Zeitung* welcomed it as a means for music lovers to enjoy the work at any time in their own living rooms.[69] By 1845 Moscheles had produced editions of Beethoven's concertos for piano and small ensemble (two violins, viola, cello, bass, and flute), or for piano alone. Unlike Mozart's concertos, Beethoven's do not invite modernizing of the passagework, although it should be remembered that each performer at least had to compose or borrow his cadenzas since Beethoven's own were not in print until 1864. Still, like the Mozart arrangements, the Beethoven arrangements, too, take the solo piano as their starting point, and at least in this way follow the norm for the virtuoso concerto. Also like the Mozart arrangements, Moscheles's Beethoven arrangements give a curiously intimate look to the concertos, especially the last two. The piano scores for all five concertos show the tuttis and orchestral interludes or accompaniment parts in small notes. Although these may be played by the chamber group, the pianist who is playing without accompaniment might take them over, as if he or she were playing a sonata rather than a concerto. But at times, for example, in the first movement of the G Major Concerto, the pianist's two hands cannot possibly take on both the elaborate passagework and the orchestral melody. Then, the performance sphere shrinks to the pianist alone, communing only with himself or herself (see Example 5.2). The very public performance medium of the concerto becomes a very, very private one; the pianist plays, perhaps sings along, or perhaps only imagines the vital orchestral part.

The reduction of Beethoven's concertos to the intimacy of the drawing room informs the one positive review Schumann gave of a performance of a Beethoven concerto. After Mendelssohn played Beethoven's G Major Concerto on 3 November 1836, he recalled the work "with its very mysterious

Example 5.2 Beethoven, Concerto in G Major, first movement, bars 157–64. Moscheles's edition.

Adagio" and Mendelssohn's "inspired and inspiring" performance as a highlight of the fall season.[70] In this middle movement the forces are reduced to piano and string accompaniment, and carry out a chamber music-like dialogue.

Schumann left no record that any other concerto by Beethoven inspired him as much as the G Major. After hearing a performance of the C Minor Concerto by Wilhelm Taubert on 31 October 1833, he dismissed it as no more than an historical curiosity.

> I find much weak, much drawn out in the C [Minor] Concerto. One would not be beside oneself, if someone came with a similar new work. ... The thing is to be praised, as an antiquity to be recommended to young composers; but spare the public thereby; at least use the E-flat Major Concerto, or the D Minor of Mozart, if you offer something old. ... As reverence for

the eminent man, who certainly, as is becoming ever clearer to us, turned all his energy to his masses and symphonies and truly yielded up his best for them, who himself perhaps did not wish to hear any more about this concerto—I laud your clapping.[71]

What Schumann suggests as a substitute for the C Minor Concerto, either Beethoven's E-flat Major Concerto (the *Emperor*) or Mozart's D Minor, he still views as "something old." The Mozart he knew from Dorn's performance, in Hummel's arrangement. The *Emperor* he probably learned from his close friend Ludwig Schuncke, who would perform it just three months later, on 27 January 1834.[72] As for the C Minor Concerto, Schumann was sure Beethoven himself grew tired of it, and that his contemporaries clap for it only out of duty. His nonengagement with this concerto hardly seems to have changed by late 1839 when he reported that Camilla Pleyel "presented it with dignity, without fault, in the German manner, so that it pleased us like a picture."[73] For Schumann, all Beethoven's concertos rank beneath his masses and symphonies.

* * *

Schumann held up both Mozart's and Beethoven's concertos as a standard for contemporary concerto composers but not one that offered any specifics for them to follow. Rather, especially with regard to Mozart, the reverse turned out to be the case: his concertos were remade in the image of contemporary virtuoso concertos. In the 1830s a performance of a Mozart concerto was a singular conglomerate of old and new styles. With Mendelssohn, restraint in elaborating Mozart's score was coupled with extravagant cadenzas ending in up-to-date bravura displays. What little Schumann left us of his reaction to these mixtures shows him tepid. In 1833, Mozart's D Minor Concerto, presumably as he knew it in Hummel's arrangement performed by Heinrich Dorn, was worth hearing as an antiquity, a thing of the past, not as a vital part of the contemporary concert scene. He rejected Beethoven's C Minor Concerto. The *Emperor* was acceptable but, as an example of something old with the drawbacks of the old style, an educational piece, not one of Beethoven's masterworks. The concerto he warms to is Beethoven's most tender, the G Major, in Mendelssohn's performance. However, for the most part Schumann stands at some distance from the concertos of Mozart and Beethoven. As his reviews of concertos by his contemporaries repeatedly attest, he views those concertos most comfortably through the mediation of an intervening generation, whose concertos follow not the style or even the method of earlier concertos, but their spirit.

6
Critical Observer:
The Old Form I

Schumann wrote a series of reviews of piano concertos that ran in the *Neue Zeitschrift für Musik* from February through April 1836, then continued under different titles in January and February 1837, January 1839, and January 1840.[1] In all the series critiqued twenty-five concertos and concertinos. We will look at every one, beginning in this and the next chapter with twelve concertos that follow the plan of the virtuoso concerto as outlined in Chapter 2, what Schumann calls the old form. The two chapters thereafter will discuss concertos that strike out in a new direction.

This chapter will discuss concertos in the old form that Schumann approved, the last concertos of Hummel, Ries, and Field, and the two concertos by Chopin. Chapter 7 will turn to concertos of the same type for which he showed less enthusiasm. We have already discussed Schumann's admiration for earlier concertos by Hummel, Ries, and Field. We will show that, in championing their later works, he was not merely engaged in special pleading for composers fondly remembered from his youth. Rather, references in his reviews to earlier concertos by these composers show him well aware of a process of new repertory formation begun already in his generation. As explained by Siegfried Kross with reference to the late nineteenth century, this process means inclusion of a new work by a composer at the price of exclusion of an older one.

> In those days of public mania for the new. ... a new work could only be presented at the cost of eliminating [another of] the same composer's work in order to keep some appearance of a balance [among] composers performed. As long as a composer was productive, his output suffered continuous erosion by his new compositions. A consolidated repertoire would thus only be formed after the entire *oeuvre* was complete.[2]

Schumann's realistic assessment of the last concertos by Hummel, Ries, and Field is that although they have merit, they will not displace earlier works by these same composers that came to the public's attention in the 1810s and 1820s when their creators were most active as performers and teachers. Posterity, as we shall see, bore Schumann out. Earlier concertos by these composers remained in the repertory through the nineteenth and into the twentieth century. Chopin's concertos, of course, are still played.

Although he ranks them below their earlier concertos, Schumann still admires the last concertos of Hummel, Ries, and Field, and recommends the old form they follow to young composers. Our main question will involve what appealed to Schumann in these concertos in the old form. The most overarching answer is that he was interested in the concerto as a serious endeavor rather than frivolous entertainment. Our survey in Chapter 1 of subscription concerts of the Gewandhaus Orchestra attended by Schumann during his first season in Leipzig (1828–29) showed that the symphonic part of the program was usually reserved for what were already then considered classics (mostly by Beethoven, but also by Mozart or Haydn, among others). The portion spotlighting an instrumental soloist consisted of a somewhat later repertory which at the time was considered more ephemeral, or at best *Gebrauchsmusik* serving the purpose of placing the performer's skills in high relief.[3]

That Schumann was aware of this frivolous function of the concerto is shown by his fanciful account to Clara Wieck of the "fall festivals and other heavenly delights" he was experiencing during a vacation in Zwickau in late summer 1835.

> I'd like you to know everything about the other parts of the trip. In one corner of my imagination there's a bird shoot, and over there a grand concerto by Schmittbach is peeping out of the Rose [tavern], and there a christening at Thierfelder's in Schneeberg, not to mention little things like the rat hunt, potato feasts, beer dithyrambs and trips out to the country.[4]

Carl Ferdinand Schmittbach (or Schmitbach) was a bassoonist in the Gewandhaus Orchestra who was featured in two different solo works of his own composition in 1830.[5] The concerto Schumann attributes to him is heard among all the festivities that come together in one grand street scene. The piece floats out from a restaurant or tavern, just like the music of the Merchant's dance which would later "[waft] out with the steam of the cabbage soup from the tavern" in the final tableau of Stravinsky's *Petrushka*.[6] The usual association of the concerto with the frivolous was not lost on Moscheles, either, who just a year later expressed surprise at the title of a work of which he was the dedicatee, Schumann's *Concert sans orchestre*, Op. 14.

> The work has less the requirements of a concerto and more the characteristic idioms of a grand sonata, like some we know by Beethoven and Weber. In concertos, beyond any unity of style, one is (unfortunately) used to seeing some concessions ceded to the brilliant bravura or coquettish elegance of the player ...[7]

How, then, to change the concerto into something more serious? The lead article of Schumann's series gives the answer. It reviews a Concerto in F Minor, Op. 1, by E. Herman Schornstein (1811–82). Although this work received considerable attention at the time of its composition, I have not been able to locate a surviving copy.[8] That is too bad, but it does not prevent us from discerning where Schumann stands on just what is acceptable in the genre.

> The beauty of form that, as is common knowledge, is so admirable in the school of Mozart and especially in Hummel's compositions, we find here in happy imitation, and not just in the sense of a stylistic reproduction, but in that of the composer's natural feel for unity and proportion. ... The path that our composer has trod remains the surest and most blessed.[9]

Schumann holds up the virtuoso concertos of an older generation (Hummel's) as admirable models to follow, and not just in a general sense. He urges conformity to the specifics of the genre, for example, in the first movement by varying the close of the recapitulation as compared to the exposition and by introducing an *espressivo* area at the beginning of the development, and in all movements by restraining the orchestral accompaniment.

> Also, it is not in good taste to bring back note for note the brilliant period, with which solos close, when it is repeated ... In the [first] movement we like the tender central idea very much ...
>   Much as the individual voices are combined, the orchestra accompanies lightly, and nowhere covers up.[10]

Our examination of concertos following the old form in this chapter and the next will not catalog these and other usual features of the virtuoso concerto, as we described them in Chapter 2, and as they were recognized and accepted by Schumann. What will interest us primarily is one particular feature that is less common, but highly prized by Schumann: a natural cohesiveness, a sense that the various parts of an individual movement relate easily to one another. Although Schumann encourages the young Schornstein (who, in fact, was only one year younger) to polish his work, he also commends details already found in its passagework, accompaniments, and orchestration, and in its connection of different ideas. The last of these is the most difficult to pinpoint, and, as we shall show, the most important to Schumann.

> As concerns details, we note the elegance of the passagework, charm of accompaniments to the melodic parts, shading in the middle voices, elaboration and working out of the themes, analogy and connection of the different ideas whether from the orchestra, the solo, or both.[11]

In a genre known for running passages *con dolore* right up against those *con furore,* building connections rather than playing up disruptions is hardly the path of least resistance. The ways Hummel, Ries, and Field do this are various. Hummel imbues his passagework with what I call a certain sweetness, the result of carrying the lyricism of his thematic areas over into the beginning of passagework areas. Ries limits the number of motives he uses across different sections of a movement. Field maintains an easy gait that often spreads from thematic into passagework areas. Whereas each of these strategies tends to lessen disjunctions between various parts of the virtuoso concerto, none obscures its familiar form. The two concertos by Chopin, which Schumann holds up as examples nonpareil in the genre, saving them for the final, crowning essay of his 1836 series, also have an easy flow from section to section, related often enough to motivic connections that are allusive rather than contrived.

* * *

Hummel's Concerto in F Major, Op. post., was the last he wrote before his death in 1837. It was composed in February 1833 for what turned out to be his final extended concert tour, a trip to England lasting from late February through mid-June. The Concerto was performed in London from manuscript on 13 May. Nearly a year later a defensive but tepid review appeared in the second issue of the newly founded *Neue Zeitschrift für Musik.*[12] This was near the time Hummel played the Concerto in Dresden, on 3 April 1834; the response to this concert by a different reviewer for the *Zeitschrift* was not so sympathetic.

> Hummel should not embark on another concert tour. ... By doing so he detracts considerably from his well-earned fame. His brilliant period is long gone. His art has decreased as his years have increased.[13]

While acknowledging Hummel's artful treatment and beautiful instrumentation, the reviewer singles out for criticism his "old, second-hand motives and passagework."

Schumann knew well what was being said about Hummel. Already in 1832 he had written his mother that he planned to go to Weimar even though everyone advised against it, saying Hummel was ten years behind the times.[14] When he reviewed the F Major Concerto in 1840 he still retained a respect for the master, even as he was aware that his style was no longer fresh.

> Here, too, the name is sufficient to know in advance what to expect. ... no one would consider [the Concerto] a work of his prime—the time of his A Minor Concerto and F-sharp Minor Sonata. ... [it] is not an advancement from the ones preceding it, but rather a step back to the oldest of them—unpretentious, its ideas confined in range, its melodies almost simple, its passagework so elegant and pure as one knows it from Hummel. It will, therefore, not elicit any reaction, let the *Allgemeine musikalische Zeitung* say what it will. But the artist's chest is decorated with so many duly acquired orders, that it is hardly necessary to want to drape a new one on him.[15]

G. W. Fink, who reviewed the concerto for the *Allgemeine musikalische Zeitung* in 1839, had heard it performed twice privately with quintet accompaniment. All the hearers, he said, found the concerto "beautiful and exceedingly effective," adding that it "must be counted with the true, genuinely clear, and generally pleasing ones of the master, those that attest to his lasting strength, sound organism, and ... best spirit."[16] But Schumann is probably closer to the truth when he says it will elicit no reaction, especially, we might add, before a larger audience. It brought none in London at the Concert Room, King's Theatre, and, as far as the *Neue Zeitschrift* correspondent was concerned, none at Hummel's public concert in Dresden.[17]

Time bore out the opinion of Schumann and his correspondents. In an overview of Hummel's concertos printed in the *Neue Zeitschrift* in 1883 the F Major is not even mentioned.[18] It receives only one sentence in Hans Engel's exhaustive overview of the nineteenth-century piano concerto, where it is described as "severely conventional," and offering "nothing worth mentioning."[19] Hummel's A Minor and B Minor Concertos, on the other hand, were popular from the time of their publication in 1821 on into the twentieth century.[20] Table 5.1 attests to their repeated performances in Leipzig in the 1820s; the popularity in England of the A Minor Concerto at the same time was already mentioned in Chapter 4. Hummel himself continued to play the A Minor Concerto abroad long after its composition in 1816, even while he toured with his newer A-flat Concerto, Op. 113, in 1830 and 1831, and F Major Concerto, in 1833.[21]

The F Major Concerto's "step back" to an older style appealed to Schumann. In form it shows nothing unusual as compared to the virtuoso concertos described in Chapter 2, and in fact, could well be included among them. As concerns style, there are no abrupt modulations, no extreme dynamic markings, the melodies and passagework are, comparatively speaking, moderate in their use of the upper register. The passagework involves mostly if not exclusively scales and arpeggios of various types. Although others considered the style old-fashioned, Schumann may rather have seen a virtue in the lack of modern pianistic feats that the Dresden correspondent declared should push Hummel out of the ranks of professional performers altogether. The alberti basses, which the reviewer from Dresden considered tiring, lend the concerto's themes a certain sweetness. The melodies over them, despite the wide reach of their ornamentation, have a basic range that is small, and harmonic vocabulary that is restricted. The passagework, too, has at times a sweetness not found in the A and B Minor Concertos.

The closing passagework of the F Major Concerto lacks the excitement generated in the A Minor and B Minor Concertos. But what the passagework of the F Major Concerto may lack in vigor is offset, again, by a certain sweetness, the result of the perception that the melodic unit immediately after the initial vamp congeals quite firmly into a full phrase (a perception underscored by Hummel's *ritardando*), at any rate, more firmly I think than at the comparable point in either the A or B Minor Concertos. The reader may wish to compare Example 6.1, bars 196–99, the four bars immediately following the vamp in the F Major Concerto, and Example 2.2, bars 220–23, the comparable place in the A Minor Concerto.

This is but one example of the passagework that Schumann calls "so elegant and pure" in Hummel, a match for what he calls his almost simple melodies. The lack of pretentiousness that Schumann admires has first of all to do with a lack of flashy display, an elegance most in evidence where the simple melodies spill over into appealing, and beautifully wrought passagework areas. In the second group the passagework eventually builds to the expected bravura close, not, however, after an abrupt break, but instead after a more natural bridge from the preceding thematic area. The listener at once recognizes the clear divisions of the old form, nothing is obscured, but at the same time is charmed by an easy ride from one section to the next, which, just as Schumann says, is not calculated to have an effect of éclat.

* * *

Like Hummel's A Minor Concerto, Ries's in C-sharp Minor was much admired by Schumann. And, as with Hummel, Schumann also considered

Example 6.1 Hummel, Concerto in F Major, Op. post., first movement solo exposition, close, following the initial vamp.

Ries's final concerto, his ninth, to be in the same tradition as his earlier ones (the C-sharp Minor is his third; Schumann's interest in it is discussed in Chapter 4).

> Even Napoleon lost his last battles, but Arcole and Wagram eclipse these. Ries has written a C-sharp minor concerto, and can rest peacefully on his laurels. ... this ninth concerto comes close to its predecessors. In no respect do we find any progress in it, neither of the composer and still less of the virtuoso. The same ideas as before, their same expression, everything firm and immovable, as if it could not be otherwise. Not a note too few, an outpouring of everything, harmony, fundamental conception, music. It is as difficult to speak of such works and one has as little to say about them as of the blue sky that looks in at me through the window. We therefore wish that the subscribers, who even now are reading this, would look out of our eyes, in order to divine the similarities between the concerto of an old master and the peacefully undulating blue yonder as quickly as we have.[22]

The Ninth Concerto was published in 1834, but the C-sharp Minor that Schumann says brought Ries his laurels continued to be played, and in fact had a long tenure in the repertory. It was composed by Ries in Russia, then went with him to London where he settled in 1813, playing it twice in that year then again as late as 1820.[23] In 1824 Ries relocated to Germany. By 1826, when he appeared in Leipzig, the C-sharp Minor Concerto had been displaced by his Seventh Concerto, Op. 132, the *Abschieds von England* (see Table 5.1). But that same year the C-sharp Minor also was heard in Leipzig in a performance by Léopoldine Blahetka. Eleven years later, on 2 July 1837, Robena Ann Laidlaw played the Concerto's final two movements in Leipzig, and then on 23 October 1838 Charles Evers played the complete concerto. Forty-one years later, in 1879, Peters printed an edition arranged for piano solo by Ferdinand August Roitzsch. Carl Reinecke included it in his four-volume collection *Clavier-Concerte alter und neuer Zeit* (1877–90),[24] and as late as 1931 an arrangement for piano solo by Charles-René was published in the *Édition nationale française: Panthéon des pianistes,* series 3 of their *Édition de concours.*

Ries's Ninth Concerto never achieved the popularity of his Third,[25] and Schumann is right that it shows no progress over the Third. His sense of the firmness and immobility of the Ninth Concerto may derive in large part from the very conventionality of its form. The first movement, for example, fits the general description given for virtuoso concertos in Chapter 2, including a long tutti introduction and thereafter three full tuttis. As the movement progresses the form unfolds clearly to the listener. At any rate, this seems to be what Fink, who reviewed the piece in the *Allgemeine musikalische Zeitung,* had in mind when he judged it easy to hear. His description gives more details than Schumann's.

[The concerto] seems to us well calculated for a mixed audience. It goes
no further than one would like in such a gathering, agreeably offering
whatever is understood readily and with pleasure, without straining oneself. ... That means, of course, that not everything in it is unheard of or
fully new. On the contrary, many things are built on motives that are of
interest as carefully manipulated reminiscences.[26]

The formal divisions of the first movement of the Concerto are well
marked. The long opening tutti presents a motto and two main themes, the
first in G minor, the second beginning in B-flat major but modulating to G
major then closing on G minor with the special tutti close. A cadenza
announces the solo entrance. The solo development settles soon after its
opening into a new, *espressivo* theme. Its main key, E major, is distant, and
the modulations that ensue in the passagework are rather far reaching. A
return to the first main theme in the tutti, followed by a bold cadenza-like
solo entrance, clearly mark the recapitulation. What were already enumer-
ated as conservative features of Hummel's F Major Concerto are heard also
in Ries's Concerto: the absence of extravagant dynamic and expression
markings, of jarring modulations and sudden shifts. The passagework is a
bit humdrum, involving, as in Ries's earlier concertos, lots of scales and
arpeggios.

A special feature of Ries's Concerto is the many motivic relations across
its various sections. In the first tutti, the second main theme begins with the
head motive of the first main theme, freely inverted (Examples 6.2b and
6.2a, cf. bars 47–48 and 7–8). Also in the first tutti, a rise from the first to
the fifth scale degree in the special close freely draws on the fall from the
fifth to the first scale degree in the opening motto (Example 6.2c, bars
67–69; cf. Example 6.2a, bars 1–5). The rising fifth motto of the special
close (Example 6.2c) is heard again in the second tutti (Example 6.2d, bars
197–98, further, bars 201–02), then in the final one (bars 360–61, 364–65).
In the second tutti, a new turn motive is introduced and combined with a
rhythm heard in the bass of the opening theme (Example 6.2d, bars
199–200; cf. Example 6.2a, bars 8, 10). The turn motive is picked up by the
solo at the beginning of the development, then freely varied to fashion the
espressivo theme (Example 6.2e, bar 236; cf. Example 6.2d, bar 199).

The motivic relationships among different thematic areas of the Concerto, although associated by Hans Engel with Beethoven's practice, are in
fact a forward-looking feature, one that became something of a fashion in
the concertos of the time.[27] It will be taken up in greater detail in Chapter 8.
For now it may be noted that, although of interest to Fink, it is not a feature
cited by Schumann. The conservation of motivic material from one section
to the next may, however be another factor, in addition to the steadfast
adherence to an older form and style, underlying his feeling that the
Concerto is "immovable." Contrary to the usual practice in virtuoso concertos, it is not extravagant in its juxtaposition of extremes in affect, nor excessive in its introduction of new themes. The special tutti close that disappears

a. first tutti, first main theme

b. first tutti, second main theme

c. first tutti, close

d. second tutti

e. solo development, *espressivo* theme

Example 6.2 Ries, Piano Concerto No. 9 in G Minor, Op. 177, first movement, motivic relationships.

completely in some concertos after one hearing returns and even spins out a link to the solo development. In sum, the first movement has motivic associations across sections, that "analogy and connection of the different ideas," that Schumann valued in Schornstein's Concerto.

* * *

From among the older generation of composers still writing in the older style, a concerto by Field, No. 7 in C Minor, is the only other work in Schumann's series that received a glowing review. As with Hummel and Ries, Schumann already held a special place for an earlier work by Field, his Second Concerto in A-flat Major. Clara Wieck began practicing that concerto in 1828, and it was known in her home as early as 1823 (her age four), the year her mother performed it.[28] As mentioned earlier, Schumann

owned a copy of the piece, too, and improvised from it.[29] He was also witness to Clara's final preparations of the Concerto for public performance.
On 16 May 1832, he wrote, "Clara [Wieck] plays the Field Concerto
divinely." He heard her play the Concerto again on 27 May, was present on
28 May at a *Soirée im Salon de M. Wieck* when she performed the first
movement before a small audience.[30] His review of her performance at the
Gewandhaus on 31 July calls the Field an "angel" among concertos, written
in the "moonlight key."[31] Of all Field's concertos, the A-flat remained the
most popular, being reprinted in different editions up to the early twentieth
century, and most recently in *Musica Britannica,* volume 17.[32]

As for Field's Seventh Concerto (composed c. 1822–32, published
1834), Schumann did not hear it in performance, and in fact Dörffel lists no
performances at Gewandhaus concerts. Field performed the Concerto on
Christmas Day 1832 in Paris when on a European sojourn undertaken in
1831–35. Afterward, François-Joseph Fétis wrote that it was "diffuse but
full of happy ideas," an assessment that has been repeated in later descriptions of the Concerto by Heinrich Dessauer, David Branson, and Patrick
Piggott.[33] The charge of diffuseness is directed mainly toward the "episodic" second movement, the finale. It may be what Schumann had in mind
when he wrote his review.

> Yes, everything is *bon* and to be kissed, and especially you, you entire last
> movement with your divine [*göttlichen*] tedium, your charm, your clumsi-
> ness, your beauty of soul—to be kissed from head to toe. Away with your
> rules of form and figured bass! First have your school benches carved
> from the cedar of genius, and more. Do your duty, that is, have talent; be
> Fields, write what you will; be poets and human beings, I beg you![34]

Today this reminds us of Schumann's later joy over the "heavenly [*him-
mlische*] length" of Schubert's Great C Major Symphony.[35] But, at the time,
his rapturous defense of the last movement of the Field may have been a
direct counter to an earlier review of the same piece that appeared in the
Allgemeine musikalische Zeitung. "We would separate the two movements
from each other, and then perform only the first for its own sake, and the
other at another time, again for its own sake. But we definitely give preference to the first movement over the second."[36]

The second movement is a rondo, *Allegro moderato,* in three-four time,
that divides roughly as shown in Figure 6.1. Each of the large, closed **A** and
B sections contains many different motives congealing into many different
themes, and the development section leads through many keys. Most striking are the abrupt orchestral interpolations, all of which interrupt or extend
a cadence by the solo. Examples 6.3a and 6.3b show two. The first, bars
221–41, turns the expected cadence on G major toward G minor. It seems to
have no motivic connection to anything that has gone before but has a clear
analogy to what follows in bars 289–96, where the solo, now also in G
minor, extends the cadence to return once more to G major. The second, the

A	bars 1–16 (tutti) + 17–92 + 93–114 (tutti) + 115–22, in C major
	transition to G major, bars 123–47
B	bars 148–364, in G major and minor
	return to C major (tutti), bars 365–90
A	bars 391–419 + 420–35 (tutti)
	transition to F (tutti), bars 436–43
development	of **A** motives, bars 444–620, beginning in F major
	(solo with tutti interludes)
	of **B** motives, bars 621–36
	of **A** motives, bars 637–56
Adagio	bars 657–71 (tutti)
coda	*a Tempo* on **A** motives, bars 672–749, in C major

Figure 6.1 Schematic representation of Field, Concerto in C Major, No. 7, Rondo.

Adagio (bars 657–71) that immediately precedes the coda, comes after an exciting retransition in which one of the **A** motives is developed in the bass by the solo (bars 637–56). The *Adagio* is recognizably related to the orchestral interpolation cited earlier (bars 221–41), and to its counterpart in the solo, notably the dotted figure beginning in bar 289.

Nonetheless, I would guess that motivic interrelatedness *per se* was not what brought Schumann's approval, but rather, despite the expansiveness of each section of the movement (save the second **A**), the flow of each idea from what precedes, or into what follows. It is a romp in which new ideas depart at a tangent from those preceding them, maintaining the affect primarily by mood rather than by any tangible motivic connections. For the solo, the tempo of the piece remains *Allegro moderato* throughout, and the easy gait of the eighth and triplet eighth notes seldom gives way to sixteenth notes, even in the coda. Dynamic and tempo indications are rare, leaving the performer to shape music that seems to stream forth naturally, that stays very much in the middle register of the instrument, or, as in the development, exploits its low rather than high reaches.

The movement's characteristic understatement was also a feature of Field's playing, as we read from the pen of Joseph d'Ortigue after he heard Field perform his Seventh Concerto in Paris.

All the ordinary mechanical procedures seem to disappear in his style of playing. It is full of carefree and good-humoured wit, and withal a precision and a surprising aplomb, grace and poetry. Field sits quite simply at the piano, as if at his own fireside. He makes no preparatory gestures, as do so many of our artists. In the first bars one is tempted to find his hand heavy, then suddenly the playing becomes agile, delicate, and of incredible cleanness in passages of extreme volubility. He remains little animated—in short he is cool, but his coolness is an essential part of his art.[37]

a. from section **B**

Example 6.3   Field, Concerto in C Major, No. 7, Rondo, tutti interpolations.

As our study up to this point has concentrated on first movements, an examination of the first movement of Field's Concerto seems in order. He gave its premiere performance in Moscow on 6 March 1822. At that time no other movement had been completed.[38] As it turns out, a middle movement was never written. Frank Merrick notes that Field's Third Concerto in E-flat Major (1816) also has no slow movement, and suggests that Field played a nocturne in its place.[39] The hypothesis has been advanced that the addition of a nocturne to the development of the first movement of the Seventh

b. from the Adagio section

Example 6.3 (*continued*)

Concerto as a kind of slow movement substitute came in 1832 when Field performed the Concerto in Paris, but no clear basis for this assumption has been given.[40] It seems questionable whether contemporary audiences even viewed this section of the first movement as a slow-movement substitute, rather than as merely an episode beginning the development. Perhaps the best answer is that they understood it to be both. Liszt, writing in 1837 about various formal innovations in the concerto, says, "Field, in his last concerto, has given the adagio by way of a second solo [*a placé l'adagio en guise de second solo*]."[41] Along these same lines Schumann simply says, in a rhapsody that alternately hangs on the physical appearance of the manuscript full score and the sounds it evokes, that "a moonlight nocturne 'woven from the fragrance of roses and snow of lilies'" is in the middle.[42]

For John A. Meyer, Field's rambling style is seen more in his first than last movements. "Field's discursive style is particularly apparent in his development sections, which almost always introduce completely new material; examples are the recitative passage in the Second Concerto, the storm episode in the Fifth, and the several self-contained episodes in the Seventh Concerto." In this way, Meyer says, Field's concertos "foreshadow the breakdown of the classical structure and the emergence of the freer forms of the romantic concerto."[43] But what strikes me is rather that Field's structure reinforces the old virtuoso model. From among first movements by various composers that we examined, the majority feature a separate, closed, *espressivo* section at or near the beginning of the development. Other features of the virtuoso concerto pattern that Field follows are found in the long opening tutti, which exposes the main themes of the first group, modulates to a new key for the main theme of the second group, and returns to the two opening themes of the first group (in reverse order) at its close. The solo exposition follows the same course as the tutti, with the usual additions: a cadenza-like gesture at the outset (over the opening motive of the tutti, a timpani roll), a new theme in the first group, expansive transition area (but one still using a motive from the comparable place in the opening tutti), then, after the theme of the second group, a separate, brilliant *con forza* close. The recapitulation is considerably truncated. After a statement of the opening theme by the tutti, the solo enters with the theme of the second group. The brilliant passagework, *con fuoco,* freely recomposes the close of the exposition.

If Field differs from the virtuoso model in his Seventh Concerto, it is in ways similar to those already described in connection with his Second Concerto: in the simple lyricism of the themes; in the structure of the development, which, after the G major nocturne episode, elaborates motives from the first theme group, then (in a *con sordino* area in A major with a new, pastoral theme) incorporates motives from the second group theme, and finally (in the retransition) again picks up motives from the first group. A special feature of the movement is that the expansive transition in the first solo consists of two full periods. The first (bars 155–70), as already noted, is derived from the transition in the first tutti. The second (bars 171–94) has a new melody, played by the woodwinds to obbligato accompaniment by the solo. Its much drawn out penultimate and final measures (Waldbauer-Riemann nos. 7 and 8) run seamlessly into the theme of the second group. The brilliant close, however, remains the property of the soloist and follows a more customary pattern, beginning with the usual vamps then going forward in conventional double thirds, scales, and arpeggios.

* * *

It seems, to sum up our findings so far, that for Schumann the attractive feature of these three concertos, by Hummel, Ries, and Field, was an easy flow in the individual movements from section to section. This derives in part from their composers' eschewing outrageous technical effects in brilliant areas and unabashed sentimentality in thematic areas. The result is a certain downplaying of the contrast between the two types of areas, which may be further aided by the introduction of quasi-thematic phrases into the passagework area, or of motives from the thematic area into the passagework. However, motivic relationships across thematic areas, or between thematic and passagework areas, is a specific compositional refinement which Schumann does not champion for its own sake. More telling for him are the overall mood and smooth flow of a movement rather than any contrived connections.

For Schumann, the crowning example in the genre of this unforced flow is found in Chopin's two concertos, which he reviewed in April 1836 in the final essay of his concerto series for that year. Leon Plantinga believes that by this time "the keen edge of [Schumann's] first excitement about Chopin seems to have been dulled." If Schumann was in fact "not altogether satisfied with these compositions" the reason would hardly seem to be the one Plantinga puts forward, namely, that "they belong to the virtuoso type."[44] As we have seen, Schumann does not slight the virtuoso concerto for being just that, and in Chopin he finds the best it has to offer. In this, posterity has upheld his judgment: Chopin's are the only two virtuoso concertos still in the repertory today. Although perhaps not the most frequently programmed among nineteenth-century concertos, they remain favorites of conservatory students and contest devisors.

It is true, to grant another point Plantinga makes, that any discussion of the specifics of Chopin's concertos is scant in Schumann's review, yet reading it one can hardly doubt the author's deep attraction to the concertos' sensual appeal, nobility, and seriousness of purpose.

> ... if an homage in words is hitherto lacking (the most beautiful homage has already been offered him in a thousand hearts), then I would look for the reason partly in the fear that befalls one with regard to an object one thinks about most often, and which one loves the most, namely, that one cannot adequately speak of the majesty of the thing, one cannot fully apprehend it in its full depth and height. In addition, I would look for the reason in the intimate artistic relationship in which we admit we stand with this composer. Finally, too, an homage in words is suppressed because in his latest compositions Chopin appears to have entered upon not another, but a higher path, about whose direction and presumed goal we first hoped to be a bit clearer before rendering an account of it to our beloved allies abroad ...[45]

Chopin's Concerto in E Minor, Op. 11, was first published in 1833. Clara and Friedrich Wieck heard Chopin play it in Paris on 14 March 1832, and reported back to Schumann when they returned to Leipzig in spring 1832.[46] Clara began studying the Concerto as soon as it was issued. On 29 September 1833 she played the finale at a Leipzig subscription concert, then on 5 May 1834, the entire piece. For the next few years the Concerto remained prominent in her repertory.[47] When Chopin stopped for a day in Leipzig, on the night of 27 September 1835, Clara played for him in private, among other things, the last movement.[48] Schumann had his first meeting with Chopin at this time, and commented in the *Neue Zeitschrift* on 6 October, "He plays just as he composes, i.e., singularly." Two weeks later Schumann revealed a more personal reaction in the *Neue Zeitschrift,* something of what seven months later in his review he called the "artistic affinity" he felt for the composer. "Chopin was here. Florestan flung himself on him. I saw them arm in arm, more floating than walking. I did not speak with him, in fact was alarmed by the very thought of it."[49]

Over the course of her career, Clara Wieck Schumann's influence on the way Chopin's music was played was enormous. According to James Methuen-Campbell, "The acceptance of Chopin in Germany was largely due to her advocacy." In Schumann's opinion she gave "almost more meaning to his compositions than Chopin himself."[50] In Leipzig she was certainly the first to play the E Minor Concerto, and nearly the only one to continue performing it at least through 1840.[51] Still, as late as 1840, she approached it with some trepidation. After a performance of the last two movements in Hamburg she wrote Schumann, "I lost all fear and played the Concerto by Chopin ... altogether beautifully and to my own satisfaction, which should say a lot indeed."[52] That the Concerto was "monstrously difficult" was already recognized by Fink when he reviewed it for the *Allgemeine musikalische Zeitung* in 1834. "Whoever undertakes it will practically give it up at the start, rather than subject his ears to so much pain before he achieves the security of performance that makes possible, first a familiarity with the contents, then a grasp of the ideas."[53]

As for Chopin's F Minor Concerto, though composed earlier than the E Minor Concerto, it was first published in 1836, an event that no doubt gave the impetus for Schumann's review of both concertos. Clara Schumann was the first in Leipzig to publicly perform this concerto, too, when she played its final two movements on 31 March 1841. Her next performance was not until 14 March 1852, when she gave all three movements under Schumann's direction in Leipzig.[54] It might be added that Chopin also favored the E Minor Concerto, which from 1830 to 1835 he played publicly in Breslau, Warsaw, Vienna, Munich, Paris, and Rouen. Of the F Minor, by contrast, he gave only two public performances according to Jean-Jacques Eigeldinger's meticulous records, in Warsaw on 17 and 22 March 1830, that is, soon after its composition.[55]

Fink points not only to the difficulty of the E Minor Concerto, but also to the "peculiar spirit" it breathes, the very "bizarreness" of its attraction. He concludes it will not please everyone, "for where, as here, so many new and often curiously disposed things resound, then the fondness for something customary, something loved does not have sufficient release or free rein so that one can simply give oneself over to one's impression without being disturbed."[56] Fétis, who heard Chopin perform the Concerto in 1832 in Paris, gave a similar assessment.

> In his concert which he gave at the salons of MM. Pleyel et Cie on the 26th of this month [February 1832], M. Chopin performed a concerto [Op. 11], which gave as much astonishment as pleasure to its audience, both by the novelty of melodic ideas and by the brilliant passages, modulations and general form of the movements. There is a soul in the melodies, fantasy in the passage work and originality in the whole. The modulations are too rich [*trop de luxe*], and there is some disorder in the sequence of phrases, so that sometimes the music seems more improvisatory than planned ...[57]

Fink and Fétis's opinion that Chopin concentrates on local contrasts at the expense of the larger form of the E Minor Concerto has come down to our day. In Jim Samson's words, he "[fails] to relate detail to whole." As a consequence, in the first movement he embarks on what Tovey calls a "suicidal" (but Samson merely an "eccentric") plan. This was already mentioned in Chapter 3, the so-called fault being a tonal scheme that does not modulate from the tonic mode (minor then major) in either the first tutti or first solo.[58] Samson concludes, as we, Fink, or Fétis might well:

> It is clear from the concertos that he viewed tonal contrast less in terms of its structural potential than as a means of local colour change, where the contrast of major and minor was often in itself a sufficient resource.[59]

Yet, Fétis, Fink, and Schumann are all silent on the overall tonal scheme of the movement.

Writing in 1936, Tovey further says that up to his day another main objection to at least the F Minor Concerto (and by implication the E Minor) has been its orchestration. This began at least as early as the comment in Berlioz's *Mémoires,* which were published posthumously in 1870. "In Chopin's compositions," he writes, "all the interest is concentrated in the piano part; the orchestra's role in his concertos is confined to a frigid and practically superfluous accompaniment."[60] Today, like Tovey, we may view ourselves as more modern for accepting Chopin's orchestration as "the correct accompaniment to his piano-forte writing."[61] Meyer (in 1982) speaks of it as a usual practice of the day, to which we could add, so usual that it is not even mentioned by contemporary reviewers.[62] That is, except for one who noted that Chopin's E Minor Concerto was better received in Paris on 26 February 1832 when he played it without an orchestra than two months later on 20 May when he played its first movement with one, because of "the somewhat heavy orchestration combined with the rather weak tone Chopin elicits from the piano."[63]

If, then, Schumann did not voice objections raised by some later commentators, namely to the form or orchestration of Chopin's concertos, what, by contrast, appealed to him about them? One hardly needs to mount an exhaustive defense of Chopin to answer this question. His concertos have a ravishing beauty, both in their thematic and passagework areas, as we already discussed in Chapter 4.[64] Here we will show that they also have a facile flow from one section to the next, that "analogy and connection of the different ideas," which Schumann found attractive in Schornstein's Concerto, and which we found in concertos by Hummel, Ries, and Field. This is not a quality that was the focus of many later commentators. According to John Rink, much twentieth-century analysis placed "a premium on synchronic structural integrity at the expense of the diachronically unfolding flow of events that characterises music in sound" and that is so important to works conceived, like Chopin's concertos (and, we should add, all virtuoso concertos) "with the medium of performance at heart."[65] He terms this an objective response, one that emphasizes music's structure. A subjective response, the one Schumann inclines toward, favors instead music's "unfolding flow of events."

In the first movement of Chopin's F Minor Concerto, the "analogy and connection of the different ideas" results from a cohesiveness of the overall mood that depends more on a general as opposed to a specific relationship among the different sections. Thus, in the recapitulation when a mere four-bar statement of the theme of the first group runs directly into the theme of the second group, the conjunction of the two affects is seamless. Along these same lines is the interconnectedness of the tuttis of the same movement. The third tutti begins with a motive obviously derived from the opening motive of the first tutti, transformed sufficiently to take on a new character—*forte* and full orchestra as opposed to the original *piano,* strings only, close together in mid-register—yet at the same time recalling the *forto* interjections of bars 5–6 in the first tutti (Example 6.4a and b). Similarly, motives from the transition of the first tutti (and exclusive to the tuttis) are mined for the second and fourth tuttis. In the second tutti, they easily slide into other new motives and, in the fourth, into a reappearance of the opening motive.

Finally, I think the *Larghetto* of the F Minor Concerto embodies all the features Schumann admired in Chopin. It is the only movement he specifically singled out in his review. "What," he wrote, "are ten editorial accolades next to the *Adagio* [*sic*] in the Second Concerto."[66] It has an expressive melody, unity of mood, clear (return) form, and in the middle section, melodic gestures in an area that at first seems only one of orchestral and harmonic coloring (in Tovey's words, "a dramatic recitative"). The middle section, with its *appassionato* melody doubled in octaves and accompanied by string tremolos, is, in Rink's words, "extraordinarily intense, exploring

a. first tutti, beginning

b. third tutti, beginning

Example 6.4 Chopin, Concerto in F Minor, Op. 21, first movement.

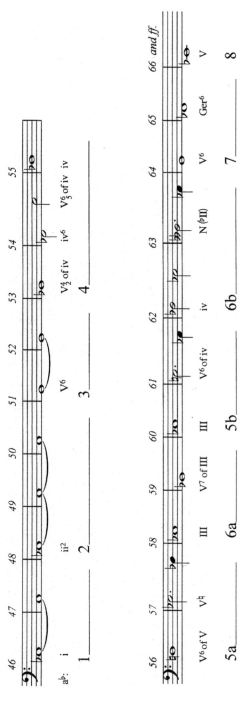

Example 6.5 Bass of Chopin, Concerto in F Minor, Op. 21, second movement, middle section.

registral and dynamic extremes in the *fioriture* interspersing the long appoggiaturas." At the same time, in addition to what Rink calls its stylized *recitativo accompagnato,* or *stromentato,* it is, as he also describes it, one large thematic period in A-flat minor, unified motivically as well as by harmonic direction.[67] A skeletal outline is given in the bass graph, Example 6.5. The first phrase is an elaborate progression from i to iv in bars 46–55 (subdivided into the segments 46–50 and 51–55, the second freely drawing on motives from the first). The consequent phrase begins with an appoggiatura bar (56), then a departure from and return to V between bars 57 and 66 (the segments being bars 56–61 and 62–66), followed by appendices in bars 67–72. The section is remarkable for its drama and passion. It shows off the skill and expressive range of the pianist, while at the same time cohering into a cogent melodic unit.

Our summary need only be brief. Schumann valued virtuoso concertos produced by an older, respected generation of composers, and pointed to them as models for younger composers. He was not alone in seeing merits in these works. As we noted, pianos concertos by Hummel, Ries, and Field were performed for the best part of a century, and Chopin's concertos are still in the repertory. All have a natural flow that smoothes away the many disruptions the genre invites. The value Schumann places on this feature reflects a response to the performer's art as it is, quite literally, played out within the design of the virtuoso concerto.

7
Critical Observer: The Old Form II

What remains in our survey of Schumann's reviews of concertos in the old style are those works that he did not like, by Hiller, Döhler, Kalkbrenner, Hartknoch, and Herz. We will begin with the young Hiller, a composer whom Schumann calls one of the most "remarkable manifestations" of Beethoven's romanticism but in whose first concerto he detects a certain lack of experience and inattention to detail. The net result is an absence of that elusive quality that we concluded appealed to Schumann in the concertos of Chopin, Hummel, Ries, and Field, what we called an "easy flow," a feel of consistency across the various sections of each movement. That it should be missing, too, in concertos by Herz, Kalkbrenner, and Döhler, especially, and also to a certain extent in one by Hartknoch, is due, Schumann thinks, to their flagrant concession to the most fashionable playing, a preoccupation with the latest technical exploits that leads to wild mood swings whereby elaborately decorated and drawn out melodies are juxtaposed with ever flashier and speedier passagework to the point that any connection between the two breaks down.

Such fiery displays are geared to the immediate response of a general audience. But Schumann was reviewing the concertos that cater to this response in the privacy of his study, either playing them for himself alone (recall that he told Hummel in 1831 he could read practically all concertos from sight), or looking at the score silently, away from the piano. In reviews, such as the one of Field's Concerto No. 7 that was discussed in Chapter 6, he often enough shows himself aware of his position as he shifts from assessing the sound of a concerto to describing its look on the page, a double perspective that an audience at a public concert would not share with him. Schumann's most famous and self-admitted miscalculation conflating these two different perspectives was his initial reaction to *Tannhäuser* in October 1845, after seeing the score. A few weeks later, after seeing the opera on stage, he wrote Mendelssohn:

> *Tannhäuser* I hope to tell you about verbally soon; *I must take back* much of what I wrote to you after reading the score; on the stage everything appears quite different. I was quite moved by much of it.[1]

Eight years later, Schumann wrote Carl van Bruyck, "But you must not judge [Wagner] from the piano reductions. Were you to hear his operas on stage, you surely would not be able to resist a profound excitement in many places."[2] One could make a similar observation about piano concertos: they come to life with the tension of a daring performance before an eager audience.

Before turning to the body of our discussion, on concertos by Hiller, Döhler, Kalkbrenner, Hartknoch, and Herz, we will briefly turn our attention to the daring pianistic feats so beloved of audiences of the 1830s, and the instruments they were performed on. We will then take up Schumann's review of Stamaty's A Minor Concerto. I have separated it out from the other concertos because I have as yet found no copy of it. It bears on our discussion as one of the few concertos Schumann heard before he reviewed its score in his series covering recently published concertos. Furthermore, Schumann's review of Stamaty's Concerto takes up a theme that is one focus of our attention in this chapter, namely, that seeing and hearing a performer can change one's perception of a concerto known previously only from looking at or sight-reading through the score.

* * *

For Schumann, the peerless pianistic technician was Henri Herz. Although he often writes sarcastically of Herz's attainments (as we have said, he never heard him play), Schumann does not deny that virtuosity is an essential element of any piano playing beyond the mediocre, nor, as we shall discuss in more detail in the next chapter, that the concerto above all is the genre that should provide a showplace for it. Schumann was intensely occupied with his own technical development during the time he studied with Wieck.[3] Later he devoted many pages to carefully assessing dozens of sets of piano etudes in the *Neue Zeitschrift*.[4] This raft of technical methods was, logically enough, to a large extent produced by the same virtuosos who composed and performed concertos: Hummel, Moscheles, Kalkbrenner, and Herz. That the most popular pianists of the 1820s and 1830s should aggressively advertise their technical finesse hardly sets them apart from earlier generations of pianists, from Mozart and Muzio Clementi, or Beethoven and Daniel Steibelt, to name only the most famous rivals of earlier times. Yet, each generation believes it has improved on the accomplishments of the last. At the time of Schumann's reviews the dominant performers of the 1830s and their audiences naturally believed they had reached the limits of technical prowess. The Parisians Herz and Kalkbrenner were in the vanguard of this group of technical wizards, and had their effect on Hiller, who lived in the city from late 1828 to early 1836. Through their published works and their concert tours, the influence of Kalkbrenner and Herz also reached beyond those near them in Paris, for example, to Döhler, who came to Vienna to study in 1829, toured Germany with his works in 1836, and eventually made it to Paris in 1838, or even to Hartknoch, who worked in Russia from 1828 to his death in 1834.

What is the link between the improved technical skills of these pianists and the instruments they played? The lighter action of all pianos of a pre-1840 vintage made rapid and even playing somewhat easier than on a modern piano. Nevertheless, the fast, brilliant areas of the virtuoso concerto are still difficult on any piano, and in the 1830s this meant both on the Viennese makes favored by Schumann, with their more responsive action and short-lived but brilliant tone, and on the English makes popular in Paris, with their heavier touch, and richer, longer-lasting tone.[5] No matter which type of piano may have been the composer's instrument of choice, the bravura fireworks always heavily feature the upper register, usually with some kind of broken-chord support in the middle or low register but with little exploitation of the low reaches of the instrument. The bass register has less reverberation and a notoriously fast decay on all pianos without the new overstringings and metal frames that were standard later in the century. In Kalkbrenner's and Herz's concertos, the upper reaches are sounded often, not just in the passagework areas, in which the gymnastics of the dexterous right hand include, in addition to the usual scales, arpeggios, and trills, wide leaps and long octave or double-third passages, but also in the wide stretch of elaborate ornaments in the thematic areas.

It may be that Kalkbrenner responded specifically to what Robert Winter (writing about Chopin) calls the "increasingly silvery, ethereal quality" of the upper register of pianos manufactured by Pleyel, a firm in which Kalkbrenner was a partner. Yet Herz, who adopted a similar style, may well have favored Erard's piano: when he founded his own firm in 1851 he produced a simplified copy of Erard's piano, an instrument Winter says lacks the gradations of color in the treble register heard in Pleyel's pianos.[6] Döhler, who wrote his concerto during the time of his studies in Vienna from 1829 to 1836, was surely playing a Viennese instrument. True, during the 1830s when a great variety of instruments were produced and technology continued to develop rapidly, one could probably uncover the perfect instrument for each composer's particular style. However, whatever the specific qualities of the instrument one settled on in each case, I think for these exhibitionistic works an important factor on any instrument is the surprise, even astonishment value of the high treble, with its natural penetrating quality.

For the traveling professional, no matter what the instrument he had in his ear when composing, he had to adapt to whatever one he found away from home. This was certainly hardest for those coming to Paris from the east, as opposed to those leaving Paris to tour Central and Eastern Europe. Clara Wieck struggled with the more "stubborn" response of the Parisian pianos on both her first and second trips to Paris, in 1832 and 1839.[7] When Chopin first came to Paris (from Warsaw via Vienna) Fétis wrote, "He draws little sound from the instrument, resembling in this the majority of German pianists."[8] But the Paris-based Herz, too, had to adapt to pianos of every sort in concert tours, which in the 1830s took him to Germany,

France, Holland, and England, and, quite naturally, he sold his works indiscriminately to owners of every make of piano.

The rush to the upper register for special effects, although not unknown in any of the concertos we have looked at so far, becomes a mannerism in concertos by Kalkbrenner (No. 4) and Herz (No. 3). It is but one effect in a full bag of tricks of the piano-playing showman, tricks that include the "splendid leaps and trills" that Schumann, in his review of Herz's Second Concerto, Op. 74, imagines an entire audience greeting with shouts of "Superb!"[9] But what thrills an audience may turn out to be merely dull to one who peruses the score in his own study. Of twelve concertos under discussion in this and the previous chapter, Schumann heard only two in concert before he wrote his review, Chopin's in E Minor, and Camille Stamaty's in A Minor. His review reels off a list of musical platitudes in Hiller's Concerto, yet Chopin reports that this same piece was enthusiastically received when Hiller played it in Paris in 1831.[10] Similarly, Schumann became increasingly "displeased" as he turned the pages of Döhler's Concerto, but a few months later the Leipzig correspondent for the *Allgemeine musikalische Zeitung* reported that Döhler's "truly extraordinary skill was ... given lively recognition after the performance of [his] Concerto."[11]

Schumann was well aware of his position as an armchair peruser of scores and its effect on his critical perception. After young Stamaty (1811–70) came to Leipzig in September 1836 to study with Mendelssohn, Schumann spent many hours in his company over some three and one-half months.[12] He grew to like him very much, even recommending him to his sister-in-law, Therese, to whom he wrote, "There is here, in addition, a young 'Stamaty,' who came to me as if he had alit from the clouds, a clever, extraordinarily handsome, cultivated and genuinely good person, born in Rome of Greek parents, raised in Paris, who now wants to complete his musical studies with Mendelssohn. You would like him very much."[13] Stamaty gave no public concerts in Leipzig, but Schumann heard him play many times in private. A few weeks after he left, Schumann reviewed his Concerto in A Minor, Op. 2.

> Only a very unyielding, indeed, a hard character could completely deny the influence of a repulsive or attractive personality on his judgment of that person's artistic achievements. ... it is no wonder that after I heard the above concerto in an exemplary fashion from the composer, that I regarded it with much more interest than perhaps would otherwise have been the case.[14]

I do not have a copy of Stamaty's Concerto, so I do not know if it follows the virtuoso model, although I suspect it does, as Schumann tells us that Stamaty lived from his early childhood in Paris, where he studied with Kalkbrenner. Furthermore, Schumann's judgment that the form of the first movement becomes confused suggests that this is in comparison to the usual course of the first movement of a virtuoso concerto.

> Imaginative as we know the composer to be, so too he leads us from
> illusion to reality, up and down hill, always breathlessly leaping over the
> next one, sometimes weary, sometimes surprising us with his frenzy. ...
> Not only are there fifths and octaves, but barbaric modulations, outlandish
> suspensions and the like, more especially in the first movement, where the
> composer did not write or play with as much passion as in the last, and
> where, whenever the form becomes somewhat confused, he sooner or
> later makes an end of it through force.[15]

What interests us, though, is not just the many unusual sounds and unexpected twists of Stamaty's Concerto as compared with the usual form of
virtuoso concertos but also that these are most obvious where the composer
not only writes, but also plays with less passion, that is, in the first movement. Any similar faults in the last movement are "delicately" concealed by
Stamaty's greater passion, when composing and also when performing for
Schumann.

In fairness to Schumann, it must be admitted that he shows some
forbearance for whatever faults he sees on paper in concertos he has not
heard performed, by Hiller, Döhler, and Hartknoch. He is less forgiving of
what he considers the calculated efforts of the more experienced Herz and
Kalkbrenner, even though he knew the latter personally. After meeting him
in spring 1833 he described Kalkbrenner as "the most well-bred and most
amiable (only vain) Frenchman."[16] By his own maxim, that should soften
any harsh judgment against him. Yet in this, and indeed in all cases we shall
consider later, Schumann's judgment remains that of the connoisseur
carefully taking the measure of a piece as he plays it to himself. His is not
the spontaneous, unstudied reaction of a crowd expectantly awaiting the
melodrama and high-wire acrobatics he finds so distasteful.

* * *

Ferdinand Hiller (1811–85) was a composer near Schumann's age whom he
repeatedly named, along with Chopin, among the romantics.[17] He first heard
reports of his playing in spring 1832 from Friedrich Wieck after he returned
from Paris.[18] In February 1835 Schumann wrote a long review of Hiller's
Twenty-Four Etudes, Op. 15, by which time the composer had published his
first works, chamber music and piano solo pieces. The review casts Hiller in
the role of Beethoven's successor, naming him "one of the young disciples
and also one of [the] most remarkable manifestations" of Beethoven's
romanticism. It also cautions him against turning the "free, unfettered language" of Beethoven to undisciplined eccentricity, a propensity that earned
him Heine's ironic epithet, "little Beethoven."[19]

When Schumann began his review of Hiller's Concerto in F Minor, Op.
5, he reminded his readers of the assessment he had made of Hiller just a
year earlier, and stated that it applied as well to the Concerto.

> To this day we do not want to dispense with a single word written then;
> the same defects, the same merits that we pointed out there, inherent as

well as acquired, are also to be found in this earlier work—except, if possible, it is yet more unclear and confused. In truth, we fear his talent will never develop naturally; he mucked it up too early to be able to set everything right again. Perhaps he himself regrets that he published this Concerto, which, just as surely as it shows traces of a bold spirit, cannot anywhere deny the strain of an early birth—perhaps it doesn't concern him, otherwise he might have shown later through his actions that he had turned away from the forceful manner that made him famous.[20]

Perhaps later, Hiller did regret that he had published the Concerto. At the very least, he may have lost interest in promoting it: copies of the piece are difficult to find today, even though, as we already mentioned, Chopin reported its enthusiastic reception. Hiller did continue to concertize on the piano, but his career also took him in other directions resulting in the composition of large vocal works, including the oratorio *Die Zerstörung Jerusalems,* which Schumann gave two favorable reviews in 1840 and 1841.[21] He also composed another piano concerto, the F-sharp Minor, Op. 69, which remained in the repertory at least through the beginning of the twentieth century. A work of a very different style and conception than Op. 5, it was first published in 1861, long after Hiller had established his fame as a conductor, first in Düsseldorf (1847–50), then in Cologne (1850–84).[22]

In form and style the first movement of the F Minor Concerto is very much like the virtuoso concertos discussed in Chapter 2, although two features are notable. In the first solo, the second group opens with a new *espressivo* theme, then (after a double period) the solo brings back a tune from the first tutti (where it was played first in A-flat major then in F minor) for a single statement, an idea surviving from the Mozart era. What follows the second solo can hardly be called a recapitulation, though it is a type of abbreviation found in concertos examined in Chapter 2. Both the third and final tuttis are lacking. No material from the first group returns: the final tonic section contains only the *espressivo* principal theme of the second group and the thoroughly recomposed brilliant solo close.

Schumann's review has no complaint about the quite conventional form of Hiller's Concerto but, rather, its content.

> In order to say something about the Concerto itself, what stands out above all, and even more than in his Etudes where he can hide himself behind figuration, is the poverty of *cantilena*. There is a dice game whereby one can put together waltzes and songs by the dozen. On the face of it they even sound good, but lifeless to the point of death. In a way, the melodic parts in Hiller remind me of that.[23]

Hiller shows both a poverty of ideas and an indifference to their development. In the first movement he falls back on the most hackneyed of formulas in both the thematic and passagework areas, then repeats them nearly or fully verbatim. Repetition, without what he considers sufficient variation, is Schumann's special peeve. His cases in point are the first two bars of the transition, which are repeated with some variation in the second two, and the first four bars of the principal theme of the second group, which are answered by four bars that vary the theme, although apparently not enough for Schumann (Example 7.1, bars 109–16). Furthermore, according to Schumann, Hiller does not "compensate for the emptiness of his melodies through harmony," but gives us instead "dull basses" he should get rid of with a "pen stroke," to wit, following Schumann's examples, downbeat octaves followed by the chugging of repeated eighth-note chords (see Example 7.1, bars 117–20).[24]

What Hiller needs to consider with greater care is the development, or flow of his various musical ideas.

> As has been said, it is sad, how next to so much that is truly ingenious and singularly charming in this Concerto, there is so much that is insipid and ugly. Not for one minute does he persevere, not for one half page does he remain the same; where one wants to rest, he pushes on, where he should carry on, he stops it, and so it goes up to the end, where one awakes frustrated as after a night of reveling, trusting only one thing, that it can hardly get worse.[25]

Schumann admires the main ideas of Hiller's first movement, including what he calls its "unusual" opening (a broad line descending in octaves, not

Example 7.1 Hiller, Concerto in F Minor, Op. 5, first movement, solo exposition, second group, principal theme (12 of 16 bars).

unlike the opening of his own F Major Concerto), but expresses frustration with their working out. He dismisses the entire *Adagio* as "sour." The opening is a dialogue between unison strings and solo passages marked *ad libitum,* something today's listener might find disturbing because of its too slavish resemblance to the middle movement of Beethoven's G Major Concerto. I suspect, however, that Schumann's displeasure stems from certain particulars in the movement (the repetitious bass of the long *agitato* middle section) and their working out, specifically, the many changes of mood: from a recitative, *ad libitum* at the opening, to a simple *dolce* melody in D-flat Major, to the middle *agitato* section in A-flat major, followed by a framing return to the *dolce* melody then *ad libitum* area.

Schumann never heard Hiller play his piano concerto, at least not in a public concert. He first met Hiller in 1840 when he came to Leipzig at Mendelssohn's invitation to conduct *Die Zerstörung Jerusalems.*[26] When he returned to Leipzig to conduct the Gewandhaus Orchestra for the 1843–44 season, he played a new concerto from manuscript, presumably his Op. 69.[27] One wonders, though, if the reaction of a large audience is of any concern to Schumann in his review of the earlier concerto, as he consistently supports his critical observation with specific references to the score. At the end of the review he invites the reader not to play or go hear the Concerto but to look it up or consult it himself [*selbst nachlesen*]. Schumann does not imagine or invite the reader to imagine the concerto as it might be heard in a concert hall, for instance, the one in Paris where it was enthusiastically received.

Schumann is still the armchair critic in his review of Theodor Döhler's Concerto in A Major, Op. 7. Removed from the immediacy of any live performance, he chides the composer for catering to audience response. Here is the conclusion of his review, addressed to Vienna, the city where Döhler went to study with Czerny in 1829, and resided until 1836.

> And you, too, gay imperial city … remind your young artists over and over that one of the greatest individuals of the age lived within your walls, as you encourage them with your amiable *bonhomie* to set out on a path that ultimately terminates at a quicksand bed into which they sink ever deeper and deeper with heavenly ease amid your thousandfold bravos![28]

Although Schumann's complaints against Döhler's Concerto are not outlined in detail as explicit as those against Hiller's, we can draw some conclusion as to what displeases him, as he moves from enjoying the physical beauty of the score to ever greater impatience with its contents, then (further on in the review, and not quoted here) turns to a discourse on the dangers of Italy's "siren songs." Schumann assumes Döhler succumbed to their allure on his travels, when in fact he had been born and lived much of his life in Italy.

> Since in opening Döhler's Concert in A Major, the key that, above all, overflows with youth and vigor, I had already discovered laurel branches

on the title page, I hoped finally to meet a friendly person who would relate to me many things about the beautiful Italy where he has traveled for so long. ... In the beginning, too, it went quite tolerably, yet already in the middle while I was playing from one page I threw a few hopeful glances onto the next one, for the man displeased me ever more. Finally I had to say to him honestly, that he as yet has no inkling of the dignity of the art for which nature has given him some talent, though no lavish amount, thus all the more reason for him to husband it.[29]

The title page has a large wreath of laurels encircling the dedication to "Sa Majesté la Reine de Naples Marie Isabelle de Bourbon, Infante d'Espagne, Mére du Roi Ferdinand II. du Royaume des Deux Siciles." The opening of the piece is quite attractive. Thereafter the form of the first movement is clear, its melodies not without charm. Likely what irritated Schumann as he turned from page to page were the extravagant decorations added to the melodies, and the etude-like, harmonically wide-ranging passagework.

By the time he reached the "middle" of the Concerto, or its second movement, Schumann's displeasure was mounting. A comparison with the *Larghetto* of Chopin's F Minor Concerto suggests the reason: Chopin's movement is fully rounded, closed off by a return of the opening melody and key. Its dramatic middle section comprises a full period. Döhler's *Adagio* is in two sections, with no return. The first section of the movement begins with a melody in the tutti sporting a prominent dotted head motive (bars 1–8). The solo starts out with a very free variant of this theme, stated simply enough in its first phrase (bars 9–12) but already heavily ornamented in the second and in a short suffix (bars 13–18 and 18–21). A yet more varied and even more heavily decorated, modulating restatement leads from F major through F minor to a D-flat major cadence (bars 21–28). The first ten bars of a second section are given in Example 7.2. It starts out with the prominent dotted motive, but as the Waldbauer-Riemann numbers show, it is no more than a series of modulatory short suffixes leading to a long, cadenza-like dominant preparation (some two pages long and not shown in the example) on V of A major that leads in turn directly to the third, rondo movement. There is no return to either the opening theme or key of the *Adagio*.

Seven months after he wrote his review, Schumann heard a public performance by Döhler of the *Adagio* and *Rondo* from his Concerto, together with several of his variation sets. There is no indication that this caused him to change his opinion of the Concerto. Yet, whereas in his review he concluded that Döhler had "no inkling of the dignity of the art for which nature has given him some talent," after his performance Schumann reported in the *Neue Zeitschrift* that he had "pleased exceedingly" and in his diary noted that he played his variations with the "greatest finish and perfection."[30] He also described Döhler as "a polite youth and very shy," following his own standard, qualities that should favorably affect his assessment of the Concerto.[31] But those could be deadly compliments, delivered to sidestep passing judgment on Döhler's music, and Schumann refrained from doing so in either

Example 7.2 Döhler, Concerto in A Major, Op. 7, second movement, second section, beginning.

his diary or the journal. No wonder. His reported pleasure in Döhler's playing leaves him with a conundrum: although he believes that falling back on crowd-pleasing pianistic feats has a deleterious effect on the Concerto, he must concede that the effectiveness of Döhler's performance resulted from his adeptness in bringing off these very same feats.

* * *

With Friedrich Kalkbrenner (1785–1849), we come to the first composer of some eminence whom Schumann heard perform publicly before he reviewed his concerto. In 1833 Kalkbrenner came to Leipzig and on 11 May played, among other things, his newest concerto, the Third, in A Minor, Op. 107 (1829).[32] On hearing one of the great Parisian virtuosos perform for the first time, Schumann gained the impulse to compare his playing with other professionals he knew, in particular Clara Wieck and Anna Caroline de Belleville (1808–80). He wrote his mother on 28 June 1833, "One thinks one will hear the newest thing from famous men and often discovers merely his favorite old mistakes cloaked in a glorious name. ... For all that, before all male virtuosos I give the palm to two girls, Belleville and Clara."[33] Some six months later, he stated publicly that he no longer considered Clara Wieck a youthful talent to be judged on the basis of her age (fourteen), but a fully accomplished artist.[34] Schumann was an intimate of the Wieck household, a friend of the young Clara. Nonetheless, his conclusion is extraordinary given the high place Kalkbrenner held in the eyes of the public and among professionals. Chopin, who was in contact with Herz, Hiller, and Kalkbrenner soon after his arrival in Paris in September 1831, was in awe of Kalkbrenner. He wrote to a friend:

> You would not believe how curious I was about Herz, Liszt, Hiller, etc.—They are all zero beside Kalkbrenner. I confess that I have played like Herz, but would wish to play like Kalkbrenner. If Paganini is perfection, Kalkbrenner is his equal, but in quite another style. It is hard to describe to you his calm, his enchanting touch, his incomparable evenness, and the mastery that is displayed in every note; he is a giant, walking over Herz and Czerny and all—and over me.[35]

One reason Schumann concluded that Clara Wieck, at least, was a better pianist than Kalkbrenner is because of the repertory she chose. On 29 April 1833, just two weeks before Kalkbrenner came to Leipzig, she played a movement from his "latest" Concerto, presumably the Third. On the same program she also performed Chopin's Variations, Op. 2; a Concert Rondo, Op. 120 by Pixis; and Herz's Bravura Variations, Op. 20.[36] We may not consider this fare for connoisseurs, but it rates above Kalkbrenner's program of 11 May, which was made up entirely of his own compositions: his Third Concerto; etudes from his Piano Method, Op. 108; a rondo; variations; and a fantasy, *Der Traum*, Op. 113.[37] In Schumann's opinion, as expressed through Eusebius, "The total of everything that Kalkbrenner played was hardly more than two-thirds in comparison to the amount of pieces Clara played, pieces that in themselves were more difficult by far."[38]

Kalkbrenner's Third Concerto conforms to the virtuoso model described in Chapter 2. Its style, according to Hans Nautsch, is one of "noble chit-chat."

> This is certainly the sphere in which Kalkbrenner, by nature, was most at home. The lack of thematic substance is therefore not of particular importance, since the manner of playing and expression bear the burden.

They are not, as in other cases, overblown by an excessive, seemingly affected passion.[39]

Although Schumann has nothing to say of the Concerto itself, we can surmise that in it he, too, witnessed a grand exhibition of Kalkbrenner's extraordinary and renowned technique. Above all, the piece is a forum for rapid broken octaves and tenths, and for right-hand scales in thirds. However, Schumann's critique is not of the technique itself but, rather, in agreement with what Nautsch writes, of Kalkbrenner's dependence on technique as the center of interest in his playing and compositions. Still, whatever the pitfalls of this strategy, in his review of Kalkbrenner's next concerto Schumann finds himself urging the composer to fall back on it, to keep his old ways and shun any attempt to imbue them with the eccentricities associated with the new generation of young romantics.

In April 1834 a notice in the *Neue Zeitschrift* informed readers that Kalkbrenner "writes to one of his friends, that with [the Fourth Concerto] he hopes to give the world his best."[40] When the Concerto came to light, the opinion was otherwise. After Kalkbrenner played it in Strasbourg on 13 April 1835, the correspondent for the *Allgemeine musikalische Zeitung* reported, "After hearing the piano concerto, admittedly with only [double] quartet accompaniment, a certain vacillation was noticeable among the large gathering, as if they wondered, is this the famous Kalkbrenner?" When Kalkbrenner reverted to his old style with a Duet and Variations on a Theme from Meyerbeer's *Robert le diable,* for Piano and Violin, Op. 111 (with Charles-François Jupin), and a Fantasy with Variations, the opinion changed. "Soon this indifference, which could only have been on account of the composition itself, was dispelled by enthusiastic applause."[41]

In April 1836, when Schumann reviewed the score of Kalkbrenner's Fourth Concerto in A-flat Major, Op. 127, he agreed with the Strasbourg audience. He was looking for the composer of the D Minor Concerto, the piece he knew so well, that he called the work of Kalkbrenner's "highest bloom ... where all the radiant facets of his congenial talent broke through." He hoped for the suavity and amiability he had found earlier in Kalkbrenner's person and in his music, "in the lively, truly musical sonatas of his youth." Instead, he discovered that the D Minor Concerto was "the boundary, where, when he wanted to pass beyond it, [Kalkbrenner's] star failed him;" his later works suffer from "artificial pathos and a certain mannered profoundness."[42] The "artificial pathos," even bathos is easily heard in Kalkbrenner's themes. But, as we shall see in our examination of Schumann's review that follows, it is also the juxtaposition of the overly dramatic, scene-shredding emotion of Kalkbrenner's themes against the exuberance of his passagework that Schumann ridicules, imagining that Kalkbrenner himself is the subject of this ever-changing soap opera, a soprano who turns from her deathbed aria to a thrilling cabaletta in the space of one short breath.

Kalkbrenner's Fourth Concerto follows the usual form of virtuoso concertos, except that the first tutti is shortened to a mere twenty bars.

Schumann has no comment on this change; as we shall see in Chapter 8 it is not unusual for concertos of the time. Rather, he calls Kalkbrenner to account for not integrating the tuttis with the solo part. His review begins with a scold for the grand old man.

> I am going to reprimand the composers of concert-concertos (no pleo-nasm intended) on two counts. First, the solos are all finished and ready to go before the tuttis—unconstitutionally enough, for after all the con-sent of the parliament, that is the orchestra, should be necessary before the piano undertakes a thing. And why not begin at the real beginning? Was our world created on the second day? ... I'll wager that Herr Kalk-brenner devised his introductory and internal tuttis later, and merely shoved them into place ...[43]

Schumann knew from experience the problems of composing the solo parts first, the method he followed with his Concerto in F Major. The conse-quence for that piece was that the tuttis never were finished. In the first movement of Kalkbrenner's Concerto the music of the four tuttis has no motivic relation to the music of the solos. Of the first tutti's two themes, only the first is heard again, in the third tutti.

In the solos, Schumann doesn't like Kalkbrenner's style—not his virtu-osic displays as such, but the extremes of expression and swings of mood, which he sees as an attempt by the aging composer (in 1836 he was forty-eight) to join the new romantic school of which Schumann counted himself a member. According to one reviewer of his first works, Schumann "has himself created a new, ideal world in which he wanders about almost rogu-ishly, sometimes in fact with queer unconventionality."[44] But for Kalkbren-ner, the epitome of gentility, the predictable result of his improbable attachment to the new school is a travesty.

> In the present concerto we see the unmistakable influence of the young romantic world that turned the Kalkbrenners out of its school, but deliv-ered Kalkbrenner himself seemingly undecided to a crossroads, wonder-ing whether he should continue on the old path with its well-earned laurels or should fight for new ones on another. ... Completely true to his accommodating character, he does not fling himself too vigorously into the new sphere, exactly as if he would want first to test what the public thinks about it. Now, if the public is like us, then it must admit that the result is an aesthetic disaster. One imagines the elegant Kalkbrenner, a pistol at his head as he wrote *con disperazione* in his piano part—or despairing on the edge of an abyss when he put three trombones in the Adagio. It won't do, it doesn't suit him; he has no talent for romantic audacity; and were he to don a diabolical mask, one would recognize him by the kid gloves with which he holds it.[45]

To clarify Schumann's musical examples: in the second movement, in A-flat minor, the trombones punctuate the funeral march of the opening tutti with a dotted-motive, then continue their somber tones when the solo enters *diminuendo sempre ed espressione.* In the first movement, the second group of the solo exposition has a theme, in E-flat major, in the form **ABA'**. Kalk-brenner writes *con disperazione* in the return, which is considerably elaborated, where it turns to the minor subdominant, in bars 104–5 (Example 7.3a). This is only one of a number of bathetic elements, including, besides the turn to minor, a move to the high register, octave doubling of the melody, *crescendo* to *forte* then *fortissimo,* and slow trill, *accelerando.*

This kind of high drama also takes place in the passagework areas, although, as Schumann describes it, in a somewhat different way.

Second, however, I disapprove of the modulation

| 7♭ | 5 |
| 5 | 3 |

X major to X+1 major [that is, as Schumann explains in a footnote, from a dominant-seventh chord in a major key to the flat-sixth degree; the example he gives is from a V^7 of F chord to D-flat major], in which young composers in particular take refuge whenever they don't really know how to continue, and which they usually employ such that, if the first half of this modulation has burst forth with loud turmoil, then suddenly in the other half notes begin to whisper with ethereal softness. Of course, we ourselves once tolerated such surprises, and think them good enough for the Mssrs. Döhler, Schornstein, Hartknoch, and Thalberg, who employ them by the dozen, but never for a maestro like Kalkbrenner, who makes claim to the title of a cultivated man of the world, and should contrive newer surprises.[46]

We could find several examples in Kalkbrenner's Concerto of a surprise deceptive cadence from the dominant-seventh to the flat-sixth degree. Where, however, it is followed by notes of ethereal softness is, as often in virtuoso concertos, in preparation for a time-out section within the brilliant close, a diversion from the final approach to the penultimate measure with its protracted six-four chord. We have already seen one example of such a time-out, introduced by a different progression, in Herz's A Major Concerto (Example 2.3, bars 171–81). Schumann is railing against this type of mood change, as much as against the hackneyed progression that introduces it. Example 7.3b shows both the progression and the beginning of the time-out in the brilliant close of Kalkbrenner's exposition. The example starts with the cadence measure of the first move away from the tonic, reached after two different vamps (eight bars and four bars long) solidly establish E-flat major. What follows after the high altitude G-flat major (bars 128–32), and not shown in the example, is a chromatic climb in the bass of a full octave and beyond, to G major, then full turn around the circle of fifths and beyond to I^6, IV then I_4^6 in E-flat major, the start of the long penultimate measure of the close.

Taken together, Schumann's two complaints show his irritation with the disjointedness of Kalkbrenner's Concerto. In the exposition, the florid ornamentation and extremes of expression found in the themes directly abut first the gay

Example 7.3 Kalkbrenner, Concerto in A-flat Major, Op. 127, first movement, solo exposition, second group.

barcarole that begins the transition then the easy vamp that starts out the close. Further intensifying these extreme contrasts are tempo and meter changes from section to section of the movement. These are listed in Figure 7.1.

Kalkbrenner's tempo changes may be no more than a record of what was already the practice of the day, fluctuating speeds as the performer moved between thematic and passagework areas. Berlioz wrote that "Chopin simply could not play in strict time."[47] An article in the *Neue Zeitschrift* comparing Clara Wieck, Thalberg, Liszt, and Adolf Henselt reported that none played metronomically.[48] Whereas in the Kalkbrenner Concerto it may at first seem that the precise 1:2 or 2:1 ratio of many of the changes nullifies any perception of tempo fluctuation, in fact, the opposite is true. All the fast sections (except the passagework in the development) are marked **¢**, which

first tutti, *Maestoso brillante*, ¢	$\jmath = 84$
solo exposition	
first group	
short cadenza-like entry	[$\jmath = 84$]
lyric theme, c	$\jmath = 84$
transition, ¢	$\jmath = 84$
second group	
theme, c	$\jmath = 84$
close, ¢	$\jmath = 84$
second tutti	[$\jmath = 84$]
solo development	
lyric episode, *Maestoso e poco più Allegro*, c	$\jmath = 100$
passagework, *Più Allegro*, c	$\jmath = 76$
third tutti, *Maestoso brillante*, ¢	$\jmath = 84$
solo recapitulation	
first group	
lyric theme, c	$\jmath = 80$
transition, ¢	$\jmath = 84$
second group	
theme, c	$\jmath = 84$
close, ¢	$\jmath = 63$
fourth tutti	[$\jmath = 63$]

Figure 7.1 Tempo changes, Kalkbrenner, Concerto in A-flat Major, Op. 127, first movement.

calls for two pulses per bar, with each pulse a half-note; all the slow sections are marked c, calling for four pulses per bar, with each pulse a quarter note. Where the ratio of metronome markings from fast to slow section is 1:2, each bar of the slow section has exactly twice as many pulses, at the same rate, as each bar of the fast section, giving a sense of drag. (Here the reader may wish to compare the theme shown in Example 7.3a to the passagework shown in Example 7.3b.) The metric change is immediately noticeable. Its aesthetic essence lies in its very disruptiveness, its rendering of the separation of sections as sharply as possible. Furthermore, the super-human speed of sixteenth notes moving at $\jmath = 84$ in the passagework areas, and the rather fast clip of the florid ornaments in thematic areas, lead one to believe that a steady tempo was hardly maintained within each section. The *rallentando*s marking the ends of all the thematic areas show that neither did it exist across the sections.[49]

The disruptions we have been describing troubled Schumann only in the first movement. He wholly approves the final, gay rondo.

> But we do concede that only the first movement fits this picture; in the third he is again entirely himself, and shows himself again in his natural, virtuosic amiability that we so value in him. Let him hold on to his old, well-earned fame as one of the most skillful composers for piano, who fashions things masterfully for fingers and hands, and who knows how to get around with light weapons so successfully, as firmly as he can—and let him delight us anew with his dazzling trills and flying triplets; we esteem them far more highly than his four-part fugue passages, his affectedly melancholy suspensions, etc.[50]

At the close of his review, Schumann says he is looking forward to a fifth concerto by Kalkbrenner (which was never written), one that continues in the manner of the D Minor Concerto.[51] For Schumann, Kalkbrenner is at his best when he does not disguise the purely virtuosic aims of his music behind false emotion, when he brings his character and his music into harmony.[52]

* * *

Like Kalkbrenner, Carl Eduard Hartknoch (1796–1834) patterns his Second Concerto in G Minor, Op. 14, after what Schumann calls the "old model," and, like Kalkbrenner, Hartknoch, too, in Schumann's words, "stands irresolutely on the threshold of two eras." With Hartknoch, however, inexperience is the cause of his "vacillating between old models and new ideals."

> On the one hand, still too absorbed in a struggle with the form to be able to allow his imagination free rein, on the other, vacillating between old models and new ideals, here he delights in the quiet of the past and the wisdom of those belonging to it, there in the excitement of the future and the courage of its youth eager for battle. Thus the restlessness, convulsiveness everywhere; thus he plucks out bits here, and sticks them in again there; thus he speaks simply and brightly here, grandiloquently and darkly again there. A clear self does not emerge, he stands irresolutely on the threshold of two eras.[53]

Schumann, although fourteen years younger than Hartknoch, speaks as if Hartknoch were the younger musician. He turned to a career in music after completing his university studies in Leipzig, then went on to study with Hummel in Weimar in 1819 when he was already twenty-three years old. In 1824 he left for St. Petersburg, relocated to Moscow in 1828, and died there in 1834. The Second Concerto was the last of his published works, appearing around 1830.[54] Despite objections to the Concerto stated by Schumann in the portion of his review just cited, he considered it

Hartknoch's best work as well as that of a talented composer who had not yet reached full maturity.

Schumann offers two examples to illustrate what he calls Hartknoch's "hypochondriac uncertainty." The first is the unexpected changes of mood that comes with the switch from minor to major at the ends of the first and last movements, and from major to minor at the end of the second. The second is the "far-fetched" relationship of the first eight bars of the first solo of the first movement "to the whole." Schumann decides they must have been a later insertion to deflect attention from a resemblance to the opening of Hummel's B Minor Concerto. The irony is that "he didn't succeed, as one sees." "And anyway," Schumann continues, "a chance reminiscence is always better than a doubtful independence."[55] The solo openings of the two concertos are shown in Examples 7.4a and b. In Hartknoch's, Schumann feels that the quiet G minor, which begins in the tutti as far back as bar 124 with a return of the opening theme, should continue through the opening of the solo. In other words, the V (of G minor) in bar 159 of the tutti should lead directly to the solo's G minor chord in bar 167. This, Schumann surmises, was the original beginning before Hartknoch inserted the solo part in bars 159–66. Eliminating these bars would maintain the quiet mood of the special tutti close, and do away with the conventional, cadenza-like solo entry with its crescendos to the high register.

Schumann further surmises that, in order to introduce a certain symmetry to the movement, Hartknoch inserted the solo's opening cadenza-like gesture into the retransition, just before the third tutti and beginning of the recapitulation. Schumann would have him instead move directly from a quiet ending of the solo on the dominant (at bar 472) to the quiet beginning of the tutti on the tonic (at bar 480), without the disruption of the solo's arpeggio climb and *crescendo* up to *forzando* then *smorzando* die at mid-register that comes in between.

> ... much as such reminiscences and little formal refinements succeed with many a great artists, and as Beethoven especially knows to whisper them ethereally, so younger artists must take good care not to lose their way in minor detail and not to disturb the flow of the whole by such decorative relationships.[56]

In one place, Schumann does not suggest the arpeggios should be eliminated. At the beginning of the solo development, they are an integral part of the musical argument: they continue a move toward V of F and *crescendo* begun by the tutti, smoothly picking up a neighbor-note motion and eighth-note rhythm, also begun by the tutti.

Hartknoch does not employ extravagant expression or dynamic markings. Although embellished, his melodies for the most part are not overly decorated or excessive in their use of the high register, considering the time period. There are no unusual turns of harmony or complex figurations in the passagework. Where Schumann finds fault is not with style but with

a. Hartknoch, Concerto in G Minor, Op. 14.

b. Hummel, Concerto in B Minor, Op. 89

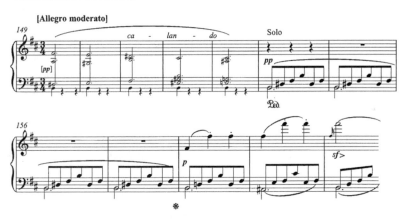

Example 7.4   First movement, close of the first tutti and entrance of the solo.

context. The end of the first movement turns to major when it should retain the minor coloring to its end. The coda of the *Adagio,* second movement is over-decorated when it should die away simply. In both cases, Hartknoch gives way to formal conventions rather than work out his material according to its inherent qualities. Perhaps, Schumann suggests, his affective inconsistencies indicate a foreboding of death, though he also cautions that the sad actual circumstances of the composer's death (at age thirty-eight) may lead us to see more in the Concerto than is actually there. All the same, this does not stop him from reading a life story into Hartknoch's Concerto.

> If one makes allowances for such mistakes ... so many excellent things still remain that we can only pity the artist who, it seems, lacked stimulation and recognition, and who also hears these words no more. During his life, separated from his homeland and left to his own resources, he perhaps dreamed of that visionary youth whom we call Chopin. And since the dream often played in contrasting scenes, it's as if on that account his old honored teacher threatened him with his finger not to turn away from the faith of his fathers. And when he awoke the concerto was done.[57]

Chopin is Schumann's example of a composer who reconciled the conventional form of the virtuoso concerto with what contemporaries considered his unconventional musical material. Following the spirit of Beethoven, he expanded the possibilities of the virtuoso concerto's traditional form without abandoning it for another, newer one. The same formal tradition constrains Hartknoch; he adheres to it at the expense of violence to his musical material. To explain his failure of nerve, Schumann conjures up an entire life of the mind for the poor man; the formal tradition in itself is not the cause.

We come finally to Herz, one of the most famous and widely traveled pianists of his time.[58] He was born in Vienna in 1803 or 1806, in 1816 came to Paris to study, and resided there for the remainder of his life. Beginning in 1818 he published a continuous stream of piano music, and by the mid-1820s was one of the most celebrated pianist in France.[59] Charles Salaman, who took lessons from Herz in 1828–29, recalls, "Herz was very charming in manner and conversation, his playing wonderfully brilliant and facile in the execution of difficult passages."[60] He was wildly received when he made his debut in London in 1833. When he first performed in New York in 1846, Henry Cood Watson, a reviewer for *The Albion*, gave a full description of his playing.

> His touch is the perfection of delicacy and lightness, united with firmness and the power of producing an extraordinary staccato either in scales, thirds, or octaves.—His execution is very rapid, and it is brilliant and distinct; there is nothing left to the imagination. ... His style is graceful and refined, and is sufficiently dignified to impart to all he does an evidence of mind. His *andantes* are given with much feeling and expression, but deep and thrilling passion is by no means characteristic of his performances,—indeed it would not be in keeping with his compositions.[61]

In New York, Herz played his Second Concerto, in C Minor, Op. 74.[62] Whatever "feeling and expression" he brought to his Third Concerto in D Minor, Op. 87, Schumann mocks in the very first sentence of his review.

> *"Herz, mein Herz* [literally, heart, my heart], why so sad," I kept singing while playing. *Con dolore* comes up three times in the first movement alone, not to mention the *espressivos* and *smorzandos*.[63]

Schumann exaggerates, but only slightly. By actual count *con dolore* occurs twice and *smorzando* once, but *espressivo* four times. The movement abounds in expression markings of the same overblown sentiment that Schumann took Kalkbrenner to task for almost a year earlier.

As Schumann tells it, the purported loftiness of Herz's endeavor in this huge concerto (the orchestra includes trumpets, trombones, and, for the march finale, bass drum, cymbals, and triangle) renders the abundant expression markings all the more bombastic.

> All the preliminaries are very exciting. Right away D minor, the Don Juan key, the rare three-four time signature, a quiet beginning, a four-page tutti—surely his most serious work I thought. And so it is, too. Our winged darling has covered himself with a sword and coat of mail, and if he borrows a lot of things for his armament from others, well, he doesn't deny it.[64]

Given the Concerto's large size and conventional form, one expects a serious endeavor. Instead, Herz's huge expansion of the form serves as an arena for the presentation of a great number of unrelated ideas. Any high-mindedness is only a pretense. The catalog of his markings shown in Figure 7.2 gives some idea of the many expressive moods, tempos, dynamics, articulations, and changes of key Herz drives the piece through.

The makeup of the thematic material further contributes to the pastiche construction of the movement. Schumann traces the source of nearly every theme to a well-known piece. His point is not just that Herz is unoriginal and therefore lacks artistic integrity, but that the Concerto lacks integrity since it does not spin out a unified mood or idea. Figure 7.3 lists the borrowings in order, labeling them according to modern terminology (note: Figure 7.3 does not represent a full, formal outline of each movement). Where modern terminology differs from Schumann's labels, his term is given, in the left-hand column, in brackets. Many passages in Herz's score he refers to by page and system number rather than formal function.[65] The first two borrowings Schumann cites for the first movement together with the comparable passages from Herz's Concerto are shown in Examples 7.5a and b. The borrowings affect only the thematic areas of the Concerto: in the first movement, all themes of the tutti and solo; in the second movement, the only theme; in the third movement, the three themes of a rondo in the form **ABCA'B'C'**. The only thematic idea Schumann does not claim Herz borrowed is a fugal subject found in the transition between sections **A** and **B** of the rondo.

Allegro moderato, $\frac{3}{4}$

cadenza-like introduction on the opening motive of the first tutti, in D minor (31 bars)

> *forte, risoluto, piano, delicato, crescendo, piano, crescendo ed appassionato, smorzando, piano, leggiero, marcato, crescendo, forte, fortissimo, poco ritenuto*

a new theme (not heard in the first tutti), in D minor (23 bars)

> *mezzo forte, con dolore, pianissimo, crescendo, piano, espressivo, dolente, agitato, un poco ritenuto, crescendo, diminuendo, sempre rallentando e sostenuto assai*

a tutti insert referring to the opening motive and leading to V of A-flat (10 bars)

> *Tempo I°, piano, crescendo, forte*

transition, beginning on A-flat major and leading to V of F (48 bars)

> *forte, con fuoco, piano, grazioso, marcato, crescendo, forte, piano, forte, marcato, piano, forte, piano, sempre piano, rinforzando, rallentando assai*

Figure 7.2   Expression and dynamic markings in Herz, Concerto in D Minor, Op. 84, first movement, solo exposition, first group.

Schumann does not begrudge Herz credit for what remains of his Concerto.

> But all the rest, to acknowledge the ornaments, chromatic purling, streams of flying arpeggios, etc., belongs fundamentally to him. One sees that he wants to learn from the best, and condescends only a little, with Kalkbrenner and Thalberg, to heroes of the second rank as well. May his valor continue and endure ... and the Concerto be properly practiced. Why does one have fingers and feeling? We ask.[66]

Similarly, the reviewer for the *Allgemeine musikalische Zeitung* observed only a few months later, "There is enough bravura in [the Herz Concerto] of a kind from which many aspiring artists could still learn a lot."[67]

* * *

The obvious and most important conclusion we have reached at the end of this chapter is that Schumann does not like the many disruptions in concertos by Kalkbrenner and Herz, whether he describes these in terms of extravagant changes of tempo and expression, or of thematic material. It is possible, when we consider the reaction in Strasbourg to Kalkbrenner's Fourth Concerto, that a listening audience would agree with Schumann. By contrast, we must consider that two other concertos by Hiller and Döhler, which Schumann takes to task for these same types of disruptions, were well received in Paris and Leipzig, respectively. Also, Herz's Third Concerto was sufficiently respected in Paris to be selected by the Conservatory as a contest

a. First tuttis, beginnings of the opening themes.

b. First tuttis, beginnings of the second themes.

Example 7.5   Herz Concerto borrowings.

first movement	
first tutti	
first theme [introduction]	Moscheles, G Minor Concerto
second [first] theme	Chopin, F Minor [recte E Minor] Concerto
solo exposition	
first group, new theme	Kalkbrenner, D Minor Concerto
transition	Weber
solo development	
theme	Thalberg
second movement	Chopin, E Minor Concerto, Romanze
third movement	
first theme [beginning] = **A**	Beethoven, Second Symphony, Scherzo
short tutti insert	Beethoven, Ninth Symphony
concluding transition	
second theme = **B**	Chopin
third theme [march] = **C**	Spohr, *Jessonda*, March
conclusion	Moscheles, G Minor Concerto

Figure 7.3   Schumann's list of borrowings in Herz, Concerto in D Minor.

piece in 1837 and 1844.[68] All of this is to say that Schumann's criteria for judging these works may have been very different from those of a listening audience, or even his peers. This brings us around to another point on which Schumann is more equivocal than he at first appears, namely, the place of bravura playing in the virtuoso concerto. Considering his reaction to Kalkbrenner's playing in 1833, we may think that he disparages pianists who depend heavily or even solely on these effects to impress their audiences. Yet, at the same time, Schumann's reviews of Kalkbrenner's Fourth Concerto and Herz's Third show he is well aware that these very effects are what bring shouts of approval from an audience. He even encourages Kalkbrenner to go on composing in this, his best vein, and compliments, if sarcastically, Herz for his fine fioritura. The question, then, is how to write a concerto that is in the virtuoso tradition but does not pander to virtuosity, does not use the form to display virtuosity for its own sake.

It is not as easily answered as it may at first appear. Schumann wants Kalkbrenner to go back to his old ways, but we should remember that we already have examples for that, in the unchanged style of the last concertos by Field, Ries, and Hummel. Although Schumann may feel these pieces maintain their formal integrity by virtue of a certain overall consistency, by the time they appeared all their composers were past their prime. Not one of these concertos had the same staying power in the repertory as earlier concertos by the very same composers. Although we today may find little difference between Hummel's, Ries's, or Field's first and last concertos, clearly contemporary audiences did. So the question remains, could the current vogue for the more modern pianism of Herz and Döhler be accommodated within the old virtuoso concerto? As we may infer from his reviews, Schumann's ultimate answer was no, and that left him with a conundrum. He is well aware that the virtuoso concerto, the concerto of his time, depends on the opportunity to exhibit superlative playing, yet he also feels that the modern, highly polished players have gone beyond what the virtuoso concerto can accommodate and still maintain its compositional integrity. He cannot deny the audience's rightful demand for a display of the latest technique in this of all genres. The only solution would seem to be to find a new form for the concerto, which would either accommodate the new virtuosity or take the focus away from the new virtuosity altogether. We can imagine that Schumann would favor the latter solution, and that will be our main subject in the next three chapters. But at the same time we also will consider that his solution existed side by side with the other school of thinking, whose ultimate exponent was Liszt.

8
Critical Observer: New Forms I

In this chapter we will begin our exploration of new forms by looking at six concertos, by Thalberg, Herz (No. 2), Moscheles (Nos. 5, 6, and 7) and Clara Wieck, which were criticized by Schumann, some severely, some only mildly. The Thalberg and Moscheles, No. 5 are virtuoso concertos outright, but with unusual motivic connections within or across their movements. Moscheles, No. 7 has subtle formal innovations, whereas those of the Herz, Moscheles, No. 6, and Wieck are radical. In the changes the last three make to the structure of their first movements in particular they are in the vanguard of their time, even if they have antecedents, most notably in Mendelssohn's Concerto in G Minor, and in Weber's *Concertstück,* two pieces we will look at in Chapter 9.

In 1839 Schumann prefaced his review of two concertos in the new form, Moscheles's Seventh and Mendelssohn's Second, with an overview of the present state of the genre under the title "Das Clavier-Concert." Two questions come under consideration in the essay, questions that will be focal points of Schumann's discussions of all concertos in the new form. First, how developments in the instrument that give it greater power, and in playing technique that give the performer greater presence are to be balanced with the role of the orchestra. Second, what form best suits these new developments.

To begin with the first point, Schumann predicts that because of advances in the instrument and in technique composers will free themselves from the "supporting orchestra" altogether, they will no longer produce concertos.[1] From his vantage this seems a likely prospect, if we consider that concertos of his time were published, and often publicly performed as solos. Of course, the dominance of solo over orchestra was not unique to Schumann's time. In his *Versuch einer Einleitung zur Composition,* volume 3 (1793), Heinrich Christoph Koch describes what he calls an abuse of the concerto, whereby its purpose is no more than to allow the performer to show off "his skill in a full and correct execution of the melodic figures and in conquering selected difficulties."[2] Over a hundred years later, Donald Francis Tovey echoed Koch's assessment. "Every virtuoso whose imagination is fired with the splendid spectacular effect of a full orchestra as a background for a display of instrumental technique has written concertos that express little else than that effect."[3]

The solution is not so simple as doing away with the bravura passages mocked by Tovey and decried by Koch. Schumann reveled in the accomplishments of virtuosos of his day, of Kalkbrenner, Döhler, Stamaty, and, as we shall see, Thalberg. In the opening paragraph of "Das Clavier-Concert" he states that the most gifted musicians of his generation and several past ones (including Bach, Handel, Mozart, and Beethoven) were accomplished keyboardists. He is not so naive as to deny the impact of their keyboard prowess on the success of their compositions. True, he dismisses all the works of Herz, including his concertos, but we recall that he never heard Herz play. When he heard Thalberg he was enthralled by the same technical feats he disapproved in his concerto. He lamented that Moscheles did not give a more fiery performance of his Fifth and Sixth Concertos, whereas an inspired performance by Wieck of her concerto persuaded him of its viability, even as he voiced objections to its construction.

Nor did the larger orchestra mustered for many newer concertos automatically effect a balance between the two forces. I have parts or know the instrumentation for eleven of the twenty-two virtuoso concertos we have looked at up to now. All eleven have trumpets, as do all but two Mozart concertos from K. 466 on, and all but one of the five Beethoven concertos. Unlike any concerto by Mozart or Beethoven, six of the eleven also use trombones. All six are newer concertos, Chopin's First and Second (1830 and 1829), Hummel's Op. post. (1833), Herz's Third (c. 1836), Kalkbrenner's Fourth (1835), and Field's Seventh (completed 1832). Schumann mocked the somber tone of the trombones in the *Adagio* of Kalkbrenner's Fourth, and in his own A Minor Concerto did not use the instrument, but Thalberg and Wieck (in Schumann's orchestration, to be sure) write for it, and Herz's Third Concerto, a bombastic affair, adds not only trombones but also bass drum, cymbals, and triangle (the last two instruments anticipating Liszt's Concerto in E-flat Major). What Schumann has in mind, though, is not raising the decibel level of the orchestra to match the power of the modern piano, but the particular deployment of the orchestra together with the piano. The orchestra should be "interwoven" with the solo, or, as he says about Moscheles's Seventh Concerto, it should "fit in everywhere." There should be, in Koch's words, "a passionate discourse of the concerto player with the orchestra that accompanies him."[4]

The new roles Schumann envisions for solo and orchestra may draw on his greater exposure to concertos by Beethoven and on his engagement with the latest works of Mendelssohn and Moscheles, both of whom he repeatedly claims were influenced by Mozart and Beethoven (also Bach and

Handel). Similarly, the new forms he imagines take as their basis an old one, the balanced sonata form found in opening allegro movements.

> One thing, however, we could reasonably demand from younger compos-
> ers: that as a substitute for that serious and worthy concerto form they
> would give us serious and worthy solo pieces. Not caprices, not varia-
> tions, but rather beautifully balanced allegro movements full of character,
> which, if need be, one could play at the opening of a concert.[5]

One could conclude that, when searching for new forms for the concerto, Schumann is at heart a conservative who balks at novelty. Yet, when he heard the concertos of Moscheles (No. 6) and Wieck, their sensuous appeal won him over, even as he called their forms faulty. His reaction was con-flicted.

None of the concertos we will examine in this chapter meet both Schu-mann's criteria for an effective concerto in the new form, to wit, a brilliant uniting of orchestra and solo forces, and beautifully balanced form. He will not tolerate concertos that give themselves over too much to technical dis-play: he rates the content of Thalberg's Concerto commonplace, and says nothing of the unusual motivic connections across sections of its move-ments; he obsesses on all Herz's compositions as no more than vehicles for technical display, and ignores the ingenious construction of his Second Concerto. In those concertos that shun technical display for effects he describes in more poetic terms, he still demands grandeur and balanced form, the formal model of the virtuoso concerto still looms large for him: although smitten by the "sparkle" of Moscheles's Sixth Concerto and "stel-lar ideas" of Wieck's Concerto, he is ill at ease with their "uncertain" or "incomplete" form; he hears "the departures in form" in Moscheles's Sev-enth Concerto "with pleasure," then wishes for the virtuoso concerto of Moscheles's prime, the G Minor.

Schumann's demand in his role as music journal critic that new concer-tos comply with his standards respecting both instrumentation and form sets his judgment at odds with that of the listening public, including his own judgment when he is part of that public. He dismisses Thalberg's Concerto without ever having heard the composer play it, then later finds himself awed by the young man's magnificent technique.[6] When ultimately he asks Clara Wieck if she is satisfied with the form of her Concerto, she firmly assures him that her audiences like it. In the face of Fink's similar defense of Herz's Concerto, he is left with nothing to reply except that his tastes are otherwise.

* * *

Thalberg's Concerto in F Minor, Op. 5, is in the old virtuoso form but includes a novel feature, multiple thematic connections across sections. In the first movement the themes of the first and second groups differ in mode as well as key, but the second group theme is a close variant of the first

(Example 8.1). Other motivic economies in the movement are the return of the opening, signature motive of the main theme of the first tutti (after a fourteen-bar introduction) in the close of the first tutti, in the solo's opening cadenza, at the beginning of the second tutti, and in the final tutti. This same motive is also extensively worked over in the solo development, after the *con espressione* theme. Additionally, a motive from the transition of the first tutti returns at the end of the first and second tuttis, and the introductory theme of the first tutti appears to be the basis for the *con espressione* theme of the solo development. In the last movement, the opening bars of the main theme of the second group, as well as the beginning and thereafter greater part of the development, derive from the main theme of the first group.

All the movements of the Concerto have other unusual features but none that place this work outside the bounds of the virtuoso genre. In the first movement the solo recapitulation follows the solo development without an intervening tutti and contains only the second group thematic area and close. The final tutti includes a two-page long, written-out cadenza. The second movement is only two pages long. Although it is a closed form (roughly, **ABA'**), it serves as hardly more than an introduction to the final movement. The final movement, although called a rondo, is one only by virtue of its thematic types. As terms used in the above paragraph suggest, it is a sonata form, somewhat reminiscent of Mozart's sonata-rondo finales.

If we think back to Schumann's interest in compositional cohesiveness as expressed in nearly all the reviews we have examined so far (and ahead to the first movement of his own Concerto in A Minor) we might imagine that he would have an interest in Thalberg's rather tidy thematic construction and neat form. Neither are mentioned in his review, which describes the Concerto as an immature product of Thalberg's youth that panders to virtuosic impulses. The reader may judge for him- or herself the aesthetic worth of Thalberg's themes as shown in Example 8.1. The passagework is, to quote Hans Engel, "totally lacking in invention," at times, in our opinion, dreadful.[7] Schumann cites no examples. He merely wishes Thalberg well along his way. "At the expense of an unenjoyable posthumous fame let him enjoy the virtuoso life's delightful mortality, and just excuse us for not discovering more than this in his works."[8]

Example 8.1 Thalberg, Concerto in F Minor, Op. 5, first movement, solo exposition.

Soon after he wrote the review of Thalberg's Concerto Schumann ran a series of reviews of capriccios and other short pieces, including Thalberg's Capriccio, Op. 15; Nocturnes, Op. 16; and Variations on Two Russian Themes, Op. 17. Concerning these Plantinga tells us Schumann "pronounced Thalberg's *Variations on Two Russian Themes* ... 'the best and most successful composition I have yet seen from him,' and honored it with the last place in the series."[9] One might conclude that Schumann considered these pieces, composed only somewhat later than the Concerto (which dates to 1829), to have greater intrinsic worth. It is true that they have a certain appeal, in that the main tune is kept in the foreground through sundry variations, and because the pianism is modern.[10] However, I think the important point is the difference in genre. What is suitable in a nocturne, caprice, or variation set is not acceptable in a concerto. Just three weeks before he ran the review of Thalberg's Concerto, Schumann admonished Döhler (whom, we recall, he said had "no inkling of the dignity of the art for which nature has given him some talent"):

> If someone writes a gay rondo, then that's his right. But if someone seeks a princely bride, then it is understood that he should be of noble birth and disposition. Or—not wanting to be unnecessarily metaphorical—if one works in so great an art form, which the best in the land approach with humility and trepidation, then he must know that. And that is what is so maddening here. Even the most talented everyday composers, Herz and Czerny, have taken the trouble to deliver something of value in their larger works.[11]

Thalberg, like Döhler, has not given the concerto its due.

About Thalberg's capabilities as a player there can be no doubt, as Schumann himself was soon to witness. At the very time he was writing the review of Thalberg's Concerto, the composer was establishing his reputation in Paris as the great rival of Liszt.[12] From his fiancée Clara Wieck Schumann knew about Thalberg's success in Vienna during the 1837–38 season.[13] Then, during his own stay in Vienna, from early October 1838 to early April 1839, he was on friendly terms with Thalberg, visiting him at his home and attending his concert on 27 November.[14]

When Thalberg came to Leipzig in 1841 Schumann was complimentary about the compositions he played (all his own) but emphasized that the real purpose of the concert was to enjoy his brilliant playing. Threads from his earlier review of Thalberg's Concerto run through this new review. By now Thalberg has decided to enjoy the "virtuoso life's delightful mortality" rather than the composer's "unenjoyable posthumous fame." Schumann does not begrudge him the choice. Compliments for Thalberg continue in a favorable review, a few months later, of his Scherzo, Op. 31; Grand Nocturne, Op. 35; Impromptu in the Form of an Etude, Op. 36; and *Souvenirs de Beethoven,* Grand Fantasy on the Seventh Symphony, Op. 39.[15] For Plantinga, such writing is "a monument to [Schumann's] integrity as a critic

... when Thalberg wrote something of merit [he] was ungrudging in his praise."[16] That may be, but I think Schumann's compliments also stem from his personal acquaintance and cordial relationship with Thalberg, and from his joy in Thalberg's great skill as a young, *au courant* pianist. I think, furthermore, that they reflect his lowered expectation when it comes to more ephemeral piano pieces. The standards were not lowered when Thalberg's Concerto was under consideration.

* * *

Schumann's reviews of Thalberg's Concerto and Herz's Second Concerto in C Minor appeared one after another in the 29 March 1836 issue of the *Neue Zeitschrift*. From then on, as we have just seen, it was yet a few more years before Schumann concluded that Thalberg had given himself over entirely to the transient fame of the virtuoso rather than devote himself to serious compositional endeavors. Already in the 1836 review he reached the same conclusion about Herz.

> What does he want other than to amuse and incidentally to grow rich? Has he thereby forced anyone to love and praise Beethoven's last quartets less? Does he invite comparison with these? Is he not much more the gay dandy, who bends a finger for no one except to play, and above all to hold onto his fame and glory.[17]

What follows is Schumann's prediction that Herz's fame will be short-lived, that it will soon burn itself out in the eyes of a fickle public. In the long run, his assessment proved correct. By the twentieth century Herz's works were no longer in the repertory. The purpose of their recent reissue has not been to change this judgment but primarily to make them "available," secondarily to understand the "ambiance" of their time, and only, it seems, by the by, to renew interest in the "music itself."[18] Throughout his career, though, Herz's performances drew audiences on three continents, and to the end of the nineteenth century his compositions remained popular with amateur players.[19]

Although Schumann's review is about Herz's C Minor Concerto, it does not touch on the piece until its final paragraph. There his summary comment reads, "The Second Concerto by Herz is in C Minor, and is recommended to those who like the first."[20] The comment is curious, given that Schumann is known to have made a thorough study of Herz's First Concerto, a matter discussed in some detail in Chapter 4. It does not seem likely that his tongue-in-cheek recommendation is a public repudiation of his earlier private pursuits. Instead, it sums up in one sentence his mockery throughout the essay of G. W. Fink's review of Herz's works for the *Allgemeine musikalische Zeitung* in January 1831. Fink writes that the music of Herz is played more than that of any of his contemporaries, and that his compositions have earned more money than all of theirs together. From among all Herz's compositions Fink singles out the First Concerto, Op. 34

as a phenomenal best-seller. He concludes that Herz must have many admirers, and that this alone speaks favorably of his compositions, at least to some degree. "Who would be so foolish as to demand that everything has to conform to his own taste? If it has some kind of spirit, then it is good, if not for us."[21]

Five years later, in the review of Herz's Second Concerto now under discussion, Schumann concedes that Herz's compositions have their uses.

> With that we should not forget that he has kept millions of fingers busy, and that by playing his variations the public acquires a mechanical polish. … We are convinced that he who has mastered Herz's bravura pieces can play a Beethoven sonata, if he understands it, that much more easily and freely than he would without that skill.[22]

In August 1836 Fink countered this dismissal of Herz as a composer of trifles in his own review of Herz's Second Concerto. "Whenever the times place someone or other too high, then another time follows which places him too low."[23] He reiterates his stand of 1831, the mere fact that Herz's compositions have a following shows they have some merit, in the case of the Second Concerto, merit that ranks it beyond use as finger exercises.

Schumann's second reply to Fink came six months later, in his review of Herz's Third Concerto, which we considered in the previous chapter. After listing the various composers from whom Herz borrows (including Moscheles, Chopin, Weber, Beethoven, and Spohr), Schumann says that he wants to learn from the best, only taking a few things from heroes of the second rank, namely, Kalkbrenner and Thalberg. "May his valor [in this regard] continue and endure," he writes. "We want to be his herald, despite the most General Musical Times [*allgemeinsten musikalischen Zeitung*], which already long ago acknowledged him and [Franz] Hünten as masters, and Handel, too, and may the Concerto be properly practiced. Why does one have fingers and feeling? We ask."[24]

No matter what the critics said, Herz's C Minor Concerto proved to be quite popular. When Herz played it in London in May and June 1833, the *Harmonicon* reacted much the same as Schumann, Herz had technique to burn but was not a superior musician.

> He crosses his hands, he weaves his fingers, with the cleverness of a juggler; an automaton constructed by Maelzel could hardly surpass him in precision. He invents and masters passages which the greatest musicians never dreamt of, which the best players never did and never will attempt …[25]

Anticipating Schumann's review by three years, the author deigns to write only one sentence about the Concerto: it is "at least on a par with most of the other compositions by the same author." Yet, two pages further on, in a write-up of another performance by Herz, which also included the C Minor Concerto, he must admit that "a large audience assembled to hear [him] …

that he was received in a most encouraging manner, and that his performances were followed by very flattering applause."[26]

When Herz played the Concerto at his first concert in the United States, on 29 October 1846, there were no reservations by the critic for *The Albion*, Henry Cood Watson.

> The Allegro is a brilliant and effective movement, with something of wild passion in its character; it is instrumented with great care, indeed all the movements in this respect exhibit a considerable knowledge of the resources of the Orchestra. ... The Andante and Rondo are admirably characteristic; the Rondo in particular, is so pleasingly melodious, and so beautifully treated, that the audience interrupted it repeatedly with bursts of applause.[27]

R. Allen Lott cites a similar reaction from Richard Grant White, the critic for the *Morning Courier and New-York Enquirer.*

> It is a beautifully chaste, simple, and symmetrical composition, and gives evidence of a capacity for orchestral writing ... the piano forte passages are brilliant and highly effective, and the orchestra is admirably handled. Indeed throughout, this composition shows thought, and is not one of those flimsy combinations—called concertos by some modern performers,—composed of rapid airs with humdrum accompaniments and unmeaning cadenzas, and which might as well be played commencing at the middle or the end, as at the beginning.[28]

George Templeton Strong was at this concert, and he, too, was carried away by the Concerto.

> *Vivat* Henri Herz! ... I never knew the power of the piano before. ... his orchestral accompaniments and introductions seem to me to be very excellent, every note telling ... composition and all very spirited and beautiful, but always subordinate to the piano—strictly in place. And in his own personal business there's no execution for execution's sake: it's all music and not sleight of hand—and beautiful music, too. And I never could say that of the concertos even of Mendelssohn and the other masters of that school.[29]

Although these reviews of performances mention the superior orchestration, brilliant piano passages, thoughtful construction, and admirable character of the Concerto, none mention the unusual form of the first movement. Nor does Schumann's review. Fink makes an observation about its unusual finish but notes nothing further.[30] Nowhere does one read in contemporary reviews the obvious fact later stated by Engel, the first movement is only "half a sonata movement."[31] Beginning in C minor, an ample tutti is followed by an ample solo exposition ending on E-flat major. Then just sixteen bars of tutti carry the movement back to C minor. An additional few bars in C major, a four-octave solo run and two chords, all *fortissimo,* confirm the return to the tonic key. Engel speculates that Herz may have found a reprise (and we may add, even a development) too boring. But a certain ingeniousness in Herz's construction suggests other reasons why he instead considered the movement finished as it stands. To support this conclusion we must first survey the movement.

The following matters need mentioning. (1) In the opening tutti, a counterstatement of the first main theme modulates to E-flat major, effecting a transition to the second main theme. (2) The solo's introductory cadenza modulates from C minor to E-flat major. (3) Following a brief tutti insert on the dominant of E-flat, the solo plays a full eight-bar theme in E-flat major. A new lyric theme at this juncture is not unusual in virtuoso concertos but a change of key is. A restatement of the theme reverses the tonal direction and modulates back to C minor. (4) The transition is yet another C minor to E-flat modulation. As in the first tutti, it is fashioned as a counterstatement of the first theme. (5) Finally, in five bars the second and last tutti of the movement confirms the solo's E-flat major cadence at the end of the exposition with a brief reference to the second theme. Thereafter, the tutti returns to C minor with the same music that returned the first tutti to C minor. A solo run in major cuts short the tutti's special close just as it starts the funeral-march rhythms that continued for twelve bars in the first tutti.

Up to this point in our study this is the first piece in which the solo portion of the first movement does not represent a full sonata form. At the same time, the movement is squarely in the virtuoso tradition described in Chapter 2. None of six contemporary writers we cited mentions any formal innovations in it. Strong even contrasts Herz's Concerto with others that do exhibit some innovation, those of the "school" of Mendelssohn. *Pace* Engel, I don't think Herz threw off the development and reprise just to get on with the piece. The drastic shortening of the movement is of a type we will see in the next concertos we examine, by Moscheles (No. 6) and Wieck. For Moscheles and Wieck this will mean that the first movement serves as little more than an introduction to what follows. In the case of Herz, though, the first movement is closed, no matter how abruptly. Furthermore, it retains an immense actual size, 259 bars in common time. The first and second tuttis, 80 and 22 bars respectively, make up about two fifths of this size. The remainder comes through the expansion of the solo in two ways. The most obvious has to do with the enormous length of the solo's *Con brio* close, two sections which together total 50 bars. The first starts with the usual vamp then veers off to E-flat minor (*piano* and *poco a poco rallentando*, then in its last bar, *crescendo assai*). A new vamp in E-flat major signals the beginning of the second section (*in tempo, piano, leggiero*).

The other expansion involves the modulation to E-flat in the first group. This may be thought of either as an extension of the solo's cadenza-like opening, or, to use John Daverio's term, as a kind of arabesque-like interruption.[32] In either case, a return from this flight of fancy to the expected course of the movement comes with the orchestral statement of the opening theme in C minor and continuation of the exposition in the usual fashion. Yet, as the exposition reaches its end the so-called flight of fancy is seen instead as an integral part of the movement, perhaps the most important determinant of its final contour. To wit, the move in the solo's first group from C minor to E-flat major and back to C minor corresponds to the move from C minor to E-flat major and back to C minor in the opening tutti. It is repeated in the solo's move away from C minor in the first group, toward E-flat major for the second group and back to C minor/major in the final tutti and closing solo bars. The symmetries of these tonal routes, and their rounding out through a return in the second tutti of the very music that leads the first tutti from E-flat major back to C minor, give a sense that the movement has run its tonal course and come to a true conclusion, rather than that it has been abruptly cut off.

The second movement of the Herz's C Minor Concerto is a closed form in the key of E major, the latter no doubt in imitation of the key of the middle movement of Beethoven's Concerto in C Minor. The final movement, though, begins with an orchestral introduction, *Allegro vivo,* which serves as a transition from E major to C major. What follows, *Un poco meno mosso,* is an abbreviated form. After an opening theme then transition, a second theme in G minor is heard. Next, much passagework in G major leads eventually to a dominant preparation and *Cadenza ad libitum* immediately preceding a return to the opening theme, which is much extended, ultimately *con bravura e sempre più crescendo.* A final *Presto* based on the first theme ends the movement.

In sum, one could say that Herz has condensed the form of the first and last movements. At the same time he has not shortened their actual length: the last movement is 516 bars in three-eight time; the entire Concerto, according to the *Albion* reviewer, took twenty-five minutes to play. The two movements have been filled out instead with long bravura passages, and in the case of the first movement, a structurally important digression. The passagework employs quite ordinary figuration, as the reader may judge by looking at Example 8.2, which shows a portion of the first section of the closing passagework of the first movement, beginning with the repeat of the opening vamp and continuing up to the move to the flat-sixth of E major. I don't think we would be wrong to surmise that above all it was this very humdrum nature of Herz's musical materials, his use of all the clichés of the time without any distinguishing grace that Schumann disliked. As early as 1834, after hearing his friend Ludwig Schuncke perform Beethoven's *Emperor* Concerto, he wrote, "It makes a difference whether Beethoven writes out pure chromatic scales, or Herz."[33]

However, whatever specific objections Schumann had remained unstated, in particular, any objections he may have had to what I consider the original form of the Herz's first movement. For all the extensions and manipulations, the form of all three movements remains remarkably clear to the listener, just as three writers who witnessed Herz's performance of the

Example 8.2 Herz, Concerto No. 2 in C Minor, Op. 74, first movement, solo exposition, portion of the close, beginning with the repeat of the opening vamp.

Concerto in New York attested. For whatever reasons Schumann may have been insensitive to this achievement (an aversion to everything by Herz; no opportunity to hear the work in concert), we will see that his unresponsiveness is consistent with his reception of works by Moscheles and Clara Wieck that similarly depart from the traditional "balanced allegro" opening in their first movements.

* * *

We have already discussed Schumann's early admiration for Moscheles in Chapter 1. His first three concertos, in F Major, E-flat Major, and G Minor, were part of the survey in Chapter 2. Some features of the F Major Concerto were also considered in Chapter 3. Our discussion here will be of Moscheles's Concerto No. 5 in C Major, Op. 87; Concerto No. 6 in B-flat Major, Op. 90, the *Fantastique;* and Concerto No. 7 in C Minor, Op. 93, the

Pathétique. Schumann reviewed the Sixth and Seventh Concertos after he
heard Moscheles play them in concert on 9 October 1835. His review of the
scores of the Fifth and Sixth Concertos appeared on 8 April 1836 as part of
his concerto series, and of the score of the Seventh on 4 January 1839 with
the continuation of that series. As we shall see, Schumann saw each of these
three concertos as departing in some way from Moscheles's earlier, virtuoso
ones, and was aware that for this reason each would have less appeal to a
large audience, just as he reported after hearing Moscheles play two of
them, the Sixth and the first movement of the Seventh, on 9 October 1835.

> Just as at one time, full of youth, he gushed forth in the E-flat Major Con-
> certo ... thereafter he fashioned [his works] more discreetly and artfully
> in the G Minor Concerto ... so now he follows darker, more mysterious
> paths, not concerned, as he was earlier, as to whether these please a large
> public. Already the Fifth Concerto inclines somewhat toward the roman-
> tic; in his latest works [including the Sixth and Seventh Concertos], what-
> ever still vacillated between old and new before, now appears completely
> strengthened and secure.[34]

Schumann's assessment was correct. The virtuosic G Minor Concerto,
and not the later ones he calls romantic, remained Moscheles's most popular, both during his lifetime and beyond. Composed in 1820, Moscheles
completely revised it in 1822 for a performance in London. Although he
wrote seven other piano concertos, the last in 1838, up to 1846 he performed the G Minor eight times in London alone, more than any of his other
concertos. One London critic deemed it "one of the noblest [concertos] ever
composed."[35] However, Moscheles's wife Charlotte wrote, "He often used
to complain that people always played only his G Minor Concerto, while he
deemed the other seven of equal merit."[36]

The G Minor Concerto was published in 1825, and continued to appear
in various editions printed in Vienna, London, and Leipzig through about
1850. Soon after 1900 it appeared in editions by Steingräber (for two
pianos, edited by E. Rudorff), H. Litolff and A. P. Schmidt (for two pianos,
edited by Clemens Schultz), and Breitkopf and Härtel (arranged for piano
solo by Carl Reinecke). In 1971 Music Treasure reissued the Litolff edition,
and advertised a recording of the Concerto by Michael Ponti.[37] Other
recordings of the G Minor Concerto were made later, but only recently have
the Fifth, Sixth and Seventh Concertos appeared.[38] I know of no recording
of the Eighth Concerto.

The Fifth Concerto was published circa 1830–32. The Sixth followed in
1836. Schumann had not seen the score when he first heard Moscheles play
it in October 1835, but by 8 March 1836 he could write Moscheles, "Daily I
regale in your Concerto *Fantastique*."[39] With the scores of the Fifth and
Sixth, or *Fantastique*, concertos in hand, Schumann proceeded to write the
review that appeared on 8 April 1836. He repeats his observation about the
separation of Moscheles's music into three creative periods, with the Fifth

Concerto on the cusp between the second and third periods, and the Sixth squarely in the third.

> We believe we can characterize precisely three periods in the artistic for-
> mation of this master. In the first, approximately in the years 1814–20. ...
> the better musician [in him] was, on the whole, obscured by the admirably
> bold virtuoso. ... he [then] crosses over into a second period—where the
> composer and the virtuoso grasp hands in an alliance of equal
> strength—the golden age, during which the G Minor Concerto ... arose.
> ... The bridge to the third period, where the poetic tendency of the
> composer began to prevail completely, consists of the Fifth Concerto in
> C and the first important work in that period, the "fantastic" [or Sixth
> Concerto].[40]

The Fifth Concerto is a virtuoso concerto, but nonetheless in the very next sentence Schumann calls both it and the Sixth Concerto "romantic."

> If we call these two romantic, then by this we mean the faint, enchanted
> illumination that hovers over them; we do not know whether it originates
> from the objects themselves or from somewhere else. One cannot grasp
> with one's hands particular places where the romantic, luminous fra-
> grance comes out most strongly; but one feels everywhere that it is there,
> especially in the rare E minor Adagio of the Fifth Concerto which stands
> very tenderly, with an almost religious character, between the other move-
> ments ...[41]

The *Adagio* opens with a somber theme in E minor played by the tutti, then a second theme in E minor played by the solo. A middle section in E major introduces a new theme, then a return to E minor brings only the first of the two themes from the opening E minor section, played by the solo in a varied form. Schumann perhaps heard a "religious character" in the funereal sound of the E minor themes, or in the hymnlike theme of the E major section. A striking moment comes with the return to E minor from E major through a section on the sixth degree, C major, at which point a variant of the opening motive of the first theme of the first movement is introduced, in the key of the first movement (Example 8.3b, in the right hand, the last two beats of bar 66 and first two of bar 67).

Schumann calls the first and last movements "more practical and fiery, and more interesting when you look into them" than the second movement. Unlike the *Adagio*, where he names a particular moment embodying that elusive "romantic" air that is everywhere but that cannot be got hold of, he points to no such place in the outer two movements. What he does single out in each is "a definite center of gravity toward which everything grows, where all the intellectual radii come together." This center, he says, is essen-tial to "a true musical work of art," and readily discernable to an attentive listener. Although he does not explain the dramatic trajectory through which this center is reached, a look at the first movement will show that the build

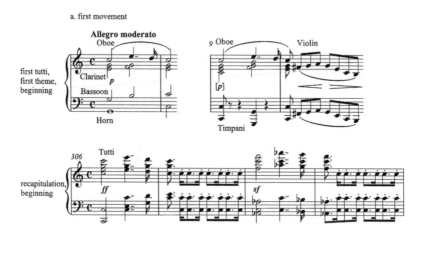

Example 8.3 Moscheles, Concerto No. 5 in C Major, Op. 87, main motive.

toward it relies on the easily heard return and transformation of key motives. The same is true of the last movement, although there Schumann says the center of gravity is "less well prepared."[42]

The first movement follows the virtuoso model. The first theme begins with a distinctive head motive, two bars long followed sometimes by a tag filling out the second bar (Example 8.3a). The tag forms the basis of the opening motive of the second, lyric theme. Thus, a single motivic entity generates the two main thematic areas of the movement. Important to Schumann's "center of gravity," however, is only the two-bar head motive. It is introduced by the oboe, *piano,* at the beginning of the first tutti, then heard again at the end of the tutti. The solo picks it up, *risoluto* and *forte,* in its grand opening cadenza and spinning forth of the first theme. In the

Example 8.3 (*continued*)

development, the oboe gives a meditative look back to the original, quiet version, then, in the bass it becomes the basis of an *animato* storm, before a return to the oboe's quieter version in the retransition. Schumann's "center of gravity" arrives with the third tutti and beginning of the recapitulation when the head motive is heard for the last time, and for the first time, full tutti (Example 8.3a).

> If you have been listening tense and straining, the moment comes, where, for the first time you can breathe freely: you have reached the summit, the view rushes by, clear and satisfying, ahead and behind. So is it in the middle of the first movement, at the place where the orchestra breaks in with the main-motive: you feel, as if the real idea is finally given vent, as if the composer proclaims with full voice: that is what I wanted.[43]

The final *fortissimo* statements of the head motive lack the tag. By way of a last sweet gasp in the drama, it is heard, *dolce,* in the two phrases of the lyric theme of the second group, the first taken by the clarinet, the second by the solo. The rest is brilliant dramatics of the solo and tutti closes.

The sprightly finale, *Allegro vivace,* is a modified sonata-rondo. The rondo theme is a hodge-podge (Example 8.3c). Consequent **a** (bars 13–16) is a reminder of the *Presto* coda, also in C major, of the Rondo movement of Beethoven's Third Concerto; it will be the basis of the opening phrase of the theme of the second group (or first episode). Antecedent and consequent **b** (bars 17–21, only the antecedent is shown) are in the so-called *volkstümlicher Stil.* And antecedent **a** (bars 9–12) is based on the opening motive of the first movement (cf. Example 8.3a, bars 1–2, 9–10). This motive further serves as the basis of the long coda, until in the final tutti it is repeated four times in succession. Thus, besides motivic links across sections of the first and last movements of his Fifth Concerto, Moscheles forges one between the first and last movements, using a motive that he also recalls in the middle of the second movement. Furthermore, the surprising choice of E minor for the key of the second movement is foreshadowed by a large section in that key at the beginning of the development of the first movement.

Schumann says that everything in the Concerto is "very like Moscheles." He singles out particular passages that show certain "stylistic idiosyncrasies," which one would recognize, even if played out of context. I believe there is also an idiosyncratic stylistic imprint on the motive Moscheles carries across his movements. In its basic form it is nothing more than a rising and falling third. In each movement it is given more characteristic features. In the first movement it is introduced by the oboe in a moderate tempo, with long note values, full chordal accompaniment and a distinctive dotted rhythm as it falls back to its initial pitch (Example 8.3a); in the third movement it is first heard in the solo, in even eighth notes and *vivace*, a single line with its distinctive ornament in the rising line (Example 8.3c, bar 8). But more important is the undistinguished building block that remains when these particular ornaments, rhythms, tempos, and instrumentations are stripped away. Its very anonymity is a recognizable style feature of the themes Moscheles fashions from it, one that will figure in his next two concertos as well, and one that, among concertos from the 1820s and 1830s we have looked at so far, is unique. In his review, Schumann skips over any description of the role of this motive as a red thread in the unfolding of the Concerto. He singles out the centers of gravity of the first and last movements, but leaves out any discussion of the process by which they are reached. The motivic connections within and across Moscheles's movements are the vital links in the dramatic progression toward those centers.

* * *

Moscheles's Sixth Concerto, the *Fantastique,* is his first that does not fall into the virtuoso pattern. Schumann noticed this as soon as he heard it in October 1835. He also noted the "difficulty and seriousness" of both Moscheles's Sixth and Seventh Concertos, and rejoiced that, in his performance of the two concertos Moscheles had left some of his youthful *Schwärmerei* behind.

> ... when it comes to youthful enthusiasm and, in general, sympathy for the latest fanciful manner of playing, whatever may be missing as compared to earlier, the man makes up for completely with sharpness of character and strength of spirit.[44]

By April 1836 Schumann had the score of the Sixth Concerto in hand. He recalls Moscheles's performance of six months earlier, repeating the earlier description he gave but changing his judgment.

> Perhaps it was due to the familiar, very tranquil and precise performance of the composer that these works, which sparkle just like his earlier ones only more faintly, did not thrill as much as they surely would have if

> played by one more spirited. It seems to us that many compositions of a fantastic sort have gained more and proved effective far more quickly through a certain bluntness of performance rather than through the fashionable neatness and smoothness of virtuosity.[45]

After seeing the score, Schumann reevaluated his memory of Moscheles's performance, especially of the Sixth, or Fantastic Concerto downward. His remembered disappointment, and desire for a more spirited performance than he recalls, denied the impact the Concerto once had on him in the concert hall.

The more spirited performance that, in retrospect, Schumann would like to have heard of Moscheles's Sixth Concerto, would have worked to disguise what he sees as the "aesthetic peril" of its experimental form. With score in hand, this is the main focus of his review.

> The Fantastic Concerto consists of four movements in different tempos joined together. We already declared ourselves against this form earlier. Even if it doesn't seem impossible to produce a pleasing whole with it, the aesthetic peril is too great compared with what can be gained. To be sure, there is a lack of smaller concert pieces in which virtuosos with one fell swoop can develop their presentation of an allegro, adagio and rondo. One would have to contrive a genre that would consist of one large movement in a moderate tempo, in which the preliminary part would take the place of the first allegro, the *cantabile* part that of the adagio, and the brilliant close that of the rondo. Perhaps the idea, which, we confess, we would prefer to realize with a special composition of our own, will arouse interest.[46]

Schumann's earlier declaration against the four-joined-movements form is found in a review of a concertino by Carl Lasekk, which we will consider in the next chapter. For now we can say that he objects mainly to the disruptiveness of "various parts in changing tempos all running into each other."[47] The form he would like to see, the one he says he would like himself to create, was indeed realized in 1841 when he composed his *Phantasie* for Piano and Orchestra (the original version of the first movement of his A Minor Concerto), which we also will discuss in a later chapter. What we will consider now are the form of Moscheles's Sixth Concerto and Schumann's particular objections to it.

The four, short movements of the Moscheles Concerto *Fantastique* are played without interruption. None, except the last, can stand on it own. Together all the movements could be considered to work as one large movement. The first, *Allegro con spirito,* common time, in B-flat major, does not have the traditional first tutti, solo exposition, second tutti, solo development, and so on, form. Instead, tutti and solo present together and in alternation a somewhat "fantastically" constructed exposition in bars 1–161 with the second group in the unusual key of D major. A tutti (bars 161–78) leads to B-flat minor, where a development section appears to begin, but is cut short after just 28 bars to lead *attacca* into the second movement. Notable is the lack of a recapitulation.

The two middle movements are transitional. The *Andante espressivo,* in three-eight time, is in two sections. The first, in G minor, is a series of continuous and evolving variations of the theme begun by the solo after a four-bar introduction. The second section introduces a new theme in G major, played first by the orchestra then varied by the solo. There is no return to the earlier, G minor theme; the second section flows directly into the next, transitional movement, *Allegro agitato.* This movement divides into two short sections, the first in twelve-eight time with the key signature C minor, the second in common time with the key signature C major, but leading eventually to V of B-flat. Both sections recall music from the first movement. The final movement, *Vivace,* two-four time, in B-flat major, is a short rondo with only one episode (the form is roughly **ABA'B'coda**). Because of its melodic connections with the first movement and tonal stability it may be considered a recapitulation of sorts.

Among the web of motives that stretch across the four movements, the most important is an ascending third, which forms the head motive of several themes in the first movement. It begins the first statement of the principal theme (Example 8.4a) and its counterstatement; the second member of the second group; and the truncated development. Another prominent motive is a fanfare of repeated-note triplets, first played in a tutti insert at the end of the transition (Example 8.4b), then in the two themes of the second group. In the third, transitional movement the first section cites the opening theme of the second group of the first movement; the second section, a portion (varied) of the second, *cantabile* theme of the second group. Both citations include the fanfare triplet motive. In the final movement, the beginning of the rondo theme incorporates an inversion and rhythmic diminution of the rising third motive from the first movement, actually a free and extended inversion of the entire first phrase of that movement (Example 8.4a). The tutti entrance which closes off the rondo refrain is also an inversion of the same motive, in a different rhythm (Example 8.4a). The return of the rondo refrain does not include the tutti that initially closed it off. This is saved until after the return of the episode, at which point the third-motive is heard in its original, rising form, in counterpoint to the falling form. Both are picked up and played repeatedly in the solo coda, which also incorporates the triplet fanfare and opening motive of the first theme of the second group of the first movement (the latter is shown in Example 8.4b, bars 81–82).

Tonally, there is considerable play of dark and light across the movements. The first movement, in B-flat major, has, as noted earlier, a somewhat unusual modulation to the major third degree, D major, for the second group. This bright coloring is balanced by darker turns to G minor in the *con fuoco* portion of the counterstatement-transition; to D minor at the beginning of the second group; and B-flat minor then G minor in the

Example 8.4   Moscheles, Concerto No. 6 in B-flat Major, *Fantastique*, Op. 90, main motives.

development. The play of dark and light continues in the second movement (G minor then G major), and the transitional, third movement, which finds its way from C minor to D major then minor before the turn to a dominant preparation of B-flat major. Tonally, the final movement is the most stable. The first statement of the episode turns for a considerable stretch to A minor (from F major), and its return statement begins in D-flat major before leading through A major and A-flat minor to the dominant of B-flat major. But on the whole these colorings seem to have a lesser structural role than the turns to the sharp keys (D and G major) or flat-side minor keys (D, G, B-flat, and C) that were explored in earlier movements.

The final movement is the only stable anchor, both as concerns fixed key and formal closure, for the three incomplete movements that precede it. The first movement has no recapitulation, the second, no return to its opening section, and the third is no more than a transition. By keeping the first three movements short and open, Moscheles generates a feeling of forward flow, which leads to the recall then return in the final two movements of music originally heard in the exposition of the first movement. Still, the separate affects of each movement, *Allegro* opening, slow middle movement, transition then rondo final movement, remain, with the passage from one to the next hardly smoothed over. In the short development of the first movement the spinning out of the *cantabile* theme of the second group to a *rallentando, dolente* cadence is followed abruptly by *agitato, con smania* passagework rising to *fortissimo,* then just as abruptly, by two bars ending the movement (which runs *attacca* into the next) *piano* and *Adagio,* with four chords, the last one V of G.

In the second movement the last three bars settle onto a tonic cadence, but at the same time the solo's thirty-second-note sextuplets flow *attacca* into the violin's sixteenth notes in twelve-eight that begin the third movement. This is not a continuous flow by which the thirty-seconds equal the sixteenths. Instead the listener feels a jolt as the beat of the second movement, $\flat = 80$ and slower, as the last three bars are also *ritenuto* and *calando,* changes to the much faster $\downarrow = 138$ beat. The steady flow of notes suddenly breaks away at something near twice their former speed. Whereas the third, transitional movement includes some dramatic and tender recalls of the first movement, it connects to the finale with less-than-inspired passagework leading to a six-bar pedal over V of B-flat.

Although Schumann concludes that the *Fantastique* is "fully effective" *despite* rather than because of its form—a view, incidentally, that I do not share—he is excited about another feature of the Concerto, the interchanges between solo and orchestra. "Together with the orchestra," he writes, "it displays an ingenious interplay, where practically every instrument has a part in the thing, something to contribute, something of consequence."[48] Already, after hearing Moscheles play the Sixth and Seventh Concertos in 1835 he wrote, "One could as good as call them duos for piano and orchestra, the latter comes forward so independently."[49] In the exposition of the first movement of the Sixth the "ingenious interplay," includes interruptions of the solo's opening cadential gestures; the initiation of the free counterstatement; the conclusion of the dominant preparation of the second group (Example 8.4b); triplet punctuations of the opening theme of the second group, and of the extended cadence of the *cantabile* theme that follows.

Yet, if Schumann liked these interjections, they also contribute to the "uncertain" form of the movement, which he did not like. Generally, the interjections are not positioned to help give structural definition to the movement. On the contrary, some are even disruptive. After various introductory gestures from the tutti then solo, the tutti's four-bar phrase with its rising third motive would seem to initiate a stable statement of the main theme in the tonic, but instead turns out to be a free counterstatement that begins modulating before it cadences. The final four bars of the dominant preparation given over to the tutti may seem to give clear definition to the beginning of the second group that follows, in bar 81 (Example 8.4b). But the first theme of the second group, though in the new tonic key, sounds more like a continuation of the dominant preparation, with the expected solo *cantabile* theme coming only in bar 90. The tutti insert after the *cantabile* theme of the second group derails rather than confirms the cadence on V of D major, sending it, with its demanding triplet, *forte* unisons, to F major and what sounds like the excited beginning of the brilliant close. The solo corrects the outburst with a return, *piano, tenero,* to V of D major and calmer mood of the mid-register *cantabile* theme, subduing the triplets which it takes up as a steady accompanimental figure.

Toward the end of his review, Schumann gives brief mention to his most and least favorite parts of the Sixth Concerto. We are not surprised that he was attracted to music in a piece whose form he "declared [himself] against." It meets one of his standards for concertos in the new form—the piano does not dominate with flashy technical displays but works together with the orchestra—but not the other—the form is not beautifully balanced. In short, he holds a different opinion of the content and effectiveness of the Concerto than of its form. But the final sentence of his review suggests that the first two matters are not as easily separated from the last as he would have it. Although unhappy with the breaking off of each of the first three movements as it moves to the next (and, we surmise, the consequent lack of return in each of these movements), he at the same times says "the whole thing closes ... as if it could still continue for a long time."[50] This particular stroke of mastery, as Schumann calls it, is a result of the very feature he rejects, namely, the reduced size of each movement and consequent small size of the entire concerto.

* * *

In closing his review of the Fifth and Sixth Concertos Schumann wrote, "We look forward with genuine joy to the new Concerto *pathétique* of this artist."[51] On 30 July 1836 he communicated his eager anticipation to Moscheles, "We are very much longing for something new from you, the Concerto *pathétique* ...," then a year later persisted in another letter to the composer, "I still see nothing advertised of the Concerto *pathétique*."[52] The Seventh or *Pathétique* Concerto was published in 1837, and a review by Schumann appeared in January 1839, more than three years after he first heard the piece in concert, in October 1835. At that time he placed the Sixth and Seventh Concertos squarely in the romantic school. By 1839 he says the Seventh Concerto only approaches the romantic, and although it is a first-rate work, does not measure up to the composer's earlier G Minor Concerto.

> In Moscheles we have a rare example of a musician, who, although elderly [he was then nearly forty-five] and still assiduously engaged in the

study of older masters, also observes the progress of newer phenomena, and has made use of their advances. As he now controls those influences with an originality born to him, from such a mixture of old, new, and what belongs to him, arises a work that is just like the latest concerto, clear and sharp in its form, approaching the romantic in its character, and once again as original as one knows the composer to be. Not to cut it too finely, the Concerto betrays its master everywhere; but everything has its prime, and he who once wrote a G Minor Concerto is no more, although he is certainly the diligent, first-rate artist, who spares no pains to make his works as good as the best.[53]

The reason for the change of perspective about the *Pathétique* may be because in some ways it is closer to the old virtuoso model than its immediate predecessor. More detailed inspection, however, will reveal considerable deviations from what we have observed to be the norm in that model, as Schumann notes in the continuation of his review.

This time [Moscheles] renounces popularity right from the start; the Concerto is called *Pathétique* and it is so; what do 99 out of 100 virtuosos care about that! The departure in form from other concertos, and from Moscheles's own earlier ones, will strike everyone at once. The first movement advances quickly, the tuttis are shorter than usual, the orchestra takes part everywhere; the second movement with its slower interludes seems to me to have been conceived with greater difficulty, it introduces the last movement, which once again takes up the pathetic character of the first movement in a more vehement tempo.[54]

We will begin with a discussion of what Schumann calls the "clear and sharp" form of Moscheles's Concerto, and its "departure in form from other concertos," following the outline of the movement given in Figure 8.1. At the same time we will show the nature of the orchestra's participation and the impact on the Concerto of Moscheles's study of earlier masters. After surveying each movement in turn, we will return to the matter of Schumann's evaluation of the Seventh Concerto as less than a work of Moscheles's prime.

In the first movement, there are four departures from the usual form in virtuoso concertos. First, the opening tutti is not a separate entity, but combines with the solo to present the principal theme of the sonata exposition. Tutti and solo thus share a single formal entity, the first group of the exposition, an area normally given over primarily if not exclusively to the solo. As Schumann observes, "the orchestra takes part everywhere." Second, the second group has two distinct members, rather than the more usual one, before the solo close begins. The first phrase of the second member, theme **C**, is played by the solo. The answering phrase, begun by the winds with the solo obbligato, delays the tonic by an enormous extension, which provides an opportunity for a graduated acceleration of pace and smooth transition to the *fieramente* close. This type of gradation in pacing from larger to

Exposition		bar nos.
first group		
Tutti	**A**, C minor	1–55
Solo	completion of **A**	56–61
	A' (counterstatement), modulation to	
	E-flat major	62–80
second group		
Tutti	**B**, E-flat major	80–87
Solo	**B'**, E-flat major	88–99
	C, E-flat major	100–25
	close	
	E-flat major (and C minor)	125–45
	E-flat major (and C minor)	145–58
Development	on **A**, E-flat major modulating to	
	C minor	158–77
Tutti	**A**, C minor modulating to D-flat major	178–99
Solo	**A'**, D-flat major modulating to D major	200–18
Tutti	**B**, D major	219–22
Solo	completion of **B**	223–24
	B', modulating from D major to F minor,	
	V of C	225–50
(Solo with Tutti)	V of C, continued	251–56
Recapitulation		
second group		
Solo	**B'**, C major	257–68
	C	269–83
	close	
	C major then minor	283–307
	on **A**, C minor	307–19
Coda		
(Solo with Tutti)	on **A**, C minor	319–33
Tutti	C minor	333–39

Figure 8.1 Schematic representation of Moscheles, Concerto No. 7 in C Minor, Op. 93, first movement.

smaller note values is characteristic of the classical masters; its presence in the *Pathétique* Concerto may be a wellspring of Schumann's observation that Moscheles is "still assiduously engaged in the study of older masters."

Third, of three segments in the solo close, the last takes over the function normally assigned the second tutti. It is constructed as one hugely expanded phrase modulating from E-flat major to C minor, a feature frequently found in second tuttis, but not solo closes. The segment is based on the head motive of theme **A**, another frequent characteristic of second tuttis. While vamps and their attendant virtuosic displays are not absent from the close, Schumann seems to have liked its original construction for he writes in his 1839 review, "We offer especial thanks to recent writers of concertos, that they no longer bore us at the end with trills, and especially with octave leaps."[55] In this concerto, and among all those to be discussed in this and the following chapter, the elimination of the emphatic ending with its "trills and octave leaps" is a signal that the expected solo conclusion is elided into a transitional area that is normally the task of the second tutti.

Fourth, the construction of the development and recapitulation is highly unusual and ingenious. From the last segment of the exposition (bars 158 ff.) up to the beginning of the coda (bar 319), the movement duplicates exactly the succession of themes heard before. It is as if the entire exposition would be replayed, but with the tonal directions changed so that two sections, the development and recapitulation, remain nevertheless discernible. In the development, a second statement of theme **B** is expanded to accommodate a long pedal on the dominant of C (bars 241–56) that signals the coming of the recapitulation not only tonally but also by assigning one three-bar segment to the tutti (251–53). The recapitulation emphasizes tonic stability. The close is somewhat shorter than in the exposition, and the place of a final tutti is taken by a coda in which both solo and tutti participate, elaborating the head motive of **A**. This final return of **A** adds much to the clarity of the movement and redresses a certain lack of balance that is often felt in those virtuoso concertos which omit the principal theme (and coincidentally, a third tutti) from the recapitulation. After the final *con forza* chords of the close, the coda returns the movement, *tranquillamente,* to a quiet mood that is appropriate to its "pathetic" character. A *fortissimo* eruption in the last two bars of the solo accentuates this mood, but also serves to usher in the traditional *sempre fortissimo* ending of the final tutti.

The second movement is a series of double variations alternating between *Allegro agitato* in common time and *Andante espressivo* in six-eight time. What Schumann may have seen as being conceived with "difficulty" in this movement is not just the juxtaposition of these two different themes in different meters and tempos, but Moscheles's far-flung modulations. The first *Allegro* begins in A-flat major and ends on open E-flat octaves. After a *lunga pausa,* the *Andante* begins in B major (a respelling of C-flat major) then ends on V of D. The second *Allegro* section proceeds in this key, ending with F-sharp octaves and a *lunga pausa.* The second *Andante* picks the octaves up as a beginning on V of V in C major. The third and final *Allegro* is again in A-flat major, but ends with a long pedal on the dominant of C minor. In sum, each section of the movement is an open-ended interlude. Taken all together, the entire movement is one large interlude which introduces the final movement, *attacca.*

The basic form of the final movement is **ABA'B'coda**. The rondo refrain, or **A**, opens with the same motive as the first theme of the second movement (Example 8.5, motive **a**). The episode, or **B**, and the transitions leading up to and away from it (except the final one leading to the coda, which makes reference to motive **a**), make prominent use of the repeat-note

Example 8.5 Moscheles, Concerto No. 7 in C Minor, *Pathétique*, motives **a** and **b**.

timpani motive from the first movement and beginning of the second movement (Example 8.5, motive **b**). The coda uses both motives.

Nowhere does Schumann directly mention the motivic connections across the three movements of the *Pathétique*. He mentions only a recall of the "character" of the first movement in the last, and not of any motives. The reason may be that he is more interested in the cogency of the form and mood of a work overall than in the intricate relationship of all motivic details. In the Seventh Concerto these are largely shaped by two factors: a lack of disruptive virtuosic outbursts (even though it does retain the traditional bravura in the closes of the exposition and recapitulation of the first movement), and a large role for the orchestra.

> In comparison to other new ones, we would not call the Concerto
> mechanically difficult: the figuration is carefully chosen, but can also be
> mastered by average players after some study; [played] together with the
> orchestra, however, it requires the greatest attention on both sides, an
> accurate knowledge of the score. Performed thus its artful interweaving of
> ideas will be of great interest, as we remember it with pleasure from the
> time Moscheles played [the Concerto] in Leipzig.[56]

Unlike in the Sixth Concerto, where interjections by the tutti tend to obfuscate the structure, in the Seventh they help clarify it. They mark important points of arrival in a movement in which, as our description and Figure 8.1 have shown, traditional divisions of the movement (the end of the exposition, beginning of the recapitulation) are not emphasized. In the first group of the exposition the timpani motive immediately precedes and signals the solo's counterstatement of the theme of the first group, **A'**; in the second group the winds present the first statement of the first theme, **B**, and the beginning of the second statement of the second theme, **C**. The same pattern is followed in the development and recapitulation: in the development the timpani motive again precedes the solo statement of **A'**, and the winds again introduce **B**; in the recapitulation the winds accompany the first and only statement of **C**.

Still, Schumann equivocated about the Seventh Concerto, lamenting that the composer of the G Minor composer "is no more." His judgment is at odds with Moscheles's (according to the testimony of his wife), with that of Engel, who calls the Seventh the "high point of [Moscheles's] concerto production," and with my own.[57] The Concerto satisfies his two requirements for works in the new form: the solo part, not "mechanically difficult," interweaves with the orchestra, and the form is "sharp and clear." But, Schumann's comparison with the G Minor Concerto suggests that what the Seventh Concerto lacks is the grandeur of the traditional virtuoso concerto: its first movement tuttis are shorter than usual, the second movement serves as a transition that cannot stand on its own as a complete movement, its finale is compact.

* * *

I have already written extensively on Clara Wieck's Concerto in A Minor, Op. 7 in a article that focused on the effect of Wieck's sex on the work's critical reception.[58] Although that is not now the purpose of this study, it is glaringly obvious that this is the first concerto of all those we have considered so far by a woman. This is not to say that Wieck was the first woman to compose a piano concerto. Her well-known contemporary Léopoldine Blahetka, a student of Joseph Czerny, performed two piano concertos of her own composition in Vienna, one in B minor (first movement) on 6 March 1825, and another in E minor on 29 March 1829. Her *Concertstück* in E Minor, Op. 25, was published around this time or soon thereafter.[59] But the achievement was rare for a woman at that time, in fact, no other examples from the early part of the nineteenth century come to mind. More normal for Wieck's female contemporaries—Emilie Reichold, Charlotte Fink, Robena Ann Laidlaw, Louise David Dulcken, Anna Caroline de Belleville, and Camilla Marie Moke Pleyel—was to play large works by other composers.[60]

I will reproduce here some of the evidence presented in my earlier study, and in Janina Klassen's thesis, that the reception of Wieck's Concerto was affected by her sex.[61] However, I think it also important to emphasize, as I did there, that the prejudice is not alone against Wieck as a woman, but has to do with the dichotomy that Schumann and many other critics perceive between those who are true composers and those who are performers, even if they also compose. The division applies to both men and women, for example, Schumann banished Herz and Thalberg from the ranks of true composers. The bias against women *per se* (as opposed to performers generally) is that they are automatically slotted into the performer category.

There is ample evidence that Wieck's self-perception was affected by this view, particularly after her marriage to Schumann. It is also clear that, whereas Schumann encouraged his wife to compose, he hardly envisioned himself married to a composer striving after the immortal laurels which he encouraged Thalberg and other young male composers to seek.[62] But before Schumann's marriage to Wieck, during the time now under consideration, I believe that his reception of her Concerto was governed less by his conditioned feelings about and socialization with regard to the role of women musicians, and more by his very specific relationship to this particular concerto and to Wieck herself as a particular woman in his life. Schumann was, first of all, involved with the Concerto from the time of its conception. On 10 January 1833 he wrote Friedrich Wieck that the key of the Concerto should be either A minor or C major.[63] He also orchestrated its final movement, the first one composed, in November 1833.[64] Second, Schumann had known Clara Wieck since she was nine years old, as a fellow student of her father and as a friend of her family. Almost exactly at the time the Concerto was completed, in fall 1835, a love relationship developed between them. Wieck took the Concerto on tour from 1837 through 1838, and during this time, on 14 August 1837, the couple marked their official engagement.

Wieck gave the first performance of her complete Concerto on 9 November 1835. This was the time of what Nancy B. Reich calls the first flush of love, when the couple exchanged their first kiss, saw each other freely, and spent hours in each other's arms.[65] It is no surprise that Schumann's passion for Wieck spilled over into his writing about her Concerto. In the *Leipziger Tageblatt* he says it "allows us a glimpse into her deepest soul."[66] In the *Neue Zeitschrift,* in one of a series of "Musing Letters" addressed to Chiara, that is, to Clara Wieck, he attributes a poetic description of the Concerto to Eusebius.

> The first strains that we heard flew before us like a young phoenix fluttering upwards. Passionate white roses and pearl lily cups leaned down, orange blossoms and myrtle nodded above, and between them, alders and

weeping willows threw their melancholy shadows. In their midst, however, a girl's radiant face bobbed and searched for flowers to make a
wreath. Often I saw skiffs floating boldly over the waves, and only a master hand at the tiller, a tautened sail was lacking that they might cut across
the waves as quickly and victoriously as they did safely. Thus I heard
ideas here that often had not chosen the proper interpreter so as to shine in
their complete splendor, but the fiery spirit that drove them on, and the
longing that directed them, finally carried them securely towards their
goal.[67]

Schumann's prose is more poetic here than in any of his writings about
concertos. His florid review gives no technical details about Wieck's Concerto. Nevertheless, the shortcoming he refers to in his description of the
first movement (an equally poetic description of the third movement follows), that Wieck does not direct her fiery musical inspiration toward a
clearly discernible goal, can be stated in more explicit terms. To begin, for
the sake of clarity, with the last movement, it is a long and self-sufficient
rondo, which Wieck performed at least three times in 1834 under the title
Concertsatz.[68] The second movement, for piano and solo cello, is in the
form **ABA'** with an added four-bar transition to the final movement. By
contrast, the first movement, after a short tutti introduction, solo exposition
and development, breaks off with no real recapitulation. The tutti entrance
at the end of the development returns to the opening theme, but in the key of
the dominant. Thereafter, the solo plays only one transitional bar, a V of E-
flat arpeggio that segues, *Adagio, a piacere senza Tempo,* into the second,
Romanze movement.

We have already discussed Schumann's objections to first movements
that are not "beautifully balanced allegros," and this may be the most obvious reason for his criticism of the form of Wieck's Concerto. Less obvious
is his likely unease with the harmonic flux of the passagework in the solo
exposition. The modulation toward the key of the second subject, F major,
is scantily prepared, coming rather suddenly at the end of the transition; the
closing group does not confirm the key of the second subject but instead
leaves it immediately and moves toward the key opening the development,
A-flat major. Both passages have a wonderfully improvisatory quality;
neither prepares the listener for the ultimate point of harmonic arrival until
the very moment of that arrival. While admitting that their free flow enrap-
tured him, Schumann all the same stands by his critical (and pedagogical)
judgment that they lack discipline, and advises the composer to take correc-
tive measures.

Soon after the love relationship blossomed between Wieck and Schumann, Wieck's father severed all relations with Schumann and forbade his
daughter to see him. By the time her Concerto appeared in print (and perhaps somewhat revised from the first time she played it), in January 1837,
they had not met or communicated in any way for nearly a year.[69]
Schumann included the Concerto among five reviewed in January and

February 1837, but he assigned it to Carl Ferdinand Becker, a regular contributor to the *Neue Zeitschrift* who normally reviewed organ music.[70] From the time he began his series on the piano concerto in 1836, it is the only work in the genre Schumann did not review himself. In a letter to Becker he excused himself on the grounds that "my relationship with the old man prevents me from writing about the Concerto myself, and makes it seem unsuitable."[71]

Becker's review is complimentary but superficial. It concentrates more on Wieck's position as a woman composer than on her work. Rather than critique the unusual features of her composition it merely lists them, and, in deference to her sex and young age, only within the nicety of quotation marks intended to indicate that these are questions raised by an unnamed, second party and not Becker himself.

> "But will you, who are always the harsher, say nothing at all about the oft-used diminished-seventh chords, about the finale—which, by its measure count, is longer than the two preceding movements—about the singular connection in writing the Allegro in A minor, the Romanze in A-flat major and the finale again in A minor? Will you say nothing about these?"—No, no, nothing more will be said than has already been said, and above all, since there may be many people who would like to know, how fast the last movement must be played.[72]

Becker, like Schumann, found much to enjoy in Wieck's Concerto, but his joy was not sufficient to overcome his reservations about certain formal procedures. He fails to credit the Concerto's careful construction which the A-flat major areas set off in high relief (although Schumann later paid them tribute in the first movement of his A Minor Concerto, whose development begins with a slow section in A-flat major). Wieck uses A-flat not only in the middle movement but also at the beginning of the development section of the first movement. Each time it signals the reappearance of thematic material derived from the first theme of the introductory tutti (Examples 8.6a and b). In the development an easily recognizable transformation of this theme in the tenor is accompanied by its own further transformation in the discant. A transformation of the discant melody, in turn, begins the second movement. The thematic connection between the first two movements and the unorthodox key used to highlight it audibly and powerfully underline the tight structure of what at first may appear a loose and unusual form. They show it to be far from capricious, despite the freedom displayed in some of its aspects, for example, in the harmonic flux of the passagework areas of the first movement.

Thematic and key connections also link the two opening movements to the finale, which may be heard as rounding out the first movement. The principal theme of the first movement is never recapitulated in the tonic key, but reappears, transformed, as the principal theme of the rondo refrain of the third movement (Example 8.6c). The unusual length of the third movement

a. first movement

b. second movement, beginning of the theme

c. third movement, begining of the rondo refrain

Example 8.6   Wieck, Concerto in A Minor, Op. 7, main theme and transformations.

and its tonal stability also serve to balance the harmonic unorthodoxies of the first two movements.[73]

Contact between Schumann and Wieck resumed at the time of their engagement in mid-August 1837, and a courtship began that had to be carried on through surreptitious meetings and secret letters.[74] By this time Wieck had already performed the Concerto in Berlin (16 February 1837), and Hamburg (1 April 1837).[75] Schumann was at the Gewandhaus when she played it there on 8 October 1837. A fevered reaction to her presence was certainly brought to a higher pitch as he listened to her perform, besides the Concerto, a piano solo, Adolph Henselt's Concert Variations on a Theme from Donizetti's *L'Elisir d'amore,* "Io son ricco e tu sei bella," Op. 1. The next day he wrote:

> I won't ever forget your "Good evening" yesterday, the look on your face when we saw each other in front of the door. Well, I thought, Clara, she's yours—*is yours,* and you can't go over to her, can't even squeeze her hand.

> I wonder whether there was anyone in the whole room who could even imagine my state of mind. Hardly even you. I was lifeless and overjoyed at the same time, so tired I wanted to drop, and almost every drop of blood was surging with fever!—[76]

Soon afterward, Wieck left with her father for Vienna. En route she played the Concerto in Prague on 23 November 1837, then three times in Vienna, on 21 December 1837, then 18 February and 5 April 1838.[77] The relationship between her and Schumann was not always easy during this trying time, and the Concerto was one bone of contention. He was suffering from the cruelty of her father's direct rebuff when he formally asked for her hand on 13 September, her eighteenth birthday, whereas she remained defensive of her father. She shared her father's anger that Schumann did not write up her 8 October concert in the *Neue Zeitschrift*, and his bitterness over Becker's review of her concerto. In particular she held up Becker's carping over the diminished-seventh chords as an example of trivia in an article that did not give her concerto the evaluation it deserved.[78]

Schumann, for his part, believed that Wieck's father prevented their marriage for selfish, exploitative reasons, and worried that, under pressure, Wieck would not remain faithful to him.[79] Already on 29 November 1837 he had asked her:

> Do you always play your Concerto of your own initiative? There are stellar ideas in the first movement—yet it did not make an impression of completeness on me.[80]

His question may reflect concern that Wieck's father was forcing her to exhibit the Concerto as a kind of curiosity piece: a young female performing a concerto of her own composition was precisely the unheard-of feat Becker drew attention to in his review.

Wieck's direct reply to Schumann's question reiterated the response she had already given to Becker's criticism. She forcefully defended the decision to play the Concerto as her own, based on the enthusiastic response of the public. On 21 December she wrote Schumann:

> You ask if I play it of my own initiative—certainly! I play it because everywhere it has so pleased, and satisfied connoisseurs as well as the general public. But, whether it satisfies me is still very much the question. Do you think that I am so weak that I do not know exactly what the faults of the Concerto are? I know precisely, but the audience does not, and furthermore does not need to know.[81]

Whether or not she would now compose her Concerto differently Wieck sticks to her point, she plays it often because it satisfies her public. In Vienna they heard the Concerto three times, the second by demand.

Wieck's defense of her Concerto is a thoroughly practical one. Although she admits to being able to take a more critical view of her work, in the end her experience as a performer is what decides her about its merit. Although Schumann recognized from his own experience as a member of her audience the deep appeal of the Concerto's beauty, imagination, and spirit, he retained his reservation about its logical structure, harmonic instability, and supposed lack of formal balance. Perhaps his judgment was residually affected by the keen competition he felt from Wieck when both were students of her father.[82] But I think his advice was sincere, not least because underlying it are the same assumptions that formed his opinion about Moscheles's Concerto *Fantastique:* no matter how ingenious her radical formal experiment, he saw it as unsatisfactory because of its very nature. Or, to state it differently, no matter how great the immediate appeal of her Concerto, even to his own sensibilities, he put greater weight on structural integrity. Although this may be the very point that Wieck concedes, she still asserts the value of the work as a medium for her performance.

If Wieck formulated her ideas about the worth of her Concerto based on her experience as a performer it is no wonder, for through most of her life she thought of herself primarily as a performer and not a composer. In Reich's words, "she composed because all professional performers of her time did so."[83] The validity of Wieck's argument still holds, even for listening audiences today, as the current surge of interest in her compositions as viable works of art and not just curiosities gives testimony. In 1970 A. J. Heuwekemeijer reissued Hofmeister's original piano part for her concerto; in 1987 Ries and Erler reprinted a copy of the full score; in 1990 Breitkopf and Härtel published Klassen's edition of the full score followed in 1993 by a reduction for two pianos, the same year Hildegard put out a two-piano edition; and in 1997 a version with string accompaniment edited by Joachim Draheim appeared from Hofmeister. There are now several recordings of the Concerto, and it continues as one of several choices in the genre for entrants in the International Clara Schumann Piano Competition first held in May 1994 in Düsseldorf.[84] Of all the concertos in this study other than those by composers who have long been considered of the first rank (Mendelssohn, Chopin, Schumann, Liszt), Wieck's is the only one I have had the opportunity to hear in concert, when it was performed by Joela Jones with the Cleveland Orchestra in fall 1995.

* * *

Our overview of innovative concertos will continue in the next chapter. For now we can summarize our discussion by saying little more than Schumann is an exacting critic. He steadfastly holds to his two main standards for new works: that each movement be wholly rounded, and that orchestra and solo participate equally. Moscheles's *Fantastique* and *Pathétique* Concertos satisfy the latter criterion, but the stumbling block is the former. Neither the seductive beauty of Wieck's performance of her Concerto nor Moscheles's spirited playing of his *Fantastique* changes Schumann's conviction that incomplete movements are aesthetically problematic: he turns from his original favorable impression as a captivated listener to a more calculated and cool judgment as a music critic with score in hand. Otherwise, we need only add that, as was the case with the older, virtuoso concerto, Schumann will not countenance heavy reliance on brilliant display. For him, Moscheles's Fifth Concerto, with its careful motivic relationships within and across movements, remains but a bridge to his more poetic, "romantic" period, I suspect because it retains the expected brilliant passagework in its outer movements. Although we may consider the motivic connections in Thalberg's Concerto unusual, or the structure of Herz's Second Concerto ingenious, they get no mention from Schumann. Since he never heard either concerto performed, he can state unequivocally that he has no use for either.

9
Critical Observer:
New Forms II

In this chapter, we will look at innovative concertos that Schumann championed, by Mendelssohn (No. 1), Wilhelm Taubert, Carl Lasekk, and William Sterndale Bennett (No. 3). Each satisfies his two criteria for "a new, more brilliant way how the orchestra may be united with the piano."[1] In each orchestra and solo have an equal share in a form that is beautifully rounded (and looks to the virtuoso concerto as a background model); and in each there is an easy flow from section to section. Although the Mendelssohn is an obvious high point among concertos of the time, and Sterndale Bennett is among the best known of what today are considered composers of the second rank, one may wonder how compositions by the obscure amateur Lasekk and little-remembered Taubert came to be championed by Schumann. To answer that I would like first, now that we are nearing the end of our survey, to step back and look over the whole of Schumann's series of reviews from 1836 to 1839 of published piano concertos. This will serve as a reminder that no one review is meant to stand on its own, but is part of a larger project that is a complete overview and assessment of the present state of the genre, and prognosis for its future. Second, I would like to turn to a review of a piano concerto by Aloys Schmitt that appeared in the *Neue Zeitschrift* before Schumann began his series and that was not written by him. The contrast with later reviews by Schumann will make clear that his interest centers as much on the contribution of each of his essays to the larger concerto project as on any judgment of a particular concerto.

The overview of Schumann's reviews of piano concertos must begin as early as 1835, when he compiled a "Börsenbericht," in Hans Lenneberg's words, "a sample report on the musical market-place, a kind of best-seller list," for a supplement to volume two of his *Neue Zeitschrift*. This is the beginning of his search for "a new, more brilliant way" for the genre.

> Instrumental music ... Concertos draw only if they are for piano, violin, or cello. Preferably they are in one movement in the form of rondos or

variations. … for piano [the composers are] Herz, Kalkbrenner and Ries although not as much as in the past.[2]

From what we now know of Schumann's later reviews of concertos by Herz, Kalkbrenner, and Ries, this report is not encouraging, especially as regards the future of the genre. It is offset by his reviews late in the same year of performances (by their respective composers) of Clara Wieck's A Minor and Mendelssohn's G Minor Concertos, in two of his four *Schwärmbriefe.* As the title, "Musing Letters," suggests, these two reviews of concerto performances are Schumann's most poetic. Nonetheless, they contain enough of substance for us to discover that Mendelssohn's Concerto satisfies the main criteria for Schumann's brilliant new way.

The first installment of Schumann's series of reviews of newly (within about the last five years) published concertos followed close on the heels of the *Schwärmbriefe,* from 26 February through 22 April 1836. Most are virtuoso concertos (and discussed in Chapters 6 and 7). The installment begins with what Schumann believes is a good example of a student work of that type and finishes with Chopin's two masterpieces (Table 9.1). It is more a discussion of the virtues of the old form than of the new, with Schumann praising concertos by Field and Ries, and, if not Kalkbrenner's Fourth Concerto his First, or if not unreservedly Moscheles's Fifth, his Third. He shows himself little interested in the formal innovations of Thalberg and Herz (discussed in the previous chapter), as they retain what he considers either the most pedestrian or the most extravagant style features of the virtuoso

Table 9.1 Piano Concerto Publications Reviewed by Schumann in 1836, the First Installment of His Series

Date	Concerto
26 February	Schornstein, First Concerto in F Minor, Op. 1
1 March	Lasekk, Concertino in B Minor, Op. 10
8 March	Döhler, First Concerto in A Major, Op. 7
	Hiller, First Concerto in F Minor, Op. 5
15 March	Hartknoch, Second Concerto in G Minor, Op. 14
29 March	Thalberg, First Concerto in F Minor, Op. 5
	Herz, Second Concerto in C Minor, Op. 74
1 April	Kalkbrenner, Fourth Concerto in A-flat Major, Op. 127
	Ries, Ninth Concerto in G Minor, Op. 177
	Taubert, First Concerto in E Major, Op. 18
8 April	Field, Seventh Concerto in C Minor
	Moscheles, Fifth Concerto in C Major, Op. 87
	Moscheles, Sixth Concerto, *Fantastique,* in B-flat Major, Op. 90
22 April	Chopin, First Concerto in E Minor, Op. 11
	Chopin, Second Concerto in F Minor, Op. 21

concerto. By contrast, although delighting in the style of Moscheles, he is not satisfied with the form of his Sixth Concerto. Instead, he holds up as a model a seemingly dull concertino composed by the amateur Carl Lasekk, even using it to mock more radical formal innovations found in Clara Wieck's Concerto. I can only surmise that, just as Schumann chose an acceptable work by a student, Schornstein, for the first review of a virtuoso concerto in his first installment, similarly he chose a passable work by an amateur as his first example of a concerto in the new form. Tellingly, in this installment there is no culminating review pointing to the best concerto in the new form comparable to the final review of Chopin's concertos.

Beginning with the second installment of his series, which ran from 31 January to 24 February 1837, Schumann turns more attention to concertos in newer forms (Table 9.2). To Clara Wieck's chagrin, he gave the place of honor to Sterndale Bennett's Third Concerto, a piece that, unlike hers, draws on the old virtuoso form, yet reflects what Schumann calls the "ideal" style of Mendelssohn, Bennett's teacher. However, much as Schumann championed Bennett's Concerto, his culminating review of a concerto in a new form would have to wait yet another two years when he resumed the series in 1839 with his essay "Das Clavier-Concert" and review of (along with Moscheles's Seventh) Mendelssohn's Second Concerto. Our discussion of that piece will await the next chapter.

The only review of a complete piano concerto that appeared in the *Neue Zeitschrift* before Schumann began his series was of Aloys Schmitt's Sixth Concerto in E-flat Major, Op. 76. Schmitt was a well-known concert pianist and composer who since 1829 had settled in Frankfurt, where he gave private lessons, and where Schumann sought him out when he visited the city in 1830.[3] In 1843 Schumann would say Schmitt was "well enough known through his collateral relationship to the school of Hummel."[4] Eight years earlier, the reviewer who signed himself "K" had higher praise for Schmitt, proclaiming that rarely had he been "so excited over a new event in the field of composition" as over Schmitt's Sixth Piano Concerto. He cites the "power of invention ... evident everywhere in [the] Concerto," calling it one of the composer's "most beautiful children." "Whoever," he concludes, "has ascended the ranks of art, or indeed just of piano playing, to the point where

Table 9.2 Piano Concerto Publications Reviewed by Schumann in 1837, the Second Installment of his Series

Date	Concerto
31 January	Stamaty, Concerto in A Minor, Op. 2
10 February	Lasekk, Concertino *brillant* in C Major
	Herz, Third Concerto in D Major, Op. 87
17 February	Wieck, First Concerto in A Minor, Op. 7 (review by Becker)
24 February	Bennett, Third Concerto in C Minor, Op. 9

he can acquaint himself with [the concerto] will find it interesting and afterwards come to like it. It will be welcomed in the chamber as in the salon, before connoisseurs and the general public."[5]

Had Schumann written the review of Schmitt's Concerto, it is not inconceivable that he, too, would have recommended it to his readers. It follows the traditional virtuoso model, and works of this type by Hummel, Ries, Chopin, and even Schornstein earned Schumann's praise. At least in the abstract, Schumann championed two features of Schmitt's Concerto to which "K" draws special attention: the "important role" of the orchestra; and, in the first movement, the continuation of the firmly established main idea "in a most natural flow" as it is gradually developed then melodically connected to the second idea.[6] However, I doubt that Schumann's enthusiasm for the Concerto would have been as great as "K"'s, nor that he would even have agreed with his assessment of the Concerto's virtues. What "K" calls a "natural flow of ideas" is the repetition of a pedestrian idea (shown in Example 9.1) to the point of saturation, so much so that a lyric episode in the development which is unrelated to anything that has gone before comes as a relief. His "important role" for the orchestra means little more than the regular interjection of a few bars that set up the solo for yet another grand entrance, in the exposition of the first movement, for example, at the beginning of the transition and before the start of the close. These do not balance solo and orchestra but, instead, serve as boosts for the solo that reinforce its advantage; they do, however, work well in the brilliant coda of the first movement.

Aside from motivic content and the formal layout of the orchestra and solo part, there remains the question of the Concerto's style, of which "K" makes no mention. It is touched on by Hans Engel in his description of the first movement.

> Conspicuous are the continual tempos changes, the many *ritardandos, tempo ad libitum,* etc. ... He dissolves in rapture, an overflow of feeling, which destroys the entire structure of the movement. ... the development completely loses all form—the pianistic embellishments, fioritura, *smorzandi* here are too rich.[7]

Engel's characterization calls to mind works in a similar style, notably by Herz (his Third Concerto) and Kalkbrenner (his Fourth), which Schumann

Example 9.1 Aloys Schmitt, Concerto in E-flat Major, Op. 76, first movement, first tutti.

panned, perhaps another reason to surmise he might have shown less enthusiasm for Schmitt's Concerto than "K."

Nonetheless, Schumann must have agreed with "K"'s positive assessment of the Concerto on some level, as his review was published in one of the first issues of the *Neue Zeitschrift* to appear after Schumann took over as chief editor in 1835.[8] Certainly there is no reason to doubt Schumann's concurrence with the review's two premises already mentioned above, namely, that meaningful participation by the orchestra is desirable in a concerto, as is a natural flow from one idea to the next. But after apprising the reader that these are two qualities to be found in Schmitt's Concerto, and enthusing over them accordingly, "K"'s review turns into a stodgy rundown of each movement, with little evaluation of the Concerto's musical content. By contrast, many of Schumann's concerto reviews give little in the way of overall description of the piece in question, but concentrate instead on its aesthetic worth. This is not a feature of his criticism that has gone unnoticed. Plantinga comments on Schumann's review of Field's Seventh Concerto, "This is an example of the sort of 'exclamatory criticism' Schlegel derided. It is unfortunate that the more Schumann likes a composition, sometimes, the less he really says about it."[9] Similar examples may be noted where Schumann does not like a composition, his review of Thalberg's Concerto or of Herz's Second Concerto, each of which concentrates more on the composer than on the piece itself.

Even if, like "K," Schumann finds one or two favorable features in a concerto, as is the case with Moscheles's Sixth or Seventh, his final judgment is based on an overall impression that he may choose to convey in other than technical terms. What he emphasizes is not what is done, but the way it is done; he was awaiting, as he wrote in 1839, "the genius who will show us in a new, more brilliant way how the orchestra may be united with the piano."[10] In this respect, in his emphasis on the evaluation of a complete musical process rather than on any one or two special features of a composition, his piano concerto reviews could be said to serve as an antidote to "K"'s more simplistic approach. The separate reviews avoid any neutral rundown of the content of an individual piece. Each is intended as part of a series, and it is only when taken together that they give a thorough picture, not of any one piece, but, as should be amply clear to us now that we are near the end of our survey, of Schumann's judgment of every aspect of the entire genre. So complete was Schumann's commitment to this project that, aside from "K"'s review of Schmitt's Concerto, and in 1837, Becker's of Clara Wieck's, during his ten-year term as editor all reviews of newly published piano concerto scores were written only by him.

* * *

The first half of our survey of concertos in this chapter will be devoted to Mendelssohn's G Minor Concerto, to the work that Schumann considered its predecessor, Carl Maria von Weber's *Concertstück* (1821), and one that copies it, Taubert's Concerto in E-flat Major. To begin with Mendelssohn, he composed his Concerto in G Minor, Op. 25 in 1831. On 17 October of that same year he gave its first performance in Munich; the next year he played it in London. Breitkopf and Härtel published the Concerto in 1833, but as late as 1 April 1835 G. W. Fink, writing for the *Allgemeine musikalische Zeitung,* said that in the vast majority of places it was not played, nor was it even owned by most pianists.[11] Schumann first learned the Concerto from the piano part. After Mendelssohn came to Leipzig on 30 August 1835 to begin his tenure as conductor of the Leipzig Gewandhaus Orchestra he opened the season on 4 October, then on 29 October, the fourth subscription concert, gave the first Leipzig performance of the Concerto.

Schumann's review of Mendelssohn's (Meritis's) performance is in the third of his *Schwärmbriefe* or musing letters to and from Chiara (Clara Wieck), which he wrote for the *Neue Zeitschrift* at the time he first declared his love to her, in late fall 1835.

> Here you should have seen Meritis playing the Mendelssohn G Minor Concerto. He sat himself down at the piano harmless as a child, and afterward he took one heart after another prisoner, and drew them in crowds behind him, and when he released them you only knew that you had flown by some Greek islands of the gods and were securely and happily set down again in the Firlenz [Leipzig] hall. ... You remember, that we never considered the mere piano part something rare and original, just as youths, on the whole, place the subjective and characteristic ahead of the general and ideal. But now that we have heard the part from Meritis and a warm, understanding orchestra, the Concerto represents nothing less than a master feeling the purest joy. With the entry of the trumpets (if it has no aesthetic relationship, admittedly it is not unaesthetic), someone next to me jumped respectfully to his feet. I know one thing, that it would never occur to me to write a concerto in three connected movements.[12]

In the most poetic language, signed by his alter ego Eusebius, Schumann dwells on the expressive beauty of Mendelssohn's Concerto, and its appeal to the audience. But he also points to some technical features of the work: the need of a warm orchestra for its proper performance; its general and idealistic character, or, presumably, Apollonian quality, which Mendelssohn's performance in turn injected with a subjective tone that Schumann did not perceive from the piano part alone; the wonderful calculation of the trumpet entry; the originality of running the movements together.

The large role given the orchestra, the warmth of Mendelssohn's performance, and the unusual form are features also mentioned by Fink in his front-page review for the *Allgemeine musikalische Zeitung.*

> [Mendelssohn's Concerto] doesn't add up at all. It is a piece of music just as the spirit of the author was given to expressing itself at the moment. It is a character piece, which requires not only competent players ... but also players who do not render it impossible for the orchestra to make its

special impression, even more ones who know, where necessary, how to blend closely with the orchestra. ... Because the orchestra often intervenes in the solo passages, and because all the movements of the work are joined to each other as closely as possible, beyond the factors mentioned, power and endurance are also part of a good performance.[13]

Mendelssohn's Concerto lacks a full opening orchestral ritornello. Instead, orchestra and solo together present the exposition, a term we use here in its broadest sense, since the first movement is more truly a two-part form, the first an exposition with a first and second theme group, and the second a recapitulation that touches on the first group and the thematic area of the second group only briefly before proceeding with a full reprise of the close. The interplay of orchestra and solo is especially notable in the first group of the exposition: after a seven-bar orchestral introduction beginning with a rising, chromatically inflected scale over a bass pedal and timpani roll on G, the solo picks up the introductory scale motive, then, *fortissimo*, continues with the first theme. This grand gesture from the solo so near the opening of the movement is reminiscent of the piano's sweeping cadential gesture at the outset of Beethoven's Fifth Concerto. However, in Beethoven's Concerto the orchestra follows the piano's cadenza with a full ritornello, which introduces the as-yet unheard main theme of the first group. In Mendelssohn's Concerto the piano is the first to sound that theme. Thereafter, the full tutti takes it up, *fortissimo* (beginning in bar 37), but is soon joined by the solo (bar 51) as the cadence of the theme is extended and switched by way of a transition to the second group. The final bars of this transition are given to the solo alone. Thereafter the second group takes, at least to all appearances, a shape usual in both the virtuoso and classical concerto—a lyric theme or themes followed by brilliant passagework— although here, too, the prominent role assigned the orchestra continues. We shall return to the second group momentarily.

Today the absence of a full opening orchestral ritornello is pointed to as one of the singular features of Mendelssohn's Concerto, yet it is one noted neither by Schumann nor Fink.[14] That neither writer speaks of the absence of an orchestral introduction raises the question whether its lack was in fact unusual, in particular, with regard to performances of concertos without accompanying instruments. It may be that for these the opening tutti was truncated or omitted, as it was when Schumann performed his F Major Concerto. In any case, the omission of a full opening ritornello was a practice soon taken up by other composers. Among those whose concertos we have already discussed are Clara Wieck, Moscheles (Sixth and Seventh Concertos), and Kalkbrenner (Fourth). In fact, it is not the possibility of detaching then ultimately doing away altogether with the customarily long opening orchestral ritornello that astonishes either reviewer of Mendelssohn's Concerto but, rather, the joining of the orchestra with the soloist in the course of the movement: both reviewers give considerable attention to the interplay between the orchestral and solo forces.

With regard to this last point, there is no reason to doubt that Mendelssohn, unlike Schumann, knew Beethoven's concertos from an early age. Already on 24 December 1829 he played Beethoven's *Emperor* Concerto in London. On 18 March 1832 he performed Beethoven's G Major Concerto in Paris, but a comparison of the close of the exposition of that concerto and his own will suggest he very probably knew it before he completed the G Minor Concerto in 1831. In each concerto the actual realization at this point is different, but the principle is the same, namely that the soloist does not participate in bringing the final trill to a close. In Beethoven's Concerto the solo drops out and the tutti continues to present a series of closing motives which draw out the preparation for the closing cadence yet another seventeen bars. In Mendelssohn's Concerto the solo continues to play, its tremolo close gradually switched from V of B-flat to V of G. Arrival on the latter immediately sets off a retransition (bar 169), which is to say, the movement lacks a true development area, even though in the course of the cadential extension and switch motives from both the first and second groups of the exposition are heard.

More interesting than his adoption of Beethoven's idea of washing away the final cadence of the solo exposition is Mendelssohn's taking from Beethoven, rather than from the virtuoso concerto, his procedure for constructing the brilliant close. Instead of following the virtuoso model whereby the close consists of a series of appendices attached to the final melodic phrase of the second group, he follows Beethoven's (and Mozart's) procedure of building the close from full phrases. To begin with the thematic area of the second group, it starts with an independent phrase, at first in B-flat but then modulating to D-flat (Example 9.2a). A varied repeat of this phrase remains in D-flat major (bars 88–98). With a second variation the phrase is drawn out for a long return to B-flat which even includes a reference to the scale motive from the introduction of the movement (bars 99–121). All three phrases are the province of the solo. Yet a third variant, now entirely in B-flat, is taken up by the winds, to *leggiero* accompaniment by the solo (Example 9.2b). Already this phrase, and another considerably extended variant which follows it (begins bar 130), constitute the expected brilliant close of the exposition. The figuration is characteristic, yet at the same time a *subito piano* cadence onto a first-inversion tonic chord washes away any demarcation of this brilliant close from the previous thematic area. The effect—the presentation of one phrase after another, each growing from the same melodic motive, and with the whole stretching from the initial thematic statement on through the brilliant closing area of the second group—is masterful. We might even note that, whereas the improvisatory quality Schumann heard in the Concerto may have derived from Mendelssohn's manner of playing, it also may have been related to this artful spinning out of its melodies.

When he looked at the piano solo score of Mendelssohn's Concerto, Schumann noted its clear outline. In the first movement the layout of the

a. first phrase of the theme of the second group

b. beginning of the close

Example 9.2 Mendelssohn, Concerto No. 1 in G Minor, Op. 25, first movement, exposition.

exposition is easily followed, with its traditional grandiose opening theme, thinning out of texture for the solo presentation of the *tranquillo* theme that begins the second group, then brilliant close leading to a long area over a six-four chord and tremolo in the solo that together appear to signal the close of the solo exposition. It is true that hereafter the formal divisions become blurred, not only because of the lack of any actual cadence closing the solo exposition, but also of a second tutti (as the solo does not drop out but continues to play) and, furthermore, of any real development. Nonetheless, a clear dominant preparation then tutti announcement of the opening theme are readily perceptible signs of a return. Thereafter, the quick move to the second theme area is not unusual, and the expected brilliant close is in place, this time with full cadential closure.

What Schumann did not have the advantage of knowing before he heard Mendelssohn's performance of the Concerto was the full contribution of the orchestra. The first edition, printed in parts by Breitkopf and Härtel in 1833, shows in the piano part the alternation of tutti and solo, and occasionally the completion of a bass line by the orchestra, but none of the instrumental melodies played over the piano obbligatos. No wonder Schumann says he formed a different perception of the piece from the piano part alone than afterward when he heard Mendelssohn play it with an orchestra. Seeing or hearing the piano part alone, one would not conclude, for example, that the ingenious construction of the passagework was "something rare and original" but, rather, that it was no more than a series of rather ordinary cadential gestures. Only on hearing the complete phrases of the orchestral melody could Schumann fully appreciate the beauty and originality of Mendelssohn's scheme.

Schumann was certainly aware, even before he heard Mendelssohn play the Concerto, of a kinship to what he deems a "general" or one might say "classical" ideal in the sense we have already discussed, that is, that much in the Concerto harks back to an earlier model. Particularly appealing to him may have been the lyric quality of the melodies. They are without any of the excessive roulades and so forth that characteristically embellish melodies of the Parisian composers, for example, Herz or Kalkbrenner, or even the London-based Moscheles, and which seem to derive, at least in spirit, from the style of *bel canto* singing then current. In the same sense, Mendelssohn's passagework, too, is "unusual" (to quote Fink), in that it consists primarily of scales and passagework, a style trait of Mozart or Beethoven, or Hummel, but not of younger composers.

In 1835 Schumann said it never would have occurred to him "to write a concerto in three connected movements." One precedent for this, of course, is not any classical model, but Weber. Four years later Schumann made the comparison when he heard Camilla Pleyel play both the Weber *Concertstück* and Mendelssohn's Concerto at the same concert, on 26 October 1839.

> ... this was of double interest because, as the forerunner of the Concerto by Mendelssohn, in many places it might have played seductively in the imagination of the composer who was still young when he wrote [his Concerto], and moreover because in tenderness and refinement of construction it can hardly be compared with the later work [by Mendelssohn]. Madame Pleyel performed it exceptionally well, with the same excited passion with which she seems to grasp all music.[15]

R. Larry Todd says that Mendelssohn, in fact, played the Weber *Concertstück* often, citing dates in 1827, 1830, and 1831, to which we may add one in 1824.[16] The last movement of his concerto, especially, calls up Weber's lively *Presto giojoso* finale.[17]

Aside from this copying, two features of the form of Mendelssohn's concertos noted by Todd, namely "the avoidance of the traditional opening orchestral tutti," and the "[linking] of the various movements by transitional passages" are also features of the *Concertstück*.[18] All the same, the parallels between the overall structure of Weber's and Mendelssohn's works are hardly exact. The Weber begins with an introduction, *Larghetto ma non troppo*, a theme played first by the orchestra then taken up by the solo, considerably ornamented and expanded, and eventually worked into an *accelerando* transition to the *Allegro passionato*. The sharing of this slow introduction by the tutti and solo, then, is not the same as the sharing of the sonata-style exposition by the orchestra and solo in Mendelssohn's Concerto. However, to continue the comparison, the *Allegro passionato* section of Weber's *Concertstück* is loosely analogous to the first movement of Mendelssohn's Concerto. Roughly speaking the form of the Weber is **ABA'**, with the first theme of the **A** section played by the solo, then the orchestra and solo sharing a transition to the **B** section, in A-flat major (begins bar 143). A return to the theme of the **A** section immediately follows the **B** section, first in A-flat major but soon returning to F minor for a varied return to the theme, now with a long passagework codetta. Although the scheme of Mendelssohn's first movement is more elaborate, it parallels Weber's first movement form in that it presents not a full sonata-form movement but, rather, a binary form movement. It exposes two main themes and two keys in the two subsections of its first part; its second part is a truncated return that emphasizes only one of the subsections, namely, the one with the most virtuosic display for the solo. Both Weber and Mendelssohn close off their *allegro* movements completely, then begin a separate transition to a middle movement. Weber's second movement is an orchestral interlude, a march theme played three times. Mendelssohn presents a traditional slow movement, an *Andante* in E major in the form **ABA'** involving both the orchestra and solo. Both movements close off, and are followed by a fast transition (in Weber, *Più moto;* in Mendelssohn, *Presto*) to the final, rondo movement.

A third feature of Mendelssohn's Concerto mentioned by Todd, cyclic thematicism, has no analogy in Weber's *Concertstück*. In the G Minor Concerto there is a general similarity between the scalar motives of the first themes of the first and last movements, and a specific reminiscence from the theme of the second group of the first movement just before the coda of the final movement (bars 219–24). Rather than the *Concertstück,* the precedent for such reminiscences is likely Beethoven, for example, the Piano Sonata in A Major, Op. 101, song cycle *An die ferne Geliebte,* or, most especially, the Fifth Symphony with its prominent use of the oft-repeated opening motive of the first movement in the third movement, then reminiscence of that same motive, as it is heard in the third movement, in the final movement.

Neither of the two cyclic links between the first and third movements of Mendelssohn's Concerto are mentioned by Schumann, but yet another one is, a repeat-note motive played by the trumpet which is heard in both the bridge between the first and second movements, and in the one between the second and third movements. "With the entry of the trumpets," Schumann writes, "someone next to me jumped respectfully to his feet," a humorous remark, perhaps intended to indicate his surprise at this militaristic effect. The instrumentation, of course, tags the motive as unforgettable, and it is easily recognized when it is heard again, in a variant form in the next bridge. Yet it is just this special coding in the two bridges between the three separate movements of Mendelssohn's Concerto that may have given Schumann some pause. He says it never would have occurred to him "to write a concerto in three connected movements." Apparently, too, it never would have occurred to him to connect them in this way, for he also writes that if the entry of the trumpets "has no aesthetic relationship, admittedly it is not unaesthetic." The lack of "aesthetic" relationship is due, seemingly, not only to the fact that the motive is new to the Concerto but also to its tone. When Schumann wrote of Mendelssohn's performance it was with the warmest words, describing his innocence, his capturing of hearts, his joy, a representation that seems at odds with the military character of the trumpet motive.

The greatest difference between Mendelssohn's Concerto and the *Concertstück* is that the latter has a program whose source is the composer. Basically, it tells the story of a châtelaine who sadly awaits the return of her knight from the crusades, and her joy at his return.[19] According to Dana Gooley, Weber's program was well known by at least 1845. Furthermore, it gave the impetus for another, parallel narrative that grew from the way the *Concertstück* was performed by its most famous exponent, Franz Liszt.[20] To this I would add that Liszt's approach was taken up by a group of virtuosos who played the piece widely, and it is their interpretation that, despite any structural or thematic similarities between the two works, sets the *Concertstück* at some distance from Mendelssohn's Concerto.

The first comments in the *Neue Zeitschrift* on the manner of this interpretation were elicited after a performance of the *Concertstück* by Adolf Henselt on 29 December 1837. The reviewer, Ernst Ferdinand Wenzel, writes, "It is noteworthy how the greatest of our piano players today keep holding firmly to this composition: Liszt, Thalberg, and Henselt play it often ... without having heard [the first two] ... we know for certain that it would not be easy to match Henselt's heroic playing."[21] By October 1839 when Schumann reviewed Pleyel's performance of the *Concertstück* he certainly had reports of Liszt's performance from Clara Wieck, who attended his concert in Vienna on 18 April 1838.[22] In a second, unsigned review of Pleyel's concert which Schumann wrote for the *Leipziger allgemeine Zeitung,* he observed, "She played [the Weber] after Liszt's example, in the most extreme tempos and with the fullest command of the instrument." By contrast, his description of Mendelssohn's performance of his own Concerto not even two weeks earlier, on 13 October 1839, is more subdued; he likens it to "silver fruits in a golden bowl."[23]

* * *

For all its innovations in form and individuality of style, Mendelssohn's Concerto stands in some relation to the virtuoso concerto, even if only as a far-flung portrait of the virtuoso model. Just how close a relation I think will become evident as we look at a concerto by Wilhelm Taubert, his Op. 18 in E Major, which copies the form of Mendelssohn's Concerto without reproducing its masterful style. This is precisely Schumann's point in his review of Taubert's Concerto: he recognizes similarities between the two concertos, even lists them point by point, but also takes Taubert to task for his old-fashioned passagework. The latter, I believe, is the primary reason that Schumann concludes Taubert's Concerto has a different spirit than Mendelssohn's.

> ... the relationship between the concertos of Taubert and Mendelssohn is too striking and interesting to permit them to be passed over. In spirit they certainly play on two fully different fields ... but outwardly they coincide so completely at the most decisive moments, that, if not an active rivalry, then one must infer a mutual knowledge of each other's work while they were working, but one such that Mendelssohn is for the most part always a few steps ahead.[24]

Based on a style analysis, Schumann assigns Mendelssohn's Concerto precedence over Taubert's in order of composition. The G Minor Concerto was completed and performed in 1831, and nothing suggests that Taubert finished his Concerto in E Major earlier.[25] Furthermore, Schumann knew one reason for the many similarities between the two: both composers were students of Ludwig Berger in Berlin.[26]

Schumann's first comments on Taubert and on his Concerto are recorded in his "Leipziger Konzertnotizen von 1833," a series of critiques of nearly all the Gewandhaus concerts from the end of September to the beginning of December 1833. These were never reworked for publication, but Schumann surely wrote them with publication in view; already at that time he had in mind the founding of the *Neue Zeitschrift*.[27] His reaction after first hearing Taubert's Concerto, at a concert given by the composer on 4 November, is general: he describes salient characteristics of each movement; notes the overall beauty of the piece; remarks on one unusual feature, to wit, the close interaction of orchestra and solo; then sums up the matter by saying the Concerto is a "Beethovenian type expanded."

> Concerto for the Piano
> I have retained little of it, except the beautiful impression of the whole. ... The first movement in six-eight time—second movement—tender adagio with oboe accompaniment in sustained notes for a wonderful effect— bound to the last movement in 2/4 [recte common time] by recitative— more a conversation with the orchestra, a sonata for piano *and* orchestra, than a concerto—Beethovenian type expanded—richness and the fullness of life in every movement—very delightful—Or do I deceive myself ...[28]

All of Schumann's original points are returned to in 1836 in his review of the published score, indeed, all are summarized in the new review's opening statement, which tells us any supposed faults in the Concerto lie with its modernity.

> "Should someone want to find fault with this concerto altogether, the most he could say is that nothing is the matter with it except what is the matter in modern times." This is about how a man expressed himself in October [recte November] 1833 as he was going down the Gewandhaus steps, even as Herr Taubert finished playing his Concerto. I cannot really say how much I indulged myself in this piece on that evening, and how much I understood the faultfinder, on whom the Concerto made no impression other than the deplorable one that it had not turned out worse. However, as I thought more precisely about those words, I discovered a sense behind them after all, about which more below.[29]

Schumann spends the rest of the review explaining just what the faults, and, by extension the virtues, in the modernity of Taubert's Concerto are. He produces, in essence, a gloss on his original pronouncement in 1833, that the concerto is an expansion of a Beethovenian type, and as his review explicitly and thoroughly demonstrates, also one after Mendelssohn's model.

To begin with, Schumann writes that while the new form of Taubert's Concerto may be considered crooked and unnatural by certain classicists, he believes it is of a type that surely would have been followed by the same classical composers whom the classicists champion, were those composers still alive. In his mind this conclusion is born out by the overall impression of the Concerto with regard to both its poetic eloquence, and its equal part-nering of orchestra and solo. He reaches this conclusion even though he believes particular aspects of the passagework and thematic areas are too old-fashioned.

> To put it plainly, I would call the Concerto one of the most excellent. ... For, looking from the old point of view, what could you reproach the Con-certo with? If it is crooked in form, unnatural, confused, mutilated—the favorite words of the classicists whenever they do not understand some-thing right away—doesn't it still have, aside from its much-prized calm and clarity, completely different qualities, which we find only isolated here and there in older concertos, for example, poetic language, well-cho-sen setting, tenderness of contrast, interweaving of the threads, and an orchestral accompaniment full of eloquence and life? ... But do we want concerto composers to imitate our ancestors in everything down to wig and queue, and, as a small concession to more modern requirements, to also throw in something new to boot, if it is good—and are we convinced that a genius like Mozart if born today would rather write Chopin concer-tos than Mozart ones. To return to our worthy composer, here and there his invention lacks what is new and attractively piquant. ... he will under-stand us, if we should wish that, for example, the passagework with which

he has clothed his ideas, were chosen with greater care and not so much of the old stamp; and if we reproach him for themes of a similar type, such as the first one in the last movement, which, as excellently as it is suited for elaboration, is somewhat outmoded and in addition given to stiffness, a thing a brilliant concert audience will not stand for any more.[30]

Immediately after this long passage defending the modernity of Taubert's Concerto, Schumann begins the comparison to Mendelssohn's Concerto. A point-by-point run-down, citing page and system in each score, revolves for the most part around the very characteristics in Mendelssohn's Concerto that set it apart as "modern": the sharing of duties by the tutti and solo at the opening of the first movement; the deceptive trill at the end of the solo exposition that initiates a bridge continued by the solo up to the beginning of the return; the bridges between movements; the extraordinary beauty of the middle movement; the return of music from an earlier movement in the final one. Only with regard to one of these points does Schumann say that Mendelssohn's Concerto is more effective than Taubert's: the bridge to the second movement. Still, the conclusion is hard to escape that the modern concerto Schumann is championing is really by Mendelssohn rather than Taubert. Indeed, comparison of the first movements of the two composers' concertos will show that it is exactly in the matter wherein Schumann faults Taubert, his outmoded passagework, which his concerto differs fundamentally from Mendelssohn's. It is in this that he leaves behind any modern, "Beethovenian expansion," and falls back rather on the old virtuoso model.

After the unusual sharing of duties by tutti and solo in their first groups, both Mendelssohn's and Taubert's concerto follow traditional formal patterns (or at any rate, ones seen in concertos by Hummel and Kalkbrenner) in their second groups: a theme played first by the solo, then by the orchestra to the solo obbligato, followed by the expected brilliant solo close. Mendelssohn's clever crafting of these two sections was already discussed, in particular, at the beginning of the second group, his smooth introduction of the theme over the dominant pedal which continues from the transition, and, later, final statements of the theme in the orchestra to a solo obbligato that marks the beginning of the brilliant close. Taubert makes a connection to what has gone on before by beginning the theme of the second group with the main motive of his introductory theme. But the transition comes to a full stop on the new tonic, B major, before this happens. Furthermore, the *leggieramente* close that follows the theme begins with the final, tonic cadence of the theme. It is, like the closes of all virtuoso concertos, a fully dependent, short suffix, even though Taubert overlays the solo fioritura with motives from the theme of the second group played by various instruments in the orchestra (see Example 9.3). The close begins with the traditional tonic-dominant vamps, then continues in two bar units on or around the tonic until a section on the flat-sixth degree (G major) leads to B minor then the final six-four chord. It is not a complete phrase but a series of

appendices to the phrase that precedes it. In this way it differs from
Mendelssohn's close, which is two long (the second, very long), independent phrases.

For Schumann, Taubert's passagework has "the stamp of the old," of the
older composers Hummel, Ries, and Kalkbrenner, not Mozart or Beethoven.
It is heard most obviously in arpeggios and broken chords, rather than more
original figuration, which make up the close, but more tellingly in the construction from small units that are heard as a string of phrase appendices,
despite the overlay of piquant melodic fragments. Schumann sees no need

Example 9.3 Taubert, Concerto in E Major, Op. 18, first movement, exposition,
beginning of the close.

to excise this passagework and its traditional place in the concerto, he wishes only that it were chosen with greater care. One can, he writes, "take full advantage of certain requirements and inclinations of the time without thereby compromising something of the finer artistic worth."[31]

Schumann's taking Taubert to task for a lack of invention in his passagework, or even the "stiffness" of one of his themes, does not negate the "beautiful impression of the whole" that remained with him after first hearing the Concerto, an impression that he conveys in some detail through a poetic synopsis.

> Allegro, E major, $\frac{6}{8}$ time, horn calls from afar—whom do they not right away draw out into the distance and deep into the green forest! Anyone who wants to get to know the joy and life of the hunter in music ... will find it here and with no more than a few passionate, pale-blue streaks of delicate Romanticism below, at the foot of the forest. By contrast, whatever darker thing may hover over the Andante is ... a truly ardent, universal melancholy, just as is wont to steal into the heart at twilight. Finally, the last movement is really only the conclusion of the first, and its minor hardly more than a veiled major, until this breaks through by itself, light and rosy.[32]

In the sonata-form last movement, the main motive of the playful theme of the first group, in E minor, is the basis for the main motive of the *scherzando* theme of the second group, in G major. The recapitulation begins, not with a return to the playful first theme, but with a recall of the darker, E minor *con espressione* theme of the second movement, then, *pianissimo,* a distant reminiscence of the horn calls that opened the first movement, echoed in the solo by a skeletal outline of the rising arpeggio motive that is common to the opening of the first and second themes of the final movement. This is the quiet moment after which the major breaks through; we hear the connection of the first and last movements, then florid arpeggios lead to the *scherzando* second theme.

To return to the very opening of Schumann's review and his quotation of the opinion of the Gewandhaus man, it is true that the form of Taubert's Concerto is modern. Yet, it also should be noted that it retains clear hallmarks of the older form. The most obvious is the fast-slow-faster sequence of movements. Even if these are connected, each has a complete tonic close. Just as obvious is that, for all the changes and truncations made to the traditional form in the first movement, it retains a full brilliant solo close in both the exposition and recapitulation, as does, incidentally, its companion concerto by Mendelssohn. However, Taubert's first movement lacks the long sweeping arc of Mendelssohn's. It is constructed instead of small individual units strung together, especially at the climactic moments of the brilliant close. If, as Schumann says, Taubert's last movement completes his first, it does so in the sense that the progression to the last movement, through the bridges leading from the first to the second and from there to the third movement, is continuous, and also because the last movement reuses material from the first movement in an integral fashion. Taubert does not follow Mendelssohn's example in the sense that the long sweep of his first movement has the feel of a preparation, an introduction even a push forward to the more traditional slow movement and finale.

* * *

Schumann's main focus in his review of Taubert's Concerto is its form, and the form of other modern concertos. In 1833 he calls Taubert's Concerto (and, by extension, the Mendelssohn Concerto on which it is modeled) an expansion on a Beethovenian type; in the 1836 review he suggests that were Mozart alive he would be writing concertos like Chopin's. We have already discussed Schumann's holding up of Mozart and Beethoven more as ideal than actual models. The background against which Taubert's innovations are made is the virtuoso concerto, that is, the concerto by Chopin that Mozart would be writing, not the ones he actually did write. For example, the orchestral participation that Schumann enthuses over is hardly the type of exchange between orchestra and solo that one finds in the solo sections of Mozart concertos but more usually the orchestra's appropriation of a melody normally given to the solo in the virtuoso concerto, while the solo continues to play, obbligato. By contrast, the aspect of style that truly copies Beethoven in Mendelssohn's Concerto, the long phrases of the second group reminiscent of Beethoven's Fourth Concerto, are seen by Schumann as a peculiar invention of Mendelssohn himself. This is to return to a point we have repeatedly made, namely, that for Schumann the virtuoso concerto represents the basic, background model for the genre. Just how highly he prizes the model will be seen in his reviews of two concertinos by Carl Lasekk, a composer whose style is undistinguished, but whose formal modifications to the concerto retain the clear, symmetrical outlines of the old virtuoso form.

Carl Lasekk is the pseudonym under which the dilettante Baron Carl von Kaskel (1797–1874) published his musical works, and an anagram of his own name. Schumann reviewed Lasekk's Concertino in B Minor in early 1836, but did not include the review in the first edition of his *Gesammelte Schriften* which he published in 1854. The first paragraph is a paean to the dilettante, who has "developed his natural gifts" and whom Schumann prefers "to many artists who high-mindedly disregard his concerto." He continues:

> We have to call it a concerto, however, on account of the fact that it consists of three separate movements, separated by caesuras. If these are quite short, then they have an added advantage. Indeed, it seems to me that this form is more artistic than that of the usual concertinos, which are put together from various parts in changing tempos, all running into each other, and which for the most part are an aesthetic disaster. Or is it something different when after the close of an Allegro, a distant drum roll

begins, then a tedious Andante, and after endless ritardandos, a Polonaise!—How much more successful is our dilettante, who gives rather three small, but finished pictures, instead of one large one, where everywhere the seams are clearly visible. If, due of such terseness, the middle movement—which in larger concertos comes in for the most attention—must be eliminated and in this case replaced by a short tutti, the way it is done is entirely natural, good and even to be recommended as worth emulating. ...

Just as this agreeable piece of music meets strict requirements with regard to the essentials of its internal and external stipulations, so, too, it in no way neglects secondary matters. We find no trace of the naive harmonies with which dilettantes often surprise us; the melodic ornaments are tastefully placed in the appropriate places; the passagework spins out quickly and fully; and the small orchestra intervenes discreetly and often in an interesting way. In short, with the best of wills, one can say nothing against the composer, excepting only that he flits about with the art which he should have embraced with all his mental powers.[33]

So far I have not been able to locate a copy of this work, but if I were to capsulize what Schumann holds up in the Concertino as a model, it would be that in every aspect it avoids extremes. In both its form and content, or as Schumann calls them, its externals and internals, it is agreeable: it shows the composer's good judgment in developing his natural gifts easily and joyously, in avoiding the melodramatic gestures, or as Schumann calls them in the same review, "painful plaints" of many artists. The Concertino is not high-minded, but neither does it pretend to be. Nonetheless, its content, as Schumann describes it in his third paragraph (the second one above), is tasteful, with respect to harmony, melody, passagework, and the role of the orchestra. The form of the Concertino is also approved by Schumann, three separate if short movements, each complete in itself, even though the second is taken by the tutti alone. The formal flow of the Concertino is not interrupted by the breaking off of any of its movements before its expected completion, nor through disruptive gestures—drum rolls or pauses—inserted to bridge the gap from one incomplete movement to the next.

Schumann calls the Lasekk a concerto rather than a concertino because each of its three movements is complete. The diminutive applies only to its size, and does not define what he considers to be the concertino form, namely a piece in which the movements run together and are not each fully independent. Whereas the exaggerated gestures he describes as found in certain concertinos are surely a fiction, his invention has some basis in fact. At least since Beethoven's Fourth Concerto, examples are numerous of concertos the second movements of which run into their final movements. In the concertos we have surveyed these include the Döhler; Herz Second; Hummel A Minor; Moscheles F Major, G Minor, and *Pathétique;* Pixis; Ries, C Minor, E-flat Major, and C-sharp Minor. None of these are called concertinos, nor would be considered such by Schumann. However, one concerto that was both called a concertino (although not published under that title, it was billed as such for performances in Vienna and Prague), and which suits Schumann's mock example only too well is Clara Wieck's Concerto, which she had just completed and performed in Leipzig on 9 November 1835.[34] Its first movement breaks off then is connected to the second movement by a short *Adagio* bridge consisting of a long arpeggio taken by the piano in one pedal, and ending with a fermata over the last note. Another bridge, involving a series of broken chords for the piano and timpani rolls, connects the second to the third movement. The timpani roll continues alone as an introduction to the third movement, joined in the final two bars by the trumpets playing a polonaise rhythm.

Exactly at the time Schumann wrote his derisive description of certain concertinos, in February 1836, was when Friedrich Wieck discovered the growing love between Schumann and his daughter, exploded in a rage against Schumann, and removed his daughter from his presence by taking her on a long concert tour.[35] It is also the time when Clara Wieck was giving the most performances of her concerto (after its November premiere in Leipzig, between 1 December 1835 and 28 March 1836 she played the second and third movements in Plauen, Chemnitz, Dresden, and Breslau) before she made final revisions to the instrumentation in October 1836.[36] If, indeed, Schumann's description is a transparent reference to Clara Wieck's showcase work, this may be one reason he omitted the essay on Lasekk when he assembled his complete prose writings nearly twenty years later.

Schumann's next review of a concertino by Lasekk was written in 1837 when he continued his piano concerto series during late January and February. He refers the reader back to his earlier review where he described all the features of Lasekk's B Minor Concertino that are again found in his new Concertino *brillant* in C Major. Two friendly reviews of an amateur's efforts suggest that he knew the composer, Dresden banker Baron von Kaskel, but the two did not meet until Schumann traveled to Dresden in September 1838.[37]

> The Concertino which is open before us now moves in the same circle as the earlier one in B minor, except that the newer one is yet more genial and glides by more quickly. Further, the same form, which at that time we called a happy one and which is to be preferred over the average among other concertinos, is adhered to. I like the look of the first movement best. In two places one finds the note, *à la Thalberg*. ... The second movement is easy and melodious. However, of the three themes of the last movement, the contrasting and main ideas are manifestly lacking in invention altogether. ... The instrumental accompaniment is simple and agreeable.[38]

Above all, Schumann praises the form of the C Major Concertino. All of its parts are abbreviated, or in his words, glide by quickly. The first movement is further shortened through the omission of a development. The second tutti instead serves as a bridge back to the recapitulation. The movement begins with a full, if short, tutti, which presents the two main themes in two keys, the first in C major, the second in G major. Dotted rhythms are prominent in both themes, the transition, and close. The layout of the solo exposition is straightforward. The solo enters with the full chords of the grand first theme. A new phrase, that starts in bar 60 and sounds at first like a cadential extension of the grand theme, begins the transition. Its second statement turns to E minor, followed by a vamp in that key from bar 69 on (see Example 9.4). The pace is relentlessly by double bars, in the grand theme, in the new phrase that begins the transition, where a near-repeat of every gesture pairs the single-bar measures, and in the vamp. For us, and perhaps for Schumann, the lack of any change of pace is a hallmark of the amateur. The only variation comes with the drawing out of the cadence onto E minor to three bars (66–69), a pause for breath before sailing into the vamp, at the same double-bar pace as before.

The theme of the second group is played by the flute to the solo obbligato, first in E-flat major followed by a modulation toward G major, then, varied and doubled by the bassoon, in G major. This may well be an example of what Schumann calls a "simple and agreeable" instrumental accompaniment by the small orchestra—strings, flute, clarinet, and bassoon. However, at *un poco meno Allegro* the solo takes over, playing brilliant passagework that begins with a variant of the same vamp that was heard in the transition, now in G major (bars 118–26). Another vamp, also in G major, follows (bars 127–31). The *à la Thalberg* passage—thick chords, staccato double octaves, diminished-seventh arpeggios, a chromatic scale, then double trills—closes the exposition (bars 132–38).

The Concertino follows patterns traditional for the first movement of a virtuoso concerto, but in an abbreviated form, and this seemed to appeal to Schumann. Although the piece is highly sectionalized, that is, it does not show the sophisticated ease in moving between melody and passagework found in Field's or Hummel's concertos, Schumann likes its lack of extremes. The pacing may be dull, with its continual returns to a downbeat emphasis every one or two bars in the passagework, but that approach also lends it an easy flow that does not allow for the exaggerated sentiment or virtuosity that is anathema to Schumann. The composer even mocks such high virtuosity by dubbing the most brilliant section of the close *à la Thalberg*. For Engel this section exemplifies the shoddy workmanship of the Concertino. Schumann, in the spirit of the joke, suggests instead that it is "a tip for the performer."[39]

* * *

Lightheartedness and the urbanity of the cultivated amateur are far from what attracts Schumann to Sterndale Bennett's Concerto No. 3 in C Minor, Op. 9. He writes instead of its poetic beauty, even supplying a long story for the second movement. His primary technical comment about the Concerto is that the first movement is cohesive, an organic whole, a feature not generally found among virtuoso concertos, which tend to be fragmented by the

Example 9.4 Lasekk, Concertino *brillant* in C Major, first movement, solo exposition theme and beginning of the transition.

many changes of mood and pacing. Yet, as with the Lasekk Concertino, all the hallmarks of the virtuoso concerto are clearly audible even in the changed guise of Bennett's work. Although the basis of its cohesiveness seems to be a knowledge of Beethoven, Schumann sees it instead as a new feature, just as he also did Mendelssohn's drawing from Beethoven in his concerto. In Bennett's case, though, any new features that draw on Beethoven combine with recognizable stylistic hallmarks of the old, virtuoso concerto that Mendelssohn left behind.

Schumann met Bennett and developed a close friendship with him during Bennett's stay in Leipzig from 29 October 1836 to 12 June 1837.[40] He opened the first issue of the *Neue Zeitshrift* for the new year of 1837 with a

Example 9.4 (*continued*)

laudatory article about the young Englishman.[41] Then on 19 January 1837 Bennett played his Third Piano Concerto with the Gewandhaus Orchestra. Mendelssohn, in a letter to his sister, reported the audience's "jubilation," and the correspondent for the *Allgemeine muskalische Zeitung,* a presentation with a "lively appeal."[42] However, five weeks later in his review of the printed score, Schumann recalls that the public was at first slow to react. They were expecting a virtuoso performance but got something quite different.

> The judgment of the public was put to the test here in an entirely different way than with other virtuosos. In this instance it meant nothing to recognize technical skill, to distinguish a school, to draw parallels with other virtuosos. In the case of our artist one must recognize much more, above all the modesty with which he rejects all display ...[43]

The audience adjusted: like Mendelssohn and the correspondent for the *Allgemeine musikalische Zeitung,* Schumann, too, reports that Bennett won them over.

> After the first movement, a purely lyric piece full of such beautiful human emotion as one finds only in the best musical works, the main thing was clear, that here it is a question of a more refined type of artist. Yet, that thunderous, all-around, roof-raising applause that bold virtuosos provoke did not follow. People demanded more, were obviously expectant. ... Thereupon began the Romanze in G minor, so simple that one could count the notes in it. Even if I had not known on the foremost authority that here, while composing, the picture of a somnambulant maiden hovered before the poet, even so, it seems every sensitive heart must be immediately overcome by all the touching things such a scene contains. ... In the last movement we gave ourselves over to the undisturbed joy which we are used to receiving from a master, whether he leads us into battle or to peace.[44]

Bennett's lack of display as a virtuoso performer and the "purely lyric" quality of his Concerto are linked, of course. But what Schumann sees as a master hand behind Bennett's composition has to do also with what he calls "the cohesion of the whole." With the exception of certain "prolixities" in the first movement, nothing, he says, is unessential.

> ... one must marvel ... over the quiet disposition, over the cohesion of the whole, over the agreeable sound of its language, the purity of its ideas. If I wished, at the very least perhaps in the first movement, that some slight prolixities were eliminated, that is personal. On the whole one meets with nothing unessential, nothing that is not intimately related to the basic conception, and even in those places where new elements come in those gold threads still shine through, carried forward as only a master hand knows how. What a pleasure ... to hit on a robust, organic, whole, and what a joy that the Leipzig audience, as little as they were prepared for it, quickly and joyously knew to recognize it.[45]

Schumann does not categorize Bennett's Concerto as belonging to an old or the new type. According to Engel, though, its obvious model is more Beethoven's C Minor than any virtuoso concerto. Engel even goes so far as to include Bennett in his history of the German piano concerto because he understood "more deeply than many Germans the spirit of Beethoven, especially in his Concerto in C Minor, Op. 9."[46] There is every reason to believe that as a student of Cipriani Potter, Bennett would have studied Beethoven and Mozart, and that, even when he performed concertos by Hummel, Dussek, and himself in London as a teenager, he also knew those of Beethoven and Mozart.[47] Although this Beethovenian influence does not overthrow the virtuoso model, it renders certain features of it very different.

To begin with is the opening motive of the tutti, **a**, two half notes separated by an upward octave leap, then, a half step lower, a dotted rhythm outlining a descending major third followed by a rising minor third. This motive forms the head of the first two phrases in the tutti (bars 1–10, Example 9.5a shows the first phrase), then continues into the transition. Although I would not say that the use of the head motive of the first theme as material for the transition is unusual, even in the virtuoso concerto, the extent to which it permeates the transition is. The pervasiveness of the motive is related to its characteristic chromatic descent by seconds, which is easily linked to several further descents by repeating the dotted rhythm. The long notes in these chromatic descents are manipulated by Bennett to carry the music forward in various ways. In the first theme they descend first the upper trichord, then upper tetrachord of a C minor scale (bars 1–3, 6–9). A trichord descent generated by the **a** motive, this time from the fifth to the third degree of an E-flat minor scale, is heard at the end of the transition (bars 45–47). The opening motive of the second theme continues the descent, from the third to the first degree, in rhythmic diminution and corrected to E-flat major (this motive can be seen in Example 9.5b, bar 62).

Or, as Schumann says, "even in those places where new elements come in those gold threads still shine through."

The dismembering of the motivic elements of a thematic phrase so that they can be used *ad infinitum* in nonthematic areas is a recognizably Beethovenian, or classical technique. It is combined here with another technique (a favorite of Mendelssohn's as we have already seen, and of many other composers, both classic and romantic), and that is the overlapping of one characteristic phrase into another. In the second theme of the first tutti the modulation from E-flat major back to C minor takes place within the second phrase of the second statement of the theme (Example 9.5b). In eight bars this leads to a surprise landing, *fortissimo,* on the Neapolitan sixth of C minor (bar 69), at which point the octave leap of motive **a** enters.

Example 9.5 Bennett, Concerto No. 3 in C Minor, Op. 9, first movement.

Imitative statements of this motive lead to a varied statement of the opening of the tutti, *pianissimo,* for the tutti close (bars 77–89). Although the imitative statements are actually a large expansion of the final phrase of the second theme before it arrives onto its final cadence (at bar 77, also the beginning of the close), the return to the head motive of the tutti opening gives them in addition the character of a prelude to the close.

The remainder of Bennett's movement follows the model of a virtuoso concerto, yet it does not sound like one. One obvious reason it does not is that it is just too lyric. This is easily heard in the melody of the second group, which is played in the middle register, without decoration. Furthermore, any melodic statement filled with pathos is absent at the beginning of the development, which centers instead on a spinning out of the main, opening motive of the movement. This smacks more of Beethoven or Mozart than the virtuoso concerto, as does, incidentally, the unadorned melodic statement of the second group. Even the addition of the coda with solo participation (heard already in Beethoven's Third Concerto) and the retention of the special close reserved for the tutti alone, could be said to be features taken over from the classical concerto. The anomaly is that, apparently, it is just these older features which sound refreshing to Schumann's ears. He sees them as bringing new life to the old, virtuoso form. In other respects he criticizes Bennett, not for drawing on that form but, rather, for not revitalizing it, for composing prolonged and conventional rather than more pointed and original passagework. In the exposition, for example, the closing *brillante* begins with a tonic-dominant vamp, and continues in short two- and four-bar segments using sequential figuration. A second tonic-dominant vamp, *tranquillo,* begins with a fragment of a melody that refers (vaguely) to the second theme. This is prelude to an *appassionato* section, which leads to a long dominant closing the first solo.

When Schumann writes that the second movement of Bennett's Concerto is "so simple that the notes can almost be counted in it," he declares his distaste for the elaborate melodic decoration of the Parisian pianists. Bennett instead projects a singing melody in every section of his movement, in either the solo or orchestra. Although the piano may play obbligato around the melody, no ornamentation infuses the melody proper. Two sections alternate in the movement, following the basic form: **A** (G minor); **B** (G major); retransition; **A'** (G minor); **B'** (G major); coda on **A** (G minor). There is no modulation to a new key, a stasis perhaps reflecting Bennett's vision of the sleepwalker, inspired, no doubt, by Bellini's opera *La sonnambula.* Like Anima, Bennett's sleeper is in some danger, as Schumann describes her, "atop a high parapet," reflected in the end of the **B** section, a dramatic cadenza-like area in G minor. The happy conclusion comes with the return to the opening motives of the **A** theme in the retransition, which begins with a bright statement by the orchestra over the dominant of G major before turning again to G minor. Thereafter, the return to the **B** theme, begins, to use Schumann's words, where "that wonderful [G major] chord came in, where the wandering maiden, out of all danger, seems to lie down on her couch and peaceful moonbeams stream over her."[48]

The last movement is a sonata rondo. Its basic form is:

A (C minor)
B (E-flat minor and major)
A' (E-flat major and modulation to V of F)
C (F minor) and developments of **A**
A" (C minor)
B' (C minor and major)
coda on **A** and **B** (C minor)

The head motive of **A** is nearly omnipresent, being heard, in addition to the areas shown in schematic, in the transition to **B** and in the closing passage-work of both **B** and **B'**. The movement has the motivic compactness Schumann praised in the first movement. The rondo theme is perhaps intentionally reminiscent, at least in its general mood and particular construction, of the rondo theme from Beethoven's Third Concerto.

Still, despite any reminiscences of Beethoven in Bennett's Concerto, whether in his choice of material or development of it, his model remains one that, in Schumann's words, takes "full advantage of certain requirements and inclinations of the time." And this, I believe is what we need to keep in mind in the next chapters as we look at the first concerted compositions Schumann produced after a nearly eight-year hiatus. What he composed in the genre, beginning with a *Concertsatz* in D minor, is directly related to what he wrote about the genre, just as we have explained it up to this point. Thus, we should not be surprised to discover that some of the features he found attractive in concertos with formal characteristics he considered modern should find their way into his own experimental works. First of all is his preference for retention of the symmetry and closure of individual movements found in older forms, a preference he retains alongside his interest in more innovative forms, for example, concertos with connected movements. Second is his preference for lyric melodies as opposed to the more elaborate style of the Parisian school, even as he at the same time recognizes that the virtuoso performer must be given something to show off his prowess on the instrument. Thus, for example, he never suggests that the usual brilliant close of the concerto first movement be done away with but, rather, that it be chosen with great care, should be infused with an original and modern stamp, and remain compact. Third is Schumann's interest in the interplay of solo and orchestra. Here we might note that the first movement examples he praises tend to revolve around a more or less equal division of labor in the first group of the exposition, and considerable obbligato playing by the soloist in the second. Finally, we see his interest in cohesiveness. This has to do with the obvious and direct derivation of one theme from another only on the most superficial level. Rather, it relates more to the sustaining of long lines that give the feel of an improvisatory spinning forth, as in Mendelssohn's First Concerto, or of an overall, unbroken mood, as in Field's Seventh Concerto.

The reader may conclude that what I have given in the above paragraph is an exact description of the first movement of Schumann's Concerto in A Minor. We shall see, though, that his first realization of these very points can be found, in a very different guise, in the *Concertsatz* he composed two years before the A Minor Concerto.

10

Concertsatz in D Minor

Although Schumann did not see every solution to what he considered the problem of how to combine piano and orchestra as acceptable, he was not willing to concede Thalberg's point, expressed to him in conversation on 28 October 1838, that "there is nothing more to be done with the combination of piano and orchestra."[1] Thalberg wrote only one piano concerto, which Schumann panned, but, like many of his contemporaries he produced numerous variations sets and fantasias for piano, often with orchestra *ad libitum.* In his article "Das Clavier-Concert," written only a few weeks after his conversation with Thalberg, Schumann partially acknowledges Thalberg's point when he says, "on the other hand we can hardly contradict the pianists if they say, 'We do not need assistance from others; our instrument is most effective by itself'." Nonetheless, he demands from young composers that "as a substitute for that serious and worthy concerto form they give us serious and worthy solo pieces [meaning, in this context, solo pieces with orchestra]. Not caprices, not variations, but rather beautifully balanced allegro movements full of character, which, if need be, one could play at the opening of a concert."[2]

We shall see in the next chapter exactly the kind of "beautifully balanced allegro movement" for the opening of a concert Schumann ultimately realized when we discuss his first completed movement for piano and orchestra, the one-movement *Phantasie.* His efforts in this direction began with a less successful endeavor, the first movement of a concerto, or *Concertsatz,* in D minor, which he never finished, and which will be a focus of discussion in this chapter. As of 1839, however, with no compositions of his own to offer, the only ones he finds acceptable for opening a concert are above all older works, that is, concertos by Bach, Beethoven, or Mozart, or more recent concertos by Mendelssohn or Moscheles.[3]

Aside from its overview of the state of the concerto, "Das Clavier-Concert" is a review of two concertos, Moscheles's Seventh, the *Pathétique,* and Mendelssohn's Second, in D Minor. We discussed Moscheles's Concerto in some detail in Chapter 8, and it will figure again in the latter part of this chapter. We turn now to Schumann's review of Mendelssohn's Concerto, as that piece stands as a forerunner to the most characteristic features of Schumann's *Concertsatz.*

> Truly, he is still the same; he still travels at his own happy pace; no one has a more beautiful smile on his lips than he. Virtuosos will hardly be able to apply their monstrous skill to this concerto: he gives them almost nothing to do which they have not already played and done a hundred times. We have often heard this complaint from them. They are quite right; opportunity to display bravura through novelty and brilliance of passagework should not be left out of the concerto. However, music is above all else. ... the pouring forth of a beautiful soul, unconcerned whether it flows in the presence of hundreds or for itself in secret. ... For this reason, too, Mendelssohn's compositions produce such an irresistible effect whenever he plays them himself; his fingers are only the carriers which could just as easily be hidden [from the eyes]; the ear alone should appraise and then the heart decide. I often imagine, Mozart must have played like that. ... this concerto belongs among [Mendelssohn's] most casual products. I would have to be greatly mistaken, if he did not write it in a few days, perhaps a few hours. It is as when one shakes a tree— the ripe, sweet fruit falls down without further ado. ... Here and there Sebastian Bach looks out in the harmonic progression. Melody, form, instrumentation, for the rest, are Mendelssohn's property. So let us rejoice over this bright, fleeting gift; it resembles completely one of those works, just as many as we know produced by the older masters whenever they rested from their larger creations. ... the D Minor Concerto by Mozart, the G Major by Beethoven ...[4]

The review hardly separates Mendelssohn's demeanor (his "happy pace" and "beautiful smile") and manner of playing (his fingers as carriers of a message intended for the listener's heart, after the manner of Mozart) from the nature of the Concerto (lacking in virtuosity, full of musicality, the pouring forth of a beautiful soul) and even the process of its composition (among his most casual products, written in a few days or hours, produced as easily as ripe fruit is shaken from a tree). With regard to each of these matters, the personality of the composer and his performance, the Concerto and its composition, Schumann writes of a beatific and easy flow. In the case of the performance, it is an outpouring of Mendelssohn's inmost soul, which just happens to be heard by an audience.

Of course, Schumann was aware, although he does not let on here, that such public displays of private emotion, no matter how candid seeming, by their very nature possess an element of the disingenuous. Thus, he writes about Mendelssohn's performance of his G Minor Concerto in 1835, "He sat down at the piano innocent as a child, and then took one heart after another captive, drawing them after him in droves."[5] The innocent child is at the same time the wily Pied Piper who entices the audience, the children of Hamelin, to follow him. A few years later, Clara Schumann was more cynical about this very public side of Mendelssohn. "The *bravos* were not lacking, and the ladies were certainly the happiest—sitting with open mouths through the entire concert and acting as if they had never in their lives seen conducting. I certainly respect Mendelssohn highly, nonetheless this stupid idolizing the way it is done by a portion of the audience here is intolerable to me."[6]

Sanna Pederson explains Schumann's representation, within the very public arena of his musical criticism, of a subjective musical experience and his framing of that criticism as a discussion among friends in an intimate circle.[7] We might add the observation that in his review of Mendelssohn's Concerto Schumann writes of the public presentation of a piece in a genre associated with performance before a broad audience, and its assumption of the nature of a private performance, embodying a more personal expression. Just as Pederson points out, that in his criticism Schumann felt the tension between the need to appeal to a general public and his own inclination to put forward the more elitist views of a small circle of cognoscenti, so too, in his review of Mendelssohn's Concerto Schumann felt the tension between the necessity of acknowledging that "opportunity to display bravura through novelty and brilliance of passagework should not remain excluded from concertos" and his own view that music must remain "above all else." As we would expect, the entire tenor of Schumann's review shows that it is the intimate, the private side, what he calls the musical side that wins out over any call for virtuosic display, however justifiable the latter may be. In defense of his position, he points to two earlier concertos that he believes resemble Mendelssohn's, Mozart's in D Minor and Beethoven's in G Major. Not coincidentally, these were two concertos in Mendelssohn's repertory.[8]

We will begin by exploring Mendelssohn's D Minor Concerto, showing how it has the easy flow that Schumann perceives as an outpouring of Mendelssohn's soul. In this it exhibits an intimacy that Schumann argued was a desirable feature, but that is also inimical to its purpose. As we shall see, this last fact must have become all too clear to him when he left off work on his nearly completed *Concertsatz,* a work that courts the intimacy of private, even lone performance to a degree greater than any concerto of its time. Still, Schumann suggests that a return to earlier concertos may be one avenue by which his ideal may be realized, and this thought seems to be shared by some of his contemporaries. It should be noted, though, that their reaction to concertos of past generations differs markedly from that of those alive at the time of their first performances.

Leopold Mozart, for example, after hearing his son play the premiere performance of his D Minor Concerto called it splendid, magnificent, hardly terms one would apply to inward music.[9] By contrast, after hearing Mendelssohn play the same piece with the Gewandhaus Orchestra on 4 February 1841, Clara Schumann wrote, "The concerto touched me extraordinarily in its simple way."[10] After Beethoven gave a private performance of his G Major Concerto in 1807, the *Journal des Luxes und der Moden* reported of it and the other pieces on two programs (the composer's first four symphonies and the Overture to *Coriolanus,* among other works) that "many found fault with lack of a noble simplicity and the all too fruitful accumulation of ideas which on account of their number were not always adequately worked out and blended, thereby creating the effect more often of rough diamonds."[11] This does not suggest the kind of personal communication that Henriette Voigt heard in the Concerto during Mendelssohn's performance with the Gewandhaus Orchestra on 3 November 1836. "Today Mendelssohn played the G Major Concerto by Beethoven with a masterfulness and perfection that transported everyone.—I enjoyed myself as seldom in my life, and I sat there, without breathing, without moving a muscle, for fear of the disturbance.—Then the anxiety afterward that I would have to speak with people, to hear mistaken judgments and remarks!—I had to leave the hall and go out into the fresh air."[12]

We have already discussed in Chapter 5 Schumann's holding up of Mozart and Beethoven as ideal rather than actual models. With this in mind, it would not seem fruitful to try to show any return to either composer's work as a literal model for Schumann's first protracted effort at composing a concerto in nearly a decade. What we will look at instead is the relationship between Schumann's *Concertsatz* and his reception of Bach, including, above all, his first hearing of Bach's instrumental works on the public stage, in particular his Solo Concerto in D Minor, BWV 1052 as performed by Mendelssohn. In this connection, again, we will not look for exact copies of style or form but, to paraphrase Carl Dahlhaus, for Schumann's interest in polyphony (and, we might add, other elements of Baroque style) as a way of enhancing the aesthetic quality of the melodious, of, in John Daverio's terms, emphasizing his essentially lyric materials.[13] To quote Dahlhaus precisely:

> Schumann's Bach reception consists ... primarily of a latent appropriation, not of a manifest style copy; the model toward which he orients himself is less the fugue than the "free composition," whose voices are not equally and unbrokenly present but instead form a hierarchy of primary and secondary voices, and not infrequently emerge unexpectedly and disappear.[14]

We will extend Dahlhaus's idea to show that Schumann was also interested in the form of Bach's concertos, once again, not so much as concerns exact imitation, but as more distant models representing one way of achieving equal balance of solo and orchestral participation, and of evening out differences, usual in concertos of Schumann's contemporaries, between heartfelt thematic statements and boisterous virtuosic flights.

The start of our discussion, about Mendelssohn's D Minor Concerto, will show that Schumann's perception of the Concerto's easy flow, its "pouring forth of a beautiful soul," was very different from that of the composer, who saw it as a product of hard, even anxious work, and who had in mind an audience expecting a display of superior pianistic skill. The discussion of Bach which follows will turn on the same point, the difference between Schumann's perceptions of Bach's music and the proper venue for its performance, and Mendelssohn's. Schumann's perceptions were, I believe, influential in shaping the *Concertsatz*. Furthermore, they offer, in addition to the circumstantial evidence I shall present, a musical reason as to why it was never completed. Stated succinctly, among the cross-overs between chamber and orchestral music that begin to emerge at this time, the movement is a miscalculation.[15]

* * *

On one point in his review of the Concerto in D Minor, Schumann was wrong: Mendelssohn did not compose it in a few days. In fact, worry over the project shadowed him for several months. In April 1837 he made a definite decision to participate in the Birmingham Music Festival to be held the following September. A performance of his oratorio *St. Paul* was planned, and he intended also to present a new piano concerto. Already on 30 April he wrote Karl Klingemann "I really would like to compose for myself a concerto for England, and cannot yet manage it. I wish I knew why it is so difficult for me."[16] To his mother, Lea Mendelssohn Bartholdy, he despaired on 15 May, "Oh Lord, would that I could get on with composing a piano concerto!" and to Ferdinand David on 2 June, "Are you writing a new concerto for your instrument? I am stuck with one for mine and curse about it—it doesn't come easily from my pen."[17] Even after composition was well under way, Mendelssohn's tribulations continued. On June 24 he reported to his sister, Fanny Hensel, "The concerto is proving to be a real pain for me ... the first movement still torments me, because it has to be brilliant ..." and to Karl Klingemann on the same day, "The new concerto is already begun and, as usual, will again be horribly hard for me—it is a misery, with the piano and its 100,000 little notes."[18] He finished the piano part only a month later, on 26 July, the orchestral score on 5 August. The performance in Birmingham followed on 21 September, and one in Leipzig on 19 October.[19]

On another point, too, Mendelssohn's assessment differs from that of Schumann, who said the Concerto gives the virtuosos "almost nothing to do" that they haven't done before. Rather, on 22 July 1837 Mendelssohn wrote his mother, "The concerto, which you ask about, will be nothing very special as a composition, but the last movement creates so much effect as a piece of pianistic pyrotechnics that I often have to laugh when I happen to play it properly. There will be once again three connected movements ..."[20] Although to us today the last movement may not be considered "a piece of pianistic pyrotechnics," we might consider just what tempo constituted for Mendelssohn a "proper" playing of this *Presto scherzando*. Furthermore, in the first movement there is the Thalberg "three-handed" effect.[21] In 1838 Moscheles referred to Mendelssohn's repeated employment of it as his "*favorite* arpeggio passages, through which the melody seems to push its way."[22]

That Mendelssohn was up on the latest in pianistic technique, and even had considerable respect for the more accomplished virtuosos, is clear from the words of encouragement he asked his mother to give his sister, Fanny.

> I was annoyed, however, to hear that Fanny says the new school of piano-playing has left her behind … but there is absolutely nothing to that. She really plays all of the little fellows such as Döhler into the ground. … Thalberg and Henselt are a rather different matter, for they are supposed to be true virtuosi in the manner of Liszt (who outclasses them all); and yet it all amounts to nothing more than a Kalkbrenner in his heyday, and blows over during their lifetime if there is not some spirit and life in it, and something better than mere dexterity. That, however, Fanny has …[23]

All the same, Schumann is right, Mendelssohn can hardly be considered a flashy composer. When in Paris, Breitkopf and Härtel's agent, Heinrich Probst, wrote repeatedly in 1838 to his employer Raymund Härtel about the difficulty of finding a Parisian publisher for Mendelssohn's Concerto. As Hans Lenneberg explains, the taste of the Parisian public ran instead to showy music, to new, programmatic potpourris.[24]

We shall see soon enough that these two perceptions of Schumann's about Mendelssohn's Concerto, that it was composed quickly and that it is not for virtuosos, even though they are, from Mendelssohn's point of view, misperceptions, will have ramifications for his *Concertsatz* in D Minor. So will a third one, namely that in Mendelssohn's Concerto "here and there Sebastian Bach looks out in the harmonic progression." True enough, the harmony of the Concerto is conservative, most notably in its favoring of harmonic motion by fifths. Where Bach is more explicitly conjured up, though, is in the free fantasy of the solo opening. Its wide-ranging descent through a D minor arpeggio then ascent through a diminished-seventh arpeggio, all over a tonic pedal, give the impression of a toccata-like opening, and call to mind the same effect in the Toccata of Bach's D Minor Toccata and Fugue, BWV 565 (Example 10.1a). Although the sound of *quasi ad libitum* arpeggios is generic enough, its association with the Baroque style is plainly indicated in the opening of Moscheles's *Hommage à Haendel,* Grand Duo for Two Pianos, Op. 82, the piece with which Mendelssohn introduced himself to the Leipzig public as a pianist when he performed it with the composer on 9 October 1835 (Example 10.1b). Another evocation of an older style in Mendelssohn's Concerto may be heard in the development of the first movement, where a variant of the opening motive of the first theme is played in a canon that is an example of the "latent polyphony" Dahlhaus describes in Schumann's works. Entries appear, marked out by the repeated eighth notes of each line's anacrusis, then disappear into a texture that supports the upper voice in sixths or thirds (Example 10.1c).[25]

Concerning a fourth perception about the Concerto, both Mendelssohn and Schumann agree, that it is similar to Mendelssohn's G Minor Concerto. All three movements of the D Minor Concerto are joined by bridges. The last

a. Mendelssohn, Concerto No. 2 in D Minor, Op. 40, first movement, beginning of the solo part

b. Moscheles, *Hommage à Haendel*, Grand Duo for Two Pianos, Op. 92, first movement, beginning

c. Mendelssohn, Concerto No. 2 in D Minor, Op. 40, first movement, from the canon in the development

Example 10.1 Baroque homages.

movement has no cyclic reminiscences, but is sparing in its material. Roughly, after an opening transition/introduction, in the form **ABA'CB'A"C'coda**, the opening of section **C** both transforms and reiterates the head motive of the theme of section **A**. Within the first movement, Mendelssohn avoids the kind of sectionalization that is normal in the virtuoso concerto, using techniques similar to those he used in the G Minor Concerto. There is no long first tutti, rather, tutti and solo share the exposition. In the first group, the solo repeats and expands the tutti's statement of the theme, but leads to V of

Example 10.1 (*continued*)

V instead of V. With this turn to a new key, in bar 75, the solo begins a long passagework area, all over V of A minor (Example 10.2 shows its beginning). At first this is accompanied by motives in the orchestra from the first theme, but in its final bars, 88–90, the solo plays alone, continuing into the *cantabile* theme of the second group. The theme is four bars long (91–94), moving by circle of fifths through A minor, D minor, G major, and ending on C (see Example 10.2). A second statement is expanded to lead to V of G minor (bars 95–102), then a new statement begins on ii^6 of F major (103–106). Now solidly grounded in F major, the four-bar theme is played yet again, then after an interlude, is heard one more time (bars 107–10; 111–16 [interlude]; 117–20). On its final hearing the theme is expanded to include a new motive (played in alternation with a variant of the opening motive of the first theme) that stretches the phrase to twelve bars (121–32) and brings it around to end on the tonic, F major. Another six bars (133–38) extend the cadence.

In retrospect, the listener realizes that the rather conventional harmony and figuration of the transition act merely as a foil against which Mendelssohn unexpectedly pushes off toward his true harmonic goal, F major, within the thematic area of the second group. In a parallel fashion it turns out that the short-breathed and again rather conventional harmony and figuration at the beginning of the close serve, too, as points of departure for the very long gesture that follows from there and leads all the way to the beginning of the recapitulation. The close begins with a tonic-dominant vamp, the solo playing obbligato arpeggios, the orchestra the head motive of the first theme (bars 138–41). A repeat of the vamp moves to V of iii, then the head motive continues, in stretto, over harmonic motion by thirds that lands on V (bars 146–50). What follows is essentially a long gesture around a six-four chord in F major (bars 151–82), begun by the solo alone which plays both the obbligato part and, *à la* Thalberg, the head motive of the second-group theme. The passage leads to a typical, even clichéd, ending including the final trill, except that the final chord is deflected to a diminished-seventh chord over the sixth degree. Solo then tutti play a motive from the first theme that leads to V of D, but the close onto D minor is delayed by the

Example 10.2 Mendelssohn, Concerto No. 2 in D Minor, Op. 40, first movement, exposition, beginning of the transition, then of the second group.

introduction of the canon described above (and shown in Example 10.1c). The bass support of the canon moves by half steps, from A to A-flat, G, F-sharp, before stabilizing around entries that define first G minor, or iv of D minor, then V of D.

What we have described here are two long gestures in the exposition and development of Mendelssohn's first movement. The first begins with the solo transition and runs through to the cadence closing the thematic area of the second group; the second begins with the close and continues through the development on up to the recapitulation, and even beyond, since the solo cadence overlaps by three bars the tutti's *fortissimo* entry. We have already noted in our discussion of Mendelssohn's G Minor Concerto that his artful spinning out of the lines of the individual sections of his concerto can be traced to his thorough understanding of procedures practiced by classical composers. For Schumann, the result is a much-prized spontaneity, even if, as we have seen, to produce it requires considerable effort and skill.

Nonetheless, after Schumann heard Mendelssohn rehearse the D Minor Concerto with the Gewandhaus Orchestra, on the day before the concert of 19 October 1837, he wrote in his diary that the new piece was "somewhat ordinary."[26] This may be related to his later, printed observation that Mendelssohn "is still the same," and could apply to any number of aspects of the concerto: its form, which is not new but follows that of the G Minor Concerto, or its content, for example, the main theme of the last movement. It also could have to do with some of the passagework we have just described, namely, the clichéd arpeggio and trill work. Although I believe the juxtaposition of these commonplace conventions against Mendelssohn's more original constructions is the most ingenious aspect of the work, it may be that Schumann heard them as part and parcel of what he called one of Mendelssohn's "most casual products." Even if the master knew well enough how to make good use of such well-worn formulae, by now we know that Schumann had no interest in incorporating them into his own style. All the same, he was not immune to the charm of Mendelssohn's Concerto, for he reproduced in his *Concertsatz* both its long, seemingly effortlessly produced lines, and its bow to an earlier period as embodied in the music of Bach. He also paid tribute to this "pouring forth of a beautiful soul" by importing one of its motives into his own "Glückes genug," literally translated as "Overflow of Happiness" (Example 10.3).

* * *

It is not surprising that Mendelssohn should evoke Bach in his Concerto, considering his work with Carl Friedrich Zelter and his *Singakademie* during his early training, and his fame since 1829 as the person who began the Bach revival in the concert hall with his performance in Berlin of the complete St. Matthew Passion.[27] Likewise, as a number of procedures followed by Mendelssohn in his concerto are taken up by Schumann, it will not surprise

a. Mendelssohn, Concerto No. 2 in D Minor, Op. 40 (1837), first movement,
  new motive in the theme of the second group.

[Allegro appassionato]

b. Schumann, *Kinderszenen*, Op. 15 (1838), No. 5, "Gluckes genug," beginning.

Example 10.3 Schumann's tribute to Mendelssohn.

us either that Schumann, too, makes some reference to Bach in his *Concertsatz.* What we will find is that Schumann's reaction to Bach and his adoption of him is from a different perspective than Mendelssohn's. This needs some explanation, which will follow before we turn to the *Concertsatz.* Although Schumann knew of Bach's music from at least his early teens, and performed it at home in his later teens, his introduction to Bach's music as viable for concert hall performance began after Mendelssohn's arrival in Leipzig in late summer 1835. This will prove to be a decisive difference.

Among the fragments of poetry, essays, travel diaries, letters, dramas, translations, aphorisms, and other literary efforts that make up Schumann's youthful collection "Blätter und Blümchen aus der goldenen Aue" is a group of "Short biographies of famous composers in alphabetical order edited by Robert Schumann: 1823." The first entry under "B" reads:

> *Bach* (Johann Sebastian) Among German composers one of the most famous and indeed the greatest of this musical family b. in Eisenach 1685 †1750; he was the Capellmeister to the Prince of Cöthen. He had 11 sons … the most famous are the following: [Here Schumann gives thumbnail sketches of Wilhelm Friedemann, Carl Philipp Emanuel, Johann Christoph Friedrich, and Johann Christian.][28]

The entries never went beyond "B." According to Corina Wenke, Schumann seems to have taken over most from an encyclopedia by Brockhaus, third and fourth editions of 1814 and 1817. His entry for Bach also resembles the text of his father August Schumann's *Bildnisse der berühmtesten Menschen aller Völker und Zeiten,* which was intended as a supplement to Brockhaus's 1814 edition, and for which the young Schumann was assigned the task of copying out biographies of famous musicians.[29]

When he undertook the copying work in 1823, Schumann probably knew none of the instrumental music of J. S. Bach. His "Älteste musikalische Erinnerungen" from 1828 refers to his first acquaintance with the music of Bach as coming only three years later: "Mozart, Haydn, Beethoven—Bach, 1826—."[30] In the "Selbstbiographische Notizen" of c. 1840 he writes, "In my 18th year [that is, beginning in late 1827] passion for Jean Paul; I also heard for the first time Franz Schubert. Until then Goethe and Bach were closed to me." Then for the year 1828, that is, after he moved to Leipzig, "Especial passion for Franz Schubert, also Beethoven, of Bach less," and "I began to understand Franz Schubert and Beethoven; I saw the light about Bach."[31]

Schumann's exposure to Bach's music began not with the concert stage, but with four-hand playing with friends, sight-reading at home, attendance at private soirées, counterpoint studies, and possibly through visits to Thibaut's home in Heidelberg.[32] On 18 February 1829 he played Bach preludes and fugues with one of his Leipzig friends, Christian Glock.[33] On 24 May 1832 he heard Clara Wieck play the "second fugue" by Bach "plain and clear and with a beautiful iridescence," then again four days later at a soirée at her father's house.[34] Three days afterward he "tore through" six Bach fugues with Clara, four-hands, *a vista prima*.[35] Schumann's early exposure to Bach also included more abstract thoughts about the manifestation of his genius in severity as opposed to Mozart's in facility, Beethoven's in warmth, and Schubert's in darkness.[36]

Schumann's idealization of Bach, as a severe genius yet at the same time a musician connected with his passion for Jean Paul and Schubert, and his enjoyment of Bach's music in private musical circles, overlapped with the beginning of his study with Heinrich Dorn in summer 1831. By the time he quit his studies in February 1832 he had progressed from figured bass and chorale harmonization to canon and fugue.[37] On 27 July 1832 he wrote to his old teacher in Zwickau, Johann Gottfried Kuntsch, of his work with Dorn up to canon, and of his study all the way through Friedrich Wilhelm Marpurg's *Abhandlung von der Fuge*. "Otherwise," he continues, "Sebastian Bach's *Well-Tempered Clavier* is my grammar, and the best besides. I have dissected the fugues themselves in order down to their finest points; this is very profitable, the equivalent of a moral fortification of one's entire person for Bach was a man—through and through; with him nothing is by halves, nothing unhealthy, everything is written for eternity."[38]

With respect to the concert stage, the first performance of a work by Bach at a Gewandhaus subscription concert was not until November 1835.[39] That fall Moscheles visited Leipzig, played through Bach's Triple Concerto in D Minor, BWV 1063 with Mendelssohn (taking the orchestral part), Clara Wieck and Louis Rakemann at Friedrich Wieck's home on the afternoon of 6 October.[40] Schumann was present at this private read-through, and recalled "with great joy" the pleasure it gave.[41] A public performance of the Triple Concerto was given by Mendelssohn, Clara Wieck, and Rakemann on 9 November 1835. Schumann drew attention to it in an announcement that appeared in the *Leipziger Tageblatt* four days before the concert.

> Aside from that, the Concerto for Three Claviers by Joh. Seb. Bach ... will be performed. It would be an interesting and remarkable experience for the inhabitants of Leipzig if the spirit of their former fellow citizen, old Bach, in its complete, deeply severe, good-naturedly capricious, peevish loveableness stepped into their midst sometime, greeting them, admonishing them, and as if bluntly asking them, "What's it like now in your artistic world? Look, that was me!"[42]

After the concert, in the fourth of his *Schwärmbriefe,* Schumann wrote, "Just don't laugh at the Concerto for Three Claviers by old Sebastian ... rather be like Florestan, who reflected concerning it: under the circumstances it becomes quite clear to a person what a scoundrel one is."[43] He does not mention the reaction of the public, only his private one, namely, that his own efforts hardly compare with those of the old master.

Ferdinand Hiller, in his autobiography of 1880, says that his public performances of the Triple Concerto in Paris with Liszt and Chopin on 23 March and 15 December 1833 were, at that time and in that city, an ungrateful task.[44]

In Leipzig, Mendelssohn writes of an enthusiastic reception, but is skeptical of the reason, as if true appreciation of Bach is limited to only a few, for example, himself and his correspondent Friedrich Schneider in Dessau:

> The Triple Keyboard Concerto by [Bach] was received (in my opinion) like everything one offers people of the correct sort, if it's really good. They clapped after both [sic] movements and appeared heartily glad. If for that reason it has made some kind of an impression, I'll leave undecided, but we have heard it once and taken pleasure in it, and so I would have been fully satisfied if it had been a bit controversial.[45]

Mendelssohn's critique of his audience reveals the proprietary air of the professionals and connoisseurs who collected and performed music of the past. Although they fostered the revival of public performances of Bach's instrumental music, they still believed that performances in private settings were greeted by a more receptive audience, that they were taking place in a more appropriate venue.

During the mid- to late 1830s, Schumann's primary engagement with Bach was away from the public eye. He played Bach with the pianist Camille Stamaty at his own home, and with the composition student Johann Verhulst at the home of Graf von Reuß-Köstritz.[46] Also at home he heard the violinist Ferdinand David play solo works by Bach from the Sonatas and Partitas.[47] At Henriette Voigt's he heard Bach sonatas played by the visiting violinist Karol Lipinski with Voigt at the keyboard, and at Mendelssohn's, Bach sonatas, again by Lipinski.[48] No works by Bach were played by Lipinski at his two Gewandhaus concerts of 7 and 15 October 1836, but rather concertos, variations, a fantasy, and a concert rondo, all of his own composition.[49]

After the Triple Concerto, the next performance of a Bach keyboard concerto on a Gewandhaus subscription concert was nearly two years later, on 9 March 1837, again by Mendelssohn, this time the D Minor Concerto for Solo Keyboard, BWV 1052. Five years earlier, on 1 December 1832, he had performed the Concerto in Berlin at the *Singakademie.*[50] At that time he was not pleased with the reaction of the Berlin public. On 19 January 1833 he wrote Franz Hauser:

> I played the D Minor Concerto publicly, the applause after the last movement just wouldn't stop, and the people were all so inspired, that I am convinced it pleased no one. In general, I have my own views about the public (I mean [about] art) and especially the Berlin public.[51]

When the Concerto was performed in Leipzig Schumann's frame of mind, at least, was perhaps more to Mendelssohn's liking than that of the Berlin public: not wild enthusiasm, but quiet, distant meditation. In an overview of the concert scene in Leipzig for the season Schumann wrote, on 5 May 1837:

> I would like to say a lot about what thoughts occurred to me in connection with this sublime work. ... But one thing the world should know. ... in the

music cabinets of the Berlin *Singakademie* to which old Zelter bequeathed his library, at least seven such concertos and aside from that uncountable other Bach compositions in manuscript are still stored away in good condition. Only a few people know it; however, they are indeed there. Really, isn't it time … to undertake a complete collection and edition of the entire works of Bach. One would think …[52]

Publication of Bach's works on a grand scale began soon enough with the formation of the Bach-Gesellschaft in 1850.[53] Schumann's efforts were on a more modest scale that involved circulating a few of Bach's unpublished works among the several hundred readers of the *Neue Zeitschrift* through musical supplements.[54]

Eventually, it may have been Mendelssohn's performance of the D Minor Concerto in Leipzig that precipitated its publication by Kistner in 1839.[55] When he reviewed the new publication, Schumann recalled Mendelssohn's performance. Rather than rejoicing in the work's wider dissemination, he pointed instead to the small and special public that would enjoy it.

A beginning of an edition of the keyboard concertos of Bach was made by Herr Kistner with the highly celebrated one in D Minor; it is the same one that Mendelssohn played publicly in Leipzig a few years ago, to the great joy of the odd individual, but in which, notwithstanding, the majority seemed to take no part.[56]

After the two concerto performances, in 1835 and 1837, Mendelssohn continued his programming of Bach works for a larger public. From 15 February to 8 March 1838 he presented a series of four historical concerts, beginning with music from the Baroque era and progressing forward chronologically as far as Weber. The first program included Bach's Suite for Orchestra in D Major, BWV 1068, and Sonata for Violin and Keyboard in E Major, BWV 1016. According to a report in the *Allgemeine musikalische Zeitung* the Suite was repeatedly applauded, and the Sonata, which concluded the first half of the first program, was given the loudest applause to that point.[57]

Schumann took a skeptical, even snobbish, attitude toward the audience's enthusiastic reaction.

As happy as what we were given to hear made us, so what here and there we had to hear about it made us really ill-tempered. Many acted as if we honor Bach in this way, as if we know more than those of earlier time, and find it curious and interesting at the same time! And moreover the connoisseurs are the worst ones, and they smile, as if Bach wrote for them,—He who pretty much carries the whole lot of us with his little finger …

About Bach's music which was played, little needs to be said; one must have it in one's hands, must study it as much as possible, and he remains as impenetrable as before.[58]

Schumann was put off that the audience deigned to believe they were doing Bach a favor, that the attendance and applause were greater than usual. For

him the real appreciation for Bach came, not through concert hall performance of his instrumental music, but through study of it at home, and
through private meditation on it.

That is just what Schumann was doing. In February 1837 he began a
renewed study of Bach that was to last many months. He copied out the Art
of the Fugue and gradually played through many of Bach's Chorale Preludes
for organ.[59] According to Uwe Martin, the stimulus for this activity was a
visit on 22 January 1837 to Mendelssohn, who played his new Preludes and
Fugues, Op. 35.[60] Later in the year Schumann began again with Marpurg's
Abhandlung von der Fuge and returned to study of the Chorale Preludes,
a preliminary to the composition of his own fugues, which he undertook with
some tribulation from 24 October to 4 November.[61] During this time his
published review of Mendelssohn's Preludes and Fugues appeared with the
declaration that he "could luxuriate for hours in Beethoven, Bach and Handel
[fugues]."[62] By spring 1838 Schumann was again studying the Chorale Preludes. He also took up the *Well-Tempered Clavier.*[63] To his fiancée, Clara
Wieck, he wrote on 18 March, "Bach is my daily bread," and recommended
that while in Vienna, she, too, learn to write fugues.[64]

For Schumann, an appropriate venue for public performance of Bach's
music was the series of Gewandhaus chamber concerts where, on 8 February
1840, David played to Mendelssohn's accompaniment (composed by himself) the Chaconne from the Partita for Solo Violin No. 2 in D Minor, BWV
1004, and the Prelude from the Partita No. 3 in E Major, BWV 1006. Schumann approves of the modernization of these two pieces "of which it was
earlier asserted that 'an added voice to them cannot be imagined'—which
Mendelssohn then in the most beautiful manner disproved, in that he played
all sorts of voices around the original, so that it was a joy to hear."[65] He also
dwells on his pleasure in their beauty. Not so the reviewer for the *Allgemeine
musikalische Zeitung,* who is at pains to explain that the accompaniments
are a concession to a wider public. "Now, to be sure, for artists, who are in a
position to understand and judge the harmonic progression and its artful work,
[the violin part] by itself is fully sufficient for comprehension, only the public
requires a help to this end, a commentary so to speak, that makes the whole
thing perceptible to them and eases their comprehension."[66]

Three weeks later, on 29 February 1840, Mendelssohn played Bach's
Chromatic Fantasy and Fugue, BWV 903, and the five-voice fugue in C-sharp
minor from the first book of the *Well-Tempered Clavier* on the chamber
series. He wrote his sister, Fanny Hensel, that the Fantasy and Fugue were
the high point.

> Can you think what I, among other things, played just a week ago? and by
> what completely furious and stormy *da capo* I was demanded? with the
> chromatic fantasy by Sebastian. ... This is unadulterated taste for the
> rococo, for it is nothing more to people; to me, however, it was important,
> because I never used to be able to stand the piece much, and a little while

ago took it in hand and so came to like it like anything else by him.
I would be delighted to play it for you sometime.[67]

Even as Mendelssohn owned up to the fickleness of the public's tumultuous
response, he continued to present Bach at his flashiest for the purpose of
eliciting that very response. Richard David Green goes so far as to assert,
"The fact that Mendelssohn would only play [the Triple Concerto in D Minor]
with two other virtuosi, here [that is, in 1840] Liszt and Hiller, indicates his
conscious effort to relate this music to the contemporary cult of bravura
music of Herz, Czerny and Hünten."[68]

Schumann's approach to Bach was more personal. He continued to asso-
ciate him with Jean Paul, noting in his diary on 23 March 1838 their shared
birthday.[69] When he heard Lipinski play an accompanied Bach violin sonata
with Henriette Voigt he complained that the violin virtuoso "played well and
beautifully, practically too theatrically," and Voigt "very dryly and without
true understanding."[70] In his review of Mendelssohn's Preludes and Fugues
he emphasized the poetic rather than learned side of a type of composition
he associated with Bach, the fugue.

> In any case, the best fugue is always the one that the audience—perchance
> takes to be a Strauss waltz, in other words, one where the artful roots are
> covered over, like those of a flower, so that we see only the flower. So once
> (truly) a, in other respects not intolerant, music connoisseur took a Bach
> fugue to be an etude by Chopin—to the credit of both ...[71]

* * *

Amid this period of new interest in performance of Bach's instrumental
music in the concert hall Schumann composed his *Concertsatz*. In October
1838 he left Leipzig for Vienna with the hope of finding a publisher for the
Neue Zeitschrift. In this he was frustrated, and ultimately unsuccessful, yet
in at least one way his six-month stay in the city bore fruit: he finished the
Arabeske, Op. 18; *Blumenstück*, Op. 19; *Humoreske*, Op. 20; *Nachtstücke*,
Op. 23; first four pieces of the *Faschungsschwank aus Wien*, Op. 26; and,
with his work on the *Concertsatz* in early 1839, returned to the concerto genre
for the first time in nearly seven years. On 16 January 1839 he wrote Clara
Wieck that he was composing, or at least thinking of composing, a concerto,
a piece which, ten days later, he calls "a cross between a symphony, a concerto and a big sonata."[72]

The *Concertsatz* is a harbinger of a group of symphonic compositions
that followed in 1841, the First Symphony, Symphony in D Minor in its
first version, Overture, Scherzo and Finale, and *Phantasie* or first movement of the Piano Concerto in A Minor. To a greater or lesser extent, the
web of motivic connections that Schumann cultivates within each of these
pieces is already in evidence in the *Concertsatz*.[73] I have made this point in a
previous article, a review of a modern edition of the work edited by Jozef De
Beenhouwer and Joachim Draheim, in two paragraphs which I quote with

little modification in the two following paragraphs. Aside from the motivic connections they point to in the *Concertsatz,* they also discuss the long and nearly unbroken sweep of its harmonic and melodic gestures, and the tendency of these to blur the outlines of the movement's sonata form.[74]

Two motives and their transformations generate almost the entire melodic life of the *Concertsatz.* One is a recognizably individuated scalewise gesture, diatonic or (less often) chromatic, the other an eighth-note motive with a rocking rhythm. Both are shown in Example 10.4 as they first appear in combination with one another. The scalar motive alone provides material for four sections. A chromatically descending form constitutes the slow introduction (*Un poco maestoso*); a threefold sequential ascent answered by a threefold chromatically inflected descent produces the theme of the first group (*Allegro passionato*); various diatonic forms are heard in the second half of the thematic area of the second group; the ascending diatonic form makes up the entire tutti following the exposition. The rocking motive is extracted from the descending sequences of the theme of the first group and appears thereafter always in some sort of combination with the scalar motive or a recognizable fragment of it. With the single exception of the first phrase of the theme of the second group, all remaining sections of the *Concertsatz* make use of this combination: the transition (bars 22–46); the close (*Animato*); and the development.

To the extent that the formal design of the *Concertsatz* conforms to a traditional classical model of sonata form, it can be said that the motivic interconnections within the movement tend to conceal the outlines of this model. The phrase syntax and harmonic structure contribute further to the blurring of these outlines. The breathtaking quality of the scalar ascents and descents of the theme of the first group seem at first to be another introductory gesture. The fairly regular periodization of the transition that follows gives an initial impression of being the real first theme. Only the modulation of its consequent from the tonic D minor to the dominant F major changes this perception. The principal theme of the second group (reminiscent of "Der Dichter spricht," No. 13 from Schumann's *Kinderszenen*) enters in such a way as to give the impression of being a mere outgrowth and continuation of the preceding dominant preparation. As shown in Example 10.5, the latter ends on the first downbeat of bar 46 with a V$^4_2$ of F chord. This chord anticipates the first note of the new theme, which is harmonized on

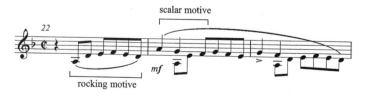

Example 10.4 Schumann, *Concertsatz* in D Minor, two main motives.

the second half-note beat of the same bar by the same V_2^4 chord. The first phrase of the new theme ends with a feminine cadence, the tonic falling on the second beat of bar 50. But when the tonic is actually sounded it is already V_2^4 of IV. This chord in turn begins a repeat of the first phrase a fourth higher in the same anticipatory manner as before. Both this particular blurring device of the local V resolving to the local V of IV and the sequential continuations, mostly by fourths and fifths and often resulting in a headlong rush, remain steady features of all further sections of the movement.

The motivic connections across the various sections of the *Concertsatz* are in evidence in earlier compositions by Schumann, for example, across the collection of pieces in *Carnaval* (which Schumann characterized as a composition "on four notes"), or, to cite a genre closer in its form to the *Concertsatz*, across the different sections of the first movement of the *Fantasie*, Op. 17.[75] Schumann noted that these types of links, within or across movements, were a fashion of the time when he reviewed Carl Loewe's *Grande sonate élégique* in 1835.

> To bring three parts together as a whole, is, I believe, the aim of sonata, also concerto and symphony writers. ... They did not stick to elaborating an idea in one movement, they also hid it in other formations and refractions in succeeding ones. ... Recently, they tied the movements together even more, and joined them to each other through a quick transition into the new movement.[76]

With regard to the last point, we can only speculate as concerns the *Concertsatz*, as later movements of the piece, beyond the first few bars of a scherzo, are not extant. We will offer some thoughts on the matter at the end of our discussion.

More generally with respect to motivic links, Schumann is usually reticent about pointing these out in his discussion of concertos by his contemporaries.

Example 10.5 Schumann, *Concertsatz* in D Minor, exposition, end of the transition and beginning of the theme of the second group.

His November 1835 review of Mendelssohn's performance of his G Minor Concerto does not mention the thematic reminiscences in the final movement; a month later his review of Clara Wieck's performance of her concerto says nothing of the thematic connection between the first and last movements.[77] In his spring 1836 series of concerto reviews he does point to the return of thematic material from the first movement in the last one of Moscheles's *Fantastique* Concerto, but says nothing of the pervasive motive that informs the first movement of Thalberg's Concerto.[78] A year later he writes that the first movement of Bennett's C Minor Concerto is cohesive without specifically noting the repeated use of a signature motive in its various sections.[79] His review of Moscheles's *Pathétique* Concerto is silent about motives shared by its three movements.[80]

Perhaps it is not surprising that Schumann does not belabor the matter of motivic unity, when we consider that he showed real enthusiasm for some of the concertos listed in the previous paragraph (Bennett's, Mendelssohn's), an ambivalent attitude toward others (Wieck's, Moscheles's), and outright disdain for one (Thalberg's). Instead of any specifics as to what constitutes cohesiveness in a concerto, it is the overall sweep, the broadly unifying gestures that interest Schumann and that he repeatedly returns to in his discussions. We may observe, as we have in the case of the *Concertsatz,* that this involves limitation of motivic material, but we should also keep in mind that Schumann's real concern is an aesthetic, not a technical one. Important to him is the flow of a movement; he values seamless transitions between its different parts, between thematic and passagework, or tutti and solo areas. Mendelssohn's concertos create this feel through overlapping and deflecting the cadences that normally separate these sections. Similarly, in the *Concertsatz* Schumann blurs the line of demarcation between the end of the solo exposition and beginning of the tutti that follows, first by having the tutti enter two bars too soon (at the pickup to bar 123), and, second, by carefully concealing the closing cadence: the C major dominant chord at the end of the solo is interrupted by the tutti, which resolves not to F major, but to V$^4_2$ of B-flat major (see Example 10.6).[81]

Innovative features of Schumann's *Concertsatz* have models in concertos by his contemporaries. Closest to hand were Mendelssohn's D Minor, and Moscheles's *Pathétique,* the two concertos that formed the touchstone for his review article "Das Clavier-Concert," which he sent off from Vienna to Leipzig on 11 December 1838, that is, less than a month before he began composing the *Concertsatz.*[82] What needs to be stressed is that Schumann takes these innovations to further extremes in the *Concertsatz* than can be found in any concertos of the time. I would like to suggest that the more extreme experiments tried by Schumann were to a certain extent prompted by the influence not just of his contemporaries but also of Bach. This is not to say that the *Concertsatz* sounds like Bach (although the fact that it is in D Minor is suggestive, given that the two Bach keyboard concertos Schumann heard performed in Leipzig were both in D Minor), nor even that it follows

Example 10.6 Schumann, *Concertsatz* in D Minor, exposition, end of the solo close and beginning of the second tutti.

any particular compositional procedure of Bach. Instead, what must be kept in mind is Schumann's idea of what Bach's music represents, or, to return to Dahlhaus's formulation, Schumann's "latent appropriation" of Bach's music as opposed to any "manifest style copy." We will look at innovative features of the *Concertsatz* in relation to concertos by Bach, beginning with two we have already discussed, motivic connections and the blurring of lines of demarcation across sections, followed by three others, the even balance between orchestra and solo, the elimination of a long opening tutti statement, and the truncation of the recapitulation.

Schumann shuns the melodic decoration and flashy passagework that came to be associated with the concerto, and that so sharply differentiated its alternating thematic and passagework areas. He tends instead to smooth out the differences between these areas. In the *Concertsatz,* cutting out a large amount of passagework is one way of closing the gap. We already mentioned the fairly regular periodization of the transition, which gives an initial impression of being the real first theme. A similar excision of passagework can be seen in Moscheles's *Pathétique* Concerto, where the solo's counterstatement of the first theme closes directly onto the theme of the second group; it may be the feature Schumann had in mind when he wrote that the Concerto's "first movement advances quickly."[83] But another precedent comes to mind in the Bach concertos Schumann heard, for solo keyboard and for three keyboards, both in D minor. Despite their alternation of tutti and solo sections, the differentiation of musical types between these areas is not great, due, in both concertos, to the dominance of the solo and simplification of the accompaniment, at least as compared to other concertos by Bach (the *Brandenburg,* or violin concertos). In the D Minor Solo Keyboard Concerto this lack of differentiation is further strengthened by the recurrence of the opening motive through much of the movement, in other words, by the same mono-motivic quality heard in the *Concertsatz*.[84]

Related to this flattening out of differences from section to section of the *Concertsatz* is the balance it strikes between solo and orchestral participation. In his overview of the genre in "Das Clavier-Concert" Schumann said he awaited "the genius who will show us in a new, more brilliant way how the orchestra may be united with the piano," a way whereby piano and orchestra would participate equally.[85] In the review that follows, Mendelssohn's D Minor Concerto, which gives the virtuosos "almost nothing to do" and Moscheles's *Pathétique,* which is not "mechanically difficult" offer two examples. Already we have noted that Schumann's view on this matter was different from Mendelssohn's who wrote of the "pianistic pyrotechnics" in the last movement of his Concerto. After a rehearsal in Birmingham he reported, "The people just about fell over themselves with pleasure after the first solo passage of the last movement—an unbelievable noise;" then after the premiere performance two days later, "They demanded the last movement to be repeated, but I was too tired."[86] Along these same lines, Moscheles wrote his wife Charlotte that "the concertos *Pathétique* and *Fantastique* were received with mounting applause" from the Leipzig audience.[87] Both these concertos exploit a chamber-music-like relationship between solo and orchestra, which is also a characteristic of Schumann's *Concertsatz*. But Schumann's mechanical simplification of the solo part that is a corollary to this relationship goes far beyond Mendelssohn's or Moscheles's, and of this he was well aware. Even as he was composing the *Concertsatz* he wrote Clara Wieck, "I cannot write a concerto for the virtuoso."[88] He did not have in mind the same public for the *Concertsatz* that received Mendelssohn's and Moscheles's concertos with audible acclaim.

The public Schumann did have in mind seems to have been closer to his ideal audience for Bach, a composer whose music he believed was not meant for the masses and which he preferred to hear played in more intimate surroundings. In the *Concertsatz* the intended intimate setting for performance is heard most conspicuously in the toning down of areas traditionally devoted to virtuosic display, the closing group and the development. The generation after Beethoven, especially, gave these areas over to lightly accompanied bravura show. Even Mendelssohn's and Moscheles's concertos save the close for bravura display, although both give the orchestra a more substantial role. In the *Concertsatz* the orchestra carries the melody, but Schumann gives the pianist only middle register eighth and quarter notes in the right hand over long notes in the left hand. These make up an obbligato part, which now reinforces, now anticipates or echoes by a short distance the orchestra melody.

The melody itself has the movement's characteristic breathless quality, which I believe has more in common with the Baroque practice of spinning out a motive "in place" before directing it toward a cadence, than with the repetition of closed melodic and harmonic cells that normally initiate closing groups in concertos of the 1830s.

Comparison of Schumann's close with a passage from the second solo episode of the first movement of Bach's Concerto for Solo Keyboard in D Minor will make the point (Examples 10.7a and b). The main motive of the Bach passage (also the signature motive of the movement) is led through the circle of fifths (from A minor, to D minor, G minor, C major, F major, and B-flat major). Then in the keyboard part a new arpeggiation in the bass is introduced and led through the same portion of the circle of fifths (though beginning now with an E major chord) at twice the pace, followed by a stepwise descent in the bass leading to the dominant of F major (this last is not shown in the example). A perpetuum mobile feeling is kept up by the constant sixteenth notes, and steady figural (and in most cases harmonic) changes every half bar. The motion begun at bar 28 or 34 (or 37 where the bass descent begins) could, presumably, go on forever, or, at least until the instrument's lower register is exhausted.

In the *Concertsatz* Schumann begins a sequential motion that rises stepwise in the bass. This seems to suggest a more definite goal than Bach's turns through the circle of fifths, and indeed, when the highpoint is reached at bar 79, the feeling is that the new sequence that follows completes (in bar 96) the phrase begun at bar 70, the beginning of the *Animato*. Yet, at the same time the very special construction, two-bar phrases that overlap in the middle of every other bar, gives the music the thrust that makes one feel, just as in Bach, that we have set in motion a chain of events that could perpetuate themselves *ad infinitum*. On the most local level, this contributes to the rush of the music, which is also heard in the overlapping cadences that push one section into the next. Add to these overlapping two-bar phrases the complex texture of the orchestra melody and piano obbligato, and the impression is similar to the complex texture of Bach's passage, where the keyboard plays obbligato first to melodies in counterpoint between the two violins, then between the first violin and viola. Schumann's passage exemplifies both Dahlhaus's "latent polyphony" and the free reign of the composer's imagination in appropriating not only the music of his contemporaries but also of an earlier era as a means of developing his own special propensities.

In addition to eliminating a long tutti introduction to his *Concertsatz,* Schumann also begins his movement in a slow tempo (*Un poco maestoso*), according to Draheim, a procedure without precedent. Draheim compares it, not to any other concerto, but to the opening of Mozart's Overture to *Don Giovanni*.[89] I believe, in addition, that a striking resemblance to Mendelssohn's D Minor Concerto should not be overlooked. While Mendelssohn's five-bar opening tutti is in the same tempo, *Allegro appassionato,* as the remainder of his movement, its opening motto, a whole note followed

a. Bach, from the second solo

b. Schumann, exposition, beginning of the close

Example 10.7 Comparison of Bach, Concerto in D Minor, BWV 1052 and Schumann, *Concertsatz* in D Minor, first movements.

by two descending half notes, has the same stately quality as Schumann's introduction. Similarly, the unaccompanied solo *ad libitum* descending and ascending arpeggios which follow Mendelssohn's introductory tutti have the same breathtaking quality as the unaccompanied solo ascending and descending scales of the first theme that follow Schumann's introduction (Example 10.8; cf. Example 10.1a). As we noted earlier, Mendelssohn's arpeggios call to mind the opening sweep of certain toccata movements by Bach: they suggest a direct link to the Baroque as conjured up in something like Moscheles's *Hommage à Haendel,* wherein, Schumann concludes, Moscheles "for a few

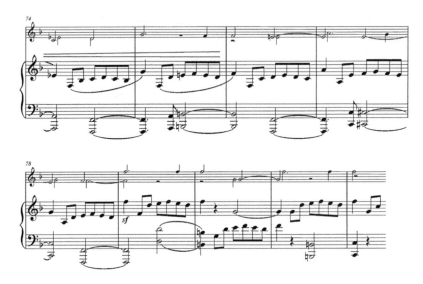

Example 10.7 (*continued*)

Example 10.8 Schumann, *Concertsatz* in D Minor, introduction, and beginning of the first theme.

moments puts himself back in that age of wholesomeness, propriety and frankness."[90] Schumann's introduction and first theme are yet one more remove away in their evocation of the Baroque. They have an improvisatory sound, a majestic opening followed by sweeping scales, that calls to mind the opening of certain virtuoso keyboard works by Bach (for example, the Toccata and Fugue in D Minor mentioned above, with its *Adagio* opening, then *prestissimo* continuation) without copying their precise musical sound.

One final novel feature of the *Concertsatz* cannot be related to any latent appropriation of the Baroque style idiom, but only to contemporary concertos, and that is the dropping or extreme truncation of the first group of the reprise. In Mendelssohn's D Minor Concerto the recapitulation moves directly from a tutti statement of the main theme of the first group to a solo statement of the first theme of the second group. In Moscheles's *Pathétique* Concerto, after a short tutti and solo exchange, the solo proceeds with the theme of the second group, in the tonic major. Schumann's recapitulation devotes just eight bars to the theme of the first group. The theme of the second group follows immediately, without any transition. In a further truncation of the reprise that goes beyond Mendelssohn or Moscheles, Schumann also eliminates the closing group. He composes only eight bars of a final tutti, then, leaving just one blank page, starts a sketch for a scherzo. That he intended this sketch as the beginning of a second movement is supported by his suggestion in "Das Clavier-Concert" that the scherzo might be effectively introduced into the concerto, just as it has already been in the symphony and sonata.[91] Furthermore, as it now stands, the brevity of the first movement suggests Schumann may have intended to connect it with succeeding ones, possibly through bridges between them, or even through thematic links or reminiscences across them. The extreme truncation of the movement's recapitulation strengthens this hypothesis. Only two other concertos match this extreme, Clara Wieck's in A Minor, and Moscheles's *Fantastique;* both have connected movements. How Schumann would have continued, though, is an open question, especially given that he was critical of the lack of balance in those two concertos.[92]

* * *

Whether Schumann broke off his composition on the *Concertsatz* for personal, business, or musical reasons is not clear. The answer may involve all three. He wrote Clara of his failing inspiration.[93] His letters are also filled with a raging jealousy over what he sees as Clara's improper relationship with a certain Dr. Gustav Schilling, whom she met during a stay in Stuttgart.[94] This obsession, as well as an increasing anxiety over his situation in Vienna, and growing realization that he would have to leave the city without fulfilling his hope of finding a publisher for the *Neue Zeitschrift,* may have soured his composing: despite the steady production of piano solo pieces neither of the two compositions he began in larger forms, the D Minor Concerto and an Allegro in C Minor for piano, was ever finished. The fatal illness of his brother Eduard, which precipitated Schumann's leaving Vienna in early April, was followed by protracted court proceedings against Friedrich Wieck, which were necessary for Schumann to pursue in order to gain legal permission to marry Clara. Not until the serene time that began with his marriage in

September 1840 did Schumann again turn to a large form of composition. By then, the *Concertsatz* was abandoned.

As a work-in-progress the *Concertsatz* shows Schumann both reacting to trends of the time, and working out his own vision of what the concerto should be. Certain structural features of the movement can be seen in other concertos of the 1830s, most notably the elimination of a full tutti exposition, and the truncation of the recapitulation. But other, less obvious aspects bear Schumann's individual thumbprint. As a counter to the virtuosic displays that were the norm in concertos of the day, he trimmed the traditional bravura areas of the movement more than any other composer, filling them instead with thematic material in which the solo is often enough given an accompanimental role. This lack of differentiation between the type of material used in what are traditionally contrasting thematic and bravura sections of the concerto first movement, together with the motivic and harmonic connections across these sections and the deliberate overlapping of cadences between them, create a movement where the traditional lines of demarcation, although still in place, are blurred. The brevity of the movement, particularly its recapitulation, suggests the possibility that both the connections and the blurring were to span across later movements.

As it now stands, the *Concertsatz* is an exciting experiment, one that is far removed from the conventionally virtuosic F major concerto movement of Schumann's youth, and that is a clear harbinger of ideas which are basic to his later symphonic works. But the experiment was never completed, and the torso that remains gives only a glimmer of its essence. What remains is a testament to Schumann's desire to compose a work for the connoisseur in a genre that traditionally plays to the masses: although he introduced into it the latest developments in the romantic concerto, he also brought to it aspects belonging to chamber compositions and even to the very private world he associated with Bach. I believe he envisioned for it the position which Daverio associates with early nineteenth-century chamber music, and specifically with Schumann's Piano Quintet, that is, a position "suspended midway between private and public spheres ... between quasi-symphonic and more properly chamber-like elements," or, we might add, between concerto and chamber elements, since the Quintet draws on performance practices associated with the concerto.[95] It is a position that also applies to Schumann's first completed concert piece, our next subject of discussion, the *Phantasie*. As we shall see, both the Quintet and *Phantasie* owe their success in reconciling the two spheres, public and private, to greater incorporation of traditional elements which accentuate the solo's virtuosity, among them some of the very elements Schumann set out to eliminate in his radical experiment, the *Concertsatz*.

11
Phantasie

Much has been written about the change in Schumann's compositional output beginning in 1840. The outflow of songs has been associated with his plans for marriage and the need to generate more income; his turn to symphonic and chamber music with a desire to achieve greater recognition as a composer.[1] Not that any of these genres were new to him; he had composed songs, a piano quartet, and a symphony in his youth. The early songs were inspired by his love for Agnes Carus, and his later songs, too, are an outpouring of love, this time for his new bride.[2] The early piano quartet grew from music making with a circle of amateurs. Likewise, the chamber pieces from the early 1840s, the string quartets and piano quintet, are music with appeal to a wide audience of amateurs. They avoid the more adventuresome turns of the solo piano works from the 1830s, their experiments in sound, their high drama and impulsive virtuosity.

When it comes to works for larger ensembles, those Schumann composed in his youth, an unfinished Symphony in G Minor, and the Piano Concerto in F Major, also were intended to have broad appeal, although to a less intimate audience. Both were composed along fairly conventional lines, the Concerto following the fashion of virtuoso concertos of the day, the Symphony following models from Beethoven's middle period. When Schumann again turned to these genres he found new models: Schubert for his First Symphony, Mendelssohn for the Overture, Scherzo and Finale. He also turned out some of his most experimental works, the *Phantasie* in A Minor for Piano and Orchestra, and the D Minor Symphony. Unlike the First Symphony, these were not an immediate success, and both underwent substantial revision before being published some years later.[3] Neither, it seems, falls into the category of broad audience appeal that characterized the First Symphony. Although they tone down the harmonic twists, high drama, and virtuosity of the solo piano works from the 1830s, like those pieces, the appeal of their unusual structures and novel strategies with their heavy reliance on what the fantasy genre connoted at the time, was still to the cognoscenti.[4]

   This chapter will explore the generic expectations circa 1840 for a work called fantasy, then show how Schumann subverts these to suit his own sensibilities precisely as he had already made them known in his reviews. We will begin our examination with a brief look at certain aspects of the D Minor Symphony. This is because I believe the aesthetic Schumann brings to the Symphony, as described by Mark Evan Bonds, can already be seen in the *Phantasie,* which was sketched and orchestrated only days before the Symphony was begun.[5] Each piece was dubbed a fantasy at some stage in its compositional history, although both emerged with more traditional names, the symphony as Symphony No. 4 (in 1851), and the *Phantasie* as the first movement of the A Minor Concerto (in 1845). In order to understand just what the name fantasy suggests, we will then look briefly at a few earlier examples in the genre, including Schumann's own *Fantasie* for Piano Solo, Op. 17. Thereafter, a discussion of the *Phantasie* for Piano and Orchestra will take up, in order, its special form; the construction of its passagework; the role of the cadenza; and the relationship of tutti and solo.

   As I have shown earlier, the *Phantasie* is an unprecedented realization of the idea of compressing all movements of an entire concerto into a single sonata movement.[6] Although the basic model for this realization is the virtuoso concerto, its most notable features—motivic cohesiveness, persistent lyricism, and balance of orchestra and solo—contradict both that model and the expectation of heightened virtuosity common to the fantasy genre by mid-century. They suggest instead a crossover into the more intimate world of chamber music, but we will see that, in its turn, chamber music of this time partakes of the concerto's more public world. Schumann's Piano Quintet, which was composed one year after the *Phantasie,* furnishes one example. The chapter will conclude with a brief look at three piano concertos by Liszt. Although unknown to Schumann when he composed his *Phantasie,* these were conceived near the same time and under many of the same artistic influences. Their vast stylistic difference from the *Phantasie* will highlight how much Schumann goes against the grain of the work's generic title by composing, to paraphrase his words describing his incomplete *Concertsatz* in D Minor, a concerto "not for the virtuoso."[7]

* * *

The year 1841 has been called Schumann's year of the symphony. He completed the First Symphony, Op. 38, the Overture, Scherzo and Finale, Op. 52, the *Phantasie* for Piano and Orchestra, and the first version of the Symphony in D Minor, published in its revised version as the Fourth Symphony, Op. 120. Jon W. Finson has suggested that Schumann was stimulated to compose the First Symphony by his discovery in early 1839 of Schubert's Great C Major Symphony.[8] Mark Evan Bonds believes the D Minor Symphony looks instead to Beethoven's Fifth Symphony, as evidenced in two salient ways: the thematic transformations and returns across its movements; the segue of the third movement into the fourth with its so-called breakthrough from minor to major.[9] Nonetheless, Schumann's aesthetic approach to the symphony is very different from Beethoven's. Bonds calls it a deliberate "misreading" (in the sense used by Harold Bloom).[10]

> By extending the principle of thematic return beyond a single movement, and by alluding so forcefully to Beethoven's Fifth in the transition from the scherzo to the finale, Schumann establishes firm expectations that this finale, like its model, will provide a culmination of the whole. But the last movement ultimately takes on a surprisingly light character, one that falls more within the tradition of the *lieto fine* [happy ending]; the movement is full of sudden shifts and surprises, including a series of buffa-like strettos toward the end. The finale, in other words, begins by following the principles of one archetype, only to decamp for another.[11]

In Bonds's words, the teleology of Schumann's final movement is different from Beethoven's, with a looser presentation of material in the finale. For Schumann, more important than culmination and summation in the last movement is balance vis-à-vis the first movement, what Bonds calls "reaffirmation and re-enactment of the analogous process of breakthrough [from minor to major] in the first movement ... not so much a resolution of what has gone before as an affirmation and continuation." The parallels he sees between the first and last movements are, aside from common thematic ideas and the breakthrough to D major: the slow introduction to each; the trombone blasts at the beginning of each development; an initial sounding of the tonic in second inversion and avoidance of a return to the opening theme at the beginning of each recapitulation; in the conclusion of each movement (the recapitulation of the first movement, coda of the last movement) the introduction of a new theme. To his thinking, the finale represents both a continuation and a recomposition of the first movement.[12]

It is the very different aesthetic in Schumann's D Minor Symphony, as opposed specifically to Beethoven's Fifth, that I believe is important in thinking about the parallels between it and his *Phantasie* for Piano and Orchestra. Both when he was working on the Symphony in 1841, and later when he returned to revise it in 1851, Schumann referred to the work as a *Symphonische Phantasie, Phantasie,* or *Phantasie für Orchester.* John Daverio makes reference to this fact, then cites Carl Czerny's definition (from his 1848 publication *School of Practical Composition*) of the fantasy as a genre "in which several thematically related sections proceed without pause."[13] This, indeed, describes the Symphony both in its final version, which has been the basis of our discussion up to now, and in what we know of its original version.[14] It also describes the *Phantasie* for Piano and Orchestra. However, before we proceed to a discussion of the *Phantasie,* further examination of the fantasy genre is needed, particularly within Schumann's oeuvre.

* * *

Nicholas Marston terms Schubert's *Wandererfantasie* of 1822 the *locus classicus* of those fantasies from the early nineteenth century whose multiple sections represent the "typical succession of movements in a four-movement sonata," that is, Allegro, Adagio, Presto (scherzo and trio), and Allegro. Furthermore, he says, if the "nineteenth-century fantasy tended to take on the multi-movement character of the piano sonata, the reverse was also true: composers tried replacing multi-movement structures with something more continuous."[15] Beethoven, he continues, provides "the most distinguished examples of the piano sonata-as-fantasy," to begin with in his Opp. 27, Nos. 1 and 2, each of which was published as *Sonata quasi una Fantasia.* Marston opines, "the fantasy element in the title seems above all to reflect Beethoven's rejection of the conventional sonata-allegro model for the opening movement," and suggests that the title *"quasi una fantasia* is also an apt description for a number of the later sonatas," for example, Op. 101.[16]

Correspondingly, Marston shows that, up to the time of its publication in 1839, Schumann called his *Fantasie,* Op. 17 by turns a fantasy, a sonata, and other, suggestive names.[17] Highlights of Marston's run-down of the changing nomenclature are: (1) in June 1836 Schumann titled a one-movement *Fantasie* (later the first movement of Op. 17) *Ruines;* (2) with the addition of two further movements by December 1836 he called his entire work a "Sonata for Beethoven" and titled the individual movements *Ruinen, Trophäen, Palmen;* (3) later he referred to the work variously as *Fata Morgana, Phantasieen, Dichtungen,* and finally *Fantasie.* Despite his settling on this last designation, in its final form Schumann's Janus-faced opus embodies more characteristics of a sonata than a fantasy.

> Examined against [the] background of sonata-fantasies and fantasy-sonatas, the organization of the *Fantasie* is remarkably clear: three substantial movements, each closing firmly in its own tonic key. There is none of the open-endedness associated with the Beethoven works just discussed [Opp. 101; 102, No. 1; and 131]. ... Also significant is the fact that in contrast to Beethoven's tendency to shift the expected weighty sonata-allegro movement from first to last place in his 'fantasy' works, the weightiest movement in the *Fantasie* is undoubtedly the first. All these features suggest that the *Fantasie* is closer to the sonata than to the genre announced by its title.[18]

The very different aesthetic in Schumann's *Fantasie* as compared to Beethoven's sonatas, in particular his *Sonata quasi una Fantasia,* Op. 27, No. 2, is, I believe, a misreading of the type Bonds describes with respect to Schumann's D Minor Symphony as compared to Beethoven's Fifth. Thus, whereas one can hear a clear reference to the Op. 27, No. 2 first movement in Schumann's final movement, the ultimate goal of the *Fantasie* is entirely different from that of Beethoven's Sonata. Rather than begin with a languid, "moonlight" movement and end in a *Presto agitato* storm, the triumph of

Schumann's second-movement march dissipates into his own *Lento soste-nuto e sempre piano* "moonlight" finale. This is not the transcendence of the final, slow movements of Beethoven's late sonatas (Opp. 109 and 111), but a contented calm that quickly yanks the movement away from two brief rises to a joyous mood in dotted rhythm (bars 68–71, 119–22), a calm that pervades and concludes the movement.

Schumann's intentional misreading of Beethoven's *Sonata quasi una Fantasia* downplays one of the two hallmarks of the genre from the early nineteenth century on, to wit, virtuosity. According to Annette Richards, "Around 1800, with public (published) improvisation increasingly intent on being impressive in large halls rather than expressive in small chambers, the genre of free fantasia proper faded from the published repertory, to be replaced by the virtuoso pot-pourri." Reviewers of the time made a distinction between fantasies played in the privacy of one's own room where "abandon to accident and strange wandering might be natural," and those "designed for 'general entertainment' [which] must have harmonic coherence and a sense of direction, 'a natural underlying connection, despite apparent diversity on the surface'."[19] Although adopting the orderliness of this newer, more coherent fantasy, Schumann resisted the virtuosity that Peter Schleuning tells us came to be foremost in defining it.

> The opera fantasia gave rise to a special branch of the genre which was most demanding pianistically and which, together with a hypertrophic species of the sonata fantasia, formed a type that was described as virtuoso fantasia in accordance with the spectacular level of the technical demands it made on the instrument and the performer.[20]

Turning now from the solo fantasy to fantasy-concertos, we note that the one we have already examined, Moscheles's *Concerto fantastique,* follows the new sonata-as-fantasy model. Like Schubert's *Wandererfantasie,* our *locus classicus* for this type, it has joined movements and recognizably transforms motives from its first sections in later sections. Only the rondo-finale is self-contained. The middle two movements are interludes, and the sonata form of the first movement is cut short near the beginning of the development. Schumann criticized these "four movements in different tempos joined together," because he felt, "even if it doesn't seem impossible to produce a pleasing whole with it, the aesthetic peril is too great compared with that which can be gained."[21] Although not called a fantasy, the three sections of Clara Wieck's concerto are also joined and related to each other through motivic transformation. As with Moscheles's Concerto, the sonata form of the first movement is cut short, in this case just before the beginning of the recapitulation. Schumann's private comment to Wieck was, "There are stellar ideas in the first movement—yet it did not impress me as complete."[22]

Those concertos with joined sections that Schumann did praise, by Mendelssohn, Taubert, and Lasekk, are made up in each case of three fully rounded movements. Yet, even though Schumann was surprised when he first heard this innovation in Mendelssohn's G Minor Concerto, he had something more radical in mind when he contemplated composing his own concerto with joined movements in 1836. "One would have to contrive," he wrote, "a genre which would consist of one large movement in a moderate tempo, in which the preliminary part would take the place of the first allegro, the *cantabile* part that of the adagio, and the brilliant close that of the rondo. Perhaps the idea, which, we confess, we would prefer to realize with a special composition of our own, will arouse interest."[23] We will examine, first, how Schumann followed this model of coherence for the fantasy concerto, just as he proposed it, then show how he subverted it by refusing to incorporate into his fantasy the usual virtuosic display.

* * *

Schumann's 1836 prescription calls for a "smaller concert piece in which virtuosos with one fell swoop can develop their presentation of an allegro, adagio and rondo." In 1840 he still had in mind a "piano concerto following its own form," then in 1841 he composed the *Phantasie* for Piano and Orchestra.[24] Before proceeding with a description of this piece we need to add the *caveat* that, although the first movement of Schumann's A Minor Piano Concerto takes as its basis what we can fairly safely assume was the solo piano part of the *Phantasie,* the music for the original *Phantasie* is no longer extant so no one knows exactly what it was like.

In his introduction to the facsimile edition of the Concerto, Bernhard R. Appel describes the composition and reception history of the *Phantasie.* After its first performance at a private rehearsal of the Leipzig Gewandhaus Orchestra on 13 August 1841 with Clara Schumann at the piano, Schumann revised the score at least twice, once immediately after the run through, then again prior to offering it to the publisher Whistling in January 1843. It was only thereafter, in July 1845, that the piano part of the *Phantasie* was copied by Carl Mehner, Schumann's Dresden copyist.[25] Schumann then used Mehner's manuscript as a working copy for the revisions that transformed the *Phantasie* into the first movement of the Concerto, and it is this autograph that is reproduced in the facsimile edition.

Mehner's procedure was to copy the piano part onto the two top staves of each page leaving twelve blank staves below it. On these Schumann added the orchestration, which is also cued into the piano part with small notes. The relationship of this orchestration to the original can only be guessed at. However, three major revisions by Schumann to Mehner's copy of the solo piano part, at the end of the exposition, in the final section of the development, and at the end of the cadenza, are suggestive as to just what the *Phantasie* was like.[26] Altogether, taking Mehner's copy as a starting point, I believe the differences between what we can surmise constituted the *Phantasie* and what is the first movement of the A Minor Concerto are not so great that Schumann's original ideas concerning the type of composition he wished to create in the *Phantasie* cannot be seen in the first movement of the Concerto. That Schumann himself held this view is suggested by his subtitle on the flyleaf of the autograph score of the Concerto, which calls the first movement *Allegro quasi Fantasia.*[27] Therefore, without any claim that we know precisely what constituted the *Phantasie* before its transformation into the first movement of the Concerto, we will take the latter to represent the *Phantasie.* Where this differs noticeably from Mehner's copy we will note this, in the appropriate context.

To return to the overall form of the *Phantasie* for Piano and Orchestra, Schumann's incorporation of an allegro, adagio, and rondo into one movement takes as its starting point a chief feature of the virtuoso concerto, the turn to an expressive theme in a remote key at the beginning of the solo development. His solo development begins with a closed section in A-flat major, *Andante espressivo,* six-four time (bar 156–85). This is the adagio "movement" of his plan, reached after the triumphant tutti in C major that closes the exposition suddenly quiets down and turns to C minor. The opening of the exposition of the *Phantasie* also follows the virtuoso model: a *forte* crash on the dominant note E, full orchestra and spread over four octaves, followed by handfuls of descending chords in the solo sound as if we have just come upon the scene at the moment of conclusion of the first tutti, of an orchestral introduction that, in fact, the *Phantasie* lacks.[28] As we have seen, Schumann never did complete the large opening tutti for his early concerto movement in F major; in the *Phantasie* he has simply done away with it, just as it would be eliminated in any solo performance of a virtuoso concerto without instrumental accompaniment.

The "allegro" section of Schumann's three-movements-in-one scheme is found in the exposition of the *Phantasie,* which begins *Allegro affettuoso,* in common time. It returns in the development, at *Allegro (Tempo I)* (bar 185), that is, just at the point where the slow section of the development closes onto the tonic and the *forte* fanfare from the opening bars of the movement returns. The "allegro" continues with the *Più animato, Passionato* (begins bar 205) that leads to the reprise, where the fanfare is not sounded. The "rondo" section of the *Phantasie* comes after the reprise and a written out cadenza. It introduces a new tempo and meter, *Allegro molto,* two-four time (bar 458).

In 1858, when Eduard Hanslick heard Clara Schumann play her husband's A Minor Concerto in Vienna, he called the succession of moderately fast, slow, and quick tempos in the first movement a "miniature representation of a complete concerto."[29] But most modern commentators have centered their attention on another aspect of Schumann's movement that, rather than direct attention to its mix of affective sections with their roots in the virtuoso concerto, instead downplays the differencesd among them, to wit, the movement's motivic unity.[30] The entire movement uses only two basic motives, shown in the table of motives given in Example 11.1. The first, motive **a** in the table, is a falling, filled-in third with a characteristic rhythm. It generates the main themes of the first ansecondgroups of the

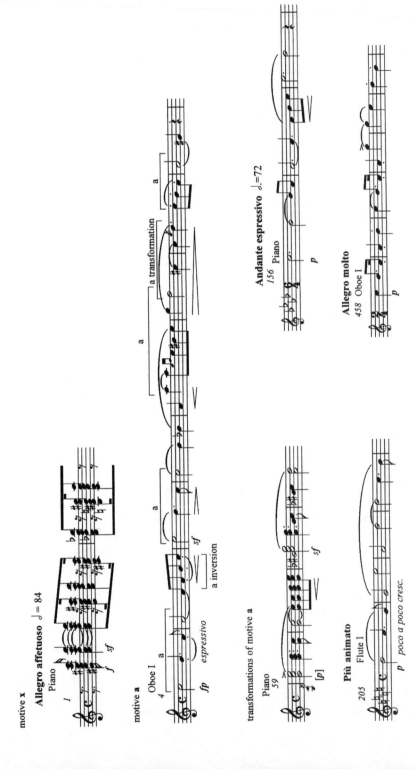

Example 11.1 Table of motives, Schumann, Concerto in A Minor, Op. 54, first movement (the *Phantasie*).

exposition and recapitulation, of the slow and quick parts of the development, and of the coda. The second motive, **b** in the table, is a free inversion of the first, a rising, filled-in third, again with a characteristic rhythm. It belongs primarily to the orchestra, and except for in the cadenza is played by the solo only in conjunction with the orchestra. Essentially, in the exposition and recapitulation motive **b** alternates with the primary thematic material generated by motive **a**,[31] which is to say, **b** is heard in various guises in the transition, and in the solo and tutti closes.[32] Both motives are prominent in the cadenza.

Despite the neatness of Schumann's motivic scheme, motivic or thematic unity across movements is not something he emphasized in his reviews of concertos. What he did emphasize, however, brings us to a second, and I believe most important reason that few modern analysts have remarked on the *Phantasie*'s representation of three movements in one, namely, its nearly unbroken lyric mood. We will examine this on two levels. The first, which will occupy us presently, has to do with the construction of the passagework at the foreground level. The second, which we will turn to later, relates to the overall structure of the movement, and will call back to mind Bonds's comments on the D Minor Symphony. Both are important in understanding how Schumann subverts expectations in a movement that takes its title from the splashiest of genres, and its defining gestures (the beginning of the exposition and beginning of the development) from the most well-worn clichés of the virtuoso concerto.

Generally, it can be said of the passagework of the *Phantasie* that it is constructed of two- or four-bar units. This is a characteristic we observed already in Schumann's F Major Concerto, and one we concluded was a hallmark of concertos of the post-Hummel generation. In most cases these small units bear highly individuated melodic profiles; in the closes of the expositions we examined we noted that, nonetheless, they do not stand alone as complete phrases but are instead a series of appendices to the thematic areas that precede them. We have seen that this type of construction of passagework can degenerate into a rather tedious formulation, usually starting off with a tonic-dominant vamp. However, we also have observed that Schumann's favorite concerto composers, Field, Mendelssohn, and Chopin, have adopted and adapted it, each in his own way, with considerable refinement: Field, through an easy segue of one idea into the next; Mendelssohn through his continual avoidance of decisive cadences; and Chopin through his unsettling harmonic clashes. Schumann's adaptation in the *Phantasie* is reminiscent of Field's Seventh Concerto in two ways: the small, one could even say singable range of his melodies, and the lack of differentiation in pacing of his passagework as compared to the thematic areas: the entire work moves in quarters and eighths, without the expected turn to sixteenths in the passagework areas. These two features bring to mind Clara Schumann's insistence "over and over again" many years later to her student Adelina de Lara "that her husband's music contained no 'passage-work' whatever."[33]

The lyric feel of Schumann's passagework is further heightened by a strategy that recalls both the classical concerto and those of Mendelssohn: the two- and four-bar units that are the basic building blocks of his passage-work areas are not, as in the virtuoso concerto, a series of appendices but are instead integral parts of full, independent phrases, in the case of the close, of a period with antecedent and consequent phrases. Yet, they retain a feel, characteristic of his passagework, of a forward rush. Examination of two different passages, the transition and close of the exposition, will show how careful manipulation of the harmonic rhythm and melodic line creates this seemingly anomalous effect.

A fanfare of three bars, characterized by the piano's full chords and dotted rhythms, serves as prefix to the opening theme, **A**. The theme is a straightforward parallel period in stately half notes, the antecedent (bars 4–11) of the winds being answered by the consequent (bars 12–19) of the solo, both playing *piano, espressivo*. The next segment, the transition in bars 20–67, is perhaps the most unusual in the entire exposition. Its two most striking features are that in spite of its length it forms one single period and, even more striking, that this single period represents both the entire transition and what is traditionally viewed as the entire first theme of the second group. As was the case with the Mendelssohn G Minor Concerto, Riemann's numbering method is too cumbersome, even in its revised form, to show the construction of this and indeed most other periods in this movement. Instead, taking a cue from Rothstein's method, a summary of the bass line between bars 20–67 is given in Example 11.2 to show its harmonic direction. There is, of course, some harmonic ornamentation of the basic chords, particularly of the F chord (IV of C, bars 42–58) and the G chord (bars 59–66) over which a variant form of the entire **A** theme (**A'**) is heard, but neither melody nor harmony allow a cadential resting point until bar 67.

Breathless melodic motion militates against cadential formations. The motive of the ascending third ("b1" from the table of motives in Example 11.1) keeps being repeated and transposed mostly in two-bar groups, tossed back and forth between tutti and solo. These melodic units are expanded somewhat after bar 35, even more after bar 48 and particularly after bar 52, where they congeal into a practically continuous line. This line leads to the contrasting stately half notes of theme **A'** in bars 59–67. Larger metric groupings, Rothstein's hyper-measures, mirror this expanding forward motion. In bars 20–35, 2 + 2 bar units are heard; these change into (2 + 2) + 2 units in bars 36–47; an even larger 4 + 4 + 3 unit in bars 48–58 prepares the entrance of theme **A'**. Thus, when theme **A'** enters in bars 59–67, it sounds like one single eight-bar unit, a large penultimate, resolving to the first bar of whatever comes next. The sense of a restless forward motion is further enhanced by the relation of basic harmonies and larger metric units.

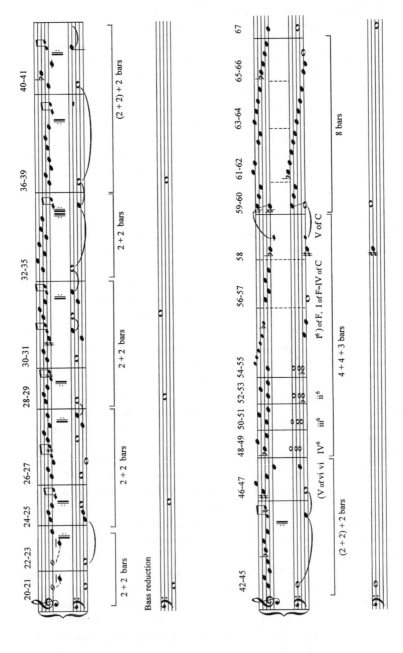

Example 11.2 Reduction of Schumann, Concerto in A Minor, Op. 54, first movement, bars 20-67 (transition).

Rather than coinciding exactly, the harmony keeps leapfrogging the hyper-measures. The E minor chord at bar 27 and the G chord at bar 31 anticipate the beginning of a metric unit by one bar, the C and F chords (bars 35 and 41), by one beat.

Schumann's close (bars 67–134), like all closes, functions in one sense as a suffix (Rothstein's term for appendix) to the first full cadence in the new key. But both its impact and its construction are different from all its predecessors. Rather than being a string of short appendices, the time-out-for-high-jinks in virtuoso concertos, or even the cadence-confirming expanded phrases of Mozart or Beethoven, it is a large and complete parallel period that summarizes all events hitherto exposed. It is a peroration rather than a mere appendix, in this sense a condensed repeat of the exposition. To facilitate discussion, once again a skeletal representation of the passage is given, in Example 11.3. The example gives the bass line, including (unlike the previous example) all the harmonic ornamentation, and, in addition, a stripped down version of the melodic lines in the upper staff. This upper staff also shows some of the inner-voice harmonies.

The overall harmonic direction of the first phrase, C (I)–e (iii)–G (V)–C (I)–G (V) (bars 67–94), is a reminder of the a (i)–C (III)–e (v)–G (VII of a = V of C)–C (I) progression of bars 20–36, except in this case, by ending with a half cadence, it requires an answering phrase. This is provided by the I–ii–V–I progression in bars 95–134. The antecedent-consequent relationship is provided by melodic forces. At the identical beginnings of the two phrases the clarinet plays the head motive of theme **A**, against which the solo presents in counterpoint a version of the ascending third, **b** motive of the transition. Thereafter, both phrases elaborate the latter motive in its various guises, the antecedent the ascending form only, the consequent also a retrograde in the long extension of its dominant. Solo and orchestra partake of the melodic presentation in equal measure, playing now together, now in staggered stages, now in counterpoint. The solo's accompanying arpeggios, rather than diluting the musical discourse as in so many earlier concertos, add to the sense of heightened density brought about by harmonic and melodic forces, and thereby to the sense of peroration created by those forces.

We turn now to the overall structure of Schumann's movement and its contribution to a nearly unbroken lyric mood. Most important is that he avoids the crashing tutti that customarily signals the beginning of the recapitulation. He does return to the crashing piano flourishes that open the movement, but at an earlier point, in the development, bars 185–204, right after the *Andante espressivo* section. This is a high point of excitement as the piano flourishes are severally repeated and shared with the orchestra. The excitement continues into the *Passionato* theme that beings in bar 205, but dies down from the dominant pedal of bar 251 on, *diminuendo* and *ritardando,* a fitting preparation for the woodwinds to play theme **A**, *piano, espressivo,* at the moment of recapitulation. As a result of the displacement

Example 11.3 Skeletal representation of Schumann, Concerto in A Minor, first movement, bars 67–134 (close).

of the flourishes from their expected place at the beginning of the recapitulation, the movement divides neatly into two halves, parallel in affect: the exposition and development are one half, the recapitulation, cadenza, and coda, the other. In the first half, a culminating point is reached with the triumphant entry of the orchestra at the end of the exposition. A lyric section (the *Andante espressivo* beginning of the development) follows, then a stretto (the *Allegro* flourishes, then *Passionato* theme of the development). Similarly, in the second half, the triumphant ending of the recapitulation dies down for the lyric beginning of the cadenza, *espressivo*. Afterward comes a stretto, the *Presto* coda.[34]

In each half of the movement, the stretto is of the *lieto fine* variety that Bonds describes in the D Minor Symphony. Furthermore, the emphasis Bonds places on balance between the first and last movements of the Symphony, on reaffirmation and reenactment of what has gone before, seems to apply equally to the two halves of the *Phantasie*. In both compositions the strategy is in keeping with Schumann's preference for the lyric, not just locally, but also on the larger scale of overall dramatic structure. It is not unusual that the climactic tutti at the end of the exposition should die down to introduce the piano's lyric solo, just as it does in nearly every concerto by Schumann's contemporaries. But Schumann's turn from a climactic tutti (with piano obbligato) at the end of the recapitulation to prepare an *espressivo* cadenza is surely unusual. It underscores Bonds's point about the importance of affirmation (as opposed to transcendence) of exactly what has gone before.

* * *

In 1839, when Schumann reviewed Moscheles's Seventh Concerto, a work he did not consider "mechanically difficult," he suggested that the old cadenza might successfully be revived.

> We offer especial thanks to recent writers of concertos, that they no longer bore us at the end with trills, and especially with octave leaps. The old cadenza, into which the old virtuosos packed whatever bravura was possible, is based on a much sounder principle, and could perhaps be used even now with success.[35]

In the *Phantasie,* Schumann follows his own advice: the close of the exposition and recapitulation build to triumphal endings without trills and octave leaps. But what does he mean when he writes of the "old virtuosos" and their custom of packing the cadenza with all possible brilliance? It is doubtful that he had in mind the generation of Mozart or even Beethoven. Mozart's cadenzas to his concertos were published in 1801,[36] but it is fairly safe to assume that any cadenzas to his concertos that Schumann knew were composed much later, by for example, Hummel, who published arrangements of Mozart's concertos, or by Mendelssohn, who performed them in Schumann's hearing. Beethoven's cadenzas to his concertos were first published in 1864.[37] Similarly, the cadenzas Schumann heard for these concertos were probably written by his own contemporaries, for example, Moscheles (b. 1794), who, despite what Schumann called his later "romantic" tendencies, was certainly one of the old virtuosos he had in mind. Although not published until 1854, Moscheles's cadenzas for Beethoven's concertos fit Schumann's characterization. They are filled with all possible brilliance. At the same time, unlike the stunning displays at the ends of closing sections of virtuoso concertos, but like cadenzas by Mozart or Beethoven, they restate and elaborate on themes and motives heard earlier in the movement. This may be what Schumann meant as concerns the "sounder principle" on which the old cadenza was based. It certainly is well exemplified in the one cadenza by Beethoven he would have known, the one not *ad libitum,* but written out at the end of the first movement of the *Emperor* preceded by the instructions *Non si fa una Cadenza ma s'attacca subito il seguente.*

Although Schumann's cadenza for the *Phantasie* takes as a starting point the "sounder principle" of the old cadenza in that it returns to and elaborates motives already heard, it also shows a different side of the performer than any cadenza by Hummel, Moscheles, or Beethoven. We have already noted that Schumann inserts the cadenza at a point that balances the lyric slow portion of the development. He composed the *Phantasie* for his wife to perform, and its lyric repose, where the piano is left to play alone, might be compared to the solo miniatures she added to her programs between larger, often concerted pieces intended to show her technical prowess. One striking example is the concert of 31 March 1841 at which Schumann's First Symphony, Op. 38 was given its premiere performance.[38] The program ran as shown in Figure 11.1. The big pieces Clara played are the two movements of the Chopin Concerto, her first number, and the Thalberg Variations, the last number on the program. Both are bravura works. One serves as a splashy introduction of the artist to her audience, the other provides an impressive conclusion to the entire show. By contrast, in between she played solo pieces, a piano four-hand duet, and accompaniment to some songs, all of which draw the audience into a more intimate type of music-making, and show to advantage what Schumann considered the most compelling aspect of her playing, a tone that "sinks into the heart and speaks to the soul."[39]

In the 1839 review cited earlier and titled "Das Clavier-Concert," Schumann also addresses the matter of balance between orchestra and solo in the piano concerto. He confidently awaited a genius who would show

> in a new, more brilliant way how the orchestra may be united with the piano so that the one dominating at the piano is able to develop the riches of his instrument and his art, while at the same time the orchestra may have more to do than merely looking on and may interweave the scene more ingeniously with its varied characters.[40]

Part I
Geistliches Stück

Concerto in F Minor, Adagio and Rondo	Chopin
Clara Schumann	
Aria	Gluck
Herr Schmidt	
Allegro	Robert Schumann
Lied ohne Worte	Mendelssohn
Klavierstück	Scarlatti
Clara Schumann	

Part II

Symphony	Robert Schumann
Introduzione and Allegro vivace	
Larghetto and Scherzo	
Allegro animato	
Duo for four hands	Mendelssohn
Mendelssohn	
Clara Schumann	
Three songs	
Die Löwenbraut (Chamisso)	Robert Schumann
Am Strand (Burns)	Clara Schumann
Widmung (Rückert)	Robert Schumann
Sophie Schloß	
Clara Schumann	
Duo Concertante for mellophone [a valved brass instrument] and cello	
Giulio Regondi	
Joseph Lidel	
Fantasy on Themes from Rossini's *Moses*	Thalberg
Clara Schumann	

Figure 11.1   Clara and Robert Schumann, program of 31 March 1841.

Schumann's prescription for a new combination of orchestra and solo is twofold: the pianist should be able "to develop the riches of his instrument and his art," and the orchestra should "have more to do than merely looking on." He, of course, is the genius who composed to fill this prescription. There is a fair amount of brilliant sounding passagework in the *Phantasie,* but it appears at all times in the subordinate role of accompaniment. It is never the protagonist, nor even the antagonist, in the musical discourse, but a mere texture-generating element, which is always subordinated to melodic movement produced now by the solo, now by the tutti. The tradition of using passagework areas to articulate particular subdivisions of the movement, typically the transition and the brilliant close, is all but gone. Instead, it is now solely the melodic motion (shared in chamber-music fashion by solo and tutti) and its underlying harmonic direction that propels the movement forward through its various sections, which are, in turn, as we have seen, determined by tradition only more or less.

Clara Schumann recognized the chamber-music quality of the *Phantasie* the first time she played her part with an orchestra in August 1841. Afterward she wrote in the marriage diary she shared with her husband, "The piano is interwoven with the orchestra in the most delicate manner—a person cannot think of one without the other."[41] Granted, there were problems. Schumann wrote Mendelssohn a month later, "The musicians played as though they had just come out of the woods (keep this to yourself), but only in the first run-through—the second was more lucid—it gave me great pleasure. You were right about the winds—at times the piano was only seen."[42] In their marriage diary Clara Schumann mentions specifically Robert's revisions to the wind parts.[43] Although Appel is surely right, we cannot know what the original instrumentation of the *Phantasie* was like, he does point out that what revisions do exist in the Mehner autograph "reveal a basic aim ... to thin the initially more sumptuous orchestration, to reduce the richness of sound ..."[44] The result, according to Wolfgang Boetticher, is a tipping of the balance to bring the piano, which at times was only to be seen in the *Phantasie,* more to the fore in the first movement of the Concerto.

Boetticher posits an original version of the *Phantasie* with a "less virtuosic piano part ... shorter cadenza and ... consequent chamber quality."[45] Two examples will make this point. The first is from the *Più animato* section of the development, bars 205–58. In Mehner's copy of the piano part these have the same phrase structure and harmonic outline as in the Concerto, but are in a lower register and do not, as in the Concerto, carry the melody. In an initial instrumentation, which presumably reflects that of the *Phantasie,* Schumann gives the melody to the first violins. Although one could argue the merits of this version, the fact is that the Concerto version gives more prominence to the piano by taking it from a role of only supplying underlying filigree accompaniment to one of prominence as a main carrier (with the flute) of the melody.[46]

The second example is the lengthening of the tutti at the end of the exposition from eight bars in Mehner's copy to twenty-two in the Concerto. Schumann crossed out the piano part that was originally to accompany the shorter tutti and did not orchestrate it in Mehner's copy. He wrote out the new tutti on a new bifolium, which was then inserted into the copyist's autograph. Thus, we cannot know what the orchestra played in the original tutti section, although it may be assumed that it had some thematic material to the piano's eight bars of tonic and dominant vamping. What is certain is that the new tutti is longer, louder, more definitive in its cadence, in sum, represents exactly what is traditionally expected in a second tutti. One could say that as Schumann tipped the balance in favor of the piano in the solo areas of the Concerto, he also strengthened this tutti, which more than any other feature defines the customary structure of the concerto. Consistent with this change he also strengthened the piano part leading up to his new tutti, adding the two bars of octave scales that we now hear in the Concerto (bars 132–33).

In taking the equality of forces suggestive of chamber music as a model for Schumann's movement we should not forget that, at a time when the piano came to dominate even the orchestra, it also took a dominating role in chamber music. Leon Plantinga points out that the two places where the piano held sway in the early nineteenth century, namely, the public world of the virtuoso and the domestic world of amateurs, come together in chamber music.

> While the accompanied keyboard sonata arose from a demand for easy music for amateurs, its offspring in the nineteenth century are all the species of chamber music with piano—sonatas for piano and one other instrument, piano trios, quartets, and the like. How persistently the patrimony of these pieces asserted itself can be gathered from a remark Schumann made in 1836 while reviewing some new piano trios by minor composers; the sort of ensemble needed to perform them, he said, is "a fiery player at the keyboard, and two understanding friends who accompany softly."[47]

Schumann seems to be describing not a piece of chamber music, but a concerto, possibly of the sort represented by the many arrangements of virtuoso concertos or embellished versions of Mozart's concertos for piano and small ensemble. In Chapter 5, we raised a question regarding the audience for arrangements of Mozart's concertos, and showed that, while they were intended for home performance, it was with a view to getting them into the public arena. Their piano parts were dazzling, and this falls in line with Plantinga's (and Schumann's) description of contemporaneous chamber music.

Within this same tradition is also Schumann's Piano Quintet, Op. 44, composed in 1842 and, like the *Phantasie* and Concerto, intended for his wife. In fact, of all the large pieces Schumann composed for piano, these were the two she played most often.[48] If Schumann's *Phantasie*, even in its version as the first movement of the A Minor Concerto, brings to mind chamber music, then by the same token the Quintet seems to take on elements of his concerto. Not, however, merely due to what Tovey calls the "preponderance of the pianoforte throughout," but because the piano takes on all the different roles associated with both the orchestra and the piano.[49] To take the first movement as an example, the piano supplies brilliant reinforcement in tutti-like areas, as seen in the opening chords (bars 1–9) and in their return at the close, *con fuoco* (bars 99–116). Often it takes the lead in playing the melody, but then turns to light accompaniment when the strings answer, *espressivo* (bars 27–50, 51–72, 73–98). Then in the development the piano comes into its own, taking on the stormy role we might expect from it in a virtuoso concerto. Earl Wild is convinced that Schumann heard the full sound of a string orchestra when he composed the Quintet, and has made an arrangement accordingly.[50] Certainly, in the concerted quality of the chamber music with piano of his day, including in his own quintet, Schumann had a ready model for the concerto as chamber music which he realized in the first movement of his A Minor Concerto.[51]

* * *

In conclusion, it is appropriate to make a few remarks about Liszt's three piano concertos, Nos. 1 and 2 in E-flat and A Major, and No. 3, in E-flat Major, Op. post. Although the E-flat Concerto was not published until 1857, the A Major until 1863, and the posthumous concerto was unknown until Jay Rosenblatt's edition of 1989, according to Rosenblatt, Liszt began composition on all three during the 1830s.[52] Schumann heard only the first of these, and that long after he began work on the *Phantasie.*[53]

The two concertos published in Liszt's lifetime have the character of fantasies: each strings together several sections, reminiscent in their order and type of the movements of a sonata. They also link these sections together through thematic transformation, which may be the reason they are closely associated with Schubert's *Wandererfantasie,* a piece Liszt had arranged for piano and orchestra by 1852. Characteristic features of the fantasy found in No. 1, the E-flat Concerto, are its division into four movements (*Allegro maestoso, Quasi adagio, Allegretto vivace,* and *Allegro marziale animato*) instead of the usual three in concertos; the running together of all four movements and lack of a closing cadence at the end of the second or third movement; the unusual form of the first movement (a sonata whose recapitulation is no more than a coda); and the return to and transformation, sometimes radically, of motives from its first two movements in its final two. More remarkable in its construction is the A Major Concerto. It resembles Liszt's B Minor Sonata, or what Dahlhaus, in his description of Liszt's *Après une lecture du Dante* or *Dante* Sonata (subtitled by Liszt *Fantasia quasi Sonata*), calls "at once a single sonata movement and a multimovement sonata cycle."[54] Similarly, the A Major Concerto is one large movement divided into six sections. These follow the usual divisions of a sonata-form movement in which are embedded the representative movements of a sonata cycle, as Figure 11.2 shows.

After the exposition, the "scherzo" and "slow movement" introduce new material, but thereafter all sections of the movement are based on previously heard themes.[55] It is the affect of these themes that is transformed. The clarinet's *dolce soave* motto which opens the Concerto, *Adagio sostenuto assai,* returns at the beginning of the recapitulation as a triple *forte* grand march for full orchestra and solo, a transformation that turns the recapitulation into an exciting finale.

Exposition (or first movement)
1. *Adagio sostenuto assai* (1st group)
   L'istesso tempo (2nd group)
2. *Allegro agitato assai* (close)

Development	
un poco più mosso (tutti then solo)	scherzo Movement
Tempo del Andante	transition
3. *Allegro moderato*	transition
in Tempo	slow movement
4. *Allegro deciso*	developmental

Recapitulation (or final movement)
5. *Marziale un poco meno Allegro*

Coda (final movement, continued)
6. *Allegro animato*

Figure 11.2 Diagram of Liszt, Piano Concerto in A Major.

The one concerto Liszt did not complete, the Op. post., remains in the form in which he left it in 1839. An overview of its form and main motives is given in Example 11.4. It shows that the main motives are exposed in the introduction. The backbone of the piece is a falling fourth motive heard in the very first bars, then as the opening motto of the somber theme of the first group in E-flat minor. On its return in the recapitulation this theme is transformed into a lively E-flat major. Similarly, the hymn-like song in the *Andante* section of the development will be turned into a gay dance in the recapitulation. One other important motive, the sextuplet turn, is heard primarily in transitional areas. The grand D major theme of the second group is heard only once.

Although Liszt's posthumous concerto is not as economical in its use of motives as Schumann's, the similarity of his formal design to that of the *Phantasie* is striking. Liszt's Concerto begins with a rather free introduction, then continues to present an exposition, a development beginning, as is traditional in the virtuoso concerto, with a slow section then continuing with a faster area, and a recapitulation that is really a stretto coda-like area. One main difference is the disjunction caused by the prominence of the piano in the cadenzas of the introduction and in those that separate each section of the piece except the final one, which is preceded instead by a general pause. Without going further into the huge differences between Liszt's and Schumann's styles, especially as concerns harmonic language, we could say that the concentration on virtuosity in this piece is much greater. In the Concerto, Op. post. the brilliant pianist is ever present, inserting cadenzas, reinforcing the tutti, playing obbligato, supplying filigree in the slow section.

Introduction
Andantino, with falling fourth motive

Recitativo del pianoforte (two different inserts),
a hint of the theme of the slow section of the
development

[**Allegro**], transition with characteristic sextuplet
turn; ending with a short solo

Exposition (QUASI FIRST MOVEMENT)
[**tempo primo**], first group in E-flat minor with
falling fourth motive

second group in D major, with a new tune; later
the sextuplet motive, and, with a move away
from D major to C-sharp major, the falling
fourth motive

solo cadenza

Development
[**Andante**] in G-flat major, ending with a short
    solo cadenza (QUASI SECOND MOVEMENT)

[**tempo primo**], development of falling fourth
    motive leading to a short solo cadenza

[**Allegro come primo**], retransition using the sextuplet
    and falling fourth motives, leading to a GP

Recapitulation (QUASI FINALE)
Allegro vivace, the falling fourth, now a lively $\frac{3}{8}$
    and in E-flat major; at bar 346, gay transformation
    of the slow theme from the development
    [*con bravura*], $\frac{2}{4}$ and [*Stretto*], $\frac{3}{8}$, rousing coda on
    the falling fourth motive

Example 11.4 Liszt, Concerto in E-flat Major, Op. post. Music reproduced by permission of Editio Musica Budapest, edition by Jay Rosenblatt.

Rosenblatt connects the "modest [orchestral] resources" of all three of Liszt's concertos from 1839 with his plans to perform them on tour.[56] This speaks to a definite need and ideal: the orchestra needs reinforcement from the piano, and the piano should be displayed. At the time he wrote the *Phantasie,* neither was Schumann's main purpose. This changed to some degree by the time the revised *Phantasie* became the first movement of the A Minor Concerto, but one is still left to wonder at the anomaly of Schumann's sally into the virtuosic world of the sonata-fantasy with a distinctly non-virtuosic composition.

By way of conclusion we might note that Liszt's type of concerto became the model for experiments among the French, in particular for Franck's Symphonic Variations, or Fauré's *Ballade.* While Schumann's *Phantasie* movement stems from interest in the same type of formal experimentation, the degree to which he masks his experiment means it is associated with works of the next generation or two that turn back to more traditional forms. Thus, whereas it is well known that Grieg consciously modeled the first movement of his Concerto in A Minor on the first movement of Schumann's Concerto, he certainly did not pick up on the more daring formal or stylistic constructions that underlie Schumann's work. Similarly, Jeremy Norris cites Schumann and Mendelssohn as principal influences on the music of Anton Rubinstein, whose five concertos he characterizes as "more conventional in design" than Liszt's.[57]

12

Concertstücke

After 1839, Schumann wrote two more installments for his piano concerto series. The first, run on 31 January 1840, reviewed Hummel's F Major Concerto, Op. post. (which we discussed in Chapter 6), Bennett's Concerto No. 4 in F Minor, Op. 19, and Mendelssohn's *Serenade und Allegro giojoso,* Op. 43. This is a small group of works by composers Schumann genuinely admired and wished to promote. Two years later, in July 1843, his last article in the series shows him weary of the whole business. It headlines reviews of Ferdinand Kufferath, *Capriccio,* Op. 1; Bennett, Caprice, Op. 22; and Aloys Schmitt, *Rondeau brilliant,* Op. 101; then lumps together reviews of Jacques (or Jacob) Rosenhain, Concertino, Op. 30; Czerny, Concertino, Op. 650; Charles (or Carl) Mayer, Concerto, Op. 70; and Jacques Schmitt, Concerto, Op. 300. Schumann begins his survey of this last group with a disheartening summary, which he repeats at the end.

> We come now to the true concertos, or concertinos, which have recently appeared, and would like to begin with a deep sigh over the barrenness which manifests itself in this area of piano music, over the little meaning of the little that has appeared, quantitatively as well as qualitatively, the situation is truly sad in this genre. ...
>
> This, then, is the yield that we have reaped from this area of music, the most important things that have been published in a period of over three years. Did we say too much above, [when we said] that the situation in this genre is dismal?[1]

Although Schumann's reviews of one-movement works by Kufferath, Bennett and Aloys Schmitt are more positive, they also say these works bring nothing new to the genre. Kufferath's *Capriccio* "does not reveal a new aspect of art," Bennett, of late "always says the same thing," and Schmitt's *Rondeau* is "10–15 years" out of date. Schumann's judgment that all seven works he reviewed in July 1843 are lacking in either quality or originality may be a backhanded way of elevating his own, spurned experiment: his *Phantasie* was rehearsed by the Gewandhaus Orchestra in August 1841, but never publicly performed. By July 1843 he had offered it to three different publishers (and in the course of 1843 was to offer it to two more) without success.[2]

This chapter will survey concerted works Schumann reviewed in 1840 and 1843, and will discuss his addition of a middle movement and finale to his revised one-movement *Phantasie* in June and July 1845. The end product is a three-movement work, his Piano Concerto in A Minor, Op. 54. Yet, even after completing it Schumann had not composed a full three-movement concerto, but rather two shorter pieces for piano and orchestra, a concertino (the first movement) and an introduction and allegro (the middle and final movements). Critics have long marveled at the unity of the two halves whose origins are separated by four years, but they may have protested too much, for in some ways the two parts of the Concerto remain two separate entities, just as they were composed.

The works we shall survey include two concertos, by Mayer and Jacques Schmitt, and two concertinos, by Rosenhain and Czerny. The remainder, by Mendelssohn, Kufferath, Bennett, and Aloys Schmitt, are one-movement works, rondos with introductions or caprices. We shall discuss the works by Rosenhain, Mayer, Czerny, and Aloys Schmitt, all reviewed in 1843, summarily. They retain the old virtuosic style, in their highly decorated melodies, their flashy but hackneyed passagework, and in the contrast, heightened by histrionic expression and tempo markings, between the two. This is a style that Schumann tolerated to a degree in less ambitious pieces for piano solo, but that he was unwilling to accept in the grand style he demanded of works for piano and orchestra. His negative views of these pieces will form a background for examination of those he promoted, both in 1840 and 1843.

Schumann's judgment of old-style works, with the exception of Jacques Schmitt's Concerto, is withering. That a composer who said he could not write a concerto for the virtuoso condemns excessive bravura and hypersentimentality in the genre is clear enough. But Schumann also wrote that the virtuoso must make a living.[3] Once our summary of his reviews of works by Rosenhain, Mayer, Czerny, and Aloys Schmitt shows again that he is not interested in excessively long and mundane passagework filler, the question remains, what exactly gives the virtuoso enough to make his living and satisfies Schumann's aesthetic sense? The answer will lie in examining those works he had better words for but reservations about, by Kufferath and Bennett, and comparing them to two works he genuinely admired, the *Capriccio brillant*, Op. 22, and *Serenade und Allegro giojoso*, Op. 43, by Mendelssohn, who set a standard for the two younger composers. Our examination will center on the brilliant closes found in both the sonata-form and rondo-design pieces, as these are often the locus of the "mechanical and bravura fingerwork" Schumann complains about.[4] We shall then see how in his own rondo finale Schumann follows procedures familiar from the works of Mendelssohn and his young followers: he retains the traditional brilliant close while at the same time changing it in ways that satisfy his aesthetic requirements.

Before proceeding, I would like to emphasize that in 1843, when he wrote the last of his essays about the piano concerto, Schumann kept to the same standards for the genre that he set forth in his essays from 1836 to 1839. These are clearly laid out in his review of the one work among those under consideration in this chapter for which I have not been able to locate a score, Jacques Schmitt's Concerto, Op. 300. Schumann's review of this work in what he calls "the large three-movement form" emphasizes the very qualities we know he values: adherence to the old model; clarity of form; flow from idea to idea; melodic invention; organic relationship between the tutti and solo parts. However, even though it follows these standards, Schmitt's Concerto comes across in Schumann's review as no more than average.

> There remains yet one concerto to discuss, by Jacques Schmitt ... which is neither new nor significant in invention, yet everywhere betrays the worthy man of ability and talent. It displays in particular a worthy form, the large three-movement one such as we would regret were it to disappear entirely from among concert music, on which account, notwithstanding, some ingenious novelties should not be championed any the less as [another] avenue. ... Besides clarity, and flow of the movement, the compositions of Jacques Schmitt are further distinguished by a distinctive euphony, and ... melodic invention. ... if the composition does not elevate the genre onto a higher plane, then it also does not add to its superfluity. ... We deem the first movement of the most value on account of the tuttis, which emerge not as a patchwork, but rather as organically growing out of the whole.[5]

Schumann values a concerto in the tried and true form, but still hopes for some "ingenious novelties." This hope was realized in his own concerto, which appeared two years later with its newly minted second part whose rondo finale both follows the old form and refashions it.

* * *

The Concertino, Op. 30, by Jacques Rosenhain, and Concerto, Op. 70, by Carl Mayer have different names, but the same form, whereby the three movements are run together, with the first movement ending after the second tutti. We first saw this type form in Herz's C Minor Concerto. It is also comparable to Clara Wieck's Concerto, which, before its publication, was sometimes billed as a concertino. Although Schumann wrote Clara asking if she thought the first movement of her concerto incomplete, he did not mention the form of Herz's Concerto in his review of that work, nor does he say anything about the form of Rosenhain's Concertino or Mayer's Concerto.

Rosenhain (1813–94) was a young composer with whom Schumann corresponded in spring 1836 when, on the strength of a Piano Trio, Op. 2, he invited him to be the Frankfurt correspondent for the *Neue Zeitschrift*.[6] In a review he called Rosenhain's Trio a masterly study after the best masters, but also warned that "the later works of this richly talented young man, insofar as they have come to our attention, hardly stand comparison to this excellent beginning."[7] He continued to chide Rosenhain in later reviews that he should be composing sonatas, concertos, and so on, that "his versatile talent, if it is to produce more dignified things, need only be advised to be more watchful over an inherent levity."[8] After Rosenhain moved to Paris, in 1837, Schumann blamed the city's influence for his failure to produce more serious music.[9]

Rosenhain played a concert in Leipzig on 26 September 1839. Two weeks later, in a review of his Twelve Characteristic Etudes, Op. 17, Schumann remembered the composer's "lively performance." With respect to his compositions, though, he still complained about Rosenhain's failure to realize his full potential, and the insidious influence of Paris.[10] Some two years later, in April 1841, Schumann received Rosenhain's Twenty-four Etudes, Op. 20, with downright hostility. "There is nothing really agreeable in the entire work."[11] By the time he reviewed Rosenhain's Concertino, Op. 30, in 1843, he relegated his productions to nonmusic.

> A Concertino by J. Rosenhain ... strengthens us in the suspicion which we already began to have some time ago, that this not untalented composer relaxes his efforts ever more, and with the years will give himself over to the unsalvageable lot of a *routinier*. ... we have nothing to say about this Concertino, except that it is a speculative work, couched in that brilliant tinsel which has an effect on the birthdays of fathers of untalented daughters. Of music there can be no question.[12]

Without going into much detail, we can say that despite its abbreviated form, the piece has all the hallmarks of the Parisian style that Schumann saw as a corrupting influence. The solo's themes are highly ornamented: in the first movement, the second melody of the second group begins *espressivo* then works its way through various changes in expression, dynamics and tempo over a range of some three octaves to a nine-bar cadenza; in the second movement, a barcarole melody begins simply but is soon extravagantly embellished. The passagework is ordinary: in the first movement, the close of the exposition begins with the usual vamp, moves rather quickly to a section over the flat-sixth degree, then, *Doppio Movimento,* the final gestures (*staccato* chords, rising scales, then trills) over the six-four chord; in the last movement, a coda is the work's crowning example of "brilliant tinsel." The orchestra has little to do.

Schumann knew Carl Mayer's works from his youth and wrote favorably of them in the *Neue Zeitschrift* as early as 1835.[13] Positive reviews, with some reservations, continued until May 1841, when, in a review of his Etudes, Op. 55, Schumann expressed the fear that the composer has "become shallow," yet hoped he still had better things in store.[14] Mayer was in Leipzig on 1 September 1841, the day the Schumanns' first child was born, hence they did not see him.[15] He brought with him a letter of introduction from Cipriano Romberg, a friend of Schumann from Leipzig who had since moved to St. Petersburg, where Mayer also resided. Romberg recommends in particular Mayer's latest concerto ("in form, a concertino") which, he writes, "is brilliant and ... in the latest taste, and [in which] the orchestra plays an important role, if not a main role."[16] The recommendation did not result in a favorable review of the Concerto two years later.

> Concerning a concerto by Carl Mayer ... we expected, likewise, more. It contains almost nothing but passagework; perhaps many praiseworthy things are to be found in the orchestral score, which did not come into our hands—the piano part, as we said, gave us little pleasure. If here and there favorable signs promising a more beautiful future of art rise up to the musical heavens, for that very reason works like this concerto, where everything repeatedly runs on to the mechanical and to bravura finger-work, put us doubly out of sorts.[17]

We can back up Schumann's judgment that Mayer's Concerto "contains almost nothing but passagework," that "everything repeatedly runs on to the mechanical and to bravura fingerwork." After a long tutti introduction, the majority of the solo part of the short first movement is filled with it, the close alone running sixty-one of its 151 bars. Similarly, much of the short rondo (327 bars in two-four time; the entire form is **ABA'coda**) is taken up by the brilliant passagework at the close of the episode or **B** (seventy-three bars), and close of **A'** plus the coda (eighty-four bars). Large portions of the *Larghetto* slow movement are filled with an inner-voice tremolo in thirty-second-note triplets that drags out the half and quarter notes of the upper-voice melody.[18]

Schumann's weariness with virtuosic showpieces reaches its height (or depth) with his review of Czerny's Concertino.

> About the Concertino of C. Czerny ... we likewise don't know what to say. Whoever writes thus, he can easily continue on up to Opus 1000."[19]

In fact, before his death in 1857 Czerny reached only Op. 861. The manner in which he writes for the Concertino is, to this listener, little distinguishable from his scale and arpeggio exercises which are still given to young pianists.

Like Schumann, we, too, can be brief with our description of the Concertino. It consists of only two movements. First is a slow introduction, *Adagio non troppo,* a theme and its two variants leading to a solo cadenza. The wide range of the ornaments (mostly scale and arpeggio figures), changing dynamics and expression marks, and sudden and far-flung key changes may be a try at what Schumann called (in his review of Kalkbrenner's Fourth Concerto) "romantic audacity," but the result is the purely maudlin. The second movement, an interminably long rondo, is filled with the brilliant dazzle of hackneyed figuration, square rhythms, and long areas with wide deviations in key and no discernible melody, at least in the solo part. From the solo part alone, it appears the orchestra has little to do.

We have already discussed (in Chapter 9) the enthusiastic review of Aloys Schmitt's Concerto in E-flat Major, Op. 76, which appeared in one of the first numbers of the *Neue Zeitschrift*. We suggested that at that time Schumann may have had no quarrel with the reviewer "K"'s high praise of a very conservative work. However, eight years later, in his own review of Schmitt's *Rondeau brillant,* Op. 101, Schumann, while still respectful of the school of Hummel and Field, tells us that we now have other notions about music.

> The composer is well enough known through his collateral relationship to the Hummelian school, which this Rondo, too, betrays most clearly. What we find in most of the output of that school, correctness, clarity and compositional flow, we also find here. Beyond that, the author himself explains the Field-like tang of the Rondo by the title, "Souvenir à John Field," he has given his work. One thing has again become very clear to us on account of his work: how demands and times have changed in the last 10–15 years. The Rondo, had it been published earlier, would have caused a splash; now, we fear, it will not succeed. ... Beethoven, the poor ridiculed Beethoven, yes it was indeed he, the one who was to be feared, who brought us around to other notions about music. However, even good, plain prose should be permitted, if out of ignorance it is not somehow compared to the poetry of an immortal like Beethoven.[20]

Schumann had already formulated his double view of Schmitt—on the one hand, a solid composer, on the other, a panderer to virtuosity—during a visit he paid to Leipzig in 1841. "Yesterday," he wrote in his marriage diary, "A. Schmitt from Frankfurt, a fatiguing man who thinks too much, visited me—half Philistine, half (true) artist. He was very polite and said many friendly things."[21]

In the *Rondeau brillant,* after a short tutti introduction, the solo plays the *alla polacca* rondo theme. Polonaise rhythms continue through the transition to the first episode, and in the theme of the episode. The middle episode, a nocturne in minor, has the Field-like character mentioned by Schumann. A return to the rondo refrain is cut short to make way for a *Presto* coda, which leaves the polonaise rhythms behind until the final few tutti bars. Although we can simply say categorically that there is little in this piece to appeal to Schumann (or ourselves), we do need to say something of Schumann's basis for his claim, that the work does not measure up to Beethoven who has taught us different standards in the last ten to fifteen years, specifically with respect to the concerto. A workaday showpiece, of which Hummel could turn out fine specimens, and his "collateral relatives," for example, Jacques and Aloys Schmitt, acceptable ones, just will not do for the genre, as it may have done some years earlier. For Schumann "good plain prose" is not enough for the modern concerto. The poetry he demands is our next subject, specifically, how to combine it with the virtuosity a short concerted movement calls for.

* * *

The four short concerted works in the Parisian style that Schumann reviewed in 1843 set a negative standard. His positive standard was Mendelssohn. Mendelssohn's achievements loom even over works Schumann judges favorably, by the younger composers Bennett (1816–75) and Kufferath (1818–96). They stand as models and examples for his continued insistence that everything smacking of the bravura be done away with, and his belief that this can be accomplished without sacrificing the viability of the genre. Schumann specifically mentions the influence of Mendelssohn in his review of Kufferath's *Capriccio,* and the work bears close comparison with Mendelssohn's *Capriccio brillant.* We shall look at these two works, then turn to Bennett's *Caprice* and Mendelssohn's *Serenade und Allegro giojoso.*

Schumann never reviewed in print Mendelssohn's *Capriccio brillant* in B Minor, Op. 22, which was composed in 1832, but he heard it numerous times, first of all because it was a mainstay of Clara Wieck's repertory. She performed it on 9 November 1835 in Leipzig, and up through 1841, sixteen more times in thirteen cities.[22] Second, aside from Clara's performances, Mendelssohn's *Capriccio* was a well-known and respected work, a very different view than nowadays.[23] Schumann's announcement of her 9 November concert tells us, "She will play ... a *Capriccio brillant* with orchestra by F. Mendelssohn-Bartholdy, rich in artistic content and original ideas ..."[24]

The *Capriccio brillant* divides into two sections, an *Andante* then *Allegro con fuoco.* The *Andante,* in B major, is not a closed movement, but an introduction that spins out variants of the opening, lyric theme (Example 12.1a) and leads to the *Allegro con fuoco.* The *Allegro con fuoco,* in B minor, is in sonata form, with its two main themes in a characteristic style associated with final movements (Examples 12.1b and d). Particular features of the movement are the introduction of a new motive that figures prominently in the transition (Example 12.1c), and in the development the incorporation of motives from both the main theme and theme of the second group.

For our purposes in thinking about how, in Schumann's view, Mendelssohn's work set a standard for the young Kufferath, three further points are important. First, the high level of orchestral participation in the *Allegro con fuoco.* In the exposition, for example, although the solo plays the main theme, the transition involves tutti and solo exchanges, then an obbligato part for the orchestra. The second-group theme, a march in D major, is played first by the tutti, then continues with tutti and solo exchanges. The close includes an obbligato orchestra part.

Second, the march theme of the second group continues seamlessly into the close, and similarly, the development moves without break into the recapitulation. The seamless move from march theme to close comes about in

a. introduction theme

b. exposition, first group, main theme

c. exposition, first group, transition motive

d. exposition, second group, march theme

Example 12.1   Mendelssohn, *Capriccio brillant*, Op. 22.

two ways: (1) because the last bars leading to the close, playing on the characteristic alternation between *fortissimo* and *piano* in the march theme, are
piano, and the close continues at this dynamic; (2) because an obbligato flute
part, begun before the close, continues with the pick-up to the close (bar 137)
and beyond, reinforcing a solo line buried among sixteenth notes. As for the
lack of break between the development and recapitulation, solo passagework,
con fuoco and *fortissimo,* drives up to the recapitulation with no announcement by the tutti of an arrival, but instead a solo statement of the opening
four bars of the first theme over a dominant pedal (bars 206–09).

Third, the mode switches from major to minor in the second group of
the recapitulation. The march begins in B major (bar 232), but is played by
the solo, *piano,* not, as in the exposition, by the tutti, *fortissimo.* A turn to the
minor mode holds through a close that includes new music, a *con fuoco*
coda that refers to motives from the main theme, the transition, and the
march, and a final short tutti with a rousing reminiscence of the march.

Schumann heard Kufferath play his *Capriccio,* Op. 1 on 5 November
1840 at a Gewandhaus subscription concert. His review of the concert
appeared just over a week later.

> [Kufferath's] compositions bear witness to decided talent and a noble
> direction, on which, whether known to him or not, a master living near us

appears to have had an influence. … In the *Capriccio* we liked the introduction especially; the Allegro had an unfortunate form; it lacked a middle part, which, like the transposition of the first brilliant passagework to
the minor mode at the end of the movement, is not and seldom can be
effective. The orchestration was skillful, sometimes refined, but sometimes too much and too contrived.[25]

A review of the score of Kufferath's *Capriccio* bore the honor of heading
Schumann's 1843 article on concertos and concertinos.

The *Capriccio* does not reveal a new aspect of art, but rather a respectable
effort. … Specifically what the *Capriccio* lacks is a charming, melodic
character, that sonorous magic as it comes pouring out to us from the serious endeavors of masters. Perhaps the keys, D-flat major and C-sharp
minor, contribute to the oppressive, gloomy effect; as it is the orchestra
works in these and similar keys unwillingly and with difficulty, as Jean
Paul would say, as if with tin gloves.[26]

If we consider that Schumann is clear about his liking the piece and its
composer it may seem strange, although quite in keeping with his customary reserve when first dealing with a promising new talent, that he addresses
many fewer positive specifics than negative. He singles out only the
Andante introduction for outright praise. The main theme is a possible reason. It seems to have that "charming melodic character" he misses in the
rest of the piece (see Example 12.2). It also may have signaled to him the
"noble direction" he expected the work to take. In this regard, we may
assume that the Mendelssohnian influence counted in Kufferath's favor. On
the surface, this is manifest in the form of the *Capriccio:* like Mendelssohn's *Capriccio brillant* it begins with a slow introduction leading,
after a long dominant preparation, to a sonata form movement. Each piece
also has a high amount of orchestral participation.

Comparison to Mendelssohn on a deeper level requires more analytical
detail. Specifically, in the *Capriccio brillant* we discussed how Mendelssohn created a seamless move from the march theme to the close, and,
in a different place in his movement, Kufferath appears to emulate this
construction. His thirty-three-bar *con fuoco* transition, a somewhat forcibly
prolonged modulation from the tonic C-sharp minor to E major, which is
interrupted by some exaggerated gestures and loud tutti interjections, eventually leads to V of E major, where without pause the first theme of the

Example 12.2 Kufferath, *Capriccio* in C-sharp Minor, Op. 1, beginning of the
main theme of the introduction.

second group begins (in bar 201). The theme cadences on an A major chord after fourteen bars, and is then answered by a phrase which is long drawn out by passagework and frequent references to the opening motive of the theme, before it finally closes in the E major tonic onto the *brillante* of bar 249. Thus, the entire thematic area of the second group appears to serve as a continuation of the transition. The reader may catch a glimpse of this in Example 12.3, the end of the transition and beginning of the second group.

It is also in the transition and second-group theme that we can find the grounds for two of Schumann's specific objections. The first, the "too con-trived" orchestration, may well be understood as referring to the kind of interruptions seen in bars 193–95 of the example. The other, the lack of a "charming melodic character" is a subtler matter. In order to appreciate Schumann's comment one may compare the entire passage of Kufferath's *Capriccio* just described with the same type passages he emulates in Men-delssohn. The small individual melodic units that are heard as singable, additive, yet inextricably connected links in Mendelssohn's long gesture, beginning with the march and continuing through the close, seem to be missing in Kufferath's transition and second theme. In fact, even though the beginning of the Kufferath's second theme in bars 201–16 may be deemed to satisfy Schumann's desire for a "charming melodic character," the contin-uation of this theme (not shown in the example), with its passagework and

Example 12.3 Kufferath, *Capriccio* in C-sharp Minor, exposition, end of the tran-sition and beginning of the second group.

many repeats of the opening motive, seems but a series of continual beginnings, so much so that in the end the impression is not that Kufferath draws the transition into the melodic area, but more the opposite: that transition and thematic area together are merely a grand preparation for the final *brillante* close.

Schumann voices two more specific objections to the *Capriccio,* both of them in the concert review, before he saw the score. One is the lack of a middle part, that is, of a development section. The other, the ineffectiveness of the turn to the minor mode at the end. The first is more an illusion than fact, stemming from Kufferath's endeavors to play down the customary lines of demarcation, actually a Mendelssohnian trait. What happens is that in the close of the exposition the piano drops out at the dominant chord and the tutti completes the close with references to the melody of the second group. The solo then picks up this theme and develops it before moving on to a twelve-bar development of the main theme, which leads directly, without break or change of texture, to the recapitulation of the main theme in C-sharp minor (at bar 335). Over this development a flute solo produces a countermelody based on the second theme, which continues beyond the point of the solo's recapitulation, effectively covering up a milestone that others usually emphasize. When Schumann speaks in his concert review of the adeptness and delicacy of the orchestration, he may well have had this passage in mind as one example. It is worth noting that in his review of the score he does not repeat his objections to any lack of a development.

Schumann's other objection, the turn to minor at the end of the piece, is a matter of opinion. In my view, it has a fantastic, fanciful quality, quite fitting in a caprice. In his review of the score, Schumann transmutes this criticism when he merely objects to the "oppressive, gloomy effect" of the keys of D-flat major and C-sharp minor.

To return to the comparison with the Mendelssohn, similarities with the Kufferath are: a slow introduction and long dominant preparation before the solo plays the first theme of the *Allegro* section; a comparatively high level of orchestral participation; references to the themes of both the first and second groups in the development; lack of a tutti announcing the recapitulation; and a turn to the minor mode for the close of the recapitulation. Schumann's point, then, is well taken, that the influence of Mendelssohn is "clearly manifest" in Kufferath's composition. The question remains why does he like one and not the other? Aside from the pat answer that Mendelssohn was a more skilled composer than Kufferath, and certainly one with a more fertile imagination, I think we need to take into consideration the standards Schumann repeatedly set forth for concerted works. Where the Mendelssohn differs from the Kufferath is in the persistent lyric quality of the introduction and resulting clear difference in feel between the introduction and start of the *Allegro con fuoco* section; in the lyric quality pervading the transition; and in the continuation of the cadence of the second-group march theme seamlessly into the beginning of the close of the exposition. This last point, I think, is the most important, for it gives the sense that the brilliant close is a mere afterthought in the exposition, rather than, as in Kufferath, its goal.

Other differences between the two *capriccio*s, are Mendelssohn's longer development, his greater imagination in reconceiving the recapitulation, and longer coda. Mendelssohn's final brilliant close and coda return his piece to the minor mode, and we might wonder why in this case Schumann seemingly had no quarrel with the strategy. Perhaps the emphatic turn away from the quiet march of the recapitulation, long coda, and forceful statement of the march theme by the orchestra at the end give some sense of triumph as opposed to Kufferath's more atmospheric ending. What we do know is that none of Schumann's completed pieces for piano and orchestra end in the minor mode. Like the Mendelssohn, and unlike the Kufferath, all have discursive codas.

* * *

It seems a mystery that the best piece, and by the composer he knew best, Sterndale Bennett, is given little praise in Schumann's 1843 review. The answer perhaps lies again in his keeping to the forefront his ideal composer in the genre, Mendelssohn. We shall look at Bennett's Caprice, then turn to Mendelssohn's *Serenade und Allegro giojoso*. When Schumann wrote his review of the Caprice in 1843, he said that he began to fear that "of late [Bennett] always says the same thing," that his compositions in the genre were becoming mannered. A brief look at Bennett's Fourth Concerto, which Schumann reviewed in 1840, will establish the basis for this observation, before we turn to its application to the Caprice.[27]

During his second, long sojourn in Leipzig, from 15 October 1838 to 2 March 1839, Bennett introduced two new works for piano and orchestra, his Fourth Concerto in F Minor, Op. 19, on 17 January 1839, and a Caprice for Piano and Orchestra, Op. 22, on 21 February 1839. During this time Schumann was in Vienna, but he received reports from Bennett about both works.[28] A year later Schumann's review of the published concerto appeared in the *Neue Zeitschrift*.

> Unfortunately I have not heard the Concerto by Bennett played by himself, and certainly not with orchestra. ... Perhaps Bennett should have indicated the orchestral parts even more often, or else he could have made them playable by the pianist. ... The form of the Concerto is the old three-movement one, the key F minor; the character tends to the serious, but not gloomy. A cheerful barcarole connects the first movement with the last; it especially, so I heard, won hearts to the Concerto when it was played here in Leipzig. ... The other movements offer nothing new in their form, or, better said, they do not seek novelty in startling effects, but rather in lack of pretense. Thus, at the end of the solo, where in other concertos trills are heaped on trills, Bennett interrupts the trill and lets it softly fade away, as if to prevent any applause. So it is that nothing in the

entire concerto is calculated for bravura display and applause. ... Neither does one find in it any new mechanical combinations or finger exercises, unless, in every case, they are important to the presentation, unless they demand more musical than manual skill, here for the purpose of subordinating itself to, there to ruling over the orchestra.

One also finds beautiful melodies in abundance; the forms are charming and flow as always in Bennett's compositions. ...[29]

Like Bennett's Third Concerto, his Fourth follows the older form of the virtuoso concerto. Yet, in his review of the latter Schumann's emphasis is not on Bennett's customizing of this form to suit his own stylistic preferences but on its lack of anything new in form. True, the Fourth Concerto uses that form to different ends than the Parisian virtuosos. There is, for example, more interplay between solo and orchestra, which Schumann refers to obliquely when he suggests that Bennett should have given more indications of the orchestral parts in the piano score, and arranged them so that a pianist playing without orchestral accompaniment could take them over. Furthermore, virtuosic display is downplayed in favor of "beautiful melodies in abundance ... forms [that] are charming and flow."

Still, the virtuoso model remains evidently in place, the usual pattern of alternating thematic and brilliant episodic areas, with emphasis on the latter. The final trill of the exposition may be interrupted by a deceptive cadence that begins, *giocoso,* the bridge to the recapitulation, but the grand build preceding it remains. While the 18-bar bridge displaces a development, this does not change the basic layout, or at least Schumann does not call attention to it as anything novel. If Schumann says Bennett's form flows, nonetheless, it is more a tribute to the art with which he conceals the disjunction between thematic and passagework areas inherent in the design, in the thematic areas through his choice of melodies that incorporate little decoration, and in the passagework areas, through the infusion of motives derived from the, comparatively speaking, stripped-down melody. It is, as it were, a dressing up of the old virtuosic form in a style suitable to Bennett, but which already Schumann saw as mannered rather than as a new direction for the genre.

Bennett's Caprice was not published until 1841. During a third sojourn in Leipzig, he performed it on 17 January 1842. Though the occasion is noted by Schumann in his diary, he makes no comment on the composition or its performance.[30] A write-up of the concert in the *Neue Zeitschrift* by "Z" describes the composition in one sentence: "The Capriccio is a lovely flower bouquet, fresh and fragrant, graceful, fine and beautifully colored, and as concerns its inner worth, at the same time so modest."[31] Schumann's review of the score appeared the next year; what "Z" saw as modest he downgrades to "dainty" and "playful."

This Capriccio shares all the excellent qualities which we have had cause to praise many times already in the compositions of this most important of all living English composers. We begin to fear only one thing: Bennett seems to be giving himself over increasingly to a habit from which eventually he will no longer recover. Of late he always says the same thing, only in a different form; the more fully he has learned to master the latter, the more the essential power of invention seems to diminish in him. In order to give his power a new stimulus, he has to apply himself to large works, to the symphony, opera, etc.; he has to turn away from the dainty, the playful in order to have the power, the passion to find a language.[32]

Bennett's Caprice is a beautifully lyric piece. It begins with two long lyric statements by the solo (bars 1–22, 23–40), an unusual opening for a concerted piece (Example 12.4). Similarly, the beginning of the development eschews the usual dramatics, and the beginning of the recapitulation has no annunciatory tutti but starts instead with quiet playing by the solo, a continuation from the *piano, rallentando, diminuendo* dominant pedal ending the retransition.

At the same time, though, the Caprice maintains the traditional passage-work areas, and these are clearly divided from the thematic areas. After the long opening lyric statements, things turns boisterous with the entrance of the tutti, *fortissimo.* The solo transition that follows continues, *risoluto,* with arpeggios, octaves, broken octaves, ending with a slow trill that is eventually reduced to one repeated pitch, V of B. In the second group, the opening *meno mosso, diminuendo* B minor melody is played by the solo cello then violin, accompanied by the piano. Though its opening lingers long around the dominant, and could be heard as a close to the transition, it is clearly divided from the quicker-paced *con forza* passagework that precedes it. A second tune in B major, shared by the piano and solo clarinet, is also clearly separated from the *brillante* close by a *fermata.* The *brillante* begins with the usual vamp, and a reference to a motive of the theme of the first group. Although it contains some other sweet melodic motives, its construction is the usual one for the virtuoso concerto.

In sum, the brilliant parts of the Caprice differ little from those found in virtuoso concertos as concerns size and construction. They are beautifully melodic, and I would say no less so than in the C Minor Concerto which Schumann praised in a review in 1837. However, just as Schumann showed little interest in the virtuosic concertos and rondos he reviewed, I think in

Example 12.4 Bennett, Caprice in E Major, Op. 22, beginning.

the case of this more lyric piece, he is also not interested in one of the hall-marks of the virtuoso concerto it displays, clear divisions between brilliant and lyric parts. What we can surmise, then, that Schumann has in mind is not just a lyric sound in the thematic areas of a movement but, rather, the lyric sound carrying the form instead of merely being one of its divisions. Perhaps Schumann was less concerned about the divide in his review of the first concerted piece he heard by Bennett, his Third Concerto in C Minor. When he heard it for the second then third time in Bennett's Fourth Concerto and Caprice, he dubbed it habitual or manneristic, the result of the composer's mastery of form to the point of diminishing the possibility of an invention that would elevate his concerted works beyond "the dainty, the playful" to a more powerful and passionate language.

Schumann's take on Mendelssohn's *Serenade und Allegro giojoso,* which he reviewed in the same article from 1840 wherein he discussed Bennett's Fourth Concerto, is very different. To begin with, his review has a poetic tone, whereby any description of the piece is reduced to only the vaguest outline.[33]

> What one can expect from it is indicated by the title: a serenade, evening music, followed by a fresh, healthy allegro. For whom the first is intended, who knows! Not for a beloved, it does not seem sufficiently secretive and furtive; also not for a great men, for that everything is lack-ing; I believe that it is offered to the evening itself, a greeting to the life that a beautiful moonlit evening may awake in the poet, and if one knows finally, that this one can see out from his room straight into Sebastian Bach's little cantor's chamber, then the piece is that much more readily accounted for. ... Those who understand the poet's speech will also understand this ...[34]

Mendelssohn's account of the genesis of the *Serenade und Allegro giojoso* is more mundane. On 2 April 1838 he wrote his family:

> —Tonight is the concert of [Caroline] Botgorscheck, an excellent contralto, who has so tortured me to play, that I agreed, and then only afterward realized that I had absolutely nothing short and suitable. So I decided, then, to compose a rondo, of which on the morning of the day before yesterday not a note was written, and which I am supposed to play tonight with the entire orchestra, and have rehearsed this morning. It sounds gay enough; how I will play, though, the gods know, and even they hardly, since at one place I have written a 15-measure rest in the accompaniment and still have no idea, what I shall play into it. But one who plays *en gros* as I do gets through a lot![35]

Mendelssohn says he depended, not on the inspiration of the moonlight, but on his own skills as an improviser. Nonetheless, like Schumann, he empha-sizes the quick "play of his imagination" in completing the piece. There is no report in the *Neue Zeitschrift* as to how his performance came off in spring 1839, but when he performed the rondo, now titled *Serenade und*

Allegro giojoso, again on 6 December 1839 Schumann recalled, in a summary of the season's concerts, that he played it "enchantingly."[36]

Despite Schumann's poetic description, the *Serenade und Allegro giojoso* follows the outlines of any number of more prosaic pieces. The *Serenade* is a closed off section in B major, beginning, just as Mendelssohn says, with the piano solo playing the opening theme alone for fifteen bars. The toccata-like spinnings forth of this tune call up Bach to Schumann, who imagines that his contemporary's gaze into the master's chamber imparted to his slow movement something of an earlier era.

The *Allegro giojoso* is a rondo in D major, with the expected divisions between its sections. The solo plays the opening theme alone, is gradually joined by the tutti, then the full tutti closes the rondo refrain and initiates a transition. The solo pushes the transition forward with cascades of wide-ranging thirty-second-note arpeggios that contrast markedly with the slower dotted-eighth note rhythm of the theme of the episode which they butt up against. The brilliant close tears away from the quarter-notes at the end of the theme, *con fuoco,* with more cascading thirty-second-note arpeggios.

Yet, for all its clear divisions, Mendelssohn also forges close connections among the sections of his rondo. The main dotted motive of the rondo theme is the same as a dotted motive that began the short transition of the *Serenade* (cf. bars 20–21 and 91–92 shown in Examples 12.5a and b). The arpeggios of the transition to the first episode alternate with a dotted figure in the orchestra derived from the opening motto of the rondo theme; they lead to a long V of A pedal (bars 180–87) and the opening of the first episode over that same pedal without any stop. Because the first phrase of the episode (bars 188–203) is a series of sequences, and because it begins with a motive heard twice in the transition, the one derived from the opening of the rondo theme (see Example 12.5c), it is not until the cadence on A major that the listener perceives he is securely in the episode rather than a continuation of the transition. Finally, the arpeggios of the close support an eight-bar melody moving in quarter and eighth notes (bars 220–27). The melody ends on I[6], which gives a feel of continuity when its repetition begins an octave higher. What begins as a second, *leggiero* repetition (over V of IV at bar 240) turns instead into a long climb to the final dominant followed by the close onto the tonic that begins an *Animato* episode.

We could observe that Mendelssohn separates off the brilliant close of his *Allegro,* as do also Kufferath and Bennett, yet Schumann seems to have no objection, but rather calls the movement "fresh and healthy." Is this in contradiction to what we have already asserted as concerns his preferences for the lyric and for continuity? I think not, for in this movement the lyric first-episode theme is imbued with the excitement of the rondo theme (even borrowing its opening motto) and the closely related transition that follows that theme. This is most evident in the recapitulation, where Mendelssohn runs the rondo statement pell-mell into the return of the first-episode theme. The two are of one piece, and if there is a slowdown with the *espressivo*

a. cadential tag to the *Serenade* theme

[**Andante**]

Violin I

b. beginning of the rondo refrain

[**Allegro giojoso**]

Solo

c. beginning of the theme of the first episode

Example 12.5 Mendelssohn, *Serenade und Allegro giojoso*, Op. 43.

solo bars just before a return of the *Animato* theme from the second, middle episode, it is no more than a pause for breath rather than a change of overall feel.

* * *

It will not be difficult to show that the next composition Schumann wrote for piano and orchestra is very different from the virtuoso concertos, concertinos, and concert rondos he rejected. The intermezzo and finale of his Piano Concerto in A Minor have an easy flow in all their parts, much like Mendelssohn's concerted pieces, and unlike the disjunct sections of virtuoso concertos, with their emphasis on the contrast between emotive lyric and spectacularly brilliant sections. At the same time, like Mendelssohn's pieces, Schumann's final movement incorporates many of the expected features of the brilliant and popular concert rondos of the day. Although he always intended his intermezzo and rondo as middle and final movements of his Concerto, their separate composition, four years after he completed the independent composition that became the Concerto's first movement, also falls into the tradition of free-standing rondo movements, often with slow introductions, for piano and orchestra. In essence, the Concerto is two separate entities welded together. When Schumann wrote Mendelssohn concerning its first Leipzig performance, on Thursday, 1 January 1846, he requested that this division be noted on the program. "My concerto breaks down into *Allegro affettuoso, Andantino* and Rondo—the latter two continuous, if perhaps you would like to note that on the program."[37]

We shall begin with a brief overview of the compositional history of the last two movements. Discussion of the movements proper will center on the standards Schumann set for new concertos. Among these, the balance of tutti and orchestra will get little attention, as we have already discussed it in connection with the *Phantasie* or first movement of the Concerto, and it is a feature easily heard. We shall concentrate instead on Schumann's combination, in the finale especially, of a "worthy [older] form," just as he said he would regret were it to disappear, and a melodic flow and invention that turn his movement into an "ingenious novelty."[38] The finale shuns virtuosity, but at the same time gives the virtuoso, in this case Clara Schumann, something to do. Its stirs up excitement not with conventional bravura, but through a dance of changing metric divisions that take a leisurely pace to a rousing climax and splendid denouement.

When he began work on his newly conceived concerto, Schumann composed the rondo movement first. Appel writes:

> Although there were no discernible reasons for the expansion and revision of the [*Phantasie*] which he then undertook, Schumann also composed a Rondo Finale during the period from 14 June at the latest to 12 July 1845. ...
>
> Clara Schumann evidently considered the concerto to be complete in this two-movement form, for she noted on 27 June: "Robert has written a beautiful final movement for his *Phantasie* for piano and orchestra in A Minor, turning it into a concerto, which I shall play next winter."[39]

Schumann then began work on the second movement, the Intermezzo, *Andante grazioso,* on 14 July 1845 and completed it by 16 July. Finally, he refashioned the *Phantasie,* the concerto's opening movement. To quote Appel again, "The expansion and recasting of the single-movement *Phantasie* into a three-movement piano concerto might thus be said to have proceeded in 'retrograde' from the third movement."[40] We, however, will begin our discussion with the Intermezzo, in F major.

The reduced orchestration (strings and winds) lends the Intermezzo an intimate quality. The form of the movement is **ABA'**, with the first **A** closed in F major. The middle, **B** section is closed in C major. It has an **aba'** form, with **b** being a development of the **a** theme. The piano carries the melody in the **A** section, the accompaniment in the **B** section. In the latter, for the most part, the cellos have the melody in part **a**; the winds in part **b**. Placing these orchestral instruments in the foreground contributes further to the intimate sound. Hans Engel calls this an unusual procedure, though he does cite precedents for giving over the melody to the cello in other concertos, including Clara Wieck's.[41] For this listener, the piano accompaniment of the middle section calls up the sweet sound of the *Andante* and Variations for Two Pianos, Op. 46 that Schumann composed in 1843, and that was repeatedly played by Clara.[42] Like that piece, its melodic lines are simple and tuneful, especially as compared to the elaborate melodic decoration that is heard in, for example, among the pieces discussed in this chapter, the introduction of Czerny's Concertino or the second movement, barcarole of Rosenhain's Concertino. The Intermezzo demands, to cite Schumann's description of Bennett's Fourth Concerto, "more musical than manual skill." This is not to say it was composed for tyros. It shows off a skill carefully cultivated by Clara Schumann, one that Robert Schumann recognized as a signature of her polished artistry, a tone that "sinks into the heart and speaks to the soul."[43]

The A' section of the Intermezzo returns to F major, but then moves to A major, the key of the final rondo, rather than closing on the tonic. The cadence on A major initiates reminiscences of the introduction and first theme of the first movement, the beginning of a bridge that leads without pause into the final movement. Appel shows from his study of the autograph that Schumann originally closed the Intermezzo on the pitch e', followed by a general rest (in Example 12.6, bar 102; the general rest originally followed in bar 103). The introduction of the first-movement reminiscences, then of an upward scalar flourish in the strings, led to the addition of eight bars at the beginning of the *Allegro vivace,* where the opening motto of the rondo theme is introduced together with the further flourishes (Example 12.6, bars 103–8 and 109–16). Appel sees the reminiscences then series of scales as lending the bridge a Janus-faced aspect in that it both looks backward (toward the first movement) and forward (to the rondo). Further mediated, he notes, are the conflicting tempi between the two movements as the reminiscences are introduced *poco a poco ritardando* (major then minor mode), followed by *stringendo* (major mode again) to *Allegro vivace.* In Appel's words, "The stroke of genius behind this celebrated transition lies in its epigrammatic combination of reminiscence and anticipation. ... The boundaries between the two movements, originally meant to be crossed *attacca,* are now overrun pell-mell ..."[44]

I would call the transition a "stroke of genius" only with some qualification, for one still clearly hears the halt in the second movement at the original final e'. Manfred Hermann Schmid calls the initial major-mode reminiscence of the first movement's main motive in the high winds (bar 103) "a point outside the foreground passing of time."[45] To this listener, the sudden appearance of the main theme of the first movement, in the major and at a slowed tempo, is jarring. One could argue that an *attacca* charge into the original *sforzando* chord opening the third movement (in the movement's final form, the chord in bar 117) would be no less so, though it has a model in the segue from the dramatic intermezzo movement of Beethoven's Fourth Concerto to its finale. In the Schumann Concerto, the original, similarly abrupt transition has the beauty of allowing the listener to discern for herself the relationship between the ascending opening motive of the rondo theme and the descending motive of the main theme of the first movement. With the addition of the transition, one feels that Schumann is tutoring the

Example 12.6 Schumann, Concerto in A Minor, Op. 54, end of the transition to and beginning of the third movement.

listener in the relationship, with perhaps too heavy a hand. The reminiscence forcefully returns the listener to the first movement, creating what seems to me an artificial link. The link depends on the three movements being played together, and perhaps this is Schumann's way, as a composer, of dictating that this practice be followed, as did his wife in every one of her performances.

The skyrocketing scales and hints of the rondo theme that introduce Schumann's finale, whatever aesthetic judgment one passes on them, are conventional gestures, similar, for example, to the rising arpeggios and hints of the rondo theme that, after a slow introduction, form a bridge to the *Allegro con fuoco* rondo theme of Mendelssohn's *Capriccio brillant.*[46] Thereafter, Schumann's long and unhurried rondo balances the long first movement. It embodies the chamber-music ideal already realized in the first movement, with the piano taking now the part of solo, now of solo obbligato or accompaniment. The leisurely lines are reminiscent of the final movement of Field's Seventh Concerto that Schumann wanted to kiss for its "divine tedium." The ease and variety with which Schumann spins out a continual string of quarter and eighth notes is remarkable. The movement is in three-four time, but underlying the rondo theme is a broad six-four meter (breaking occasionally into hemiolas in three-two time; see Example 12.7a). The famous syncopated first episode moves in large measures in three-two time (Example 12.7b). The main theme of the central episode follows the three-four meter marked in the score (Example 12.7c).

As the form of Schumann's sonata-rondo finale unfolds, it incorporates every one of the gestures expected in a concerto last movement while at the same time subverting them. The rondo refrain closes off before the transition begins; the thematic area of the first episode cadences onto the beginning of the close, and the close is brought to a firm halt by a conventional trill. Yet, through it all, Schumann keeps up an unbroken, joyous patter of eighth- and quarter-notes, shuffled about in various metric patterns, avoiding even the emphatic cadence that traditionally jump starts the close. The cadence comes instead on a weak beat, *piano,* with no slow down then speed up of the tempo. The close continues with the traditional tonic-dominant vamp, in E major (at bar 253), starts again with the same vamp forty-three bars later, on F major (bar 295), then another twenty bars along, on F-sharp major. The feel is one of moving forward, but ever so slowly. When the expected fireworks come, they are with a surprise turn to A major and a sounding of the opening of the rondo theme by the tutti (begins bar 327). Rather than bringing a full statement of the rondo theme, this only initiates the solo's final syncopated octaves and brilliant trills preceding the final cadence of the close onto E major. Under the trills, the solo plays the main motive of the rondo, horn-call-like, a conventional gesture used already by Beethoven at the end of the solo exposition of the first movement of his Third Concerto, and by Schumann in the coda of his F Major Concerto movement, except now the head motive is not a quiet reminder from the distance but a brilliant stand-in for a grand return to the rondo refrain. When the solo is done, the tutti picks up the rondo motive *forte,* but then quickly turns to quiet development.

The ever so gradual build in Schumann's exposition leads to a grand statement of the rondo theme, which then is not fully realized. The gradual build will continue, with Schumann artfully delaying what I believe he

a. beginning of the rondo theme with dashed barlines to show the 6/4 measures

b. beginning of the first episode with dashed barlines to show the 3/2 measures

c. beginning of the central episode

d. from the coda, lyric gloss on the rondo theme

Example 12.7 Schumann, Concerto in A Minor, Op. 54, third movement.

would call the "center of gravity" of his movement until the beginning of the coda. After a central episode, the opening rondo motive returns in A major, a call in the medium distance by the winds accompanied by low rumbles and swells in the piano (begins bar 485). But when the entire theme bursts out, for the first time full force in the tutti, it is in a surprise D major (bars 497–513, the solo follows in bars 513–28). After the transition, the second episode returns in the tonic, A major, as does the close.

The coda, at last, presents a full *fortissimo* statement of the rondo theme in A major played by the tutti. In what follows for the solo Schumann builds excitement not by heaping pyrotechnics on pyrotechnics, but through ever-increasing rhythmic energy of the constant eighth notes, coming in two waves. In the first, the solo begins with broad eight-bar phrases starting on D but eventually moving toward A major (bars 771–810), where the opening motive of the rondo appears in free rhythmic diminution, although still with the swing of broad six-four meter double bars (bars 811–30). Cross-rhythms in bars 831–34 (bars with a six-eight feel in the solo; three-four bars in the orchestra) break the flow into single bars, and lead to the theme of the central episode. After a rise to *fortissimo,* an abrupt drop to *piano* brings a return to the broad eight-bar phrases (begins bar 859) from the beginning of the coda, again in D major, the start of the second wave.

With some changes the various motives of the first wave are heard again in the second wave, in the same order, but leaving out the central episode theme and leading instead to a wonderfully free and lyric gloss on the rondo theme (beginning in bar 911, see Example 12.7d). At *sempre brillante* (bar 927) the central-episode theme returns, varied, its two-count upbeat cutting into the expected continuation of the two-bar units of the free lyric gloss of the rondo theme. The contraction, anticipated by accents on every downbeat of the four bars preceding the cadence of the free lyric gloss (923–26), begins a headlong rush of single-bar measures, accented on every downbeat beginning in bar 937. Afterward come ever closer reiterations of downbeat tonic chords (beginning in bar 943) until the end of the movement.

Over the entire movement, Schumann avoids the intermediate climaxes that usually come at the end of the exposition, and beginning and end of the recapitulation, crafting instead one long build. He avoids a full climax early in the movement by quickly turning the brilliant tutti climax at the end of the exposition to quiet development, a strategy not unlike Bennett's in his Fourth Concerto. He then pushes the movement's "center of gravity," beyond the beginning of the recapitulation (where he located it in the *fortissimo* return by the tutti to the opening theme in the first movement of Moscheles's Fifth Concerto), to the beginning of the coda.[47] The delay results from the return, after the central episode, to the rondo refrain by the tutti *fortissimo* but in the subdominant. In the retransition winds sound the opening motto of the rondo theme in the tonic, A major, but this turns out to be V of IV. When the tutti actually begins the refrain in D major we feel we have sat down very comfortably rather than found our way to an exciting return, that the real return has been delayed by what Plantinga calls "that Schumannian meditative tilt toward the subdominant."[48] Only at the end of the recapitulation is the tutti finally pushed into its first full statement, *fortissimo* and in the tonic, of the rondo refrain. Everything that follows is afterthought, building in energy yet retaining the easy flow of the entire movement. "Never," wrote Tovey, "has a long and voluble peroration been more masterly in its proportions and more perfectly in character with the great whole which it crowns with so light a touch."[49]

* * *

Clara Schumann described the Concerto in her diary just the day after Robert finished, but had not orchestrated the Rondo. "I am very glad about it, since I have always lacked a large *Bravourstück* by him."[50] Although Clara saw the work as a "bravura piece," some eighty years later (in 1927) Engel writes, "If, now, we ask whether Schumann fulfills the rightful claims of the virtuoso for effect and brilliance, then we can only answer this partly in the affirmative."[51] The public reaction to the Concerto's first performances underscores Engel's qualification. After the premiere in Dresden, on 4 December 1845, the correspondent for the *Allgemeine musikalische Zeitung*, Julius Schladebach, gave the work high praise for its artistry among "the innumerable quantity of ephemera which the field of pianoforte composition generates every week." He also complained about the poor attendance at the concert, and observed that were it a virtuoso performer or a concert of Strauss waltzes the public would come. He even wondered how much longer Clara could continue concertizing and still cover her costs.

> We have every reason to rate this composition very high ... because it happily forgoes the usual monotony of the genre and gives to the completely obbligato orchestral part, which is worked out with great love and care, its full due, without lessening the sensation of the piano's effect, and because it allows both parts to maintain their independence in beautiful union. Among the innumerable quantity of ephemera which the field of pianoforte composition generates every week, it is a true pleasure to meet for once such a solid, sound work that gives new proof to the old assertion as to how well form and thoroughness of schooling can be united with gifted understanding, expressive invention, and every brilliance of the recent and newest technique. It would be difficult for us, if we had to designate the most successful of the three movements—Allegro affettuoso, in A minor; Andantino, in F major; Rondo, in A major—as such. They are all so characteristically bound, have such happily invented and cleverly developed motives, and keep building to the most complete satisfaction without slackening, are at the same time so intimately bound with each other through a basic idea that to want a separation would be foolish.[52]

Schladebach's praise for the concerto encompasses every one of the criteria Schumann campaigned for in the concerto: equality of tutti and solo; form and thorough schooling; "expressive invention;" "brilliance of the ... newest technique;" and "cleverly developed motives" that are "intimately bound ... through a basic idea." However, although these qualities may elevate his concerto above "the innumerable quantity of ephemera which the field of pianoforte composition generates every week," they also mean it was not a crowd pleaser.

In Leipzig, when Clara played the Concerto on 1 January 1846, what pleased the public was not the performance but the performer, one of their own natives whom they greeted with noisy signs of approval when she came out to the piano, and with a storm of applause after each number (aside from the Concerto, an Impromptu by Ferdinand Hiller and two *Lieder ohne Worte* by Mendelssohn).[53] A reviewer of the performance, L. R., points to the same features as the correspondent for the *Neue Zeitschrift:* the Concerto is "beautifully sensitive, profoundly thought out and ingenious," "in a symphonic manner," "a beautiful rounded-off whole," "'brilliant' … only on account of the truly artistic treatment of the pianoforte."[54] He also adds a qualification that the work is not immediately apprehensible.

> It is difficult, after only a single hearing, to confer the prize on one of the three movements; each of them speaks for itself with spirit and life; yet it seems possible to explain, that the high energy of the Allegro affettuoso and the simple, charming song of the Andantino first and most of all claim the interest of the audience, while the Rondo, despite its playful and fleeting character, requires a deeper understanding of the intentions of the composer.[55]

From the standpoint of critical reception, the low point in the squaring off with popular judgment came when Clara played the Concerto in Vienna just a year later on 1 January 1847. Eduard Hanslick reports, "The attendance was very moderate, the applause cool and apparently given only for Clara." Schumann's Piano Concerto and Symphony No. 1 in B-flat Major, Op. 38, "both new to Vienna, found little sympathy," a fact Hanslick attributes in part to Schumann's poor conducting and rehearsal technique.

> After the concert I accompanied the Schumann couple from the concert hall home; two courageous, understanding Schumann fans, [Gustav] Nottebohm and [Franz] Jüllig, came along. The first minutes elapsed in an uncomfortable silence, for each one of us was impressed by the lukewarm reception of this so splendid musical evening. Clara broke the silence first, as she complained bitterly over the coolness and ungratefulness of the audience. Whatever we others tried to say as appeasement, it only increased her audibly ill-humor. Then Schumann spoke the words which were unforgettable to us: "Calm yourself, dear Clara; in ten years everything will be different!" And he was right. Ten years later there was hardly a piano virtuoso who did not have Schumann on his program, and no concert institute that did not play Schumann's orchestra pieces.[56]

Although in 1894 Hanslick could say with confidence that Schumann's prediction came true, Schumann did not live long enough to see his prophecy fulfilled. He took a risk in writing a concerto "not for the virtuoso": his grumpy rejection of anything with even a whiff of the Parisian virtuosity, and because of this, subtle refashioning of the traditional form, set him at odds with contemporary audiences. If, in Hanslick's version of his friend's pronouncement, Schumann, too, sounds confident, we also should recall that he never again offered the public a three-movement work for piano and orchestra.

13

Team Programs

Schumann's last two works for piano and orchestra were the *Introduction und Allegro appassionato, Concertstück für Clavier und Orchester* in G Major, Op. 92, which he completed in late 1849, and the *Concert-Allegro mit Introduction* in D Minor, Op. 134, which he completed in late summer 1853. Both are one, movement pieces consisting of a slow introduction then faster section in sonata form. Neither are performed nearly as often as Schumann's Piano Concerto. The reasons could be several: (1) the standard repertory only has room for one Schumann concerto; (2) programming practices today, whereby at each appearance a piano soloist usually plays only one piece with an orchestra, call for larger works; (3) Opp. 92 and 134 are not good enough to warrant more performances.

The first reason did not have application in Schumann's lifetime, simply because he did not live long enough after Opp. 92 and 134 were composed. In March 1854 he committed himself to Dr. Franz Richarz's facility in Endenich, and remained there until he died in July 1856. However, as we shall see, soon after Robert's institutionalization Opp. 92 and 134 were all but dropped from Clara's repertory, whereas she continued to play his A Minor Concerto repeatedly until near the end of her long concert career, in 1891. The second reason also did not have application in Schumann's lifetime. The explanation for this is twofold. Opp. 92 and 134 were composed for his wife to perform, and she often, at least until about 1860, performed more than one concerted work on a program. More important, though, is that at the time of their composition her role as a touring virtuosa was often to support her husband as an assisting artist on programs featuring his symphonic works.

Concerning the third reason, that Opp. 92 and 134 are less performed because they are not good enough, we can only say this may have been the opinion early in the last century, but we emphatically disagree.[1] What we will show is that both pieces followed Schumann's prescription for an allegro movement that could be played by a soloist at the beginning of an orchestral concert: they are formally balanced movements; have connection among their parts; flow from one part to the next; and give both solo and orchestra enough to do.

Still, the *Introduction und Allegro appassionato,* Op. 92 and *Concert-Allegro,* Op. 134 are two very different pieces. Op. 92 is symphonic in its ambition. The piano does not take the lead so much as participate with the orchestra. In this respect it is, as we will show, similar to two other concerted works Schumann wrote near the time of its composition, the *Concertstück* in F Major for Four Horns, Op. 86, and the Cello Concerto in A Minor, Op. 129. Both works consist of three compact, joined movements. The *Concertstück* was at one time dubbed a concerto by Schumann in his diary; conversely, the Concerto was at times dubbed a *Concertstück.*[2] The terms are flexible, as we know. Clara Wieck sometime called the three-joined movements of her Concerto in A Minor a concertino. In a form similar to her composition are Herz's Concerto No. 2 in C Minor, Op. 74; Rosenhain's Concertino, Op. 30; and Mayer's Concerto, Op. 70. What both the *Concertstück* for Four Horns and the Cello Concerto share with the *Introduction und Allegro appassionato* is a toning down of the expected virtuosity, and, consequently, a compacting of those places that, in the virtuoso concerto, are usually more expansive because of the extensive bravura playing.

Unlike the *Introduction und Allegro appassionato,* the *Concert-Allegro* is a display piece for the solo. In it Schumann follows every one of the patterns expected in the virtuoso concerto. At the same time, he keeps to his ideals, not breaking the flow as is usual in virtuoso concertos, forging tight connections among the various sections of his movement, and balancing, after his own fashion, the roles of tutti and solo. The work is a *tour de force,* satisfying the critics who gave him a drubbing over the piano's unassuming role in Op. 92, but true to his own aesthetics. It follows old customs, but not in the manner of a stilted retrospective. Schumann despised back-to movements, as he stated forthrightly in January 1836 when he wrote about a manuscript sent him by Wilhelm Schüler, the last two movements, Adagio and Rondo, of a concerto.

> As for the Rondo, the composer admits in a letter accompanying the score, that with it he had in view a return to the simplicity of old. Here he will have to pound on the door to be let in. We are no friends of returns to, and would rather overcome sickness by relying on a strong constitution than find relief for a few moments by turning to little artificial remedies. So then, forward, friends![3]

Schumann's effort of seventeen years later could not be construed as any kind of return to an older style, because that style had been the basis of his concerted works all along. He continued to mold it to suit his own purposes, to move forward with it to the summit from where he could look around on all that came before.

* * *

Clara Wieck's concert programs from fall 1831, the time she undertook her first tour to Paris, up through fall 1840, the time of her marriage, show that if she played with an orchestra she more likely played two, rather than only one concerted piece. Until the time she first performed her Concert Rondo (later, the last movement of her Concerto) in May 1834, she frequently played the Pixis Concerto and Chopin's *Là ci darem* Variations on the same program. All along she had several one-movement concerted pieces in her repertory: Kalkbrenner's *Rondo brillant,* Op. 101; Pixis's Variations and Rondo, Op. 20, *Rondo brillant,* Op. 120, and *Fantasie militaire,* Op. 121; Herz's Variations, Opp. 20, 23, and 76; Mendelssohn's *Capriccio brillant.* She sometimes played excerpts from concertos, for example, the Polonaise (third movement) from Moscheles's Concerto No. 2 in E-flat Major; the first movement of Field's Second Concerto; the *Adagio* and Rondo from Pixis's Concerto; or the finale of the "newest" concerto by Chopin, his E minor.

Up to the end of 1836, most of Clara Wieck's concerts included a concerted piece, a total of 84 out of 108. The programs were generally potpourris, a mix of short orchestral pieces (overtures, excerpts from symphonies); vocal numbers (choral or chamber, arias or songs); solo instrumental music (accompanied and unaccompanied); occasionally a recitation. After 1836 she played solo programs more frequently, nearly always assisted by other artists, including for her trips to Berlin and Northern Germany (late winter and spring 1837) and Vienna (winter 1837 through early spring 1838), then, after her break with her father, on her tours to Paris (winter and early spring 1839) then Berlin and Northern Germany (fall 1839 through spring 1840). Of the eighty-two concerts she gave from 1837 until she was married in September 1840, only twenty-two include concerted works.

The pattern set beginning in 1837 obtained during the first nine years of Clara's marriage (1840–49). She played more concerts as a soloist assisted by or assisting other artists, than as a featured artist with an orchestra. The number of concerts she played without orchestra picked up noticeably during her tour to Russia (winter and spring 1844). In Dresden, where she lived from late 1844 to September 1850, the number of chamber concerts rose considerably. Furthermore, of the concerted works she did play, Table 13.1 shows that up through the trip to Russia, she still favored smaller ones: the Weber *Concertstück,* pieces by Mendelssohn, the last two movements of Chopin's F Minor Concerto.

Many factors determine what pieces make up a program: the artists' repertory; the nature of the occasion and audience; the practice of the time. However, I believe one particular matter having to do with the Schumanns suggests why short concerted pieces suited their purposes, and why, for a time, they were favored by Clara: they often performed as a husband and wife team. Many times when a new symphonic work by Robert was given its first hearings, Clara played on the same program. It is true that around the time Robert's Concerto was completed and given its premiere, in Dresden on 4 December 1845, Clara took into her repertory three more large

Table 13.1 Clara Schumann's Programs with Concerted Keyboard Pieces, 1840–49, showing any large symphonic works by Robert Schumann performed on each program

Date and Place	Concerted Work(s), and Any Symphonic Work(s) by Schumann
19 October 1840, Leipzig	Moscheles, Concerto in G Minor (played by Moscheles) Bach, Triple Concerto [in D Minor] (with Moscheles and Mendelssohn)
31 March 1841, Leipzig	Chopin, Concerto in F Minor, *Adagio* and Rondo Schumann, Symphony No. 1 (premiere)
6 December 1841, Leipzig	Schumann, Overture, Scherzo and Finale (premiere) Mendelssohn, *Capriccio brillant* Schumann, Symphony No. 4 (first version, premiere)
1 January 1842, Leipzig	Mendelssohn, Concerto in G Minor
25 February 1842, Bremen	Schumann, Symphony No. 1 Weber, *Concertstück*
5 March 1842, Hamburg	Schumann, Symphony No. 1 Weber, *Concertstück*
3 April 1842, Copenhagen	Weber, *Concertstück*
2 October 1842, Leipzig	Weber, *Concertstück*
2 February 1844, Königsberg	Weber, *Concertstück*
15 February 1844, Riga	Weber, *Concertstück*
21 March 1844, St. Petersburg	Schumann, Symphony No. 1 Bernhard Molique, Violin Concerto No. 4 (played by Molique) Mendelssohn, Concerto in G Minor
29 March 1844, St. Petersburg	Mendelssohn, Concerto in G Minor Weber, *Concertstück*
5 December 1844, Leipzig	Beethoven, Concerto No. 5
6 January 1845, Dresden	Bach, Triple Concerto [in D Minor] (with Ferdinand Hiller and ?) Beethoven, Concerto No. 5
25 November 1845, Dresden	Henselt, Concerto (premiere)
4 December 1845, Dresden	Schumann, Concerto (premiere) Schumann, Overture, Scherzo and Finale
1 January 1846, Leipzig	Schumann, Concerto
5 October 1846, Leipzig	Henselt, Concerto
22 October 1846, Leipzig	Beethoven, Concerto No. 4

Table 13.1 Clara Schumann's Programs with Concerted Keyboard Pieces, 1840–49, showing any large symphonic works by Robert Schumann performed on each program (*continued*)

Date and Place	Concerted Work(s), and Any Symphonic Work(s) by Schumann
16 November 1846, Leipzig	Schumann, Symphony No. 2 Mendelssohn, Concerto in G Minor
10 December 1846, Vienna	Beethoven, Concerto No. 4
1 January 1847, Vienna	Schumann, Symphony No. 1 Schumann, Concerto
10 July 1847, Zwickau	Schumann, Symphony No. 2 Schumann, Concerto
6 April 1848, Leipzig	Schumann, Concerto
18 January 1849, Leipzig	Mendelssohn, Concerto in D Minor Schumann, Symphony No. 2

concertos: Beethoven's *Emperor;* Henselt's Concerto in F Minor, Op. 16; and Beethoven's Fourth Concerto in G Major. But her programming remained flexible, including, besides these larger concertos, shorter concerted works by Mendelssohn.

Table 13.2 shows Clara's programs with concerted works from 1850 through 1855. Within these years Robert conducted the city orchestra in Düsseldorf (1850–53), the couple undertook a tour of Holland (winter 1853), then Clara toured alone after Robert's confinement. Her programs during this time include a single performance of Moscheles's G Minor Concerto (18 March 1852 in Leipzig) and of Henselt's Concerto (28 October 1852 in Düsseldorf), her last performance of each piece. The other concerted works listed in Table 13.2 constitute nearly her entire repertory in the genre for the remainder of her career. From 1850 through 1855, the concerto she played most often was Beethoven's *Emperor* (sixteen times). She played her old favorite, Weber's *Concertstück*, eleven times, Robert's Concerto six times. Other performances were of Beethoven's Fourth Concerto (five); Mendelssohn's G Minor (two) and D Minor (one); and Chopin's F Minor (one). Aside from its premiere (on 14 February 1850 in Leipzig), Table 13.2 shows only two other performances of Schumann's Op. 92. The *Concert-Allegro*, Op. 134, fared slightly better. After its premiere on 26 November 1853 in Utrecht, Clara played it three more times during the Holland tour, then again three times during her tour in the fall of 1854.

Although it is difficult to make rigid classification, I think we can say generally that before her husband's institutionalization in March 1854, beginning from the time of her marriage, Clara generally played one concerto, long or short, on a program (forty-two of forty-seven times). Although data on this are scant, as soon after Schumann composed Op. 134 he was institutionalized, it also could be said that, up to 1854, Opp. 92 and 134

Table 13.2 Clara Schumann's Programs with Concerted Keyboard Pieces, 1850–55, showing any large symphonic works by Robert Schumann performed on each program

Date and Place	Concerted Work(s), and Any Symphonic Work by Schumann
14 February 1850, Leipzig	Schumann, *Introduction und Allegro appassionato,* Op. 92 (premiere)
24 October 1850, Düsseldorf	Mendelssohn, Concerto in G Minor
5 November 1850, Cologne	Schumann, Concerto
20 February 1851, Düsseldorf	Weber, *Concertstück*
13 March 1851, Düsseldorf	Schumann, Op. 92 Schumann, Symphony No. 3 (repeated on demand)
18 May 1851, Düsseldorf	Mendelssohn, Concerto in D Minor
4 March 1852, Leipzig	Chopin, Concerto No. 2 in F Minor
18 March 1852, Leipzig	Moscheles, Concerto in G Minor Schumann, Symphony No. 3
6 May 1852, Düsseldorf	Beethoven, Concerto No. 5 Schumann, Symphony No. 1
3 August 1852, Düsseldorf	Beethoven, Concerto No. 5
16 October 1852, Elberfeld	Weber, *Concertstück*
28 October 1852, Düsseldorf	Henselt, Concerto
3 May 1853, Düsseldorf	Beethoven, Concerto No. 4 Schumann, *Vom Pagen und der Königstochter*
17 May 1853, Düsseldorf *Niederrheinisches Musikfest*	Schumann, Concerto Beethoven, Violin Concerto (Joseph Joachim)
8 November 1853, Cologne	Beethoven, Concerto No. 5 Schumann, Symphony No. 4
26 November 1853, Utrecht	Schumann, Symphony No. 3 Schumann, *Concert-Allegro,* Op. 134 (premiere)
30 November 1853, The Hague	Schumann, Symphony No. 2 Schumann, Op. 134
1 December 1853, Rotterdam	Schumann, Concerto Schumann, Symphony No. 3
2 December 1853, Amsterdam	Schumann, Symphony No. 2 Beethoven, Concerto No. 5 Schumann, Op. 134
10 December 1853, Utrecht	Mendelssohn, Concerto in G Minor Bernhard Romberg, Concerto *Suisse* for Cello (played by Romberg)

Table 13.2 Clara Schumann's Programs with Concerted Keyboard Pieces, 1850–55, showing any large symphonic works by Robert Schumann performed on each program (*continued*)

Date and Place	Concerted Work(s), and Any Symphonic Work by Schumann
16 December 1853, Amsterdam	Schumann, Op. 134 Weber, *Concertstück*
21 January 1854, Hanover	Beethoven, Concerto No. 5 Schumann, Symphony No. 4
23 October 1854, Leipzig	Schumann, Op. 134 Weber, *Concertstück*
27 October 1854, Weimar	Schumann, Concerto Schumann, Symphony No. 4
3 November 1854, Frankfurt	Beethoven, Concerto No. 5
13 November 1854, Hamburg	Beethoven, Concerto No. 4 Weber, *Concertstück*
18 November 1854, Lübeck	Beethoven, Concerto No. 5 Schumann, Op. 134
21 November 1854, Bremen	Beethoven, Concerto No. 4 Schumann, Op. 134
29 November 1854, Breslau (theater intermission concert)	Beethoven, Concerto No. 5 Weber, *Concertstück*
1 December 1854, Breslau (theater intermission concert)	Schumann, Concerto
4 December 1854, Berlin	Beethoven, Concerto No. 4 Weber, *Concertstück*
18 January 1855, Rotterdam	Beethoven, Violin Concerto (Henri Vieuxtemps) Beethoven, Choral Fantasy Schumann, Symphony No. 4 Weber, *Concertstück*
24 January 1855, The Hague	Beethoven, Concerto No. 5 Beethoven, Violin Concerto (Vieuxtemps) Weber, *Concertstück*
27 January 1855, Utrecht	Beethoven, Concerto No. 5
2 February 1855, Amsterdam	Beethoven, Concerto No. 4 Weber, *Concertstück*
8 February 1855, Rotterdam	Beethoven, Concerto No. 5
5 March 1855, Danzig	Beethoven, Concerto No. 5 Beethoven, Violin Concerto (Joachim)
26 June 1855, Detmold	Beethoven, Concerto No. 5 Weber, *Concertstück*

Table 13.2 Clara Schumann's Programs with Concerted Keyboard Pieces, 1850–55, showing any large symphonic works by Robert Schumann performed on each program (*continued*)

Date and Place	Concerted Work(s), and Any Symphonic Work by Schumann
3 November 1855, Berlin	Schumann, Concerto Beethoven, Violin Concerto (Joachim)
22 November 1855, Berlin	Beethoven, Concerto No. 5 Schumann, *Phantaise* for Violin (Joachim)
6 December 1855, Leipzig	Schumann, Op. 92 Beethoven, Concerto No. 5 Schumann Symphony No. 2
12 December 1855, Rostock	Beethoven, Concerto No. 5 Schumann, Symphony No. 4

generally show up on programs where a symphony by Schumann is performed (on four programs out of six performances of either piece). On other occasions, from 1840 to the beginning of 1854, when she played a concerto on the same program as a symphony by her husband, the concerto may have been long or short, for example, the Beethoven *Emperor* or a concerted work by Mendelssohn, but generally there is place for only one concerted work for piano (eighteen of nineteen programs), and by a slight majority her preference is for shorter works, even when she plays only one concerted work (ten of eighteen programs). After her husband's institutionalization, from the end of 1854 through 1855, Table 13.2 shows that Clara often reverted to her old habit of programming two concerted works, if at least one was short. Thus, all eight performances of Weber's *Concertstück,* one of Schumann's Op. 92, and three of his Op. 134 are paired with another concerted work for piano.

A look at programs from 1856 to the end of Clara Schumann's concert career in 1891 shows that in this regard she became more rigid. There are only nine concerts with two concerted works for piano, most in the 1860s, the last on 23 November 1875. Her concerto repertory came down to a few masterworks. Most often she played Schumann's Concerto (ninety times); then Mendelssohn's G Minor (forty-eight times); Beethoven's G Major (forty-six); Beethoven's *Emperor* (thirty-six); Weber's *Concertstück* (fourteen); Mendelssohn's D Minor (thirteen); Chopin's F Minor (six). New works added to her repertory are Beethoven's C Minor Concerto (fourteen performances); Mozart's D Minor and C Minor Concertos (thirteen and four); Brahms's D Minor (two); Beethoven's C Major (one). Schumann's shorter concerted works are crowded out. After 1855 there are only four more performances of Op. 92, the last on 1 March 1873, and no more of Op. 134. Although no hard and fast conclusions can be reached as to practical reasons why the smaller pieces by Schumann were dropped, I would suggest that they were of less use to Clara (as was the Weber *Concertstück* which she last played on 23 April 1870, although not the Mendelssohn G Minor Concerto) after she could no longer tour with her husband, and after she, and presumably other performers, too, rarely programmed more than one concerted work on a program.

* * *

Clara Schumann first played her husband's *Introduction und Allegro appassionato* for Piano and Orchestra, Op. 92, in Leipzig on 14 February 1850, and then, as we have already noted, played it only six more times in the next forty years. The problem may not have been its length alone, about eighteen minutes, which is at least one reason it is not often heard in American concert halls today. We have already shown that from 1856 to 1891 she repeatedly programmed pieces of similar length, most notably Mendelssohn's G Minor Concerto (twenty minutes) but also the Weber *Concertstück* (sixteen minutes), and Mendelssohn's D Minor Concerto (twenty-one minutes). Although she favored longer concertos, by her husband, Beethoven, or Mozart, she did not exclude the shorter concerted works from her repertory, and on any one concert usually programmed them as the only work she played together with the orchestra.

The main reason that Op. 92 never found a prominent place in the repertory, not even in Clara's, is the balance between solo and orchestra: the piano is not given due brilliance, it is overshadowed by the orchestra. The piece is hardly a concerto at all, a complaint lodged by critics from the beginning. E. Bernsdorf begins his review of the Leipzig premiere by saying that to speak one's mind to the wide world about Clara Schumann's splendid playing is like carrying water to the ocean. In other words, the faults of Op. 92 are not hers. He continues:

> Because of its beautiful melodies, whose articulation the various orchestral voices share while the piano holds to mere accompaniment, we liked the Introduction best. In the Allegro itself one recognized the effort to make the piano and orchestra equal in rank, that is, to subordinate neither absolutely to the other. To us it didn't seem to succeed to the degree it does in the A Minor Concerto. Both parts are in some way constrained, the piano part does not offer enough brilliant things. Of course, we don't want the passagework rubbish of the older practice ... but we would also like to see the claim of the solo instrument protected, for as such it has the right to brilliant and effective things.[4]

Moscheles, who moved to Leipzig in 1846 and was also present at the premiere, wrote in his diary: "It is strikingly orchestrated, could practically even be called orchestral music, since the constant arpeggios are too covered by the accompaniment for a piano piece; the performance was excellent."[5]

Clara, too, evidently recognized the problem, but blamed herself for not warming the audience to a beautiful chamberlike piece when they expected bravura. After the premiere she wrote:

> I was very unhappy today, and the reason lay first of all in the vexation, or much more grief, over the fact that I could let myself be so overcome by anxiety, and second in the feeling that the audience did not value the beautiful *Concertstück* as it itself merited, and I kept thinking, in the end I carry the blame for that; in short, I was deeply distressed.[6]

Clara's discomfort at the premiere, and possibly at later performances of Op. 92, may be one reason she eventually dropped it. Another must be that while Robert lived the two shared concert appearances. These usually highlighted one or more symphonic works by him, a purpose well served by her intentionally stepping into the background with the decidedly nonsoloistic Op. 92. After these joint appearances came to an end, Clara's independent concert career had little room for such a piece. In time she may have come to agree with the critics' assessment that because the *Introduction und Allegro appassionato* does not give enough to the piano it is inferior to the A Minor Concerto. At least, if her thinking was similar to that of her half-sister Marie Wieck, who wrote:

> About the little *Konzertstück, Introduktion und Allegro app.,*—which truly does not equal the Concerto in A Minor, but nonetheless offers many lyrical beauties, and which Clara played from manuscript in Leipzig—a critic there wrote: "This piece for piano and orchestra, still in manuscript, belongs to those things of the composer painted gray on gray, which, at least to us, always leave behind an unpleasant mood; this outright sterile musical combination, this restless pushing and driving and plunging of oneself into an artificially concocted night is unspeakably joyless, and we do not envy those who can deceive themselves into an enthusiasm for this kind of thing."[7]

Although few would agree, now or in 1850, that Op. 92 is "unspeakably joyless," the charge that the piano is overshadowed by the orchestra is true: although the piece takes the traditional layout of the virtuoso concerto as its point of departure, its ambition is symphonic. Its motivic connections across sections are more comprehensive, its development and coda more complex than in any concerto we have encountered hitherto. In nearly every part of the piece, the orchestra takes the lead, the piano either playing obbligato or responding to statements from the orchestra. Through most of it, the piano is confined to its middle register, even at those places where registral extremes are a time-honored tradition, namely, at the conclusions of the exposition and recapitulation.

To give substance to these observations about the symphonic nature of Op. 92 requires a more detailed description. For reference, Figure 13.1 provides a synoptic outline. Already the key scheme it shows, G major for the introduction, E minor and C major for the exposition, then E minor and a return to G major for the recapitulation, makes evident that the introduction is an integral part of Op. 92, not merely a slow prelude to a faster movement. Thematic-motive interconnections between the introduction and *Allegro* will confirm this.

The introduction is a complete slow movement, with three presentations of its theme, the second two varied. Examples 13.1a and 13.1b show its two main motives, one played by the clarinet (bars 1–4), the other a horn call (bars 4–7). Both have important roles in the following *Allegro*. Throughout the introduction the piano is reduced to arpeggio accompaniment, coming to the fore only in a few cadenza-like bars at the end of the second version of the theme, and in four bars of a bridge to the *Allegro*. The falling diminished-fifth motive of the bridge is inverted to serve as the rising opening motive of the *Allegro*'s first fanfare-like theme with its signature trumpet tattoo upbeat (Example 13.1c).

The exposition's three most noteworthy features are the dual nature of the first thematic section, the harmonic direction of the transition, and the construction of the second theme and close. The first theme begins with a tutti fanfare, with minimal replies from the solo, that closes onto a deceptive cadence (bars 43–50). It continues from the sixth degree, C major, with a new, ruminating melody for the solo, also harmonically open and occasionally accompanied or punctuated by the orchestra (bars 50–81). It then closes with the fanfare, this time played by the tutti alone, on the tonic E minor (bars 82–89). In sum, the tutti has the first and last word in this first thematic section. The transition belongs to the lightly accompanied solo. It is another ruminating melody, punctuated by the motive of the descending

bars	1–42	slow introduction	in G major
	43–89	first themes	in E minor
	90–119	transition	modulation to G major
	120–51	second theme	in C major
	151–88	close	in C major
	188–99	tutti	modulation to A minor
	200–99	development	modulatory, beginning in F (VI of A minor), ending in E minor
	300–42	first themes	in E minor
	343–72	transition	modulation to G major
	373–404	second theme	in G major
	404–41	close	in G major
	442–519	coda	modulatory, beginning and ending in G major

Figure 13.1 Synoptic outline of Schumann, *Introduction und Allergo appassionato*, Op. 92.

a. opening melody

b. horn call

c. diminished fifth and fanfare (end of the *Introduction* and beginning of the *Allegro*)

Example 13.1 Schumann, *Introduction und Allegro appassionato*, Op. 92, main motives.

diminished fifth remembered from the bridge. When the new key, G major, is reached, the fifth turns perfect. Because of the emphatic ending cadence on G, and because the second group follows in C major, the transition sounds less like a preparation of something new and more like a conclusion to what has come before.

The second theme again belongs to the solo, but is introduced by two bars of horn calls, played by the horns and bassoons. The horn calls announce the new direction of the piece, and prepare the reinterpretation of the G tonic of the transition as the dominant of the key of the second group (Example 13.2a). Similarly, as the theme progresses, the horns and bassoons do not wait for the solo to complete its cadences before entering to provide the melodic element, in bars 131–33 and 145–51, the latter over the solo's finishing chords and trills (Example 13.2b). Even the close is not entirely dominated by the solo. The orchestra comes to the fore in bars 155–60 with the characteristic fanfare, and the final trill, by long custom the property of the solo, is given to the timpani.

a. end of the transition and beginning of the second theme

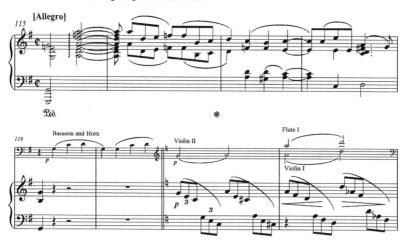

b. end of the second theme and beginning of the close

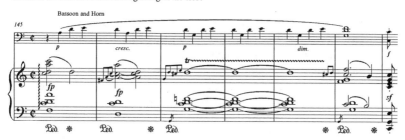

Example 13.2   Schumann, *Introduction und Allegro appassionato*, Op. 92.

The complexity of the development can perhaps best be grasped by look-ing at the long list of keys touched on and thematic entities called up or developed within its 112 bars (including the tutti ending the exposition). The last point of tonal stasis is represented by the C major of the tutti. Then come in quick succession: F major (bar 200); E minor (208); B minor (212); F-sharp minor (216); E minor (220); F major (224); V of B minor/major (232); B major (244); C-sharp minor (258); E-flat minor (recte D-sharp minor, 262); E major (273); V of E (284), preparing the recapitulation. The list of thematic entities begins with the tutti's development of the fanfare theme. Then come (with the dominating instruments and initial bar given in parentheses) the first ruminating theme of the first group (piano, bar 200); the second ruminating theme, from the transition (piano, 208); a variant of the horn call, punctuated by the bridge's diminished-fifth motive (piano and tutti, 220); the opening theme of the introduction (woodwinds) and the horn call (horn and strings, the piano merely accompanies, 244); the second ruminating theme (piano, 262); the diminished-fifth motive (piano then woodwinds, 269); the opening theme of the introduction (woodwinds, accompanied by piano and viola, 273); the tattoo fanfare (strings alternating with piano, 278). Finally, the diminished-fifth motive followed by the variant of the horn call (piano) together with the opening rhythm of the tattoo motive (woodwinds) usher in the recapitulation (288–99).

Not a note in the development comes from outside the already exposed materials; the indulgent piano flourishes of earlier piano concertos are totally absent. More than that, the piano is distinctly subordinate to the orchestra, or works in close conjunction with it, throughout. Add to this the circumstance, already noted by Tovey, that the stiffnesses (in form and orchestration) that can sometimes be detected in other Schumann developments are absent, and both the symphonic breadth and immense aesthetic success of this development are manifest.[8] The only thing that needs to be added to this overview of the *Introduction and Allegro appassionato* is that the recapitulation closely parallels the exposition, and the construction of the coda is equal in ingenuity to the development.

John Daverio succinctly summarizes Op. 92 as a play of motivic and tonal references across the slow introduction and into the *Allegro* with its complex development and coda. The G major of the introduction ultimately displaces the E minor of the *Allegro;* the clarinet's opening phrase in the introduction "recurs as the dreamy aside (for winds supported by pizzicato strings) first during the development, in B major, and next near the outset of the coda, in B♭." In the closing peroration the "dreamy aside" is "brought into line with the exuberant affect of the *Allegro*." In sum, "the *Introduction und Allegro appassionato* goes a long way toward recasting the conventional tonal-thematic polarity of the sonata style into a contrast between distance (as represented by the evocative introductory music) and presence (as asserted in the martial first theme of the *Allegro*)."[9] However, what is not resolved is the balance of orchestra and solo. The orchestra has the memorable tunes, both dreamy and martial, in the introduction and in the fanfare opening of the *Allegro*. Even in that section where the piano traditionally takes on both roles, lyric second-group theme and militant close, the orchestra takes the lead by initiating then sealing its every move. By the closing peroration when the opening clarinet phrase is "restored to the tonic, G major," and the piano takes the opening tune for the first time (in the *sehr markirt* style that characterizes its ruminating melodies), the turn to G major is already well established; the piano confirms a done deed.

On a practical level, the consequences of the symphonic nature of Op. 92 are that we today seem to agree with earlier critics. The role of the solo is too thoroughly inverted; this ravishingly beautiful piece is too much neglected. Whereas many piano students of a certain age take on the Schumann Piano Concerto, the *Introduction und Allegro appassionato* has not once in the last ten years seeped through the practice room floor above me.

* * *

Schumann completed a first sketch for the *Concertstück* for Four Horns, Op. 86, on 20 February 1849 then finished work on the orchestration on 11 March, only six months before he began the *Introduction und Allegro appassionato* in September.[10] On 10 April 1849, he wrote Ferdinand Hiller that the *Concertstück* "seems to me one of my best pieces."[11] Like the *Introduction und Allegro appassionato,* the *Concertstück* also plays down the role of the virtuoso. This, again, can be explained to some degree by the programming Schumann had in mind for the piece.

Schumann first proposed a program for the premiere of the *Concertstück* in a letter to Dr. Hermann Härtel of 27 February 1849, that is, while he was still in the midst of composing the piece. The concert was to take place in the final weeks of March, in Leipzig, and to include the closing scene of Schumann's *Faust,* the *Concertstück,* perhaps a scene from his opera *Genoveva,* numbers performed by his wife and by the singer Wilhelmine Schröder-Devrient. Because Schumann's proposed program includes the traditional vocal and instrumental solos, he likely had the horn piece in mind as an orchestral introduction or overture. He did tell Härtel it was "something completely singular," not, I believe, on account of its form, but rather its instrumentation.[12]

The *Concertstück* did not have its premiere until 25 February 1850, in Leipzig under the direction of Julius Rietz. Schumann worked out the details of the program with Ferdinand David, the orchestra's concertmaster. He proposed it include the *Concertstück,* and Beethoven's E-flat Concerto performed by his wife.[13] This again suggests that he saw the piece not as the central solo showpiece of the program, but rather as one of its framing orchestral works. David replied to Schumann that since the second half of the program was to be Mendelssohn's *Oedipus at Colonus,* which is an hour and a half long, the first half would need to be shorter. To include the Beethoven Concerto, the *Concertstück,* the indispensable overture and two sung works to separate the instrumental works was just too long. Instead of the Beethoven Concerto, a shorter work for the piano was agreed on, together with an overture, aria, the *Concertstück,* and short songs.[14] The final order was, Schumann's Overture to *Genoveva,* Beethoven's Sonata in C Major [presumably, Op. 53, the *Waldstein*], an aria by Stradella sung by Henriette Nissen, and the *Concertstück,* then on the second half, Mendelssohn's *Oedipus.*

As concerns the nature of the *Concertstück,* it represents in every way one of Schumann's "beautifully balanced allegro movements full of character, which, if need be, one could play at the opening of a concert."[15] The three movements are played without pause. The outer movements are in sonata form with recapitulations equal in size and weight to their expositions. Each has a long and complex development, more in the manner of a symphony than a concerto. They balance solos and orchestra, and, above all, they move forward with a continuous flow that does not emphasize virtuosic feats.

There are also connections across the movements, specifically, the final movement recalls music from the second movement in its development.

The continuous flow of music is easily heard in the first movement. After opening fanfares from both the tutti and solo group, the tutti alone states the grand theme in F major, closing on the dominant. The horns play a succession of small melodic motives, very soon turning away from F major. When they arrive on C major, the key of the second group, the theme turns out to be merely one cadence formula after another, continuing on into the close without any clear signal as to just where the close begins. The feel is of a long gesture that leads from V of F major at the end of the first tutti to a close on C major at the end of the exposition. In the closing gestures, both the tutti and solo group take up the solo group's initial rising, triplet fanfare; the closing tutti is the same as the opening one, transposed to the key of C major. The sense is that we never really left the opening, but only elaborated on it. The third movement is constructed similarly. The first theme is shared by the tutti and solo group, then closed off by the tutti on the tonic. Thereafter, the solos begin a transition leading to a lyric second theme that starts on V of C and continues on, incorporating other motives but with no real stopping point until the cadence that overlaps with a return to the opening tutti fanfares of the movement and marks the end of the solo exposition.

Schumann's downplaying of virtuosity in the *Concertstück* does not mean it is easy. He composed the piece to show off the equality of tone of all the chromatic notes of the valve horn, a relatively new invention at the time.[16] Before its first rehearsal Schumann wrote David that if the four hornists in Leipzig were to perform the work they must have the parts right away in order to begin studying them as soon as possible.[17] David's reply confirms the difficulty of the piece. After a first rehearsal with the hornists, he writes he still has faith in them despite a "million blunders and false notes."[18] Seemingly, though, the concert came off well. The *Neue Zeitschrift* reviewer reported, "This excellent, but extraordinarily difficult piece was performed very valiantly by *HH*. [Eduard] Pohle, Jehnichen, [E. J.] Leichsenring, and [C.] Wilke, and brought to these same gentlemen deserved applause."[19] To this day the problems for horn players are daunting.[20]

*   *   *

Schumann completed the Cello Concerto in A Minor, Op. 129 in October 1850. Its first public performance was not until June 1860, and Joachim Draheim believes the first performance with orchestra was only in December 1867.[21] A private rehearsal of the Concerto took place at the Schumanns' home on 23 March 1851.[22] In October 1851 Schumann began a correspondence with the cellist Emil Bockmühl, who twice planned public performances of the Concerto in Düsseldorf, in May 1852 and March 1853, which did not take place.[23]

Already as he was making arrangements for the first performance of the Concerto, Schumann began negotiations to publish it, but it was only in late 1853 that it was accepted by Breitkopf and Härtel. On 15 November Schumann suggested publication of an arrangement with quartet that could be played in "private circles," in addition to publication of a cello and piano version, and of the orchestral parts. In a reply of 13 December, the publisher turned the idea down.

> To speak candidly, for the time being at least we would like to forgo this, since on the one hand there is, of course, in general a far smaller market for violoncello music than for pianoforte and violin music. On the other hand, in our humble opinion a violoncello concerto, that is, a concerto for a string instrument, would probably not be played very often with string quartet accompaniment.[24]

For Schumann, the Cello Concerto crosses the line from public to private arena, not in a version in which the piano serves as a stand-in for the orchestra, but one in which a quartet, taking the parts of the orchestra strings and obbligato winds, turns it into chamber music.

In three connected movement and originally called *Concertstück* by Schumann, the Cello Concerto has some parallels to the *Concertstück* for Four Horns. Like the *Concertstück* it follows Schumann's ideal for the genre, in its motivic connections, continuous flow, well-rounded formal scheme, and balance of orchestra and solo. Contemporary critics rejected it for precisely this reason. They called for the solo instrument to come more to the fore, whereas Schumann had in mind something more like chamber music. We will begin with a brief description of the Concerto, considering first its form, overall flow, and motivic connections, and second its balance of orchestra and solo, then turn to its reception history.

Both the first and last movements are sonata forms with full recapitulations. They are joined by bridges to the short middle movement, a closed form that, in Tovey's words, "consists of a single lyrical melody in F major."[25] In the exposition of the first movement, orchestra and solo share equally in the first group; in the second group the solo takes the lead. The passagework of the close begins with the usual tonic-dominant vamp but not the usual fanfare. Rather, it continues the figuration already begun in the second theme with no break (Example 13.3, the vamp begins in bar 74). The development is symphonic, longer and more complex than is usual for concertos, including a false recapitulation in F-sharp minor. The recapitulation proper, like the exposition, begins quietly. The bridge to the third movement includes a reminiscence of the main theme of the first movement. The vigorous opening theme of the third movement is the basis of its lyric second theme, and entire development. Nearly the entire exposition is an unbroken flow: a single gesture begins with the counterstatement of the theme of the first group, and does not reach a full cadence until the tutti close of the exposition.

Example 13.3 Schumann, Concerto in A Minor for Violoncello and Orchestra, Op. 129, first movement, exposition, end of the second group theme and beginning of the close (at bar 74).

As to the balance of solo and orchestra, the continuous flow of the first and last movements means that virtuosity is downplayed at key points. In each movement the beginning of the close of the exposition and of the recapitulation is nearly imperceptible. In each the closes build to grand endings. However, in the first movement these are not affirmed by a rousing tutti, but one that enters *piano,* not on the tonic but with a deceptive cadence. In the third movement the tutti entries, though *forte,* similarly derail the tonic endings of the two closes. The cadenza at the end of the finale is not flashy, but meditative and lyric, though the coda (*schneller*) supplies a bright ending.

The unsatisfactory nature of the solo cello part for a public expecting more bravura is a matter taken up in a review of the published score of the Concerto in the *Neue Berliner Musikzeitung* of 17 January 1855.

> While it is certain that the work will enjoy full recognition as a piece of music, on the other hand its very nature dictates that it will not succeed as a concert piece. The invention of the cantilena and the passages … very often leaves one feeling just a bit unsatisfied. Thus, the player can do proper justice neither to them nor to himself. … Whereas it might well be a very interesting exercise for the violoncello virtuoso to play this concerto publicly, the possibility of success before a larger public is too doubtful to suggest as wide a dissemination as that of the Violin Concerto by Mendelssohn.[26]

Over a hundred years later, Gerhard Heldt's assessment is essentially the same as that of the reviewer for the *Neue Berliner Musikzeitung.* The Concerto does not show off the cello's bravura. Rather, he says, it is only in the most lyric moments that it takes on a truly soloistic role.

> It becomes apparent for the first time in the middle movement, where, with its presentation of tuneful, wide-swinging cantilenas, the solo clearly emerges from the orchestral group, to what degree Schumann composes in the "concertante" style. In the outer movements, on the other hand, either the deep register of the violoncello conceals its soloistic radiance, or the audible virtuosic passagework—sometimes without orchestral accompaniment, sometimes merely supported by chords—lies so exposed that little in the way of a partnership-like match can be detected.[27]

Early in the twentieth century, Tovey suggested that one option for the solo was to compose a new cadenza.[28] In our time, Michael Steinberg condemns Pablo Casals, Gregor Piatigorsky, and Janos Starker because they "have struck out thirty-two measures of Schumann's music at this point and substituted grandly rhetorical unaccompanied cadenzas of their own."[29] Similarly Draheim, who promotes an edition of the Cello Concerto for violin by presenting evidence that Schumann was involved in its preparation, condemns Dmitry Shostakovich's reorchestration.

> In 1963, Dmitry Shostakovich, at the suggestion of Mstislav Rostropovich, newly orchestrated the Cello Concerto and added to it a harp, piccolo, and two horns. Moreover, at the most inappropriate places he stuck in drum rolls, shrill flute passages, harp tinklings, awkward wind inserts and excited string figuration, and attempted thereby to bring Schumann's work down to the *niveau* of cheap film music.[30]

Shostakovich turned the Cello Concerto into an orchestral extravaganza. Noted cellists have beefed it up by composing their own rousing cadenzas. Steinberg and Draheim reject any changes, defending Schumann *qua* Schumann. But it may be that both they and the Concerto's detractors are asking the wrong question. To wit, not whether the piece works as a concerto or should be changed to sound more like a concerto but, rather, whether Schumann intended this piece, which he also envisioned as a chamber work, to have that place on a program that shines the central spotlight on a virtuoso. The program he outlined for the projected premiere on 20 May 1852 under his direction was to include, besides some songs, either Mendelssohn's overture *Die Hebriden* or Cherubini's Overture to *Medea,* the Cello Concerto, a Bach concerto for two keyboards (perhaps the C Minor, BWV 1060), and in the second half, Beethoven's Ninth Symphony.[31] The Concerto finds its place on a program, not where the soloist is center stage, but shares the platform with a singer and two pianists, all as a warmup act for Beethoven's gigantic Symphony.

* * *

Schumann composed the *Concert-Allegro mit Introduction,* Op. 134 in a few days beginning on 24 August 1853, finishing it on the 27th, when he noted his joy in the work, then completing the instrumentation on the 30th.[32]

Clara took the piece with her when she and Robert toured Holland, gave its first performance in Utrecht on 26 November 1853, played it a second time in The Hague on 30 November, then a third and a fourth time in Amsterdam on 2 and 16 December. The diaries tell of the enthusiastic reception Schumann's works received on these concerts (besides the *Concert-Allegro,* the Second and Third Symphonies).[33] When the Schumanns traveled in early 1854 to Hanover to see Joseph Joachim and Johannes Brahms, another performance of the *Concert-Allegro* was planned but did not take place.[34]

The next performances of the *Concert-Allegro* were not until after Schumann's hospitalization, on 23 October 1854 in Leipzig, 18 November 1854 in Lübeck, and 21 November 1854 in Bremen, all from manuscript, as the piece was not published until 1855 when it was prepared for the publisher by Clara Schumann and Brahms.[35] After these performances it does not show up on any of the nearly one thousand programs gathered in Clara's collection from that time on.

The *Concert-Allegro* follows the pattern of the virtuoso concerto, displaying all of its traditional gestures. The introduction, unlike that of Op. 92, is not a spun-out slow movement but a piano prelude. True, the strings start out the piece with light pizzicato, and briefly insert themselves, ritornello-like, at each of the solo's stopping points. But otherwise, the piano is left on its own to spin out from its opening tune, *sehr gehalten,* a toccata-like beginning involving many thirty-second- and sixty-fourth-note arpeggios. After the opening, the introduction never rests on the tonic, D minor, but moves continually forward. Over the final dominant pedal Schumann calls for the tempo to gradually accelerate until it reaches *Lebhaft.*

Just as in any virtuoso concerto, the piano begins the *Lebhaft* with an excited cadenza-like gesture. What follows takes a leaf from Mendelssohn's *Capriccio brillant* or *Serenade und Allegro giojoso,* or any number of rondo last movements (for example, the one in Beethoven's Third Concerto), where the solo gets the first crack at the tune. The tutti gives a bold reply, then the solo plays alone, leading into the theme of the second group. As in many virtuoso concertos the solo plays the first statement of the theme, then gives it over to the winds while it plays obbligato sixteenth notes. The solo concludes this second statement of the theme with a long and florid drawing out of the cadence (bars 68–75), yet again, after the manner of any number of virtuoso concertos. The usual tonic-dominant vamp begins the close, where the solo continues with a cavalcade of sixteenth notes until the expected charge up and back down the entire keyboard which prepares the crashing tutti entrance confirming the final tonic cadence of the section. The tutti serves its usual function of first triumphantly ending the exposition, then quietly beginning the development. The solo begins its part in the development with the long rhetorical gesture usual in virtuoso concertos, although in this case it also calls up something of the toccata-like introduction. Abruptly, this changes to the passagework section, *forte* and *mit Kraft.* This goes by quickly, although Schumann does put the brakes on when he halts the action temporarily to have the oboe play the theme of the second group (bars 126–33).

It may seem that Schumann went full out to answer the critics, and composed a virtuoso concert piece. Yet, a closer look shows that he stuck to his aesthetic ideals. First, by making obvious motivic connections across the different sections of the movement: the opening motive of the theme of the introduction is transformed into the opening motive of the theme of the second group and is prominent in the development (Example 13.4). Second, and most important, despite all the clear sectional divisions, by spinning the piece out from one long gesture beginning with the introduction and continuing through the development and recapitulation until the beginning of the coda. After the introduction leads from I to V in D minor, the solo's cadenza-like extension of the cadence leads to a first theme that begins over a first inversion tonic chord in D minor. From this point on Schumann does not close onto a full root-position tonic cadence until the beginning of the coda. The first theme leads to V of D minor, which the tutti sustains. The solo then leads to the theme of the second group, which begins on and continually returns to C, the dominant of the new key, F major. The tonic cadence ending the second theme and beginning the close is onto a first inversion chord, as is also the cadence that begins the tutti close. And so it continues, through the development and recapitulation.

A feature Schumann added that is usually not found in the virtuoso concerto is the cadenza. Its opening harks back to the introduction, with its sighing tune and toccata-like spinning forths, and its turn to minor after the close of the recapitulation in D major. Marked *mit freiem Vortrag,* the cadenza alternates between accelerations and returns to tempo. The middle

a. introduction, beginning of the solo theme

b. exposition, end of the transition and beginning of the theme of the second group (pickup to bar 53)

Example 13.4 Schumann, *Concert-Allegro mit Introduction*, Op. 134.

turns, *dolce,* to the theme of the second group which is soon accompanied, Thalberg-like, by cascades of thirty-second notes in the middle register. The end, where the orchestra quietly comes in, returns to the second-group theme, *piano, dolce* above tremolos and trills, then plunges to the depths of the keyboard and rises triumphant to signal, *fortissimo,* the first full tonic cadence in the piece.

The long coda is the first turn to something more symphonic. Up to this point, after the fashion of virtuoso concertos, the orchestral part has been confined to a few blocks and light accompaniment. With the beginning of the coda the solo announces a new chorale melody in D major related, according to Michael Struck, to "Du meine Seele, singe [You, my soul, sing]" (Example 13.5a).[36] The trumpets and trombones, saved for this moment, pick up the melody in rhythmic augmentation, reinforced by solo obbligato, a *Durchbruch* reminiscent of the chorale that breaks through in the coda of the final movement of Schumann's Third Symphony, the *Rhenish* (completed in late 1850) and a melody that Richard Strauss would later transform to depict the grand resurrection in his tone poem *Tod und Verklärung* (1888–89). But, for all its calling up of the symphonic style, the triumph in the coda is the solo's, who finishes off the piece with little support from the orchestra, bounding over the entire keyboard with dazzling arpeggio leaps and runs, radiantly topping off the last statement of the chorale motive by the strings.

Schumann was happy with his new, virtuoso piece. In letters from Endenich he asks Clara if it was a dream that she played it so splendidly, and how it is going with the publication of the *Concertstück* she played so wonderfully in Amsterdam.[37] The critics, too, received the work well. The first German-language reviews were of Clara's performance in Leipzig on 23 October 1854. The critic for the *Signale für die musikalische Welt* reports:

> ... the *Concertstück* for Pianoforte ... interested us especially. It is a slowly developed, passionately moving piece, full of energy, singular effects, and deep feeling. The treatment of the piano is difficult, but grateful, although in some places the solo instrument is obscured by a somewhat opaque accompaniment.[38]

Struck suggests that, in view of the relatively light weight of the orchestral part, the obscuring of the solo instrument may have been because of particular conditions at this performance.[39] A similarly glowing review of the same concert published in the *Neue Zeitschrift* does not mention it.[40] Neither mentions Schumann's illness or suggests that the *Concert-Allegro* is of lesser quality because of it. Both, instead, accept it as a "valid, new composition."[41]

Schumann gave the *Concert-Allegro* to his wife on her birthday, 13 September 1853. The opening motive in the piano recalls the opening of Weber's *Concertstück* (Example 13.5b), a piece that was a favorite in her repertory

a. chorale melody, "Du meine Seele, singe," and Schumann, beginning of the coda

b. Weber, *Concertstück* for Piano and Orchestra in F Minor, Op. 79, beginning
(cf. example 13.4a, Schumann, Op. 134, solo beginning)

c. Schumann, exposition, solo entrance with the main theme; and
Mendelssohn, Concerto in D Minor, Op. 40, first movement, solo entrance with the main theme

Example 13.5 References in Schumann, *Concert-Allegro mit Introduction*, Op. 134.

since their marriage: from September 1840 to September 1853, she played it more times (nine) than any other concerto. Also, the main theme of the *Lebhaft* section of the *Concert-Allegro* calls to mind the main theme of Mendelssohn's Second Concerto, which Clara first played in 1849 in Leipzig, then again in Düsseldorf in 1851 (Example 13.5c). When the *Concert-Allegro* was published in 1855, at Robert's request it was dedicated to Brahms, who wrote to Clara of his joy over the dedication of the piece that, together with Schumann's Violin *Phantasie,* was his "favorite of [Schumann's] concertos."[42]

After the *Concert-Allegro* was published by Senff, a long review appeared in his house journal *Signale für die musikalische Welt*. The writer calls the work ingenious, engaging, compelling, beautiful, full of life. He also suggests the solo could just as well do without the orchestra.

> If the work truly makes the full effect inherent in it only with full orchestra, it will also, nonetheless, prove itself excellent as a solo piece, even if the cue notes of the orchestra melody given with the passages are not played along ...[43]

Of the three works Schumann completed for piano and orchestra, the *Concert-Allegro* is the one with a popular audience most in view. It adheres audibly to the old norms of the virtuoso concerto, delivering bravura at all the expected places; it brings the piano so much to the fore that the publisher's in-house reviewer suggested it could as well be played as a solo piece. At the same time, the *Concert-Allegro* is intimately tied to Schumann's private life. He gave it to his wife on her birthday, then dedicated it to a young soulmate, Johannes Brahms, who came into his life on 30 September 1853, just after he finished the piece. An intimacy in the music is heard at the opening, the free sound of preluding, as if the pianist were alone, the pizzicato strings mere voyeurs. The inwardness of the prelude comes face-to-face with the high drama of the *Lebhaft*: over the stormy dominant pedal that leads into this section, plaintive sighs from the oboe return to the opening motive, as if desperately trying to hold back the flood. In the development, as the solo launches into gruff passagework the orchestra layers on top of it the sweet theme of the second group with its opening sigh. The harmony is temporarily frozen over a dominant pedal, but the sixteenth motion in the solo just keeps going and emerges as raging as before.

The two sides of the *Concert-Allegro* play out audibly at the same time, one over the other. The grand drama is never resolved, instead the gods are invoked in a glorious chorale that chases away both storm and pathetic sighs. In the coda, we move out of the realm of the concerto and into a drama worthy of the stage. The distress and battle that Weber portrayed in his popular *Concertstück* come to mind. Schumann, perhaps thinking to compose a piece that could stand in for or even replace the Weber in his wife's repertory, leads us not to the heights of victory on the battlefield but to a glorious place where the soul sings.

Epilogue

To the end of his composing career, Schumann's concertos and concert pieces for piano and orchestra adhered to the virtuoso model, as to the disposition of tuttis and solos and the pattern of alternating thematic and passagework areas. He kept working out this basic design in different ways, never holding to any one formula. Thus, his first effort, the F major movement, follows the traditional virtuoso model; his unfinished movement in D minor and the A Minor Concerto are more in the style of chamber music; the *Introduction und Allegro appassionato* is symphonic (as are the *Concertstück* for Four Horns and the Cello Concerto), and his final work, the *Concert-Allegro,* follows the surface characteristics of the virtuoso concerto while incorporating modifications he had worked out in his other concerted pieces. What is the same in each piece, after his student work, is the easy flow from section to section, and connection of ideas across sections, two features he repeatedly advocated in his writings about the concerto.

For all the modifications Schumann makes to the sound of the virtuoso concerto, primarily through his eschewing of hackneyed fioritura, he does not change its basic conception. He retains the traditional affect and structure of the individual movements. His sonata and rondo movements have full developments or middle sections, and balancing returns. Although he repeatedly says he is looking for something new in the genre, the changes he approves are subtle. Faced with modifications to the traditional form found in concertos by Herz, Moscheles, and Wieck, his response is that they are incomplete, hazardous, or unworthy of attention.

Someone else will have to write the history of the more radical changes to the genre during the mid- to late nineteenth century, in the concerted works of Liszt, and, among others, César Franck, Camille Saint-Saëns, Gabriel Fauré, Cécile Chaminade, and Edward MacDowell. Our study closes with, first, for the sake of completeness, a look at Schumann's final two concerted works, the *Phantasie* for Violin and Orchestra, Op. 131, and Concerto for Violin, both composed in the fall of 1853. We will then turn to the First Piano Concerto in D Minor, Op. 15, by Johannes Brahms, the young composer who showed up at the Schumanns' doorstep in Düsseldorf on 30 September 1853, and who within a month Schumann pronounced "the one who has been called to give ideal voice to the noblest expression of his time."[1] A brief examination of his Concerto, which was begun on the very heals of Schumann's final efforts in the genre, seems a fitting end to our study, as it embodies Schumann's ideals, but also makes a decisive break from the background model Schumann always followed.

* * *

The *Phantasie* in A Minor for Violin and Orchestra is a twin to the *Concert-Allegro,* Op. 134. Schumann composed it in early September 1853, just a few days after he completed a draft of the *Concert-Allegro,* then gave the two pieces to his wife on her birthday, 13 September. The work was inspired by a visit from the young violinist and friend of the Schumanns, Joseph Joachim (1831–1907), and dedicated to him. He was the first to play it, in a private performance with Clara Schumann at the piano on 23 September, then publicly, together with the Beethoven Violin Concerto, under Robert's direction on 27 October in Düsseldorf. Never a favorite in the violin repertory, the *Phantasie* had an inauspicious start. Its premiere was the last concert Schumann conducted in Düsseldorf. The next day he wrote August Strackerjan that Joachim had played "in a most enchanting manner," then three weeks later told his publisher Friedrich Kistner, "Joachim played [the *Phantasie*] not long ago with the greatest effect in one of our concerts here."[2] The *Niederrheinische Musik-Zeitung,* however, after praising Joachim's "incomparable" playing, called it compensation for an accompaniment to both concertos which "went so badly that one was repeatedly overcome with distress for fear of a complete breakdown."[3] Soon after the concert difficulties with the executive committee of the Musikverein, who negotiated Schumann's contract as music director of the Municipal Orchestra and Chorus, reached a head when they decided to take action in response to complaints about his competence.

Schumann and those close to him—his wife, Brahms, and Joachim—cherished the *Phantasie.* In January 1854 Joachim wrote of the "great pleasure" of playing it through with Brahms.[4] After a performance in Hanover on 21 January, Clara Schumann declared Joachim had played it "wonderfully," and months later Robert recalled his "splendid" playing.[5] A performance by Joachim in Leipzig on 12 January brought a positive response from the reviewer for the *Neue Zeitschrift,* who called the *Phantasie* a "splendid work," one that "gives the player the opportunity to show himself an all-around artist, and the listener to delight in true beauty."[6] But a critic in Hanover judged the *Phantasie* "utterly crude" and repellent throughout.[7] Joachim kept the *Phantasie* in his repertory through his long career, even reporting to Clara Schumann in 1887 that it was well received in Paris.[8] However, according to Michael Struck, positive assessments of the *Phantasie* virtually disappeared with Schumann's death in July 1856. The only explanation, he surmises, is the dominating influence of Schumann's mental decline during his last years on any evaluation of his late works.[9]

A few salient points about the *Phantasie* need to be mentioned. After a slow introduction beginning in A minor, the *Lebhaft,* in C major, is patterned after the virtuoso concerto, especially in the sharp divides between thematic and passagework areas. At the same time, Schumann's fingerprint can be seen in the motivic recalls: a reminiscence of the *dolce* theme of the introduction at the opening of the development; a coda devoted mostly to variants of the opening motives of that same theme, but that also incorporates the jauntier opening motive of the *Lebhaft* (see Examples E.1a, b, d). Struck relates the figuration of the *Phantasie,* mostly scales and arpeggios, to Schumann's interest in the Baroque, in particular, his composition of accompaniments to Bach's solo cello sonatas in spring 1853.[10] Also, the cadenza, in the manner of a free improvisation, conjures up a romantic idea of the Baroque.

a. introduction, opening theme

b. exposition, main theme

c. exposition, beginning of the transition

d. exposition, beginning of the theme of the second group

e. exposition, beginning of the close

Example E.1 Schumann, *Phantasie* in A Minor for Violin and Orchestra, Op. 131.

The exposition of the *Phantasie* has a long gesture characteristic of Schumann, which runs from the start of the transition to the cadence ending the exposition. The transition begins with scale figures in C major (Example E.1c), which quickly run into a thematic area that continues for the next two dozen bars without cadencing. The theme finally settles down onto closing passagework that, in its first bar, is a transposition of the beginning of the transition, but to A minor rather than the expected tonic key of the second group, G major (see Example E.1e). This is a bit of a joke. The transition leads to a lyric theme that never settles down onto its tonic key. Instead, the moment for the cadence passes, and we are thrown back to the beginning of the transition. We have gone nowhere. The lyric theme was a mere tease, an insert into the passagework that, after the sleight of hand, continues up to the usual grand close of the exposition.

After she played the piece with Joachim, Clara Schumann called the *Phantasie* "a really ingenious, humorous piece."[11] Helmut Haack has traced the opening theme of the *Lebhaft,* played by the tutti, to a tune sung at carnival time.[12] Aside from the lively spirit of this tune, the humor of the *Phantasie,* I think, is also in the solo's part: the tease of the sentimental second theme, then sudden landing right back into the grind of passagework, a forceful jolt that unmasks the sentimental pose as a mere caper. More than any concerted piece Schumann wrote, the *Phantasie* is about virtuosity, about the performer commenting on and good-naturedly sporting with his own role as a virtuoso. At the very end, the virtuoso is allowed the grand sweep of a couple of arpeggios to excite the audience for his bow, but most of the coda is devoted to a sweet song, to assurance that the joke was very gentle and is quite over.

* * *

The Violin Concerto was not published until long after Schumann's death. He composed it in fall 1853 and sent the score to Joachim on 7 October. A public performance was planned on 27 October 1853 in Düsseldorf, and there were rehearsals in Hanover on 25 and 30 January.[13] Soon afterward, Schumann was hospitalized, and the score was never published. The manuscript passed from Joachim to his son, Johannes, who sold it to the Preußischer Staatsbibliothek Berlin, with the stipulation that it not be published until the hundred-year anniversary of Schumann's death. However, with Johannes Joachim's concurrence, the Concerto was published in July 1937 and given its first public performance with orchestra on 26 November 1937 in Berlin. Eugenie Schumann, in 1937 the Schumanns' only surviving child, wrote a letter protesting the performance as an injustice to the dead and against the wishes of her mother.[14]

Although Clara Schumann ultimately decided, according to her daughter, "that the Concerto should not be published, not now and not at all," her first reaction was different. She wrote in her diary on 7 October 1853, "Robert has composed a highly interesting concerto for violin; he played me a little of it;

but I don't dare to pronounce more detailed judgment, until first I have heard it. The *Adagio* and the last movement were completely clear to me right away; the first, not so completely."[15] Joachim, too, was initially attracted to the work. Apparently he played it through with Clara Schumann at the piano when she was in Hanover in mid-October 1854. On 17 November 1854 he reported to Robert:

> If only I could play your D Minor Concerto for you; I have internalized it more than that time in Hanover, when I was obliged to play it so shamefully for you in the rehearsal, to my great chagrin, because I had tired my arm so from conducting. Now the 3/4 meter sounds much grander. Do you still remember, when we said the last movement sounded as if [Tadeusz] Kosciuszko, published a polonaise with [Jan] Sobieski: so grand![16]

Clara must have been similarly excited about the run-through, as Robert wrote Joachim on 25 November, "Oh, if only I could hear my D Minor Concerto from you, about which my Clara has written with such great joy."[17]

Joachim kept working on the Concerto; in October 1857 he wrote Clara, "It is really dreadfully difficult for the violin in the last movement, but I have pretty much played it into my fingers. [There are] wonderful places in the first and second movement."[18] He arranged a rehearsal with the Gewandhaus Orchestra in Leipzig, which Clara attended.[19] Afterward, in a turnaround from her original impression, she despaired about the "defect" of the last movement, and even asked Joachim if he could compose a new one.[20]

The Violin Concerto, too, follows the pattern of virtuoso concertos, ingeniously modified by Schumann. The long opening tutti presents the main theme in D minor, sets it directly against the second theme in F major, then returns to the opening theme, in D minor (Examples E.2a and b). The first solo proceeds similarly, beginning with the first theme, the solo playing mostly obbligato, then slipping into the second theme, which continues on through the close. The second tutti returns to the first theme, the development is devoted to the second theme, the recapitulation follows the pattern of the exposition, the final tutti returns to the first theme, and the coda is on the second then first theme. Thus, the entire movement is a continual alternation between the two themes, clearly defined by the blocklike tuttis, which always begin with the first theme. In between the second theme prepares each return. It consists of two parts, the first entirely over the dominant. In the exposition and recapitulation, after a full playing of the two parts (the second much extended), the first returns (solo with extravagant obbligato and some reinforcement from the orchestra) in place of closing passagework.

The second movement is an intermezzo, with reduced orchestration. The third movement is a sonata-rondo. The rondo refrain, with polonaise rhythms, is firmly grounded in the tonic, D major; the theme of the episode is unstable, even skittish (Examples E.2c and d). It begins on the new tonic, A major,

a. first movement, beginning

b. first movement, first tutti, beginning of the second theme

c. third movement, beginning

d. third movement, exposition, beginning of the second group theme

Example E.2   Schumann, Violin Concerto in D Minor.

two bars played by the winds in thirds. The solo answers freely, statements by the winds return, but these never settle down onto the tonic again until the solo's answer is stretched out to become the long closing cadence of the exposition. Near its opening, the development refers to the opening of the second movement.

For all its ingenious constructions, the Violin Concerto in many places has the feel common in the virtuoso concerto—that we are marching in place. The unstable second themes of the first and last movements contrast with harmonically stable, more solid statements of the first themes which are primarily the province of the orchestra. Yet, by continuing the thematic areas into the close, the second themes seem mere holding patterns in preparation for the final, grand closing gestures.

The Violin Concerto was never performed publicly by Joachim, who, as Struck has observed, in time changed from thinking that the Concerto had technical difficulties which needed to be overcome, to believing that it was not an aesthetically viable work. On 5 August 1898, at the request of his biographer, Andreas Moser, Joachim explained why the work was never published: though it would be a joy to have a new violin concerto by Schumann, his reputation must be protected.

> It must even be said, unfortunately, that one cannot fail to recognize a certain exhaustion, whose intellectual energy still strives wearily to wrestle out something. Particular places (how could it be otherwise!) bear witness to the deep spirit of the creation; all the more sorrowful, then, is the contrast with the work as a whole.

Joachim then gives a detailed rundown of the Concerto, showing the weakness of each movement: in the first, a rhythmic capriciousness, now taking a violent course, now standing still, that allows full realization of neither the lyric theme nor the brilliant passagework, and a development that is too intimate and does not allow the solo to come to the fore in the climax; a tender second movement that gives way to sickly brooding as it begins a transition to the final movement; and a last movement that is rhythmically rigid, repetitious, pompous in its main theme, ineffective in its brilliant figuration and lacking in joy all around.[21]

Joachim's complaint is that the Concerto, although in the virtuoso mold, does not give the virtuoso enough to do. In the last movement especially, the one he saw as most problematic, Schumann's scheme of combining second group thematic area and close does not give the solo sufficient time to fully display his potential as either a lyricist or a technician. In the end, the complaint is not about inspiration or lack of it but about a virtuoso concerto that pays too little heed to traditional expectations.

* * *

Soon after Schumann was institutionalized, on 4 March 1854, Brahms began a sonata for two pianos, then orchestrated its first movement, which, in 1856, he turned into the first movement of his Piano Concerto in D Minor, Op. 15.[22] At that time he also composed a new middle and final movement. Charles Rosen, following a suggestion by Donald Francis Tovey, has shown that the structure of the third movement of the Concerto follows the structure of the rondo of Beethoven's Third Concerto, a traditional model.[23] The opening melody of the second movement, as Christopher Reynolds has shown, transforms the first five melody notes played by the strings in the first movement (bars 2–3) into a moving tune, supposed by different authors to be a portrait of Clara Schumann, Robert Schumann, or Brahms himself.[24]

What interests us is the first movement. How did Brahms transform it from a sonata movement, orchestrated to become a symphony movement, into a concerto movement? The scores of the two-piano sonata and the symphony are no longer extant. But, it is clear that, even after the changes Brahms made, the work is symphonic in origin: in its length (some twenty-four minutes) and multiplicity of ideas; in its heavy and diverse orchestration; and most

importantly, in its programmatic conception. This is not the usual story of
the solo taking on and conquering the orchestra. It is about the threatening
and terrifying forces of nature heard in the thunder of the opening. Joachim
told Max Kalbeck, Brahms's first biographer, it was a response to Schumann's
attempted suicide, on 27 February 1853.[25]

In the first tutti the thunder of the opening gives way suddenly to an
espressivo theme in D minor which sounds then quickly converts to minor
first a D major then an A major chord. Another theme in the same mood
turns to a subdued B-flat minor, suspended for its entire duration over a
dominant pedal until a short modulation leads to the unleashing of the storm
once again for the close. The solo enters with the usual cadenza-like gestures, completing the tutti's close, then plays, in some form, each of the first
three themes that were heard in the opening tutti. The dominant preparation
of the second group is prolonged in the usual way, with the solo reduced to
a single line, in this case, doubled at the octave. The solo plays the opening
(as yet, unheard) theme of the second group alone, and in a second statement
it is taken up by the orchestra.

Brahms rehearsed the entire Concerto under Joachim's direction in
Hanover on 30 March 1858. Afterward, he made further changes before the
public premiere in Leipzig on 27 January 1859. Seemingly, some of the
changes were concessions to the usual order of things in the concerto. On
3 January 1858, Joachim wrote Clara Schumann:

> A new recasting by Joh. of the first movement of the Concerto has brought
> me great joy. There are exquisite quiet places and connecting passages
> with which you, too, will certainly be happy. In particular, the second
> theme has become broader and more pleasing. Now, the whole thing just
> seems a bit too rich to me. But that is a good reproach![26]

We can surmise from Joachim's letter that what Brahms added (connecting
passages, as between the end of the first tutti and beginning of the solo
exposition, or at the end of the first group of the solo exposition; a broader
second theme), bring the movement more into conformity with the usual
pattern of the virtuoso concerto and its predecessor, a more likely model for
Brahms, the classical concertos of Mozart and Beethoven.

What the additions do not change is the piano's position as merely one of
the players, and not the star, in what is a grand pastoral drama, the contrast
of a raging storm and the hymn of thanksgiving that the piano gives out as
the first theme of the second group (Examples E.3a and b). Nowhere is the
piano given a place to lead the orchestra to a grand climax, in particular
not in the place where it does in every other concerto of the time, including
those by Schumann, namely, the close. This begins after the orchestral statement of the hymn, in bar 199, with a motive that was already heard at the
close of the first tutti (bars 82–83), then as the basis of a *dolce* theme following the solo statement of the hymn (bars 165–83), and again as the main
component of an extension of the orchestral statement of the hymn (bars

193–96). In each case, the motive initiates an area that dissolves away what has come before. In the close, this happens first in bars 199–210, then in a shortened form in bars 210–15, which melt into a *pianissimo* second tutti. The motive itself is a vamp (Example E.3c), but hardly like those beginning the closes of numerous virtuoso concertos. Rather than build, it fades away, which is to say, the second group is devoted entirely to the hymn and its dissolution.

The hymn is nowhere present in the development, which begins with the storm of the opening, then continues with the two quiet themes of the opening tutti. It works up not to a climax led by the solo but to a grand symphonic crisis that leads only to a return of the storm. As there is no apotheosis with the recapitulation, so there is none in the coda, but only a raging on of the storm. The solo does get its moment, as much of the coda is based on the introductory theme played by the solo between the first tutti and solo exposition. But

a. first movement, beginning

b. first movement, solo exposition, beginning of the second group theme

c. first movement, solo exposition, beginning of the close

d. third movement, beginning of the coda

Example E.3 Brahms, Concerto in D Minor, Op. 15.

one hardly feels a resolution of the grand problem that the movement has presented. That, symphonic-, and not concerto-like, awaits further developments in other movements.

In Leipzig, where Brahms played the premiere public performance of the Concerto, he waited in vain for Clara Schumann to come to the city where, he wrote her, he knew "nothing and no one." His letter of 2 February 1859 continues:

> My concerto went very well, I had 2 rehearsals. You probably know already that it was a complete failure, because of the deepest silence at the rehearsal and outright hissing at the performance (where 3 people tried to applaud). ...
> No one said anything to me, only [Ferdinand] David, of course, genuinely nice things. [Julius] Rietz and [Heinrich von] Sahr, whom I asked, said that they did not like it.[27]

What was wrong? The audience and even the musicians did not get what they wanted. No place to cheer for the solo in the first movement, to exclaim over the beauty of the second movement, whose sentiment is too deep for such compliments, nor even to be roused by the third movement, which ends with no gay *Presto* like Beethoven's Third Concerto, but another hymn, drawn from the theme of the middle episode but calling up the beginning of the coda of Schumann's *Concert-Allegro* in the same key (Example E.3d, cf. Example 13.5a). The religious moment continues as the rondo theme is turned into a steady march, then its opening leap echoes back and forth across the cathedral. Arnfried Edler hears in these hymnal tones a musical expression of liberal thinking, a belief that the spirit of the 1848 revolutions will dawn again and begin a renewal.[28] It is a stirring call to humankind that we expect in a symphony, not a piano concerto.

In one sense, Brahms kept every aspect of the concerto model created by Mozart, and followed by Beethoven and the virtuoso composers. He also incorporated all the features called for by Schumann: balance of orchestra and solo, while still giving the solo enough to do; flow and connection of ideas; balanced return form. But he also modified the model in a way that no one before him had, a way more radical even than anything Liszt and his followers produced, for he turned the concerto from entertainment, whether silly or more serious, to a profound statement about weighty matters. The outlines of the old model are still there, but Brahms is the first to change its essence.

Schumann did not live to hear Brahms's Concerto. If he had, he would have recognized the young master's apotheosis of his own honest and profound hope for the genre, that in dignity and worth it find its place alongside the great symphonic works of its day.

Notes

Chapter 1

1. See Daverio, *Crossing Paths*, 15–16, 19–31.
2. Schumann, *Selbstbiographische Notizen*, [6]. The editor of the *Notizen*, Martin Schoppe, dates them after 1840.
3. Eugenie Schumann, *Robert Schumann*, 20 (letter from Johanne Christiane Schumann to Robert Schumann of 8 June 1835); Robert Schumann, "Älteste musikalische Erinnerungen," 1.
4. See Kapp, *Studien zum Spätwerk Robert Schumanns*, 13.
5. Schumann, "Fest in Zwickau am 12ten Juli," *Neue Zeitschrift für Musik* (hereafter *NZfM*) 7 (1837): 31.
6. Kuntsch, "Aus dem Verzeichnis ... musikalische-declamatorischen Abend Unterhaltungen." Program of 25 January 1828 in Eismann, *Quellenwerk*, 1: 20. The variation sets are: G. C. Leutsch, Variations on "Liebes Mädchen hör mir zu," Op. 1; Jean Baptist Cramer, Introduction and Ten Variations on "Le songe," by J. J. Rousseau; Ferdinand Ries, Fifth Fantasie on the Favorite Air, "Come Live with me and Be my Love," by Henry R. Bishop, Op. 92, No. 2, and A Rhenish Song ("Bekränzt mit Laub") with Grand Variations, Op. 75; Hieronymus Payer, Variations on a Polonaise by Keller; and Ignaz Moscheles, Introduction and Concertante Variations for Piano, Violin and Violoncello, Op. 17.
7. Bischoff, *Monument für Beethoven*, 31–33.
8. "Das Glück, vorspielen zu können" (Schumann, "Älteste musikalische Erinnerungen," 1).
9. Wasielewski, *Schumanniana*, 75 ("Bericht des Musiklehrers Piltzing in Zwickau"); Wasielewski, *Robert Schumann: Eine Biographie*, 26 n. The Herz Variations are on the tune "Ich war Jüngling noch an Jahren" (the Romance, "A peine au sortir de l'enfance" from Étienne Méhul's opera *Joseph*).
10. Karl Gottlob Meißner may have been instead Johann Gottlieb. See Wenke, "Aspekte zu Robert Schumanns Entwicklung," 25, 48 n. 40. On the flute and cello lessons, see Schumann, "Älteste musikalische Erinnerungen," 1.
11. Jansen, "Aus Robert Schumanns Schulzeit," 85–86.
12. Schumann, "J. F.[*sic*] Carus," *NZfM* 18 (1843): 27.
13. Schumann, "Älteste musikalische Erinnerungen," 2; "Materialien," 2. Bischoff dates the "Materialien" to c. 1846 (*Monument für Beethoven*, 36 n. 26).
14. Although Piltzing remembers a public performance of the Weber (Wasielewski, *Schumanniana*, 75), it is a genre suitable for music-making among a circle of amateurs. Furthermore, the pet name of the Caruses (Agnes and her husband Ernst August) for Schumann was Fridolin, a gentle character in the Schiller ballad "Der Gang nach dem Eisenhammer." This may have come about as a result of their hearing or participating in Schumann's performances of Weber's melodramatic setting. See Niecks, *Robert Schumann*, 36.
15. Schumann, "Materialien," 1.
16. Wasielewski, *Schumanniana*, 72.
17. "- in der freyen Phantasie am stärksten [-] hinreißendes Feuer meines Vortrags -" Schumann, "Älteste musikalische Erinnerungen," 2; also, Eismann, *Quellenwerk*, 1: 18 ("Aus selbstbiographischen Aufzeichnungen").

18. Schumann, *Tagebücher*, 1: 158.
19. Ibid., 1: 159.
20. Schumann, "Materialien," 1; also, Eismann, *Quellenwerk*, 1: 18 ("Aus selbstbiographischen Aufzeichungen").
21. Wasielewski, *Schumanniana*, 73–74 ("Bericht des Musiklehrers Piltzing"); Eismann, *Quellenwerk*, 1: 17 ("Aus dem Projektenbuch"). A description of the autograph of the Psalm setting and of an overture dated 1822 is given by Wenke, "Aspekte zu Robert Schumanns Entwicklung," 66 n. 5.
22. Jansen, "Aus Robert Schumanns Schulzeit," 86–87.
23. According to Piltzing, the normal complement was two violins, two flutes, one clarinet, and two horns, with Schumann directing from the piano and filling in the bass (Wasielewski, *Schumanniana*, 73).
24. On the audience, see Wasielewski, *Schumanniana*, 73 ("Bericht des Musiklehrers Piltzing").
25. Schumann, "Älteste musikalische Erinnerungen," 1; "Materialien," 2.
26. The program is given in Eismann, *Quellenwerk*, 1: 17. The date 1824 was added later by Schumann to the printed original, now in the Robert-Schumann-Haus Zwickau. On Pierre Lecourt, see the brief article in Francois-Joseph Fétis, *Biographie universelle des musiciens et bibliographie generale de la musique*, 2nd rev. ed. (Paris: Firmin Didot, 1867–83).
27. "Fast möcht' ich sagen, hatte ich wie jener heute unsern beau jour, denn, um mich nicht eigen zu loben, ich spielte mit ziemlicher Leichtigkeit und Fertigkeit und ich möchte fast sagen mit noch mehr Gelindheit spielte P[iltzing]. diese Variationen" (Schumann, "Blätter und Blümchen," 103–6).
28. Wasielewski, *Schumanniana*, 73.
29. See Taylor, *Robert Schumann*, 24–32.
30. What remains of his efforts in the Archiv des Robert-Schumann-Hauses Zwickau, including some metrical translations, is listed in Wenke, "Aspekte zu Robert Schumanns Entwicklung," 223–24.
31. For a transcription of Schumann's "Protokolbuch des literarischen Schülervereins" see Schoppe, "Schumanns *Litterarischer Verein*," 20–31. A further description of the make-up and purpose of the group is given by Wenke, "Aspekte zu Robert Schumanns Entwicklung," 38–39.
32. A description and full transcription of the contents of "Blätter und Blümchen" is given in Wenke, "Aspekte zu Robert Schumanns Entwicklung," 60–61, 70–193. Other poetic, dramatic, or prose texts extant in the Archiv des Robert-Schumann-Hauses Zwickau are listed in Wenke, "Aspekte zu Robert Schumanns Entwicklung," 224–27. Portions of the "Juniusabende" are in Schumann, *Tagebücher*, 1: 99–102, 105, 115 (under 1, 6, 16 August 1828); see also 98 (29 July 1828).
33. "Poetische Versuche verdrängen manchmal die musikalischen." Schumann, "Materialien," 2. Schumann, *Tagebücher*, 1: 30 (24 January 1827).
34. See Niecks, *Robert Schumann*, 11–14; also Burger, *Robert Schumann*, 12–13.
35. Schumann, "Älteste musikalische Erinnerungen," 2; Blank, "Bedeutung und Besonderheiten," 145.
36. "Aufnahme des Jünglings unter Ältern" (Schumann, "Älteste musikalische Erinnerungen," 2). On the close relationship and poetic talents of the four friends, see Schumann, *Tagebücher*, 1: 29–30 (24 January 1827); 156 (13 December 1828). Wenke explains that when the *Verein* was formed in 1825, all its members were in the *Sekunda*; Flechsig and Röller were *Primaner* ("Aspekte zu Robert Schumanns Entwicklung," 38).
37. Eismann, *Quellenwerk*, 1: 16 ("Schulfreund Flechsig erzählt").
38. Wasielewski, *Schumanniana*, 78 ("Bericht von F.[sic] Röller").
39. Schumann, *Briefe: Neue Folge*, 31 (letter to Johann Nepomuk Hummel of 20 August 1831).
40. Schumann, *Selbstbiographische Notizen*, [6]; "Älteste musikalische Erinnerungen," 1.
41. Wasielewski, *Schumanniana*, 75 ("Bericht des Musiklehrers Piltzing").
42. Schumann, *Selbstbiographische Notizen*, [6].
43. Schumann, "Materialien," 1, 2; "Älteste musikalische Erinnerungen," 1, 2. The two sources gives dates for some of the meetings as follows, with some discrepancies between them: Ernst Köhler (1820 or 1821, or 1821 or 1822); and Friedrich August Kummer (1819 or 1820); Johann Gottfried Bergmann (1821 or 1822, or 1822 or 1823).

44. Nitschkova-Goleminova, "Schumann-Moscheles-Paganini," 17–21.
45. Schumann, *Tagebücher*, 1: 181, 185 (17 March, 3 April 1829: practice in Leipzig); 192 (28 April 1829: public performance in Zwickau); 209, 210, 213, 215, 217, 221–22 (27, 28, 30 November, 1, 29, 30 December 1829; 4, 14, 18, 24 January 1830: practice and performance in Heidelberg).
46. Ibid., 1: 146, 153 (20 November, 11 December 1828); 109, 112, 117, 119 (14, 20 August 1828). On Schumann's early songs, see McCorkle, *Schumann: Werkverzeichnis*, 726–31.
47. Schumann, *Tagebücher*, 1: 172, 174 (2, 16 February 1829: with Probst); 115, 116 (17 August 1828: with Täglichbeck); 116, 117, 120; 170 (19, 21 August 1828; 25 January 1829: with Böhner); 144, 157 (19 November, 17 December 1828: with Knorr); 152 (7 December 1828: with Glock); and *Jugendbriefe*, 82 (letter to Wieck of 6 November 1829: with Probst).
48. Schumann, *Tagebücher*, 1: 125, 128, 152, 156 (9, 27 October, 7, 14 December 1828: the polonaises); 125, 133, 152 (9 October, 8 November, 7 December 1828: the variations). Bischoff lists the other works and performance dates in *Monument für Beethoven*, 47–49 (table 2). On Schumann's early four-hand works, see McCorkle, *Schumann: Werkverzeichnis*, 694–97.
49. Schumann, "Leipziger Quartettabende." See also Bischoff, *Monument für Beethoven*, 67–68, 69–71 (table 3). Besides the Schubert, the other pieces performed more than once were Prince Louis Ferdinand, Nocturne in F Major for Flute, Violin, Viola, Cello, Piano, two Horns ad lib., Op. 8; Pixis, Piano Trio No. 2 in F Major, Op. 86; and Ries, Piano Quartet in E-flat Major, Op. 17.
50. Schumann, *Tagebücher*, 1: 171, 172, 175, 177, 179, 180, 180–81, 182, 184 (31 January, 7, 21, 28 February, 7, 13, 15, 21, 28 March 1829). An edition of the piano quartet (1829) was published by Wolfgang Boetticher as *Quartett c-Moll für Pianoforte, Violino, Viola und Violoncello*, Quellenkataloge zur Musikgeschichte. Urtextausgaben praktischer Musik, supp. 4 (Wilhelmshaven: Heinrichshofen, [c. 1979]).
51. Performances of the Kalkbrenner or Hummel Concerto are noted in Schumann, *Tagebücher*, 1: 152, 178, 182 (7 December 1828; 6, 21 March 1829). Performances of other solo piano works are listed in Bischoff, *Monument für Beethoven*, 47–49 (table 2).
52. Schumann's improvisations were primarily for himself (*Tagebücher*, 1: 148, 149, 153, 156; 172, 177, 178, 179, 180, 182, 184, 186, 187 [25, 27 November, 9, 14 December 1828; 4 February, 2, 6, 9, 10, 11, 20, 29 March, 5, 8 April 1829]), but some were for his friends (*Tagebücher*, 1: 146 [20 November 1828, at Carus's?], 157 [15 December 1828, at Wieck's with Reichold listening], 178 [4 March 1829, at Carus's], 182 [21 March 1829, for the *Quartettunterhaltung*]). In the "Materialien" (p. 3), Schumann says in Leipzig he improvised daily ("Freyes Phantasiren unausgesetzt täglich").
53. Schumann, *Selbstbiographische Notizen*, [6].
54. The Beethoven symphonies were performed as a cycle on 31 October (the Second), 12 November (Third) 1828; 15 January (Fifth), 29 January (Sixth), 26 February (Seventh), 10 March (Eighth), 2 April (Ninth) 1829 (Schumann, *Tagebücher*, 1: 128, 138, 167, 171, 176, 179, 185). Schumann was in Zwickau on 12 October 1828 when the First Symphony was performed, and again on 1 January 1829 when the Fourth was played (*Tagebücher*, 1: 445 n. 92, 449 n. 138). See also Dörffel, *Geschichte der Gewandhausconcerte*, "Statistik," 4–5.
55. Schumann, *Tagebücher*, 1: 128 (31 October 1828, the Crusell Concertino played by W. H. Heinze, a clarinetist in the Gewandhaus Orchestra), 171 (29 January 1829, the Müller Concertino played by Carl Queisser, first trombonist in the Orchestra), 172 (5 February 1829, the Kummer Concertino played by Carl Heinrich Rückner, oboist in the Orchestra), 176 (26 February 1829, the Belcke Concertino, played by the composer, a flutist in the Orchestra), 184 (30 March 1829, the Mayseder Concerto, performer unknown). The Ries Piano Concerto in E-flat Major, Op. 42, was performed by Emilie Reichold, a student of Friedrich Wieck (*Tagebücher*, 1: 168 [22 January 1829]). Kalliwoda played his own Concertino in E Major for Violin, Op. 15, and Adagio and Variations for Violin (*Tagebücher*, 1: 178, 179 [5, 10 March 1829]). Wörlitzer performed on 29 May 1828 (*Tagebücher*, 1: 84).
56. "Erster Bekanntschaft durch Dr. Carus mit dem alten Wieck, Clara noch Kind" (Schumann, "Projektenbuch," 31); Schumann, *Tagebücher*, 1: 149 (29 November 1828).
57. On Emilie Reichold, see Schumann, *Tagebücher*, 1: 109, 110, 157 (15 August, 15 December 1828).

58. Schumann, *Briefe: Neue Folge*, 31–32 (letter to Hummel of 20 August 1831); *Tage-bücher*, 1: 149 (26, 27 November 1828).

59. Schumann, *Tagebücher*, 1: 153, 174, 175, 176 (11 December 1829; 13, 18, 19, 27 February 1829); Wasielewski, *Schumanniana*, 78–79 ("Bericht von F. Röller"). What Schumann refers to as Hummel's *Clavierschule* is the *Ausführliche theoretisch-praktische Anweisung zum Piano-Forte-Spiel, vom ersten Elementar-Unterricht an bis zur vollkommensten Ausbildung* (Vienna: Haslinger, 1828).

60. "Eifrigste Studien im Technischen des Clavierspiels u. große Fortschritte" (Schumann, "Materialien," 3); Schumann, *Selbstbiographische Notizen*, [6]. For Wieck's letter, see Joß, *Der Musikpädigoge Friedrich Wieck*, 30.

61. Clara Schumann and Robert Schumann, *Briefwechsel*, 2: 148 (letter from Robert to Clara of 16 April 1838).

62. Schumann, *Tagebücher*, 1: 158, 177, 178, 182 (22 December 1828; 2, 4, 5, 21 March 1829).

63. Ibid., 1: 181 (17 March 1829).

64. Ibid., 1: 182, 185, 187 (23 March, 3, 9 April 1829).

65. Schumann, *Tagebücher*, 1: 189, 191, 192 (14, 15, 23, 28 April 1829).

66. Schumann, *Briefe: Neue Folge*, 15 (letter of 29 April 1829).

67. Schumann, *Tagebücher*, 1: 354 (18 July 1831).

68. Draheim, "Robert Schumann in Heidelberg," 145.

69. Schumann, *Briefe: Neue Folge*, 3, 12–13, 14–15 (letters to Rosen of 5 June, 7 November 1828; 29 April 1829); *Jugendbriefe*, 91 (letter to his mother of 11 November 1829).

70. Schumann's first lesson (*erste Stunde*) with Thibaut was on Monday, 25 May 1829 (*Tagebücher*, 1: 50, 198). The performances were of Handel's *Samson*, in two parts, on Thursday, 25 February and Thursday, 4 March 1830 (ibid., 1: 228, 230, 232).

71. Schumann, *Jugendbriefe*, 105 (letter of 24 February 1830). The diary entries show only four visits to Thibaut's, the three cited in note 70 of this chapter, and one other on 13 July 1829 (Schumann, *Tagebücher*, 1: 205). See also Bischoff, *Monument für Beethoven*, 88–89. Bischoff reckons Schumann's encounter with Thibaut at a ball (*Tagebücher*, 1: 225 [4 February 1830]) as a fifth visit.

72. Schumann, *Jugendbriefe*, 80–81, 85 (letter to Wieck of 6 November 1829); *Tagebücher*, 1: 230 [25 February 1830]).

73. Wasielewski, *Schumanniana*, 79.

74. Schumann, *Tagebücher*, 1: 207, 208, 221, 223 (24 July, 13 August 1829; 21, 30 January 1830).

75. Ibid., 1: 215, 223 (13, 30 January 1830).

76. Ibid., 1: 208, 209, 210, 212, 214, 215, 216, 222, 223, 226, 233 (13 August, 26, 27, 30 November, 25 December 1829; 8, 13, 16, 24, 29 January, 7 February, 7 March 1830). On Schumann's known repertory in Heidelberg, see Bischoff, *Monument für Beethoven*, 92–93 (table 4).

77. Eismann, *Quellenwerk*, 1: 55 ("Studienfreund Töpken an Wasielewski"). For Schumann's account of reactions to his playing, see his *Tagebücher*, 1: 210–12 (29 December 1829).

78. Eismann, *Quellenwerk*, 1: 54 ("Studienfreund Töpken an Wasielewski").

79. Schumann, *Jugendbriefe*, 78, 80.

80. Schumann, *Briefe: Neue Folge*, 31 (letter to Hummel of 20 August 1831).

81. Schumann, *Tagebücher*, 1: 221–22, 230–31 (24 January, 3 March 1830).

82. Ibid., 1: 209, 210, 213, 221–22 (27, 30 November, 1, 29–30 December 1829; 4, 24 January 1830). See also Eismann, *Quellenwerk*, 1: 55 ("Studienfreund Töpken an Wasielewski"), and Schumann, *Jugendbriefe*, 104 (letter to his brother, Julius, of 11 February 1830).

83. Schumann, *Tagebücher*, 1: 232. Before this, the last entry recording practice is 29 January 1830 (p. 223).

84. Ibid., 1: 222 (26 January 1830). See further Robert and Clara Schumann, *Briefe und Notizen*, 28 (letter to Dr. Ernst August Carus of 25 September 1830). Also, Eismann, *Quellenwerk*, 55 ("Studienfreund Töpken an Wasielewski"), and cf. Schumann, *Briefe: Neue Folge*, 40–41 (letter to Töpken of 5 April 1833).

85. Schumann, *Tagebücher*, 1: 222–39 (entries of 25 January to 31 March 1830).

86. Schumann, *Jugendbriefe*, 100 (letter to his mother of 4 December 1829), 104 (letter to his brother, Julius, of 11 February 1830).

87. Nitschkova-Goleminova, "Schumann—Moscheles—Paganini," 24–28.

88. Wasielewski, *Schumanniana*, 79.

89. Schumann, *Jugendbriefe*, 111 (letter to Carl), also 114 (letter to his mother of 1 July 1830); Robert and Clara Schumann, *Briefe und Notizen*, 28 (letter to Carus from Robert).
90. Schumann, *Jugendbriefe*, 116–19.
91. For Christiane Schumann's letter to Wieck of 7 August 1830, and Wieck's reply of 9 August, see Eismann, *Quellenwerk*, 1: 62–65.
92. Ibid., 1: 81 ("Aus Schumanns Projektenbuch").
93. Schumann, *Tagebücher*, 1: 228 (22 February 1830).
94. See Mayeda, *Schumanns Weg zur Symphonie*, 76–81.
95. Jansen, *Die Davidsbündler*, 7, 71.

Chapter 2

1. The concertos by Field, Ries, Kalkbrenner, and Herz, two of the three concertos by Moscheles (in G Minor and E-flat Major), and Hummel's Concerto in A Minor are listed in the inventory of Schumann's personal library that he drew up in 1830 or 1831 (*Tagebücher*, 1: 315–16; Bischoff, *Monument für Beethoven*, 99–103). Additionally, under the entry "Concert v. Ries. C. moll. Op. 115" in the inventory is the note, "u.[nd] andere in einem Heft," that is, further concertos by Ries besides Opp. 42 and 55 which are entered under separate headings (Op. 55 is incorrectly transcribed by the editor of the *Tagebücher* as Op. 54).
   The Pixis was a staple of Clara Wieck's repertory. Schumann likely knew it through contact with her before he reviewed her performance in Leipzig on 9 July 1832 for the *Komet* (Schumann, *Gesammelte Schriften*, 2: 350 ["Reminiszenzen aus Klara Wiecks letzten Konzerten in Leipzig"]). On 25 April 1831, she played the rondo final movement in Leipzig (Clara Schumann, "Konzertprogramm-Sammlung," no. 6). Schumann requested a copy of Hummel's Concerto in B Minor from Friedrich Wieck on 6 November 1829 (*Jugendbriefe*, 84–85). Only Moscheles's Concerto in F Major is not mentioned in Schumann's early writings; his acquaintance with it will be discussed in Chapter 3.
2. Clara Wieck played Mozart's Concerto in E-flat Major, K. 449, for an invited audience on 9 September 1827, that is, before Schumann moved to Leipzig (Litzmann, *Clara Schumann*, 1: 11–12, 3: 616 ["Studienwerke and Repertoire"]; Roßner, "Clara Wiecks frühe Virtuosenjahre," 262). Schumann may have heard the rondo movement of Beethoven's Third Concerto from Clara as early as 1829 (Bischoff, *Monument für Beethoven*, 108, 419). Friedrich Wieck's student Emilie Reichold performed Beethoven's *Emperor* Concerto with the Leipzig Gewandhaus Orchestra on 21 December 1826 and 11 October 1829. Schumann was not present at either concert but may have heard her play the concerto as he, too, was a student of Wieck (*Tagebücher*, 1: 109-10, 152, 156, 157, 168, 179, 182, 183 [15 August, 4, 14, 15 December 1828; 22 January, 10, 21, 23 March 1829]).
3. Bischoff and Nauhaus, "Robert Schumanns Leipziger Konzertnotizen von 1833," 43–45.
4. The setting apart of Mozart and Beethoven's concertos into a category of their own has a long tradition. As early as 1810, E. T. A. Hoffmann wrote, "I harbour a real aversion to what are called piano concertos. (Those by Mozart and Beethoven are not so much concertos as symphonies with piano obbligato.)" (*Musical Writings*, 101 [from *Kreisleriana*, Part I]).
5. On these home performances, see Chapter 1, pp. 4–5.
6. On the Böhner, see Engel, *Die Entwicklung des Deutschen Klavierkonzertes*, 169–70. On concertos for amateurs, see Milligan, *The Concerto and London's Musical Culture*, 32. Another concerto suitable for amateur performance is Carl Czerny's Four-Hand Piano Concerto in C Major, Op. 153, which Schumann heard performed by Emilie Reichold at Wieck's home on 15 August 1828, presumably without accompanying instruments (orchestra or quartet) and perhaps with Clara Wieck as her partner (*Tagebücher*, 1: 109).
7. Schumann, "Variationen für Pianoforte," *NZfM* 6 (1837): 176; "Phantasieen, Capricen usw. für Pianoforte," *NZfM* 7 (1838): 167. On the inventory, see note 1, this chapter.
8. Rothstein, *Phrase Rhythm*, 70–73.
9. Tovey, who is at pains to rebut the notion of two expositions, believes that Mozart's and Beethoven's immediate successors all chose Beethoven's C Minor Concerto as their point of departure (*Essays in Musical Analysis*, 3: 16–20 ["The Classical Concerto"], 70–73 ["Beethoven, Pianoforte Concerto in C Minor"]). However, already in 1793 Heinrich Christoph Koch considered keeping the opening ritornello in the home tonic or modulating temporarily to a new key as two equally valid procedures, with the latter more usual in modern concertos (*Versuch einer Anleitung zur Composition*, 3: 334–35).

10. Mozart's A Major Concerto, K. 488, is an exception. Its second tutti ends with a new theme, which then forms the basis of the development section.

11. This difference has been noted by Tovey (*Essays in Musical Analysis*, 3: 21 ["The Classical Concerto"]).

12. The Field alternates between thematic and passagework areas, then has a false tutti recapitulation in F minor before one more passagework area leads back to the tonic, A-flat. The Moscheles turns to a *dolce ed espressivo* theme, a variant of the theme of the second group, only after an opening cadenza and passagework based on the first theme; following the *espressivo* theme, passagework leads in just twelve bars to the retransition then tutti recapitulation.

13. On standards generally, see Meyer, "The Concerto," 244–45. On the situation in Paris, see Cooper, *The Rise of Instrumental Music*, 19; in London, Ehrlich, *First Philharmonic*, 29; in Leipzig, "Nachrichten: Leipzig:" *Allgemeine musikalische Zeitung* (hereafter *AmZ*) 36 (1834): col. 131; in Holland, Charlotte Moscheles, ed., *Aus Moscheles' Leben*, 1: 314; and in Darmstadt, Litzmann, *Clara Schumann*, 1: 40.

14. See Sachs, introduction to *Piano Concerto, Op. 113*, by Hummel, ix.

15. Refer to note 9, this chapter.

16. On Hummel's relation to Mozart and Beethoven, see Joel Sachs, "Hummel, Johann Nepomuk," in *New Grove*, 2nd ed.

17. On Herz's education and residency in Paris, see Steve Lindeman, "Herz, Henri [Heinrich]," in *New Grove*, 2nd ed.

18. Particularly, Lerdahl and Jackendoff, *A Generative Theory of Tonal Music*, and Schachter, "Rhythm and Linear Analysis."

19. Rothstein, *Phrase Rhythm*, 70–73.

20. Waldbauer, "Riemann's Periodization," 338, 340.

21. See further on pacing and density, Waldbauer, "Riemann's Periodization," 342–43.

22. Parenthetical insertions are amply discussed by Rothstein, particularly in *Phrase Rhythm*, 87–92.

23. Kerman, *Concerto Conversations*, 50–52.

24. Some recent recordings of concertos by these composers include: Hummel A and B Minor Concertos, Dana Protopopescu, Slovak Radio New Philharmonic Orchestra, Alexander Rahbar conducting (Discover DICD 920117 [recorded 1993]), and Stephen Hough, English Chamber Orchestra, Bryden Thomson conducting (Chandos CHAN 8507 [recorded 1986]); Moscheles, G Minor and E-flat Major Concertos, Howard Shelley, Tasmanian Symphony Orchestra, Shelley conducting ("The Romantic Piano Concerto— 29"; Hyperion CDA 67276 [2002, recorded 2001]); Moscheles, G Minor Concerto, Ian Hobson, Sinfonia da Camera, Hobson conducting (Zephyr Z-119–01 [2001, recorded 1999]); Moscheles, F Major Concerto, Howard Shelley, Tasmanian Symphony Orchestra, Shelley conducting ("The Romantic Piano Concerto—32"; Hyperion CDA C7385 [2003, recorded 1999]). There are also older recordings (dating from c. 1960 on) of some of these concertos and of the Ries, C-sharp Minor Concerto. There are modern editions of Moscheles's G Minor Concerto (Music Treasure Publications, 1971) and Hummel's A Minor and B Minor Concertos (Paragon Music Publishers, 1966 and 1969).

     Of the other concertos discussed in this chapter, *Musica Britannica* has published the first three concertos by Field in full score (vol. 17, ed. Frank Merrick [London: Stainer and Bell, 1961]). In 1990, John O'Conor recorded the complete Field concertos with the New Irish Chamber Orchestra, Janos Fürst conducting (Onyx CD 101/103); Hans Kann recorded Kalkbrenner's D Minor Concerto with the Hamburg Symphony, Herbert Beissel conducting ("The Romantic Piano Concerto," vol. 1; VoxBox CDX 5064 [1992, recorded 1973]). There also are older recordings of the Field and Kalkbrenner. I know of no available recordings of the remaining concertos (by Pixis, Herz, and those not already mentioned by Ries and Moscheles).

Chapter 3

1. Eismann, *Quellenwerk*, 1: 81 ("Aus dem Projektenbuch"). The dating of the two fair copies is based on the handwriting style as assessed by Dr. Matthias Wendt (oral communication).

2. Schumann, *Tagebücher*, 1: 360–62.

3. Schumann, "Skizzenbuch I," 5–8, and "Skizzenbuch III," 41–44.

4. Schumann, *Briefe: Neue Folge*, 31 (letter to Hummel of 20 August 1831).

5. Kapp, *Spätwerk Robert Schumanns*, 12–13. The title page of Schumann's Psalm is dated 1822, but in 1846 he wrote in his diary that he began work on it in 1821. See the facsimile in Eismann, *Robert Schumann: Eine Biographie*, 38; also, Schumann, *Tagebücher*, 2: 402.
6. Kapp, *Spätwerk Robert Schumanns*, 16. The theater opened with Weber's *Der Freischütz*. The productions Schumann lists seeing thereafter under the heading "Theaterpassion (1823–27)" are [*Der*] *Wasserträger* [*Les deux journées*] by Cherubini, *Jacob* [recte *Joseph*] *in Egypten* by Méhul, *Das Donauweibchen* by Ferdinand Kauer, *Fanchon* [*das Leyermädchen*] by Friedrich Heinrich Himmel, [*Die*] *Entführung* [*aus dem Serail*] by Mozart, *Die Dorfsängerinnen* [*Le cantatrici villane*] by Valentino Fioravanti, and *Preciosa*, a play by P. A. Wolff with incidental music by Weber ("Materialien," 2). Under "Theater im Zwickau" in his "Älteste musikalische Erinnerungen" he further lists *Don Juan* by Mozart, and *Aschenbrödel* [*La Cenerentola*] by Rossini (p. 2).
7. See Chapter 1, p. 7.
8. McCorkle, *Schumann: Werkverzeichnis*, 658; Eismann, *Quellenwerk*, 1: 20 ("Programm einer Musikalisch-deklamatorischen Abendunterhaltung auf dem Gymnasium").
9. Schumann, *Tagebücher*, 1: 157 (15, 16 and 17 December 1828); McCorkle, *Schumann. Werkverzeichnis*, 658.
10. Rosen, "Influence: Plagiarism and Inspiration," 88.
11. Kallberg, "The Rhetoric of Genre," 243.
12. Burkholder, "'Quotation' and Emulation," 2–3.
13. See Chapter 1, pp. 7, 9–10.
14. Schumann, "Pianoforte: Concerte," review of Piano Concertos Nos. 5 and 6, by Moscheles, *NZfM* 4 (1836): 123.
15. Schumann, *Tagebücher*, 1: 361 (14 August 1831). Examples 3.1 and 3.2 show portions of the exposition from Sketchbook III. Although Schumann had abandoned this version by August 1831, he did retain, with minimal alteration, its first thirty-three bars, including the lyric theme.
16. Litzmann, *Clara Schumann*, 1: 32–33; 3: 616 ("Studienwerke und Repertoire"). She may have played the first movement of the Field in Dresden as early as 1830 (I am grateful to Nancy Reich for sharing this information from a transcription of Clara Wieck's "Tagebücher"). On the school of Field see Nicholas Temperley, "Field, John," in *New Grove*.
17. Schumann, *Tagebücher*, 1: 207 (19 July 1829).
18. Engel, *Die Entwicklung des Deutschen Klavierkonzertes*, 175.
19. Schumann, *Briefe: Neue Folge*, 32 (letter of 20 August 1831).
20. See Wendt, "Zu Robert Schumanns Skizzenbüchern," 114.
21. The complaint against Chopin goes back at least as far as Frederick Niecks (*Frederick Chopin*, 1: 210); is then continued by a number of English authors, namely, Tovey (*Essays in Musical Analysis*, 3: 103); Abraham (*Chopin's Musical Style*, 36); and Samson (*The Music of Chopin*, 55).
22. Schumann, *Jugendbriefe*, 134.
23. Schumann, *Briefe: Neue Folge*, 32.
24. The dedication is found in Schumann, "Skizzenbuch I," 29. A reproduction is in Hans Schneider, Catalog No. 188, p. 79.
25. The letter, which is drafted in Schumann's "Briefkonzeptbuch," 28–29, is unpublished. It is transcribed in appendix 1 of my dissertation, "Robert Schumann's F-Major Piano Concerto." For a partial transcription, see Boetticher, *Schumanns Klavierwerke*, 1: 26.
26. See Chapter 2, note 1.

Chapter 4

1. Clara Wieck, "Tagebücher" (refer to Chapter 3, note 16). Schumann records the occasion, but does not mention the Herz. See his *Tagebücher*, 1: 362–63.
2. Schumann, *Gesammelte Schriften*, 1: 1 ("Einleitendes").
3. Plantinga, *Schumann as Critic*, 17.
4. None of Hünten's works are listed in the index of compositions compiled by Kreisig in Schumann, *Gesammelte Schriften*.
5. Schumann, *Tagebücher*, 1: 344 (1 July 1831).
6. Schumann, "Pianoforte: Concerte," review of First Concerto, by Döhler, *NZfM* 4 (1836): 83.
7. Schumann, "Kritik: Sonaten für Pianoforte," *NZfM* 2 (1835): 127 (signed Florestan).

8. Schumann, *Tagebücher*, 1: 331, 349, 363 (13 May, 9 July, 19 August 1831). See also my article, "Schumann's Piano Practice," 547–49.

9. Schumann, *Tagebücher*, 1: 333 (24 May 1831).

10. Schumann, "Pianoforte: Concerte," review of Ninth Concerto, Op. 177, by Ries, *NZfM* 4 (1836): 114.

11. Macdonald, "The Models for Schumann's F-Major Piano Concerto," 171–74.

12. The correct count, twenty-nine bars, is recorded on the page 61 chart (Figure 4.1, line 4). The theme and postlude remained the same through all changes to the second fair copy of the exposition, just as it was recorded on that chart. They also were transposed nearly exactly in the recapitulation, hence the count of bars for the theme and postlude in the recapitulation (twenty-one bars, see Figure 4.4, line 16) is also incorrect.

13. The first revision to the close of the exposition is recorded on the page 43 chart, line 3, then copied onto the page 46 chart, line 8: a count of thirty-five bars as compared with the thirty-six bars given on the page 61 chart, which is the actual number in the close on pages 7–8 (Example 3.8, bars 96–131). This first revision consists of an insert replacing twenty-two bars of the original thirty-six-bar closing period with twenty-one bars written in Sketchbook I, page 83. On the page 46 chart, Schumann indicated a second revision by crossing out the number 35 and substituting for it the number 42 (Figure 4.4, line 8). This second revision is found on page 76. It involves a rewriting of and changes to the remaining areas of the closing period on pages 7–8 (those surrounding the revision on p. 83), including a cue indicating where the already revised portion on page 83 is to be inserted. For further explanation of the sketch sources for the final version of the close of the exposition, see my dissertation, "Robert Schumann's F-Major Piano Concerto," 339–54.

14. The bars of the transition in Sketchbook I, page 6, are similarly numbered.

15. Schumann, *Tagebücher*, 1: 361–62.

16. Schumann, "Zum neuen Jahr," *NZfM* 10 (1839): 1. See also Plantinga, *Schumann as Critic*, 100-10.

17. Schumann, "Zur Eröffnung des Jahrganges 1835," *NZfM* 2 (1835): 3.

18. Schumann, *Tagebücher*, 1: 361 (14 August 1831).

19. Petzoldt, "Klassik, Romantik und Klassizismus bei Robert Schumann," 108-10.

20. Macdonald, "The Models for Schumann's F-Major Piano Concerto," 175–78.

21. Evidently this count does not include the last two bars of the close, which are marked tutti. On the sketch sources for the final version of the close of the recapitulation, see my dissertation, "Robert Schumann's F-Major Piano Concerto," 403–10.

22. Schumann, "Pianoforte: Concerte," review of concertos by Chopin, *NZfM* 4 (1836): 138.

23. Plantinga, *Schumann as Critic*, 159.

24. Meyer, "The Concerto," 240. See also, Rink, *Chopin: The Piano Concertos*, 5.

25. See Engel, *Die Entwicklung des Deutschen Klavierkonzertes*, 212; Schering, *Geschichte des Instrumentalkonzertes*, 186–87; Abraham, *Chopin's Musical Style*, 31–32; Samson, *The Music of Chopin*, 51; Headington, "The Virtuoso Concerto," 144, 147.

26. Sachs, *Kapellmeister Hummel*, 40–42.

27. Ibid., 36–38.

28. Paul Dekeyser, "Kalkbrenner, Frédéric," in *New Grove*, 2nd ed. Nautsch, *Friedrich Kalkbrenner*, 125–26.

29. Schumann, "Pianoforte: Concerte," *NZfM* 4 (1836): 138.

30. Ibid.

31. Litzmann, *Clara Schumann*, 1: 42; Roßner, "Clara Wiecks frühe Virtuosenjahre," 265. Wieck heard a performance in Paris at Abbé Bertin's on 14 March 1832, apparently by the composer, though Roßner says it was by Mendelssohn. See also Wieck's comment to Schumann in Schumann, *Tagebücher*, 1: 383 (3 May 1832).

32. G. W. Fink, "Concerte für das Pianoforte," review of Concerto in F Minor, Op. 21, by Chopin, *AmZ* 38 (1836): cols. 538–39. See also Engel, *Die Entwicklung des Deutschen Klavierkonzertes*, 212.

33. Schumann, *Tagebücher*, 1: 333 (24 May 1831).

34. Schumann, *Jugendbriefe*, 155–56.

35. Schumann, *Tagebücher*, 1: 376 (12 November 1831); 413 (9 August 1832).

36. Ostwald, "Schumann's Right Hand," 22.

37. Eismann, *Quellenwerk*, 1: 78 ("Projektenbuch" entry); *Jugendbriefe*, 184, 188–89, 210–11 (letters to his mother of 14 June, 9 August 1832; 28 June 1833); Daverio, *Robert Schumann*, 77–79.

38. Schumann, *Briefe: Neue Folge*, 40–41 (letter to Töpken of 5 April 1833).
39. Eismann, *Quellenwerk*, 1: 74 (letter from Dorn to Wasielewski of 7 September 1856).
40. Schumann, *Tagebücher*, 1: 397, 399 (26, 28 May 1832).
41. Finson, *Robert Schumann and the Study of Orchestral Composition*, 4–9.
42. Reich, *Clara Schumann*, rev. ed., 227–28.
43. Newcomb, "Schumann and the Marketplace," 268–69. Concerning Schumann's playing, see Johann Peter Lyser's description in Schumann, *Gesammelte Schriften*, 2: 423 n. 368.
44. Newcomb, "Schumann and the Marketplace," 308 n. 43.

Chapter 5

1. Schumann, "Zum neuen Jahr 1839," *NZfM* 10 (1839): 1.
2. Schumann, "Pianoforte: Concerte," review of piano concertos by Chopin, *NZfM* 4 (1836): 137–38.
3. Schumann, "Pianoforte: Concerte," review of Piano Concerto, by Taubert, *NZfM* 4 (1 April 1836): 115.
4. Schumann, "Pianoforte: Concerte," review of Piano Concerto No. 1, by Schornstein, *NZfM* 4 (1836): 71.
5. Schumann, "Das Clavier-Concert," *NZfM* 10 (1839): 5–6.
6. Ibid., 6.
7. Schumann, "Concerte für das Pianoforte," review of Concerto No. 3 in D Minor, by Herz, *NZfM* 6 (1837): 50; "Pianoforte: Concerte," review of Concerto No. 2, by Hartknoch, *NZfM* 4 (1836): 93.
8. Schumann, "Pianoforte: Concerte," review of Concerto No. 2 in C Minor, Op. 74, by Herz, *NZfM* 4 (1836): 111.
9. Schumann, "Pianoforte: Concerte," review of Concerto in F Minor, Op. 5, by Hiller, *NZfM* 4 (1836): 84.
10. Pederson, "A. B. Marx," 100-2.
11. Dörffel, *Geschichte der Gewandhausconcerte*, "Statistik," 42–43.
12. The five performances of Beethoven concertos were: 8 February 1821 and 13 October 1823 (*Emperor*, by Friedrich Schneider); 1 January 1826 (C Minor, by Louise David); 21 December 1826 and 11 October 1829 (*Emperor*, by Emilie Reichold). The two performances of Mozart concertos were: 21 March 1822 (D Minor, soloist unknown); 16 February 1826 (C Major, K. 467, by Moritz Adolph Fuhrmann). These figures were garnered primarily from the "Statistik" section of Dörffel's *Geschichte der Gewandhausconcerte*, with some amplification from the "Chronik" section, and from reports in the *AmZ*.
13. Some other, newer piano concertos performed in Leipzig from 1821 to 1830 were by Field, Conradin Kreutzer, Pixis, Aloys Schmitt, and Weber. However, none of these composers had near the popularity with their concertos as Hummel, Ries, Kalkbrenner, or Moscheles.
14. Table 5.1 is based on the "Statistik" section of Dörffel's *Geschichte der Gewandhausconcerte*. To the performances he lists I have added those by Joseph Krogulski of the Kalkbrenner D Minor and Hummel A Minor concertos (first movements only) that apparently were not part of the regular subscription series or extra concerts at the Gewandhaus ("Nachrichten: Leipzig—bis zum 10. December," *AmZ* 28 [1826]: col. 850).
15. Willi Kahl, "Berger, Ludwig," in *Die Musik in Geschichte und Gegenwart*.
16. Jansen, *Die Davidsbündler*, 123–26.
17. Burnham, "Criticism, Faith, and the *Idee*," 190–92.
18. Pederson, "A. B. Marx," 97–98.
19. Kropfinger, "Klassik-Rezeption in Berlin," 374; "Nachrichten: Berlin," *AmZ* 34 (1832): col. 361; 35 (1833): col. 368.
20. Kropfinger, "Klassik-Rezeption in Berlin," 375.
21. Holoman, *Berlioz*, 48–49.
22. Cairns, *Berlioz*, 1: 305–8, 338–41. On a planned performance of the *Emperor* a year earlier by Liszt, see Walker, *Franz Liszt*, 1: 135.
23. Keeling, "Liszt's Appearances in Parisian Concerts," 31.
24. Ranft, *Felix Mendelssohn Bartholdy*, 31. Mendelssohn, *Briefe*, 1: 329 (letter to his family of 31 March 1832).
25. Hiller, *Felix Mendelssohn-Bartholdy*, 17.

26. Cooper, *The Rise of Instrumental Music*, 123, 127.
27. W. H. Husk and Bruce Carr, "Neate, Charles," in *New Grove*, 2nd ed. Foster, *History of the Philharmonic Society*, 4–5, 43, 46.
28. Philip H. Peter and Julian Rushton, "Potter: (4) (Philip) Cipriani (Hambly) Potter," in *New Grove*, 2nd ed. Foster, *History of the Philharmonic Society*, 56, 67, 73.
29. Ellsworth, "The Piano Concerto in London Concert Life," 158, 220.
30. Ehrlich, *First Philharmonic*, 47.
31. Ellsworth, "The Piano Concerto in London Concert Life," 150–52. See also her Appendix 2 ("List of Piano Concerto Performances in Order by Composer"), and Foster, *History of the Philharmonic Society*, 44, 50, 61.
32. "Nachrichten: Wien," *AmZ* 22 (1820): col. 479 (Blahetka); 29 (1827): cols. 370 (Czerny) and 453 (Bocklet); 31 (1829): col. 328 (Blahetka).
33. "Nachrichten: Wien," *AmZ* 33 (1831): col. 437; 35 (1833): col. 411 (Thalberg); 36 (1834): col. 418 (Thalberg); 37 (1835): col. 202 (Sallomon) and col. 444 (Thalberg); 38 (1836): cols. 464 (Hoffmann) and 478 (Henselt); 39 (1837): col. 321 (Bocklet); 41 (1839): cols. 167 (Bocklet) and 447; 42 (1840): cols. 92–93 (Liszt).
34. "Nachrichten: Wien," *AmZ* 37 (1835): col. 380 (Tedesco); 38 (1836): col. 248 (Bocklet); 41 (1839): col. 447 (Mozart, Jr.).
35. On the cadenzas published by Artaria, see Köchel's *Mozart Verzeichnis*, 733. The set of cadenzas and elaborations published by André were for Mozart's concertos K. 503, 595, 491, 482, 488, and 467. In 1959 Hinrichsen published a modern edition edited by A. Hyatt King. See his essay, "Philipp Karl Hoffmann: His Cadenzas to some of Mozart's Piano Concertos and Elaborations of their Slow Movements," which is tipped in as an introduction.
36. King, "Philipp Karl Hoffmann," [2].
37. A. E. Müller, *Anweisung zum genauen Vortrage der Mozartschen Clavierconcerte hauptsächlich in Absicht richtiger Applicatur* (Leipzig: Breitkopf and Härtel, 1796), introduction and p. 4. The translations are from Broder, "The First Guide to Mozart," 227, 228.
38. "Nachrichten: Leipzig," *AmZ* 22 (1820): col. 222 (review of concert of 11 March).
39. Ibid., cols. 219–20 (review of concert of 21 February).
40. Sachs, "Authentic English and French Editions," 205–9.
41. Benyovszky, *J. N. Hummel*, 232 (letter of 15 April 1823).
42. Ibid., 312–13 (letter of 15 April 1823).
43. Ibid., 231 (letter of 15 April 1823).
44. The concertos are, in order of publication, the D Minor, K.466; C major, K. 503; E-flat Major for Two Pianos, K. 365 (316a); C Minor, K. 491; D Major, K. 537 (*Krönungskonzert*); E-flat Major, K. 482; and B-flat Major, K. 456. No arrangements by Kalkbrenner or Moscheles were included in Hummel's series.
45. Cramer's arrangements are also for solo piano, with optional flute, violin, and cello. They are of Mozart's concertos in F Major, K. 459; B-flat Major, K. 450; C Major, K. 467; E-flat Major, K. 482; D Minor, K. 466; and C Minor, K. 491.
46. Macdonald, "Mozart's Piano Concertos," 306–13.
47. Grayson, "Whose Authenticity?"
48. Cramer's arrangements have first-movement cadenzas for only three of the six concertos (the E-flat Major, K. 482, D Minor, and C Minor); for the other three, no fermata indicates where a cadenza would fall. Five of Hummel's arrangements have first-movement cadenzas (the exceptions are K. 365 and 537).
49. "Nachrichten: Berlin," *AmZ* 35 (1833): col. 521. On the identification of the critic and date of the concert, see Nautsch, *Friedrich Kalkbrenner*, 81, 239.
50. G. W. Fink, review of Piano Concerto in C Major, by Mozart, arranged by Kalkbrenner, *AmZ* 31 (1829): cols. 542, 543. See also Grayson, "Whose Authenticity?" 379.
51. Gottfried Weber, review of Concerto in C Minor, by Mozart, edited by Hummel, *Caecilia, eine Zeitschrift für die musikalische Welt* 14 (1832): 309–11.
52. "Nachrichten: Berlin," *AmZ* 32 (1830): col. 137.
53. *Haude- und Spenersche Zeitung* of 30 January 1830. Citation from Kropfinger, "Klassik-Rezeption in Berlin," 375.
54. "Philharmonic Concerts," *The Harmonicon* 11 (1833): part 1, p. 135.
55. Macfarren, "Cipriani Potter," 46.
56. See, for example, Carl Reinecke, *Zur Wiederbelebung der Mozart'schen Clavier-Concerte: Ein Wort der Anregung an die clavierspielende Welt* (Leipzig: Gebrüder Reinecke, [1891]). Also my article, "Mozart's Piano Concertos," 319.

57. Wieck, *Piano and Song*, 146.
58. Litzmann, *Clara Schumann*, 2: 95 (quoted from her diary entry of 9 December 1845).
59. G. W. Fink, "Funfzigjährige Jubelfeyer des Instituts der Abonnement-Concerte Leipzigs in Saale des Gewandhauses, am 24sten Novbr. 1831," *AmZ* 33 (1838): col. 802.
60. "Nachrichten: Leipzig," *AmZ* 38 (1836): col. 105.
61. Schumann, *Tagebücher*, 2: 31 (January 1837). "Nachrichten: Leipzig," *AmZ* 39 (1837): col. 46.
62. "Nachrichten: Leipzig," *AmZ* (1835): col. 267.
63. "Nachrichten," *AmZ* 40 (1838): col. 168.
64. Schumann, *Gesammelte Schriften*, 2: 165 and 448 n. 496. See also Grayson, "Whose Authenticity?" 382.
65. Kinsky and Halm, *Beethoven Verzeichnis*, 35 (Op. 15), 47 (Op. 19), 93 (Op. 37), 137 (Op. 58), 196 (Op. 73).
66. "Bedeutende Werke," review of *Sämmtliche Concerte von Lud. von Beethoven* in score, *AmZ* 37 (1835): col. 261.
67. Horst Heussner, *Kritischer Bericht, Neue Mozart-Ausgabe*, ser. V, work group 15, vol. 6 (K. 466, K. 467, K. 482) (Kassel: Barenreiter, 1986), f/21–22, f/76–77.
68. Four-hand arrangements of the rondo movements of the Third and Fifth Concertos by F. Mockwitz were published in 1824 and 1826 by Breitkopf and Härtel, and Probst. Four-hand arrangements of Beethoven's First and Third Concertos by J. P. Schmidt were published in 1829 and 1830 by Breitkopf and Härtel, and Brüggemann. Xaver Gleichauf's arrangement of Beethoven's Second Concerto for four hands was published by Peters in 1835. See Kinsky and Halm, *Beethoven Verzeichnis*, 35 (Op. 15), 47 (Op. 19), 93 (Op. 37), 196 (Op. 73).
69. "Arrangirtes für Pianoforte zu 4 Händen," review of Piano Concerto, Op. 73, by Beethoven, arranged for piano four-hands by Xaver Gleichauf, *AmZ* 41 (1839): cols. 996–97.
70. Schumann, "Fragmente aus Leipzig," *NZfM* 5 (1836): 185.
71. Bischoff and Nauhaus, "Robert Schumanns Leipziger Konzertnotizen," 45.
72. "Nachrichten: Leipzig," *AmZ* 36 (1834): col. 131.
73. Schumann, "Camilla Pleyel," *NZfM* 11 (1839): 155. Pleyel performed Beethoven's C Minor Concerto on 2 November.

Chapter 6

1. The series titles are "Pianoforte: Concerte" (1836), "Concerte für das Pianoforte" (1837), "Das Clavier-Concert" (1839), and "Concertstücke und Concerte für Pianoforte" (1840). One of the twenty-five reviews, of Clara Wieck's Concerto in the 1837 series, was by Carl Ferdinand Becker.
2. Kross, "The Establishment of a Brahms Repertoire," 25.
3. See Chapter 1, notes 54 and 55. In addition to most of a cycle of Beethoven's symphonies, Schumann also heard Haydn, *Military* Symphony, No. 100; Mozart, Symphony in C Major, and Symphony in G Minor, K. 550; Abt Vogler, Symphony; Spohr, Symphony No. 3 in C Minor, Op. 78; and J. W. Kalliwoda, Symphony No. 2 in E-flat Major, Op. 17 (*Tagebücher*, 1: 132 [6 November 1828], 446 n. 106; 158 [18 December 1828], 449 nn. 137, and 172 [5 February 1829], 450 n. 156; 168 [22 January 1829], 450 n. 152; 175 [19 February 1829], 451 n. 163; 178 [5 March 1829], 452 n. 167).
4. Clara and Robert Schumann, *The Complete Correspondence*, 1: 14 (letter of 28 August 1835).
5. Dörffel, *Geschichte der Gewandhausconcerte*, "Chronik," 239; "Statistik," 63, 87. See also Koenigsbeck, *Bassoon Bibliography*, 382.
6. Stravinsky and Craft, *Stravinsky in Pictures and Documents*, 69 (letter from Stravinsky to Alexandre Benois of 26 January 1911).
7. Schumann, "Concerte für das Pianoforte," *NZfM* 6 (1837): 65. Schumann printed Moscheles's letter as an addendum to his review of William Sterndale Bennett's Third Concerto. Moscheles wrote the letter on 20 December 1836 (Boetticher, ed., *Briefe und Gedichte*, 295). On the title of the work see Nauhaus, "Schumanns Klaviersonate f-Moll," 53–58; also Roesner, "The Autograph of Schumann's Piano Sonata in F Minor."
8. The Concerto also was reviewed by G. W. Fink in the *AmZ* 38 (1836): cols. 542–43. It was originally published by F. W. Betzhold in Elberfeld (where Schornstein was *Musikdirektor*).

In his *Universal-Handbuch der Musikliteratur* Pazdírek lists it in an edition by Hofmeister. No Leipzig performances of the work are recorded in Dörffel's *Geschichte der Gewandhausconcerte*. Already in 1927 Engel reported that there were no extant copies of the concerto in Germany (*Die Entwicklung des Deutschen Klavierkonzertes*, 241).

9. Schumann, "Pianoforte: Concerte," review of Concerto in F Minor, by Schornstein, Op. 1, *NZfM* 4 (1836): 71.
10. Ibid., 72.
11. Ibid.
12. "Englische Briefe von D. G.," *NZfM* 1 (1834): 7–8.
13. "Correspondenz: Dresden: Anfang April," *NZfM* 1 (1834): 38–39 (signed 28).
14. Schumann, *Jugendbriefe*, 176–77 (letter to his mother of 5 May 1832).
15. Schumann, "Concertstücke und Concerte für Pianoforte," review of Concerto in F Major, Op. post., by Hummel, *NZfM* 12 (1840): 39.
16. G. W. Fink, "Oeuvres posthumes de J. N. Hummel," *AmZ* 41 (1839): col. 622.
17. Hummel also played the F Major Concerto at a private concert in Dresden on 31 March 1834. Carl Borromäus von Miltitz, the correspondent for the *Allegemine musikalische Zeitung*, lauded the performance (vol. 36 [1834]: col. 320). Although less enthusiastic, the correspondent for the *Neue Zeitschrift* also had some praise for it (vol. 1 [1834]: 24). On the reaction at the King's Theatre, see Sachs, *Kapellmeister Hummel*, 87–89.
18. Carl Richter, "Hummel's Clavierconcerte und ihre Bedeutung für die jetzige Zeit," *NZfM* 79 (1883): 445–46, 458–60.
19. Engel, *Die Entwicklung des Deutschen Klavierkonzertes*, 184–85, on Hummel generally, 180–85.
20. In the late nineteenth century, Carl Reinecke issued a four-volume set, *Clavier-Concerte alter und neuer Zeit*, for use at the Leipzig Conservatory where he was a professor of pianoforte and free composition. Among its twenty concertos arranged for two pianos, in addition to eleven by Bach, Mozart, and Beethoven, are Hummel's A Minor, B Minor, and A-flat Major Concertos. In 1896 Reinecke's edition of the A Minor Concerto was published as volume 47 of *Schirmer's Library of Musical Classics*, and in 1903 Xaver Schwarenka's edition of the first movement of the B Minor Concerto was published by Breitkopf and Härtel in the series *Partitur-Bibliothek für Pianoforte mit Orchester*. Later still, in 1966 and 1969, arrangements of the two concertos appeared in the Paragon Library of Musical Classics, volumes 26 and 28, though by then they were called, in an introduction by T. J. G., "long neglected."
21. Sachs, *Kapellmeister Hummel*, 33, 35, 45, 50, 68, 75 (on the A-flat Concerto); 87–88 (on the F Major); 66, 72–73, 75 (on the A Minor).
22. Schumann, "Pianoforte: Concerte," review of Concerto No. 9 in G Minor, Op. 177, by Ries, *NZfM* 4 (1836): 114.
23. Ellsworth, "The Piano Concerto in London Concert Life," 306–307 (Appendix 2).
24. See note 20, this chapter.
25. Dörffel does not list any performances of the Ninth Concerto in his *Geschichte der Gewandhausconcerte zu Leipzig*.
26. Fink, "Concertmusik für Pianoforte," *AmZ* 37 (1835): col. 210.
27. Engel, *Die Entwicklung des Deutschen Klavierkonzertes*, 178.
28. Litzmann, *Clara Schumann*, 3: 616 ("Studienwerke und Repertoire").
29. See Chapter 3, pp. 41–42.
30. Schumann, *Tagebücher*, 1: 390, 398, 399.
31. Schumann, *Gesammelte Schriften*, 2: 352 (review for the *Komet*, August 1832, "Reminiszenzen aus Klara Wiecks letzten Konzerten in Leipzig").
32. On the popularity of the Concerto, see Piggott, *The Life and Music of John Field*, 152–53; also Hopkinson, *Catalogue of the Works of John Field*, 77–79 (no. 31). On the *Musica Britannica* volume, see Chapter 2, note 24.
33. Dessauer, *John Field*, 99; Branson, *John Field and Chopin*, 130–31, 138; Piggott, *Life and Music of John Field*, 179.
34. Schumann, "Pianoforte: Concerte," review of Piano Concerto No. 7, by Field, *NZfM* (1836): 122.
35. Schumann, "Die 7te Symphonie von Franz Schubert," *NZfM* 12 (1840): 82.
36. "Recensionen," *AmZ* 37 (1835): col. 526.
37. Piggott, *Life and Music of John Field*, 76. Piggott does not give an exact citation for the quote, which is from a review of Field's three Paris concerts.

38. "Nachrichten: Moskau, im März," *AmZ* 24 (1822): col. 343.

39. Frank Merrick, *Musica Britannica,* 17: xiii (Preface). For support of Merrick's sugges-
    tion, see Piggott, *The Life and Music of John Field,* 157–58; and Nicholas Temperley,
    "Field, John," in *New Grove.* Branson argues that Field may have played his Third Con-
    certo without the addition of a nocturne to substitute for a slow movement (*John Field
    and Chopin,* 80).

40. Differing opinions about the possibility are given, in different sources, by Piggott. See his
    notes for John Field, "The Complete Piano Concertos," John O'Conor, piano, New Irish
    Chamber Orchestra conducted by Janos Fürst (Onyx CD 101/103 [1990, recorded 1982]);
    The Life and Music of John Field, 134–35, and "John Field and the Nocturne," 61.

41. Liszt, *Sämtliche Schriften,* 1: 380 ("Compositions pour piano, de M. Robert Schumann,"
    Gazette musicale, 12 November 1837). Translation from Wasielewski, *Life of Robert
    Schumann,* 268 ("Franz Liszt on R. Schumann's … Concerto without Orchestral Accom-
    paniment [Op. 14]"). In his review of the Concerto in 1835, the writer for the *Allgemeine
    musikalische Zeitung* merely states that the *Adagio* movement is lacking without going
    on to suggest that the nocturne episode substitutes for it. In an accompanying review of a
    separate edition of this episode published as Nocturne No. 12, the same writer calls it
    "ein Mittelsatz aus dem ersten Theil," which, like Liszt's description, show its dual func-
    tion. It is a middle movement (or section) but it is in the first part (or movement).
    "Recensionen," *AmZ* 37 (1835): cols. 525, 526. Note, however, that more recently Hopkin-
    son calls the nocturne episode the second movement of the Seventh Concerto (*Catalogue
    of the Works of John Field,* 135 [no. 58]).

42. Schumann, "Pianoforte: Concerte," *NZfM* 4 (1836): 122. Schumann says the quotation is
    from Wieland.

43. Meyer, "The Concerto," 220–21.

44. Plantinga, *Schumann as Critic,* 230.

45. Schumann, "Pianoforte: Concerte," review of Piano Concertos, Opp. 11 and 21, by
    Chopin, *NZfM* 4 (1833): 138.

46. Litzmann, *Clara Schumann,* 1: 42; Schumann, *Tagebücher,* 1: 383 (3 May 1832). See
    also Chapter 4, note 31.

47. Clara Schumann, "Konzertprogramm-Sammlung," nos. 36 and 43 (Leipzig), 49 and 55
    (Magdeburg, late November and 3 December 1834, finale only), 61 (Hanover, 24 Janu-
    ary 1835, finale), 66 (Bremen, 18 February 1835), 70 (Hamburg, 20 March 1835, second
    movement and finale).

48. Litzmann, *Clara Schumann,* 1: 89.

49. Schumann, "Vermischtes," and "Schwärmbriefe: Eusebius an Chiara," *NZfM* 3 (1835):
    112 and 127.

50. Methuen-Campbell, *Chopin Playing,* 37. The citation is from Schumann's letter of
    14 September 1836 to Heinrich Dorn in Riga. Methuen-Campbell wrongly states that
    Schumann wrote the letter from Paris. He was, rather, in Leipzig. See Schumann, *Briefe:
    Neue Folge,* 78–79.

51. Louis Rakemann performed the final two movements of Chopin's E Minor Concerto on
    8 September 1836. See "Vermischtes," *NZfM* 5 (1836): 89; also Schumann, *Tagebücher,*
    2: 25 and 454 n. 16. Performances in Leipzig by Clara were on 8 September (first move-
    ment), and 6 December 1838 (second and third movements). See Schumann, *Tagebücher,*
    3: 48 (8 September 1838) and 690 n. 25; "Chronik," *NZfM* 9 (1838): 194.

52. Litzmann, *Clara Schumann,* 1: 399 (letter from Clara to Robert of 12 February 1840).
    The concert was on February 11 ("Konzertprogramm-Sammlung," no. 167).

53. Fink, "Recension," review of Concerto No. 1, by Chopin, *AmZ* 36 (1834): col. 541.

54. Clara Schumann, "Konzertprogramm-Sammlung," nos. 183, 293.

55. Eigeldinger, *Chopin: Pianist and Teacher,* 142–43 n. 158. On the performances of the
    E Minor Concerto in Breslau and Rouen, see also Rink, *Chopin: The Piano Concertos,*
    14–15.

56. Fink, "Recension," *AmZ* 36 (1834): cols. 542.

57. Eigeldinger, *Chopin: Pianist and Teacher,* 290 (*Revue musicale* 6, no. 5 [3 March 1832]:
    38–39).

58. See further Chapter 3, note 21.

59. Samson, *The Music of Chopin,* 55. See also Rink, *Chopin: The Piano Concertos,* 63.

60. Berlioz, *Memoirs,* 476 (St. Petersburg, 1847).

61. Tovey, *Essays in Musical Analysis,* 3: 103–4.

62. Meyer, "The Concerto," 243–46.
63. Atwood, *Fryderyk Chopin,* 220 (*Revue Musicale,* 6, no. 17 [26 May 1832]: 133–34), and cf. pp. 60, 63–64. Atwood says these were both performances of the F Minor Concerto; Eigeldinger says they were of the E Minor, however he gives 30 May as the date of the 20 May 1832 concert (*Chopin: Pianist and Teacher,* 142–43 n. 157). Contemporary confirmation that Chopin played his E Minor Concerto on at least the February concert (at Salle Pleyel) is given by Hiller, *Felix Mendelssohn-Bartholdy,* 22.
64. See Chapter 4, pp. 66–69.
65. Rink, *Chopin: The Piano Concertos,* 26.
66. Schumann, "Pianoforte: Concerte," *NZfM* 4 (1833): 137.
67. Rink, *Chopin: The Piano Concertos,* 55–57.

Chapter 7

1. Barth, Mack, and Voss, eds., *Wagner: A Documentary Study,* 167. The letter is erroneously dated 12 November 1845; it was written, rather, on 12 December, after Schumann attended the fifth performance of *Tannhäuser,* on 22 November. See Schumann, *Tagebücher,* 3: 755 n. 567.
2. Schumann, *Briefe: Neue Folge,* 373 (letter of 8 May 1853).
3. See my article, "Schumann's Piano Practice."
4. For some discussion of Schumann's reviews of piano etudes, see Plantinga, *Schumann as Critic,* 138–47, 250–53.
5. Colt and Miall, *The Early Piano,* 112.
6. Winter, "The 19th-Century: Keyboards," 359; further in "Striking It Rich," 286–87.
7. Litzmann, *Clara Schumann,* 1: 43, 286 (letter to Robert Schumann of 14 February 1839).
8. Eigeldinger, *Chopin: Pianist and Teacher,* 290 (*Revue musicale* 6, no. 5 [March 1832]).
9. Schumann, "Pianoforte: Concerto," review of Piano Concerto No. 2 in C Minor, Op. 74, by Herz, *NZfM* 4 (1836): 111.
10. Chopin, *Letters,* 156 (letter to Tytus Wojciechowski of 12 December 1831). See also Heinrich Heine's report of the same concert (*Sämtliche Schriften,* 5: 127 ["F. Hillers Konzert"]).
11. "Nachrichten," *AmZ* 38 (1836): cols. 694–95.
12. Schumann, *Tagebücher,* 2: 26–30 (19 September to 3 December 1836). According to Katharine Ellis, Stamaty returned to Paris in early 1837 ("Stamaty, Camille [Marie]," in *New Grove,* 2nd ed.).
13. Schumann, *Briefe: Neue Folge,* 80 (letter of 15 November 1836).
14. Schumann, "Concerte für das Pianoforte," review of Concerto, Op. 2, by Stamaty, *NZfM* 6 (1837): 35.
15. Ibid., 35–36.
16. Schumann, *Jugendbriefe,* 211 (letter to his mother of 28 June 1833).
17. Schumann, *Briefe: Neue Folge,* 177–78 (letter to Gustav Adolf Keferstein of 31 January 1840), also 149 (letter to Simonin de Sire of 15 March 1839). See also Schumann's letter to his mother of 2 July 1834 (*Jugendbriefe,* 242).
18. Schumann, *Tagebücher,* 1: 383 (3 May 1832).
19. Schumann, "Kritik," review of XXIV Etudes, Op. 15, by Hiller, *NZfM* 2 (1835): 5–6, 53. The reference to Heine's epithet is found in Schumann, "Pianoforte: Concerto," review of Concerto in F Minor, Op. 5, by Hiller, *NZfM* 4 (1836): 84.
20. Schumann, "Pianoforte: Concerto," *NZfM* 4 (1836): 84.
21. Schumann, performance review of *Die Zerstörung Jerusalems,* by Hiller, *NZfM* 12 (1840): 120; "Neue Oratorien," review of *Die Zerstörung Jerusalems,* *NZfM* 14 (1841): 2–4.
22. Later editions of Op. 69 were published in 1907 by A. Cranz in Leipzig, and in 1909, by Schirmer in New York (a two-piano arrangement by Rafael Joseffy). For a full description of the F-sharp Minor Concerto, see Engel, *Die Entwicklung des Deutschen Klavierkonzertes,* 238–41. It was recorded in 1974 by Michael Ponti with the Orchestra of Radio Luxembourg, Louis de Froment conducting ("The Romantic Piano Concerto," vol. 2; VoxBox2 CDX 5065 [1992]).
23. Schumann, "Pianoforte: Concerto," *NZfM* 4 (1836): 84.
24. Ibid.
25. Ibid.

26. The performance took place on 2 April 1840, by which time Hiller had been in town for several months.
27. Hering, *Die Klavierwerke F. v. Hillers*, 41. He played the Concerto on 26 October 1843.
28. Schumann, "Pianoforte: Concerte," review of First Concerto, by Döhler, *NZfM* 4 (1836): 83–84.
29. Ibid., 83.
30. "Vermischtes," *NZfM* 5 (1836): 122; Schumann, *Tagebücher*, 2: 29 (9 October 1836).
31. Schumann, *Tagebücher*, 2: 28 (5 October 1836).
32. "Nachrichten," *AmZ* 35 (1833): col. 433.
33. Schumann, *Jugendbriefe*, 211.
34. See Schumann's report, "Der Davidsbündler," from the *Komet* (14 December 1833 and 12 January 1834), in his *Gesammelte Schriften*, 2: 261.
35. Chopin, *Letters*, 154 (to Tytus Wojciechowski of 12 December 1831).
36. Clara Schumann, "Konzertprogramm-Sammlung," no. 32. A review of the score of Kalkbrenner's Third Concerto, published by Kistner in Leipzig and Pleyel in Paris, appeared in the *AmZ* on 19 June 1833 (vol. 35: cols. 405–7). Apparently, the Concerto came into the hands of the reviewer, G. W. Fink, and Clara Wieck at about the same time.
37. "Nachrichten: Leipzig," *AmZ* 35 (1833): col. 433; Nautsch, *Friedrich Kalkbrenner*, 80–81.
38. Schumann, *Gesammelte Schriften*, 2: 263 ("Der Davidsbündler," from the *Komet*, 14 December 1833 and 12 January 1834).
39. Nautsch, *Friedrich Kalkbrenner*, 153–54.
40. "Vermischtes," *NZfM* 1 (1834): 16.
41. "Nachrichten: Strassburg," *AmZ* 37 (1835): cols. 654–55. Schumann surely read this review before his own appeared several months later.
42. Schumann, "Pianoforte: Concerto," review of Concerto No. 4, by Kalkbrenner, *NZfM* 4 (1836): 113, 114.
43. Ibid., 113. Translation from Plantinga, *Schumann as Critic*, 204–205.
44. Schumann, *Tagebücher*, 1: 426 (Schumann's copy of a review of his *Abegg* Variations and *Papillons* from the *Allgemeiner musikalische Anzeiger Wien*, no. 26 [28 June 1832]: 101–2).
45. Schumann, "Pianoforte: Concerto," *NZfM* 4 (1836): 114.
46. Ibid., 113.
47. Berlioz, *Memoirs*, 476 (St. Petersburg, 1847).
48. "Liszt in Wien: A. e. Privatbriefe von 13ten," *NZfM* 8 (1838): 136. See also, Litzmann, *Clara Schumann*, 1: 201–2.
49. This does not mean Kalkbrenner was unable to maintain the high speed. Charles Hallé reported in 1836, "He began the Allegro of the Rondo [*Gage d'amitié*, Grand Rondo in E-flat Major, Op. 66] at a speed that made my hair stand on end; he carried it on at the same pace, which he soon increased towards the close, with such bell-like clearness, and such great expression, that I cannot understand how any one could do it better" (*Autobiography*, 71–72).
50. Schumann, "Pianoforte: Concerto," *NZfM* 4 (1836): 114. The "four-part fugue passages" refers to the central section of the rondo, where a stately four-bar motive in half notes and accented quarter notes, and a four-bar motive of running sixteenths are traded between the hands (bars 260–78).
51. Kalkbrenner did, however, compose a Grand Concerto for Two Pianos in C Major, Op. 125, which was published at nearly the same time as the Fourth Concerto.
52. At an imagined thirty-eighth meeting of the *Davidsbund*, Schumann has Gustav Bergen (Bg.) saying, "I don't like the person whose life and works do not harmonize" (*Gesammelte Schriften*, 2: 262 ["Der Davidsbündler," published in the *Komet*, December 1833 and January 1834]).
53. Schumann, "Pianoforte: Concerte," review of Second Concerto, Op. 14, by Hartknoch, *NZfM* 4 (1836): 93.
54. Heinz Becker, "Hartknoch," in *Die Musik in Geschichte und Gegenwart*.
55. Schumann, "Pianoforte: Concerte," *NZfM* 4 (1836): 93.
56. Ibid.
57. Ibid.
58. Augustini, *Die Klavieretüde im 19. Jahrhundert*, 145.
59. See Christoph Kammertöns, "Herz, Henri, [Heinrich]," in *Die Musik in Geschichte und Gegenwart*, 2nd. rev. ed. Also, Reinhold Seitz, "Herz, Henri," in *Die Musik in Geschichte*

und Gegenwart. The register of the Paris Conservatory gives Herz's birth year as 1803, Herz himself gave 1806. Neither is verifiable by documents.

60. Donald Garvelmann, introduction to Variations on "Non più mesta," 4.
61. Ibid., 6 ("Full text of review of Herz's American debut, as it appeared in *The Albion*, October 31, 1846"). The reviewer is identified by Lawrence in *Strong on Music*, 1: 381.
62. Lawrence, *Strong on Music*, 1: 381.
63. Schumann, "Concerte für das Pianoforte," review of Concerto in D Minor, Op. 87, by Herz, *NZfM* 6 (1837): 49.
64. Ibid., 49–50.
65. Note that Schumann says Herz borrows the first theme (what we would call the first theme of the second group) from Chopin's F Minor Concerto. As the example bears out, he meant, rather, the E Minor Concerto. This is further proved by his reference to "the same Concerto" a few lines later. "Aber das Andante müssen auch seine Freunde als eine Apotheose der Romanze aus demselben Concert von Chopin erklären." The Romanze is, of course, the middle movement of the E Minor Concerto. Ibid., 50.
66. Ibid.
67. "Uebersicht für das Pianoforte," review of Concerto in D Minor, Op. 87, by Herz, *AmZ* 40 (1838): col. 455.
68. Garvelmann, introduction to Variations on "Non più mesta," 5.

Chapter 8

1. Schumann, "Das Clavier-Concert," review of Concerto No. 7, by Moscheles, and Concerto No. 2, by Mendelssohn, *NZfM* 10 (1839): 5.
2. Koch, *Versuch einer Anleitung zur Composition*, 3: 329.
3. Tovey, *Essays in Musical Analysis*, 3: 3.
4. Koch, *Versuch einer Anleitung zur Composition*, 3: 332.
5. Schumann, "Das Clavier-Concert," *NZfM* 10 (1839): 5.
6. Schumann may have heard the young Clara Wieck's performance of the Adagio and Rondo from Thalberg's Concerto on 25 May 1833 in Leipzig at the Hôtel de Pologne, likely with quartet accompaniment. The opening number on the program is titled simply *Quartett-Satz*; the Thalberg is the second number (Clara Schumann, "Konzertprogramm-Sammlung," no. 33).
7. Engel, *Die Entwicklung des Deutschen Klavierkonzertes*, 221.
8. Schumann, "Pianoforte: Concerte," review of Concerto in F Minor, by Thalberg, *NZfM* 4 (1836): 111.
9. Plantinga, *Schumann as Critic*, 208.
10. The interested reader may peruse these pieces in *Sigismond Thalberg (1812–1871): Selected Works*, ed. Jeffrey Kallberg, *Piano Music of the Parisian Virtuosos, 1810–1860*, vol. 1 (New York: Garland, 1993).
11. Schumann, "Pianoforte: Concerte," review of Concerto in A Major, Op. 7, by Döhler, *NZfM* 4 (1836): 83.
12. Alan Walker, *Franz Liszt*, 1: 232–38; Bomberger, "The Thalberg Effect," 198–201.
13. Clara and Robert Schumann, *Briefwechsel*, 1: 54, 79, 163 (12 December 1837; 21 January, 2 May 1838). See also, Litzmann, *Clara Schumann*, 1: 158, 170, 204.
14. Schumann, *Tagebücher*, 2: 73, 77–78 (24, 27, 29 October), 79 (5 November), 83 (24 November, 6 December 1838); 3: 51 (27 November 1838). Clara and Robert Schumann, *Briefwechsel*, 1: 328 (26 December 1828).
15. Schumann, "Kürzere Stücke für Pianoforte," review of Opp. 34, 35, 36, 37, by Thalberg, *NZfM* 15 (1841): 126–27.
16. Plantinga, *Schumann as Critic*, 214.
17. Schumann, "Pianoforte: Concerte," review of Concerto No. 2 in C Minor, Op. 74, by Herz, *NZfM* 4 (1836): 111.
18. See Kallberg, introduction to *Henri Herz: Selected Works*, vii; and Garvelmann, introduction to Variations on "Non più mesta," 13.
19. Garvelmann, introduction to Variations on "Non più mesta," 11; Lott, *From Paris to Peoria*, 55–56; Reinhold Sietz, "Herz," in *Die Musik in Geschichte und Gegenwart*.
20. Schumann, "Pianoforte: Concerte." *NZJM* 4 (1836):111.

21. G. W. Fink, "Recensionen," review of Bravour Variations, Op. 20; Exercises, Op. 21; Brilliant Variations, Op. 23; and Characteristic Variations, Op. 58, by Herz, *AmZ* 33 (1831): col. 9.
22. Schumann, "Pianoforte: Concerte," *NZfM* (1836): 111.
23. Fink, "Concerte für das Pianoforte," review of Concerto No. 2, by Herz, *AmZ* 38 (1836): cols. 543–44.
24. Schumann, "Concerte für das Pianoforte," review of Concerto No. 3 in D Minor, Op. 87, by Herz, *NZfM* 6 (1837): 50.
25. "Philharmonic Concerts," review of 10 June 1833 concert, *The Harmonicon* 11 (1833), part 1, p. 155.
26. "Benefit Concerts of the Season," review of 29 May 1833 concert of M. Henri Herz, *The Harmonicon* 11 (1833), part 1, p. 157.
27. Garvelmann, introduction to Herz, Variations on "Non più mesta," 6. The date of the review is 31 October 1831. On the identity of the reviewer, see Chapter 7, n. 61.
28. Lott, "The American Concert Tours," 186–87.
29. Lawrence, *Strong on Music*, 1: 381 (diary entry of 29 October 1846).
30. Fink, "Concerte für das Pianoforte," *AmZ* 38 (1836): col. 544.
31. Engel, *Die Entwicklung des Deutschen Klavierkonzertes*, 218.
32. Daverio, "Schumann's 'Im Legendenton'," 153–56.
33. Schumann, *Gesammelte Schriften*, 1: 28 ("Aus Meister Raros, Florestans und Eusebius' Denk- und Dichtbüchlein"). The performance by Schuncke was on 27 January 1834.
34. Schumann, "Concert des Hrn. Ignaz Moscheles am 9. Octbr.," *NZfM* 3 (1835): 130.
35. Ellsworth, "The Piano Concerto in London Concert Life," 87, 169, appendix 3. The critic cited writes in *The Musical World*, 20 June 1846, p. 186.
36. Charlotte Moscheles, ed., *Aus Moscheles' Leben*, 1: 204.
37. Made in 1968 with Othmar Maga conducting the Philharmonia Hungarica, the recording (Candide CE 31010) was reissued in 1992 on compact disk (VoxBox 2). In 1982 Ivan Klansky recorded the Concerto with the Dvorák Chamber Orchestra conducted by Ivan Parik (Supraphon 11 1195–2 [1982]). For other recordings, see Chapter 2, n. 24.
38. Ignaz Moscheles, Piano Concerto No. 5 in C Major, Op. 87, Ian Hobson, pianist and conductor, Sinfonia da Camera (Zephyr Z-119–01 [2001, recorded 1999]). In 1975 Mary Louise Boehm recorded the Fifth Concerto with Moscheles's arrangement for string quintet accompaniment (Kees Kooper and Judith Yanchus, violins; Paul Doktor, viola; Janos Scholz, cello; and Jeffrey Levine, double bass) (Turnabout 34867). In the first movement, this recording cuts the second theme area of the first tutti, and replaces the final tutti with a reference to the opening motive. Moscheles, Piano Concerto No. 6 in B-flat Major, Op. 90, *Fantastique*, and No. 7 in C Minor, Op. 93, *Pathétique*, Howard Shelley, Tasmanian Symphony Orchestra, Shelley conducting ("The Romantic Piano Concerto—32"; Hyperion CDA C7385 [2003, recorded 1999]).
39. Wasielewski, *Robert Schumann: Eine Biographie*, 353.
40. Schumann, "Pianoforte: Concerte," review of Concerto No. 5 in C Major, Op. 87, and No. 6 in B-flat Major, Op. 90, by Moscheles, *NZfM* 4 (1836): 123.
41. Ibid.
42. Ibid.
43. Ibid.
44. Schumann, "Concert des Hrn. Ignaz Moscheles am 9. Octbr.," *NZfM* 3 (1835): 130.
45. Schumann, "Pianoforte: Concerte," *NZfM* 4 (1836): 122–23.
46. Ibid., 123.
47. Schumann, "Pianoforte: Concerte," review of Concertino in B Minor, Op. 10, by Lasekk, *NZfM* 4 (1836): 77.
48. Schumann, "Pianoforte: Concerte," *NZfM* 4 (1836): 123.
49. Schumann, "Concert des Hrn. Ignaz Moscheles am 9. Octbr.," *NZfM* 3 (1835): 130.
50. Schumann, "Pianoforte: Concerte," *NZfM* 4 (1836): 124.
51. Ibid.
52. Wasielewski, *Robert Schumann: Eine Biographie*, 357, 366 (letters to Moscheles of 30 July 1836 and 23 August 1837).
53. Schumann, "Das Clavier-Concert," *NZfM* 10 (1839): 6.
54. Ibid.
55. Ibid.
56. Ibid.

57. Engel, *Die Entwicklung des Deutschen Klavierkonzertes*, 207.
58. Macdonald, "Critical Perception and the Woman Composer."
59. "Nachrichten: Wien," *AmZ* 27 (1825): col. 240; and 31 (1829): col. 328. It is possible that the Concerto in E Minor that Blahetka played in 1829 was the work she published as her *Concertstück* in E Minor. See Amster, *Das Virtuosenkonzert*, 85.
60. Which is not to say that these women did not compose. Among the works of Belleville, Dulcken, and Pleyel are piano, voice, and chamber pieces.
61. Klassen, *Clara Wieck-Schumann*, 114.
62. Reich, *Clara Schumann*, rev. ed., 215–19.
63. Schumann, *Jugendbriefe*, 201.
64. Klassen, "'Schumann will es nun instrumentieren'."
65. Reich, *Clara Schumann*, rev. ed., 47–48.
66. Schumann, *Gesammelte Schriften*, 2: 356 ("Ankündigung eines Konzertes von Klara Wieck," *Leipziger Tageblatt*, 5 November 1835).
67. Schumann, "Schwärmbriefe: An Chiara," *NZfM* 3 (1835): 182.
68. On 5 May and 11 September 1834 in Leipzig, and 26 November 1834 in Magdeburg (Clara Schumann, "Konzertprogramm-Sammlung," nos. 43, 44, and 49).
69. Reich, *Clara Schumann*, rev. ed., 49. On possible revisions to the Concerto, see Klassen, preface to *Konzert für Klavier*, by Clara Schumann, VII.
70. On Becker, see Plantinga, *Schumann as Critic*, 39 n., 55, 58, 84.
71. Schumann, *Briefe: Neue Folge*, 85 (letter to Becker of 10 February 1837).
72. Carl Ferdinand Becker, "Concerte für das Pianoforte," review of First Concerto for the Pianoforte, by Clara Wieck, *NZfM* 6 (1837): 56–57.
73. A-flat major also resurfaces briefly in the finale. See Walker-Hill, "Neglected Treasure," 26.
74. Reich, *Clara Schumann*, rev. ed., 53, 58.
75. Clara Schumann, "Konzertprogramm-Sammlung," nos. 102 and 110.
76. Clara and Robert Schumann, *Complete Correspondence*, 1: 31.
77. Clara Schumann, "Konzertprogramm-Sammlung," nos. 120, 123, 129, and 141.
78. Clara and Robert Schumann, *Briefwechsel*, 1: 57 (letter to Robert of 15 December 1837).
79. Ibid., 1: 38–39, 52 (letters to Clara of 8, 29 November 1837). See also Reich, *Clara Schumann*, rev. ed., 53–60.
80. Clara and Robert Schumann, *Briefwechsel*, 1: 53.
81. Ibid., 1: 58.
82. See my article, "Schumann's Piano Practice," 541–45.
83. Reich, *Clara Schumann*, 229.
84. There are recordings of Wieck's Concerto by Michael Ponti with the Berlin Symphony Orchestra conducted by Völker Schmidt-Gertenbach (Vox STGBY 6491971 [197-]); Veronica Jochum with the Bamberger Symphoniker conducted by Joseph Silverstein (Tudor 788 [1988]); Susanne Launhardt with the Kammerorchester Merck conducted by Zdenek Simane (Bayer Records 100 096 [1990, recorded 1989]); Angela Cheng with The Women's Philharmonic conducted by JoAnn Falletta (Koch International Classics 3-7169-2 H1 [1992]); Enrica Ciccarelli with the Orchestre Philharmonique de Montpellier Languedoc-Roussillon conducted by Friedemann Layer (Agora AG014.1 [1995]); Elizabeth Rich with the Janácek Philharmonic Orchestra conducted by Dennis Burkh (Centaur CRC 2283 [1996, recorded 1995]); and Margarita Höhenrieder with the Neue Philharmonie Westfalen conducted by Johannes Wildner (RCA Red Seal 74321 89793 2 [2002, recorded 2000–01]).
    For information on the International Clara Schumann Piano Competition, go to <http://members.aol.com/schumannga/englisch/ccse.htm>.

Chapter 9

1. Schumann, "Das Clavier-Concert," review of Concerto No. 7 by Moscheles, and Concerto No. 2, by Mendelssohn, *NZfM* 10 (1839): 5.
2. The translation is by Lenneberg, as is the attribution to Schumann. See his *Breitkopf und Härtel in Paris*, xxii–xxiv.
3. Schumann, *Tagebücher*, 1: 280, 283 (Easter Week 1830).
4. Schumann, "Concerte und Concertstücke mit Orchesterbegleitung," review of Brilliant Rondo for Piano and Orchestra, Op. 101, by Schmitt, *NZfM* 19 (1843): 18.

5. "Kritik," review of Piano Concerto in E-flat Major, Op. 76, by Schmitt, signed "K", *NZfM* 2 (1835): 9.
6. Ibid., 9, 10. "K" goes so far as to say that all the movements of the Concerto stem from the *Grundstoffe* of the first tutti, although I find any thematic relationship between the first and second movements obscure, and believe any between the first and last movements to be tenuous at best.
7. Engel, *Die Entwicklung des Deutschen Klavierkonzertes*, 191.
8. Plantinga, *Schumann as Critic*, 10–15. See also Kross, "Aus der Frühgeschichte von Robert Schumanns Neuer Zeitschrift."
9. Plantinga, *Schumann as Critic*, 159.
10. See note 1, this chapter.
11. G. W. Fink, "Concertmusik für das Pianoforte," review of Concerto, Op. 25, by Mendelssohn, *AmZ* 37 (1835): col. 209.
12. Schumann, "Schwärmbriefe: An Chiara," *NZfM* 3 (1835): 151.
13. Fink, "Concertmusik für das Pianoforte," *AmZ* 37 (1835): cols. 210–11.
14. Nor is it noted by the Berlin correspondent for the *Allgemeine musikalische Zeitung* after he heard the first performance of Mendelssohn's Concerto in that city (vol. 35 [1833]: cols. 22–23).
15. Schumann, "Leipzig, d. 28sten," *NZfM* 11 (1839): 152.
16. Todd, "The Instrumental Music of Felix Mendelssohn-Bartholdy," 362 n. 22. "Nachrichten: Berlin," *AmZ* 26 (1824): col. 107. The performance was on 15 January 1824 for the benefit of the four hundred children in the Wadzeck-Anstalt.
17. See also, Engel, *Die Entwicklung des Deutschen Klavierkonzertes*, 230.
18. Todd, "The Instrumental Music of Felix Mendelssohn-Bartholdy," 361–62.
19. Benedict, *Carl Maria von Weber*, 66. Cf. Max Maria von Weber, *Carl Maria von Weber*, 2: 311–12.
20. Gooley, "Warhorses," 67–73, 74.
21. Ernst Ferdinand Wenzel, "Adolph Henselt," *NZfM* 8 (1838): 7. The review is signed "W"; on the attribution, see Jansen, *Die Davidsbündler*, 217 n. 14.
22. Clara and Robert Schumann, *Briefwechsel*, 1: 158–59 (letter from Clara of 26 April 1838). The triumphant nature of Liszt's performance is described by the correspondent for the *Allgemeine musikalische Zeitung*, who contrasts it with the first Viennese performance by the composer, at which, he says, the *Concertstück* was received with indifference, and even coldness ("Nachrichten: Wien," vol. 40 [1838]: cols. 321–22; cf. "Nachrichten: Wien," *AmZ* 24 [1822]: col. 306).
23. Boetticher, *Robert Schumann*, 668–69 (from the *Leipziger allgemeine Zeitung*, 29 October 1839, p. 3527). See also, *Tagebücher*, 3: 137, and 702 n. 160. Schumann did not hear Liszt play the *Concertstück* until he performed it in Leipzig on 24 March 1840.
24. Schumann, "Pianoforte: Concerte," review of Concerto in E Major, Op. 18, by Taubert, *NZfM* 4 (1836): 115.
25. I have no precise date of composition for Taubert's Concerto, but see Reinhold Sietz, who says only Taubert's first six opuses appeared in 1831 ("Taubert, Carl Gottfried Wilhelm," in *Die Musik in Geschichte und Gegenwart*). The Concerto is Op. 18.
26. Schumann, "Pianoforte: Concerte," *NZfM* 4 (1836): 116.
27. Bischoff and Nauhaus, "Robert Schumanns Leipziger Konzertnotizen," 23–24.
28. Ibid., 47–49.
29. Schumann, "Pianoforte: Concerte," *NZfM* 4 (1836): 114.
30. Ibid., 115.
31. Ibid.
32. Ibid.
33. Schumann, "Pianoforte: Concerte," review of Concertino in B Minor, Op. 10, by Lasekk, *NZfM* 4 (1836): 77.
34. Clara Schumann, "Konzertprogramm-Sammlung," nos. 120 (Prague, 23 November 1837); 123, 129 and 141 (Vienna, 21 December 1837; 18 February and 5 April 1838).
35. Reich, *Clara Schumann*, rev. ed., 47–49.
36. Clara Schumann, "Konzertprogramm-Sammlung," nos. 81, 84, 87, 91 96 (Plauen and Chemnitz, 1 and 10 December 1835; Dresden and Breslau [twice], 30 January and 5, 28 March 1836). Klassen, preface to *Konzert für Klavier*, by Clara Schumann, VIII.
37. Schumann, *Tagebücher*, 2: 68, 69 (28, 29 September 1838). Schumann received a letter from Kaskel on 27 April 1838 (*Tagebücher*, 2: 54).

38. Schumann, "Concerte für das Pianoforte," review of Concertino *brillant*, by Lasekk, *NZfM* 6 (1837): 49.

39. Engel, *Die Entwicklung des Deutschen Klavierkonzertes*, 194; Schumann, "Concerte für das Pianoforte," *NZfM* 6 (1837): 49.

40. Schumann, *Tagebücher*, 2: 29–35. On the friendship, see J. R. Sterndale Bennett, *The Life of William Sterndale Bennett*, 53–54; also Temperley, "Schumann and Sterndale Bennett."

41. Schumann, "Wm. Sterndale Bennett," *NZfM* 6 (1837): 2–3.

42. Hensel, *Die Familie Mendelssohn*, 2: 38; "Nachrichten: Leipzig," *AmZ* 39 (1837): col. 242.

43. Schumann, "Concerte für das Pianoforte," review of Concerto No. 3 in C Minor, Op. 9, by Bennett, *NZfM* 6 (1837): 64.

44. Ibid., 64–65.

45. Ibid., 64.

46. Engel, *Die Entwicklung des Deutschen Klavierkonzertes*, 236.

47. Ellsworth, "The Piano Concerto in London Concert Life," 316–17.

48. Schumann, "Concerte für das Pianoforte," *NZfM* 6 (1837): 64–65.

Chapter 10

1. Schumann, *Tagebücher*, 2: 78 (entry of 29 October 1838).

2. Schumann, "Das Clavier-Concert," *NZfM* 10 (1839): 5.

3. Ibid., 5–6.

4. Ibid., 6–7.

5. Schumann, "Schwärmbriefe: An Chiara," *NZfM* (1835): 151.

6. Schumann, *Tagebücher*, 2: 191 (entry by Clara Schumann of 24 October to 14 November 1841).

7. Pederson, "Enlightened and Romantic German Music Criticism," 81–86.

8. Mendelssohn performed Mozart's D Minor Concerto on 28 January 1836 at the Gewandhaus, and Beethoven's G Major on 3 November 1836.

9. See Köchel's *Mozart Verzeichnis*, 505 (K. 466).

10. Schumann, *Tagebücher*, 2: 145 (entry by Clara Schumann of 31 January to 7 February 1841).

11. Cited from Thayer, *Life of Beethoven*, 416.

12. Schumann, "Erinnerung an eine Freundin: Von Eusebius," *NZfM* 11 (1839): 159.

13. Daverio, *Robert Schumann*, 227–29.

14. Dahlhaus, "Bach und der romantische Kontrapunkt," 16.

15. See Daverio, *Robert Schumann*, 254–57.

16. Todd, "The Instrumental Music of Felix Mendelssohn-Bartholdy," 364–65.

17. *The Mendelssohns on Honeymoon*, 156; Todd, "The Instrumental Music of Felix Mendelssohn-Bartholdy," 365.

18. *The Mendelssohns on Honeymoon*, 170–71; Todd, "The Instrumental Music of Felix Mendelssohn-Bartholdy," 366 (the translation is my own).

19. Todd, "The Instrumental Music of Felix Mendelssohn-Bartholdy," 368.

20. *The Mendelssohns on Honeymoon*, 177.

21. See Todd, "The Instrumental Music of Felix Mendelssohn-Bartholdy," 370–71, and Parkins, "Mendelssohn and the Érard Piano," 54, 56.

22. Mendelssohn, *Letters to Ignaz and Charlotte Moscheles*, 168 (undated letter from Moscheles to Mendelssohn of summer 1838).

23. *The Mendelssohns on Honeymoon*, 156 (letter of 15 May 1837).

24. Lenneberg, *Breitkopf und Härtel in Paris*, 33, 35, 41, 43, 44 (letters of 6 February, 3 March, 31 May, 11 and 27 June). See also Lenneberg's assessment of the situation on p. xxvii; Mendelssohn's, on pp. 42–43 n. 2.

25. Further on Mendelssohn's canon, see Todd, "The Instrumental Music of Felix Mendelssohn-Bartholdy," 376–79.

26. Schumann, *Tagebücher*, 2: 39.

27. Further on the Bach revival, see Nicholas Temperley and Peter Wollny, "Bach Revival," in *New Grove*, 2nd ed.

28. Wenke, "Aspekte zu Robert Schumanns Entwicklung," 119–20.

29. Ibid., 195–96 n. 12. See also Chapter 1, p. 6.

30. Schumann, "Älteste musikalische Erinnerungen," 2.

31. Schumann, *Selbstbiographische Notizen*, [6].

32. On the last point, see Bischoff, "Das Bach-Bild Robert Schumanns," 422–24.

33. Schumann, *Tagebücher*, 1: 175.

34. Ibid., 1: 396, 399. The "second fugue" is, presumably, the C Minor from the first book of *The Well-Tempered Clavier.*

35. Schumann, *Tagebücher*, 1: 400 (29 May 1832).

36. Ibid., 1: 375 (31 October 1831).

37. What written evidence remains of Schumann's studies with Dorn is found primarily in his third sketchbook, including an entire two-voice fugue, titled "Erste Fuge" ("Skizzenbuch III," pp. 67–68). For a description of the book's contents, see Hans Schneider, Catalog No. 188, pp. 80–83.

38. Schumann, *Jugendbriefe*, 187. Corroborating the letter to Kuntsch are analyses of the first three fugues from the *Well-Tempered Clavier*, Book 1 in "Skizzenbuch V" which likely date from mid-1832. On the dating of the sketchbook, see Wendt, "Zu Robert Schumanns Skizzenbüchern," 108. For a description of its contents, see Hans Schneider, Catalog No. 188, pp. 85–88. On Schumann's study of Marpurg, see Bischoff, "Das Bach-Bild Robert Schumanns," 430.

39. Dörffel, *Geschichte der Gewandhausconcerte*, "Chronik," 88; "Statistik," 3–4.

40. Charlotte Moscheles, ed., *Aus Moscheles' Leben*, 1: 304. See also Mendelssohn, *Briefe*, 2: 103 (letter of 6 October 1835). Neither source mentions Louis Rakemann's participation, but see the citation in n. 41, this chapter.

41. Schumann, "Concert des Hrn. Ignaz Moscheles am 9. Octbr.," *NZfM* 3 (1835): 131.

42. Schumann, *Gesammelte Schriften*, 2: 356.

43. Schumann, "Schwärmbriefe: An Chiara," *NZfM* 3 (1835): 182.

44. Hiller, *Künstlerleben*, 206. Keeling, "Liszt's Appearances in Parisian Concerts," 31, 33–34. Programs for the two concerts read only "Allegro de concerto pour trois pianos, composé par Sébastien Bach," and "Allegro de concerto, pour 3 pianos, de J. S. Bach." Eigeldinger identifies the piece as the D Minor Concerto, BWV 1063 ("Les Premiers Concerts de Chopin," 272–74).

45. Großmann-Vendrey, *Felix Mendelssohn Bartholdy*, 140–41 (letter to Friedrich Schneider of 6 December 1835). Note, the second and third movements of the concerto are connected by a brief transition.

46. Schumann, *Tagebücher*, 2: 26, 52 (21 September 1836 with Stamaty; 6, 7 March 1838 with Verhulst).

47. Ibid., 2: 26 (20 September 1836).

48. Ibid., 2: 27, 28 (1, 5 October 1836).

49. Dörffel, *Geschichte der Gewandhausconcerte*, "Chronik," 211 (nos. 394 and 396).

50. Ranft, *Felix Mendelssohn Bartholdy*, 33.

51. Großmann-Vendrey, *Felix Mendelssohn Bartholdy*, 210.

52. Schumann, "Fragmente aus Leipzig: 2," *NZfM* 6 (1837): 145–46. On the keyboard concertos in Zelter's collection see Neumann, "Welche Handschriften J. S. Bachscher Werke besaß die Berliner Singakademie?" 141.

53. Nicholas Temperley and Peter Wollny, "Bach Revival," in *New Grove*, 2nd ed.

54. For a list, see Plantinga, *Schumann as Critic*, 89.

55. Großmann-Vendrey, *Felix Mendelssohn Bartholdy*, 143.

56. Schumann, "Aeltere Claviermusik: Domenico Scarlatti, J. Seb. Bach," *NZfM* 10 (1839): 154.

57. "Nachrichten: Leipzig," *AmZ* 40 (1838): col. 129.

58. Schumann, "Rückblick auf das Leipziger Musikleben im Winter 1837/1838," *NZfM* 8 (1838): 108.

59. Schumann, *Tagebücher*, 2: 31 (February 1837), 34 (mid-March to 1 October 1837) and 465 n. 93. For a description of Schumann's copy of the Art of the Fugue, see Martin, "Ein unbekanntes Schumann-Autograph," 406–8, 409–10. Schumann studied the Chorale Preludes assembled by Johann Gottfried Schicht in a four-volume anthology, *J. S. Bach's Choral-Vorspiele für die Orgel* (Leipzig, 1800–1806), from various collections compiled by Bach (private communication from Russell Stinson).

60. Martin, "Ein unbekanntes Schumann-Autograph," 405–6, 408. Schumann, *Tagebücher*, 2: 31.

61. Schumann, *Tagebücher*, 2: 39, 40, 41, 44 (17, 21, 24, 26, 29, 30 October, 2, 4 November 1837).

62. Schumann, "Museum: 4. Präludien und Fugen für das Pianoforte von Felix Mendelssohn Bartholdy," *NZfM* 7 (1837): 135 (signed "Jeanquirit").
63. Schumann, *Tagebücher*, 2: 53, 55 (31 March, 6 May 1838).
64. Clara and Robert Schumann, *Briefwechsel*, 1: 126.
65. Schumann, "Musikleben in Leipzig während des Winters 1839/40," *NZfM* 12 (1840): 160.
66. "Nachrichten: Leipzig," *AmZ* 42 (1840): cols. 162–63.
67. Großmann-Vendrey, *Felix Mendelssohn Bartholdy*, 145 (letter to Fanny Hensel of 7 March 1840).
68. Green, "Robert Schumann's Historical Awareness," 147.
69. Schumann, *Tagebücher*, 2: 52. Bach was born on 21 March 1685, Johann Paul Friedrich Richter on 21 March 1763.
70. Schumann, *Tagebücher*, 2: 27 (1 October 1836).
71. Schumann, "Präludien und Fugen für das Pianoforte von Felix Mendelssohn Bartholdy," *NZfM* 7 (1837): 135–36.
72. Clara and Robert Schumann, *Briefwechsel*, 2: 358, 359, 367 (16, 19, 26 January 1839).
73. On the First Symphony, see Finson, *Robert Schumann and the Study of Orchestral Composition*, 46–56. On the Overture, Scherzo, and Finale, see Finson, "Schumann, Popularity, and the *Ouverture, Scherzo, und Finale*," 17–18.
74. Macdonald, review of Schumann, *Konzertsatz*, 145–46.
75. Schumann's original title for *Carnaval* was "Fasching: Schwänke auf vier Noten f. Pfte von Florestan" (Jansen, *Die Davidsbündler*, 44). On the *Phantasie*, see Marston, *Schumann: Fantasie*, 64–67.
76. Schumann, "Kritik: (9) Sonaten für Pianoforte," review of *Grande sonate élégique* in F Minor, Op. 33, by Carl Loewe, *NZfM* 2 (1835): 127.
77. Schumann, "Schwärmbriefe: An Chiara," *NZfM* 3 (1835): 151, 182.
78. Schumann, "Pianoforte: Concerte," *NZfM* 4 (1836): 110–11 (on Thalberg's Concerto), 123–24 (on Moscheles's).
79. Schumann, "Concerte für das Pianoforte," *NZfM* 6 (1837): 64.
80. Schumann, "Das Clavier-Concert," *NZfM* 10 (1839): 6.
81. Example 10.6 is based on Schumann's holograph. It differs from De Beenhouwer and Draheim's edition of the *Concertsatz*, which adds two extra bars between bars 119 and 120, and a fuller orchestration. On both points see my review of Draheim's edition, 148–49.
82. Schumann, *Tagebücher*, 2: 83 and 491 n. 311.
83. Schumann, "Das Clavier-Concert," *NZfM* 10 (1839): 6. See also Chapter 8, pp. 156–57.
84. For a summary description of Bach's keyboard concertos, see Roeder, *A History of the Concerto*, 96–100.
85. Schumann, "Das Clavier-Concert," *NZfM* (1839): 5.
86. *The Mendelssohns on Honeymoon*, 110, 114 (diary entries of 19, 21 September 1837).
87. Charlotte Moscheles, ed., *Aus Moscheles' Leben*, 1: 305 (entry of 10 October 1835).
88. Clara and Robert Schumann, *Briefwechsel*, 2: 367 (26 January 1839).
89. Draheim, introduction to *Konzertsatz*, by Robert Schumann, X.
90. Schumann, "Duo's," review of *Hommage à Händel*, by Moscheles, *NZfM* 4 (1836): 191–92.
91. Schumann, "Das Clavier-Concert," *NZfM* 10 (1839): 6.
92. See Chapter 8, p. 151 and pp. 161–62.
93. Clara and Robert Schumann, *Briefwechsel*, 2: 385 (7 February 1839).
94. Ibid., 2: 378–81 (6 February 1839), 407–9 (10 February), 314–15 (20 February), 398–400 and 402–6 (23 February).
95. Daverio, *Robert Schumann*, 256.

Chapter 11

1. On the songs, see Finson, review of *Tagebücher, Band III*, 460–61; Turchin, "Schumann's Conversion to Vocal Music." On the instrumental music, see Finson, *Robert Schumann and the Study of Orchestral Composition*, 27.
2. Daverio, *Robert Schumann*, 203.
3. On the initial reception of the First Symphony, the D Minor Symphony, and the Overture, Scherzo and Finale, see Finson, "Schumann, Popularity, and the *Ouverture, Scherzo, und Finale*," 3–7. For a history of the composition of the D Minor Symphony, see Roesner, "Ästhetisches Ideal und sinfonische Gestalt," 55–57.

4. The appeal of the first version of the D Minor Symphony to the cognoscenti was pointed out by Jon W. Finson in his presentation at the Annual Meeting of the American Musicological Society in Columbus, November 2002, "'To Our Sincere Regret': New Documents on the Publication of Robert Schumann's D minor Symphony."

5. Schumann completed his initial sketching and orchestration of the *Phantasie* on 20 May; the Symphony was begun on 29 May (*Tagebücher*, 3: 183, 184).

6. Macdonald, "'Mit einer eignen außerordentlichen Composition'."

7. Schumann wrote, "Ich kann kein Concert schreiben für den Virtuosen" (Clara and Robert Schumann, *Briefwechsel*, 2: 367 [26 January 1839]).

8. Finson, *Robert Schumann and the Study of Orchestral Composition*, 37–38.

9. Bonds, *After Beethoven*, 120–22.

10. On Bonds's adoption of Bloom's terminology, see *After Beethoven*, 1–8.

11. Ibid., 131. See also p. 122.

12. Ibid., 132–33.

13. Daverio, *Robert Schumann*, 239.

14. For a description of the differences between the two versions, see Andreae, "Die vierte Symphonie Robert Schumanns," and Abraham, "The Three Scores of Schumann's D minor Symphony." Also, Bonds, *After Beethoven*, 135–36.

15. Marston, *Schumann: Fantasie*, 27.

16. Ibid., 28.

17. Ibid., 23.

18. Ibid., 29.

19. Richards, *The Free Fantasia*, 185–86.

20. Schleuning, *The Fantasia*, 2: 18.

21. Schumann, "Pianoforte: Concerte," *NZfM* (1836): 123.

22. Clara and Robert Schumann, *Briefwechsel*, 1: 53 (29 November 1837).

23. Schumann, "Pianoforte: Concerte," *NZfM* 4 (1836): 123.

24. Schumann, "Pianoforte: Concerte," *NZfM* 4 (1836): 123; "Projektenbuch," 14.

25. Appel, introduction to *Klavierkonzert a-Moll Opus 54: Faksimile*, by Robert Schumann, XVII–XVIII, XX.

26. On both the orchestration and changes to the piano solo part, see Appel, introduction to *Klavierkonzert a-Moll,* XIX–XXI.

27. Ibid., XIX.

28. The opening orchestral chord may have been absent in the *Phantasie*, so that the piano solo began the movement, supported by the orchestra. See Boetticher, preface to *Phantasie for Piano and Orchestra*, by Robert Schumann, XII. Even so, the comparison of the solo opening to that of any virtuoso concerto stands.

29. Hanslick, *Aus dem Concertsaal*, 166 ("Clara Schumann").

30. An exception is August Gerstmeier. See his *Robert Schumann: Klavierkonzert a-Moll*, 11, 25–26. For other descriptions and analyses of the A Minor Concerto see, for example, Engel, *Die Entwicklung des Deutschen Klavierkonzertes*, 244–45; Tovey, *Essays in Musical Analysis*, 3: 182–83; Nieman, "The Concertos," 245–52; Voss, "Analyse und Interpretation," 198–206.

31. See Kroó, "Gemeinsame Formprobleme," 138–39.

32. The tutti following the close of the solo exposition in Mehner's copy of the *Phantasie* is eight bars long and survives in that version only as an alternation between arpeggiated tonic and dominant chords in the piano part (see pp. 29–30 of the facsimile score, edited by Appel). Harmonically, these bars are roughly equivalent to bars 134–37 and 150–53 in the Concerto. Thus, it is logical to suppose that at least the first four of these bars were written as accompaniment to the tutti playing of the "b2" motive in Example 11.1, just as they were in the equivalent spot in the recapitulation (bars 385–88).

33. Lara, "Clara Schumann's Teaching," 146.

34. This may call to mind the parallel forms Linda Correll Roesner describes in some of Schumann's sonata-form piano pieces in her article "Schumann's 'Parallel' Forms." Here, however, we are only pointing to the parallel affects in each half, not to any parallelisms of thematic or harmonic material.

35. Schumann, "Das Clavier-Concert," *NZfM* 10 (1839): 6.

36. According to Köchel's *Mozart Verzeichnis*, Artaria published eighteen of Mozart's own cadenzas in 1801; this set was enlarged to thirty-five by André in 1804 (see under 626a = 624, pp. 732–33).

37. See Kinsky and Halm's *Beethoven Verzeichnis*, 36 (Op. 15), 48 (Op. 19), 94 (Op. 37), 139 (Op. 58).
38. Clara Schumann, "Konzertprogramm-Sammlung," no. 183.
39. Schumann, *Gesammelte Schriften*, 2: 350 ("Reminiszenzen aus Klara Wiecks letzten Konzerten in Leipzig," from the *Komet*, August 1832).
40. Schumann, "Das Clavier-Concert," *NZfM* 10 (1839): 5.
41. Schumann, *Tagebücher*, 2: 180 (entry by Clara Schumann of 22 August 1841).
42. Cited from Appel, introduction to *Klavierkonzert a-Moll Opus 54: Faksimile*, by Robert Schumann, XVII.
43. Schumann, *Tagebücher*, 2: 183 (entry by Clara Schumann of 21 August 1841).
44. Appel, introduction to *Klavierkonzert a-Moll Opus 54: Faksimile*, by Robert Schumann, XX.
45. Boetticher, preface to *Concerto for Piano and Orchestra*, by Robert Schumann, VI. See also his preface to *Phantasie for Piano and Orchestra*, by Schumann, VII–VIII. I would like to repeat that, despite Boetticher's edition of the *Phantasie*, the original version cannot be known. See Appel's critical report to *Klavierkonzert a-Moll op. 54*, by Robert Schumann, 189–92.
46. For a transcription of the original piano part, see Appel's critical report to *Klavierkonzert a-Moll op. 54*, by Robert Schumann, 253–55.
47. Plantinga, "The Piano and the Nineteenth Century," 8–9. The reference is to Schumann's article "Trio's," review of Trio for Piano and Strings, Op. 2, by J. Rosenhain, *NZfM* 5 (1836): 4.
48. According to Reich, "[Clara Schumann] performed the Quintet so regularly that it could almost be said to have been her signature piece" (*Clara Schumann*, rev. ed., 261). In her program books I counted eighty-seven performances of the Quintet, and of the Concerto, one hundred (Clara Schumann, "Konzertprogramm-Sammlung," *passim* [from the time of the public premiere of the Piano Quintet on 8 January 1843, 988 programs]).
49. Tovey, *Essays in Musical Analysis: Chamber Music*, 151.
50. Schumann, Piano Quintet, Opus 44, American String Orchestra/Isaiah Jackson, Earl Wild (Ivory Classics 64405–71003 [2000]). The citation is from Wild's liner notes.
51. On the public nature of the Quintet, see further, Brown, "'A Higher Echo of the Past'," 115.
52. Rosenblatt, "The Concerto as Crucible," 109–15, 123.
53. On 31 August 1851 Liszt paid the Schumann family a surprise visit at their home in Düsseldorf, where, Clara says, he played them "a new *Konzertstück*" (Litzmann, *Clara Schumann*, 2: 263; see also *Tagebücher*, 3: 570 [31 August 1851]). According to Marie Wieck this was his Concerto in E-flat (*Aus dem Kreise Wieck-Schumann*, 170).
54. Dahlhaus, *Nineteenth-Century Music*, 135–36.
55. For an overview of the layout and themes of both Liszt concertos, see Roeder, *A History of the Concerto*, 243–47.
56. Rosenblatt, "The Concerto as Crucible," 158. Along with his Concerto, Op. post, Rosenblatt says that Liszt's Concertos No. 1 and No. 2 were composed and orchestrated by 1839, with the latter two rewritten in 1849 (p. 3).
57. Norris, *The Russian Piano Concerto*, 1: 23–24, 29–30.

Chapter 12

1. Schumann, "Concerte und Concertstücke für Pianoforte mit Orchesterbegleitung," *NZfM* 19 (1843): 18.
2. Schumann, *Tagebücher* 3: 725 n. 350.
3. See Schumann's review of Taubert's Concerto, *NZfM* 4 (1836): 115.
4. Schumann, "Concerte und Concertstücke für Pianoforte mit Orchesterbegleitung," *NZfM* 19 (1843): 18.
5. Ibid., review of Concerto, Op. 300, by Jacques Schmitt.
6. Rosenhain's response to Schumann's invitation is printed in Boetticher, ed., *Briefe und Gedichte*, 159–60 (letter of 24 May 1836).
7. Schumann, "Trio's," review of Trio, Op. 2, by Rosenhain, *NZfM* 5 (1836): 4.
8. Schumann, "Pianoforte: Phantasieen, Capricen etc.," *NZfM* 5 (1836): 131; "Fragmente aus Leipzig: 2," *NZfM* 6 (1837): 145.
9. Schumann, "Phantasieen, Capricen etc. für Pianoforte," *NZfM* 10, (1839): 198.

10. Schumann, "Etuden für das Pianoforte," review of Twelve Characteristic Etudes, Op. 17, by Rosenhain, *NZfM* 11 (1839): 113.

11. Schumann, "Etüden für das Pianoforte," review of Twenty-four Etudes, Op. 20, by Rosenhain, *NZfM* 14 (1841): 120.

12. Schumann, "Concerte und Concertstücke für Pianoforte mit Orchesterbegleitung," review of Concertino, Op. 30, by Rosenhain, *NZfM* 19 (1843): 18.

13. Schumann, *Tagebücher*, 1: 144, 152, 158, 159, 178 (19 November, 6, 22, 23 December 1828; 6 March 1829); "Kürzeres und Rhapsodisches für Pianoforte," *NZfM* 2 (1835): 154.

14. Schumann, "Etuden für das Pianoforte," review of Etudes, Op. 55, by Mayer, *NZfM* 14 (1841): 175–76. Other reviews of Mayer's compositions written by Schumann before 1841 are: "Pianoforte: Etuden," review of Six Etudes, Op. 31, *NZfM* 4 (1836): 24; "Rondo's für Pianoforte," review of Three Rondos, *NZfM* 4 (1836): 217; "Variations für Pianoforte," review of Variations, Opp. 31 and 32, *NZfM* 5 (1836): 79–80; "Phantasieen, Capricen etc. für Pianoforte," review of Fantasy, Op. 54, *NZfM* 9 (1838): 179.

15. Schumann, *Tagebücher*, 2: 184–85 (entry by Robert of 17 September 1841); 3: 192 (1 September 1841).

16. Boetticher, ed., *Briefe und Gedichte*, 155 (letter from Cipriano Romberg of 23 May 1841), and 306.

17. Schumann, "Concerte und Concertstücke für Pianoforte mit Orchesterbegleitung," review of Concerto in D Major, Op. 70, by Mayer, *NZfM* 19 (1843): 18.

18. Years earlier, Schumann cited Mayer as famous for this technique. See his "Noten," *NZfM* 5 (1836): 26. The article is unsigned, however, the two-part series is headed by a quotation attributed to Florestan (vol. 4 [1836]: 198).

19. Schumann, "Concerte und Concertstücke für Pianoforte mit Orchesterbegleitung," review of Concertino, Op. 650, by Czerny, *NZfM* 19 (1843): 18.

20. Ibid., review of *Rondo brillant*, Op. 101, by Aloys Schmitt.

21. Schumann, *Tagebücher*, 2: 155 (14–21 March 1841).

22. Clara Schumann, "Konzertprogramm-Sammlung," nos. 80, 81, 84, 87, 91, 94, 100, 108, 128, 133, 143, 157, 166, 169, 181, 184, 186.

23. See, for example, Mercer-Taylor, "Mendelssohn and the Musical Discourse of the German Restoration," 89, 90.

24. Schumann, *Gesammelte Schriften*, 2: 356 ("Ankündigung eines Konzertes von Klara Wieck," *Leipziger Tageblatt*, 5 November 1835).

25. Schumann, "Fünftes Abonnementconcert, den 5. November," *NZfM* 13 (1840): 160.

26. Schumann, "Concerte und Concertstücke für Pianoforte mit Orchesterbegleitung," review of Capriccio, Op. 1, by Kufferath, *NZfM* 19 (1843): 17.

27. Bennett's Fourth Concerto was recorded in 1986 by Malcolm Binns with The Milton Keynes Chamber Orchestra, conducted by Hilary Davan Wetton (Milton Keynes Music Series MKM 861D [1988]).

28. See J. R. Sterndale Bennett, *Life of Bennett*, 72–73, 76.

29. Schumann, "Concertstücke und Concerte für Pianoforte," review of Fourth Concerto, by Bennett, *NZfM* 12 (1840): 39.

30. Schumann, *Tagebücher*, 2: 199; 3: 205 (17 January 1842).

31. "Z", "Concert von Elisa Meerti, d. 17. January 1842," *NZfM* 16 (1842): 48.

32. Schumann, "Concerte und Concertstücke für Pianoforte mit Orchesterbegleitung," review of Capriccio for Piano and Orchestra, Op. 22, by Bennett, *NZfM* 19 (1843): 17–18.

33. On this point, see Plantinga, *Schumann as Critic*, 159.

34. Schumann, "Concertstücke und Concerte für Pianoforte," review of *Serenade und Allegro giojoso*, Op. 43, by Mendelssohn *NZfM* 12 (1840): 38–39.

35. Mendelssohn, *Briefe*, 2: 168.

36. Schumann, "Musikleben in Leipzig während des Winters 1839/40," *NZfM* 12 (1840): 152.

37. Schumann, *Briefe: Neue Folge*, 255 (18 November [recte December] 1845). On both the program for this concert and for the premiere performance of the Concerto in Dresden on 4 December 1845, the movements are listed as:

    Allegro affettuoso

    Andantino und Rondo

    See the reproductions in Appel, introduction to *Klavierkonzert a-Moll Opus 54: Faksimile*, by Robert Schumann, V. In that same volume, the correct date for the Schumann's letter to Mendelssohn is given by Appel (XIX, XXV n. 48).

38. See note 5, this chapter.
39. Appel, critical report to *Klavierkonzert a-Moll*, by Robert Schumann, 188–89.
40. Appel, introduction to *Klavierkonzert a-Moll Opus 54. Faksimile*, by Robert Schumann, XVIII.
41. Engel, *Die Entwicklung des Deutschen Klavierkonzertes*, 245.
42. I counted nearly three dozen performances of the *Andante* and Variations, Op. 46, in Clara Schumann's program books ("Konzertprogramm-Sammlung"), most concentrated in the 1850s and 1860s.
43. Schumann, *Gesammelte Schriften*, 2: 350 ("Reminiszenzen aus Klara Wiecks letzten Konzerten in Leipzig," from the *Komet*, August 1832).
44. Appel, introduction to *Klavierkonzert a-Moll Opus 54: Faksimile*, by Robert Schumann, XXII. See also his critical report to *Klavierkonzert a-Moll*, by Schumann, 279–85.
45. Schmid, *Musik als Abbild*, 61.
46. Carl Czerny, Prelude No. 11, from his *Präludien, Cadenzen und kleine Fantasien im brillanten Style für das Piano-Forte*, Op. 61 (Vienna, 1824), composed "als Einleitung zum Finale [*Air russe*: Rondo] des Ries-schen Concerts in Es [Op. 42] vorzutragen anstatt dem Adagio [recte *Larghetto*]," furnishes another example.
47. On Moscheles's Fifth Concerto, see Chapter 8, pp. 147–49.
48. Plantinga, review of *Robert Schumann*, by John Daverio, 387.
49. Tovey, *Essays in Musical Analysis*, 3: 184.
50. Litzmann, *Clara Schumann*, 2: 133. The entry was made on 27 June 1845.
51. Engel, *Die Entwicklung des Deutschen Klavierkonzertes*, 248.
52. Wise [Dr. Jul. Schladebach], "Nachrichten: Aus Dresden: Concerte," *AmZ* 47 (1845): cols. 927–28.
53. Schumann, *Briefe: Neue Folge*, 255 (letter to Mendelssohn; on the date of the letter, see n. 37, this chapter).
54. L. R., "Nachrichten: Leipzig, den 2. Januar 1846," *AmZ* 48 (1846): col. 12.
55. Ibid.
56. Hanslick, *Aus meinem Leben*, 1: 106–8.

Chapter 13

1. See, for example, Engel, *Die Entwicklung des Deutschen Klavierkonzertes* (1927), 249; Abert, *Robert Schumann* (1920), 108; Philipp Spitta, "Schumann, Robert Alexander," in *Grove's Dictionary*, 2nd ed. (1908).
2. Schumann, *Tagebücher* 3: 506 (15 October 1849); 541 (11, 14, 16 October 1850). On the Cello Concerto, see also McCorkle's description of the autograph sources (*Schumann: Werkverzeichnis*, 546).
3. Schumann, "Manuscripte," review of Piano Concerto, Adagio und Rondo, by Schüler," *NZfM* 4 (1836): 11–12. The article is signed "12".
4. E. Bernsdorf, "Leipziger Musikleben," *NZfM* 32 (1850): 103.
5. Charlotte Moscheles, ed., *Aus Moscheles' Leben*, 2: 210.
6. Litzmann, *Clara Schumann*, 2: 203.
7. Marie Wieck, *Aus dem Kreise Wieck-Schumann*, 172.
8. Tovey, *Essays in Musical Analysis*, 3: 189.
9. Daverio, *Robert Schumann*, 420.
10. McCorkle, *Schumann: Werkverzeichnis*, 381.
11. Wasielewski, *Robert Schumann: Eine Biographie*, 417.
12. Schumann, *Briefe: Neue Folge*, 458 (letter of 27 February 1849).
13. Ibid., 325 (letter to David of 14 January 1850).
14. Schwarz, "Eine Musikerfreundschaft," 297, 298 (letters from David to Schumann of 18 and 29 January 1850).
15. Schumann, "Das Clavier-Concert," *NZfM* 10 (1839): 5.
16. On Schumann's writing for the horns in the *Concertstück*, see Ahrens, "Innovative Elemente in Schumanns 'Konzertstück für vier Hörner'."
17. Schumann, *Briefe: Neue Folge*, 325 (letter of 14 January 1850).
18. Schwarz, "Eine Musikerfreundschaft," 298 (letters from David to Schumann of 21 and 29 January 1850).
19. C. F. Becker, "Leipziger Musikleben," *NZfM* 32 (1850): 142.

20. Nearly a century and a half after its premiere, the reviewer Allan Kozinn complained about "tenuous intonation and imprecise attacks" by the horn section of the New York Philharmonic in a performance of the *Concertstück* ("Spotlight on an Orchestra's French Horn Players," *New York Times*, 15 April 1995).
21. Draheim, "'Dies Concert is auch für Violine transscribirt erschienen'," 7.
22. Ibid., 6.
23. McCorkle, *Schumann: Werkverzeichnis*, 544.
24. Cited from Draheim, "Das Cellokonzert," 260; see also p. 259.
25. Tovey, *Essays in Musical Analysis*, 3: 186.
26. Cited from Draheim, "Das Cellokonzert," 262.
27. Heldt, "Konzertante Elemente," 134–35.
28. Tovey, *Essays in Musical Analysis*, 3: 187.
29. Steinberg, *The Concerto*, 413.
30. Draheim, "Das Cellokonzert," 263–64.
31. Ibid., 254 n. 25.
32. Schumann, *Tagebücher*, 3: 633–34. Cf. Eismann, *Quellenwerk*, 1: 189 ("Aus dem Projektenbuch").
33. Schumann, *Tagebücher*, 2: 441–43 (entries by Robert).
34. Schumann, *Briefe: Neue Folge*, 390 (letter to Joseph Joachim of 6 January 1854).
35. Schumann, *Tagebücher*, 3: 658 (entry by Brahms of 24 March 1855), 685 (entry by Clara Schumann of 10 May 1855).
36. Struck, *Die umstrittenen späten Instrumentalwerke*, 234.
37. Schumann, *Briefe: Neue Folge*, 397–98, 401 (14 September, 10 October 1854).
38. Cited from Struck, *Die umstrittenen späten Instrumentalwerke*, 203.
39. Ibid., 204.
40. F. G[leich], "Kleine Zeitung: Correspondenz, Leipzig," *NZfM* 41 (1854): 206–7. See also Struck, *Die umstrittenen späten Instrumentalwerke*, 203.
41. Struck, *Die umstrittenen späten Instrumentalwerke*, 204.
42. Clara Schumann and Brahms, *Briefe*, 1: 67 (letter to Clara of 29 January 1855). See also Brahms's letters to Clara of 30 January and 23/24 February 1855 (pp. 68 and 81).
43. Cited from Struck, *Die umstrittenen späten Instrumentalwerke*, 207–8.

Epilogue

1. Schumann, "Neue Bahnen," *NZfM* 39 (1853): 185.
2. Erler, *Robert Schumann's Leben*, 2: 202–3, 205.
3. *Niederrheinische Musik-Zeitung* 1 (1853): 158. Cited from Federhofer-Königs, *Wilhelm Joseph von Wasielewski*, 59 n. 156.
4. Joachim, *Briefe*, 1: 143 (letter to Robert Schumann of 9 January 1854).
5. Litzmann, *Clara Schumann*, 2: 290; Schumann, *Briefe: Neue Folge*, 398 (letter to Clara of 18 September 1854).
6. F. G[leich]., "Kleine Zeitung," *NZfM* 40 (1854): 42.
7. *Hannoversche Zeitung*, No. 41 (25 January 1854). Cited from Struck, *Die umstrittenen späten Instrumentalwerke*, 250.
8. Joachim, *Briefe*, 3: 302 (letter to Clara Schumann of 31 January 1887).
9. Struck, *Die umstrittenen späten Instrumentalwerke*, 254–55.
10. Struck, "'Gewichtsverlagerungen'," 45.
11. Federhofer-Königs, *Wilhelm Joseph von Wasielewski*, 57 (letter to Wasielewski of 28 September 1853).
12. Haack, "Schumann's Late Violin Works," 10.
13. Schumann, *Tagebücher*, 2: 448, 449 (entries by Robert of 25 and 30 January 1854).
14. Eugenie Schumann, "Eugenie Schumann über das letzte Werk ihres Vaters," 8–9.
15. Litzmann, *Clara Schumann*, 2: 282.
16. Joachim, *Briefe*, 1: 228–29. Tadeusz Kosciuszko (1746–1817) was a well-known Polish patriot; Jan Sobieski was elected King of Poland, ruling as John III from 1674–96. In 1683, as supreme commander of the allied forces, he won a victory over the Turks that marked the beginning of their withdrawal from Europe.
17. Ibid., 1: 231.
18. Ibid., 1: 453 (letter to Clara Schumann of 15 October 1857).

19. Ibid., 1: 454 (letter to Clara Schumann of 21 October 1857). See also Struck, *Die umstrittenen späten Instrumentalwerke Schumanns*, 308–9.
20. Joachim, *Briefe*, 1: 465–66 (letter to Joachim of 27 November 1857).
21. Ibid., 3: 486–88.
22. Brahms and Joachim, *Briefwechsel*, 1: 31 (letter from J. O. Grimm to Joachim of 9 March 1854).
23. Rosen, "Influence: Plagiarism and Inspiration," 91–93. Tovey, *Essays in Musical Analysis*, 3: 118.
24. Reynolds, "A Choral Symphony," 4–7.
25. Kalbeck, *Johannes Brahms*, 1: 166.
26. Joachim, *Briefe*, 2: 1.
27. Clara Schumann and Brahms, *Briefe*, 1: 242.
28. Edler, "Anmerkungen zu Struktur," 421–23.

Works Cited

Manuscript Sources

Kuntsch, Johann Gottfried. "Aus dem Verzeichnis der in den Jahren 1818 bis 1829 in dem Lyseo zu Zwickau statt gefunden musikalische-declamatorischen Abend Unterhaltungen." Archiv des Robert-Schumann-Hauses Zwickau. 4876–A3.

Schumann, Clara. "Konzertprogramm-Sammlung." 3 vols. Archiv des Robert-Schumann-Hauses Zwickau. 10 463 1, A, 3, C3.

Schumann, Robert. "Älteste musikalische Erinnerungen - Rückblick (Sommer 1828)." Transcription by Martin Kreisig. Archiv des Robert-Schumann-Hauses Zwickau. 4871 VII, B, 4 A3.

———. "Blätter und Blümchen aus der goldenen Aue. Zusammengesucht und in einen Strauß verbunden von Robert Schumann 1823." Archiv des Robert-Schumann-Hauses Zwickau. 4871 I, 1 A3.

———. "Briefkonzeptbuch." Archiv des Robert-Schumann-Hauses Zwickau. 4871 VII, C, 9 A3.

———. "Concertsatz für Pianoforte." Universitäts- und Landesbibliothek Bonn, Handschriftenabteilung. Schumann 18.

———. "Leipziger Quartettabende." Archiv des Robert-Schumann-Hauses Zwickau. 4871 VII, C1 A3.

———. "Materialien [-1829]." Archiv des Robert-Schumann-Hauses Zwickau. 4871 VII B, 3 A3.

———. "Projektenbuch," begun December 1840. Archiv des Robert-Schumann-Hauses Zwickau. 4871 VII C, 8 A3.

———. "Skizzenbücher," Nos. I, III and V. Universitäts- und Landesbibliothek Bonn, Handschriftenabteilung. Schumann 13, 15 and 17.

Published Sources

Abert, Hermann. *Robert Schumann.* 4th rev. ed. Berlin: Schlesische, 1920.

Abraham, Gerald. *Chopin's Musical Style.* 1939. Corrected reprint, London: Oxford University Press, 1968.

———. "The Three Scores of Schumann's D minor Symphony." *Musical Times* 81 (1940): 105–9.

Ahrens, Christian. "Innovative Elemente in Schumanns 'Konzertstück für vier Hörner und Orchester' F-Dur op. 86." *Schweizerische Musikzeitung* 123 (1983): 148–56.

Amster, Isabella. *Das Virtuosenkonzert in der ersten Hälfte des 19. Jahrhunderts.* Wolfenbüttel and Berlin: Georg Kallmeyer, 1931.

Andreae, Marc. "Die vierte Symphonie Robert Schumanns, ihre Fassungen, ihre Interpretationsprobleme." In *Robert Schumann - Ein romantisches Erbe in neuer Forschung: Acht Studien,* edited by the Robert-Schumann-Gesellschaft, Düsseldorf. Mainz: Schott, 1984.

Appel, Bernhard R. Critical report to *Klavierkonzert a-Moll op. 54,* by Robert Schumann. *Robert Schumann: Neue Ausgabe sämtliche Werke,* series 1, group 2, vol. 1. Mainz: Schott, 2003.

―――. Introduction to _Klavierkonzert a-Moll Opus 54: Faksimile der autographen Partitur,_ by Robert Schumann, edited by the Heinrich-Heine-Institut, Düsseldorf, translated by Bradford Robinson. Kassel: Barenreiter, 1996.

Atwood, William G. _Fryderyk Chopin: Pianist from Warsaw._ New York: Columbia University Press, 1987.

Augustini, Folke. _Die Klavieretüde im 19. Jahrhundert: Studien zu ihrer Entwicklung und Bedeutung._ Duisberg: Gilles and Francke, 1986.

Barth, Herbert, Dietrich Mack, and Egon Voss, eds. _Wagner: A Documentary Study._ New York: Oxford University Press, 1975.

Benedict, Julius. _Carl Maria von Weber._ New York: Scribner and Welford, 1881.

Bennett, J. R. Sterndale. _The Life of William Sterndale Bennett._ Cambridge: Cambridge University Press, 1907.

Benyovszky, Karl. _J. N. Hummel: Der Mensch und Künstler._ Bratislava: EOS Verlag, 1934.

Berlioz, Hector. _The Memoirs of Hector Berlioz._ Edited and translated by David Cairns. New York: Alfred A. Knopf, 2002.

Bischoff, Bodo. "Das Bach-Bild Robert Schumanns." In _Bach und die Nachwelt,_ edited by Michael Heinemann and Hans-Joachim Hinrichsen, vol. 1, _1750–1850._ Laaber: Laaber-Verlag, 1997.

―――. _Monument für Beethoven: Die Entwicklung der Beethoven-Rezeption Robert Schumanns._ Cologne: Christoph Dohr, 1994.

Bischoff, Bodo, and Gerd Nauhaus. "Robert Schumanns Leipziger Konzertnotizen von 1833: Faksimile, Übertragung und Kommentar (Erstveröffentlichung)." In _Schumann-Studien_ 3/4, edited by Nauhaus. Cologne: Dr. Gisela Schewe, 1994.

Blank, Gerhardt. "Bedeutung und Besonderheiten des Fremdsprachenunterrichts im Entwicklungsgang Schumanns." In _Schumann-Studien_ 3/4, edited by Gerd Nauhaus. Cologne: Dr. Gisela Schewe, 1994.

Boetticher, Wolfgang. Preface to _Concerto for Piano and Orchestra, A minor,_ by Robert Schumann. Translated by Richard Deveson. London: Eulenburg, 1988.

―――. Preface to _Phantasie for Piano and Orchestra, A minor, WoO,_ by Robert Schumann. Translated by Lionel Salter. London: Eulenburg, 1994.

―――. _Robert Schumann: Einführung in Persönlichkeit und Werk._ Berlin: B. Hahnefeld, 1941.

―――. _Robert Schumanns Klavierwerke: Neue biographische und texkritische Untersuchungen._ Part 1 (Opus 1–6). Wilhelmshaven: Heinrichshofen's Verlag, 1976.

―――, ed. _Briefe und Gedichte aus dem Album Robert und Clara Schumanns._ 2nd rev. ed. Leipzig: Deutscher Verlag für Musik, 1981.

Bomberger, E. Douglas. "The Thalberg Effect: Playing the Violin on the Piano." _Musical Quarterly_ 75 (1991): 198–208.

Bonds, Mark Evan. _After Beethoven: Imperatives of Originality in the Symphony._ Cambridge, Mass.: Harvard University Press, 1996.

Brahms, Johannes, and Joseph Joachim. _Johannes Brahms in Briefwechsel mit Joseph Joachim._ 3rd rev. ed. 2 vols. Edited by Andreas Moser. 1908. Reprint, Tutzing: Hans Schneider, 1974.

Branson, David. _John Field and Chopin._ New York: St. Martin's Press, 1972.

Broder, Nathan. "The First Guide to Mozart." _Musical Quarterly_ 42 (1956): 223–29.

Brown, Julie Hedges. "'A Higher Echo of the Past': Schumann's 1842 Chamber Music and the Rethinking of Classical Form." Ph.D. diss., Yale University, 2000.

Burger, Ernst. _Robert Schumann: Eine Lebenschronik in Bildern und Dokumenten._ Mainz: Schott, 1999.

Burkholder, J. Peter. "'Quotation' and Emulation: Charles Ives's Uses of His Models." _Musical Quarterly_ 71 (1985): 1–26.

Burnham, Scott. "Criticism, Faith, and the _Idee_: A. B. Marx's Early Reception of Beethoven." _19th Century Music_ 13 (1989–90): 183–92.

Cairns, David. _Berlioz._ 2 vols. Berkeley, University of California Press, 2000.

Chopin, Frédéric. _Chopin's Letters._ Collected by Henryk Opienski. Edited and translated by E. L. Voynich. 1931. Reprint, New York: Dover Publications, 1988.

Colt, C. F., and Antony Miall. _The Early Piano._ London: Stainer and Bell, 1981.

Cooper, Jeffrey. _The Rise of Instrumental Music and Concert Series in Paris, 1828–1871._ Ann Arbor: UMI Research Press, 1983.

Dahlhaus, Carl. "Bach und der romantische Kontrapunkt." _Musica_ 43 (1989): 10–22.

———. *Nineteenth-Century Music.* Translated by J. Bradford Robinson. Berkeley: University of California Press, 1989.

Daverio, John. *Crossing Paths: Schubert, Schumann, and Brahms.* Oxford: Oxford University Press, 2002.

———. *Robert Schumann: Herald of a "New Poetic Age."* New York: Oxford University Press, 1997.

———. "Schumann's 'Im Legendenton' and Friedrich Schlegel's *Arabeske.*" *19th Century Music* 11 (1987–88): 150–63.

Dessauer, Heinrich. *John Field, sein Leben und seine Werke.* Langensalza: Hermann Beyer, 1912.

Dörffel, Alfred. *Geschichte der Gewandhausconcerte zu Leipzig vom 25. November 1781 bis 25. November 1881.* 1884. Reprint, Leipzig: Deutscher Verlag für Musik, 1980.

Draheim, Joachim. "Das Cellokonzert a-Moll op. 129 von Robert Schumann: neue Quellen und Materialien." In *Schumann in Düsseldorf: Werke - Texte - Interpretationen,* edited by Bernhard R. Appel. Mainz: Schott, 1993.

———. "'Dies Concert is auch für Violine transscribirt erschienen': Robert Schumanns Cellokonzert und seine neuentdeckte Fassung für Violine." *Neue Zeitschrift für Musik* 148, no. 11 (November 1987): 4–10.

———. Introduction to *Konzertsatz für Klavier und Orchester d-moll,* by Robert Schumann. Wiesbaden: Breitkopf and Härtel, 1988.

———. "Robert Schumann in Heidelberg." In *Musik in Heidelberg, 1777–1885.* Exhibition Catalog, edited by Susanne Himmelheber und Barbara Böckmann. Heidelberg: Kurpfälzisches Museum, 1985.

Edler, Arnfried. "Anmerkungen zu Struktur und Funktion von Schumanns Konzert-Allegro op. 134." In *Schumann in Düsseldorf: Werke - Texte - Interpretation,* edited by Bernhard R. Appel. Mainz: Schott, 1993.

Ehrlich, Cyril. *First Philharmonic: A History of the Royal Philharmonic Society.* Oxford: Clarendon Press, 1995.

Eigeldinger, Jean-Jacques. *Chopin: Pianist and Teacher as Seen by his Pupils.* Edited by Roy Howat. Translated by Naomi Shohet. Cambridge: Cambridge University Press, 1986.

———. "Les Premiers Concerts de Chopin à Paris (1832–1838): Essai de mise au point." In *Music in Paris in the Eighteen-Thirties,* edited by Peter Bloom. Stuyvesant: Pendragon Press, 1987.

Eismann, Georg. *Robert Schumann: Eine Biographie in Wort und Bild.* Leipzig: Deutscher Verlag für Musik, 1964.

———. *Robert Schumann: Ein Quellenwerk über sein Leben und Schaffen.* 2 vols. Leipzig: Breitkopf and Härtel, 1956.

Ellsworth, Therese Marie. "The Piano Concerto in London Concert Life between 1801 and 1850." Ph.D. diss., University of Cincinnati, 1991.

Engel, Hans. *Die Entwicklung des Deutschen Klavierkonzertes von Mozart bis Liszt.* 1927. Reprint, Hildesheim: Georg Olms, 1970.

Erler, Hermann. *Robert Schumann's Leben aus seinen Briefen geschildert.* 2 vols. Berlin: Ries and Erler, 1887.

Federhofer-Königs, Renate. *Wilhelm Joseph von Wasielewski (1822–1896) im Spiegel seiner Korrespondenz.* Tutzing: Hans Schneider, 1975.

Finson, Jon. W. Review of *Tagebücher, Band III: Haushaltbücher, 1837–1856,* by Robert Schumann, edited by Gerd Nauhaus. *Journal of Musicology* 2 (1983): 459–62.

———. *Robert Schumann and the Study of Orchestral Composition: The Genesis of the First Symphony, Op. 38.* Oxford: Clarendon Press, 1989.

———. "Schumann, Popularity, and the *Ouverture, Scherzo, und Finale,* Opus 52." *Musical Quarterly* 69 (1983): 1–26.

Foster, Myles B. *History of the Philharmonic Society of London: 1813–1912.* London: John Lane, [1912].

Garvelmann, Donald. Introduction to Variations on "Non più mesta" from Rossini's *La Cenerentola,* Op. 60, by Henri Herz. New York: Music Treasure Publications, 1970.

Gerstmeier, August. *Robert Schumann: Klavierkonzert a-Moll op. 54.* Munich: Wilhelm Fink, 1986.

Gooley, Dana. "Warhorses: Liszt, Weber's *Konzertstück,* and the Cult of Napoléon." *19th Century Music* 24 (2000–1): 62–88.

Grayson, David. "Whose Authenticity? Ornaments by Hummel and Cramer for Mozart's Piano Concertos." In *Mozart's Piano Concertos: Text, Context, Interpretation,* edited by Neal Zaslaw. Ann Arbor: University of Michigan, 1996.

Green, Richard David. "Robert Schumann's Historical Awareness." Ph.D. diss., University of Illinois at Urbana-Champaign, 1978.

Großmann-Vendrey, Susanna. *Felix Mendelssohn Bartholdy und die Musik der Vergangenheit.* Regensburg: Gustav Bosse, 1969.

Grove's Dictionary of Music and Musicians. 2nd ed. Edited by J. A. Fuller Maitland. 5 vols. New York: Macmillan, 1904–10.

Haack, Helmut. "Schumann's Late Violin Works." Liner notes for *Konzert für Violine und Orchester d-moll,* and *Fantasie für Violine und Orchester C-dur, op. 131* by Robert Schumann. Teldec Classics 244–190–2 (1989, recorded 1988).

Hallé, Charles. *The Autobiography of Charles Hallé.* Edited by Michael Kennedy. London: Paul Elek, 1972.

Hans Schneider. Catalog No. 188. *Robert Schumann: Manuskripte, Briefe, Schumanniana.* Tutzing: Musikantiquariat Hans Schneider, 1974.

Hanslick, Eduard. *Aus dem Concertsaal: Kritiken und Schilderungen aus den letzten 20 Jahren des Wiener Musiklebens.* Vienna: Wilhelm Braumüller, 1870.

———. *Aus meinem Leben.* 2 vols. 1894. Reprint, Farnsborough: Gregg, 1971.

Headington, Christopher. "The Virtuoso Concerto." In *A Companion to the Concerto,* edited by Robert Layton. New York: Schirmer, 1989.

Heine, Heinrich. *Sämtliche Schriften.* 6 vols. Edited by Klaus Briegleb, Günter Häntzschel, and Karl Pörnbacher. Munich: Carl Hanser, 1968–76.

Heldt, Gerhardt. "Konzertante Elemente in Robert Schumanns Instrumentalwerke." In *Robert Schumann: Universalgeist der Romantik,* edited by Julius Alf and Joseph A. Kruse. Düsseldorf: Droste, 1981.

Hensel, Sebastian. *Die Familie Mendelssohn, 1729 bis 1847; Nach Briefen und Tagebüchern.* 16th ed. 2 vols. Berlin: Georg Reimer, 1918.

Hering, Hans. *Die Klavierwerke F. v. Hillers.* Düsseldorf: Otto Fritz, 1928.

Hiller, Ferdinand. *Felix Mendelssohn-Bartholdy. Briefe und Erinnerungen.* Cologne: M. Du Mont-Schauberg, 1874.

———. *Künstlerleben.* Cologne: DuMont-Schauberg, 1880.

Hoffmann, E. T. A. *E. T. A. Hoffmann's Musical Writings: Kreisleriana, The Poet and the Composer, Music Criticism.* Edited by David Charlton. Translated by Martyn Clarke. Cambridge: Cambridge University Press, 1989.

Holoman, D. Kern. *Berlioz.* Cambridge, Mass.: Harvard University Press, 1989.

Hopkinson, Cecil. *A Bibliographical Thematic Catalogue of the Works of John Field, 1782–1837.* London: the author, 1961.

Jansen, F. Gustav. "Aus Robert Schumanns Schulzeit." *Die Musik* 5 (1905/1906): 83–99.

———. *Die Davidsbündler: Aus Robert Schumann's Sturm- und Drangperiode.* Leipzig: Breitkopf and Härtel, 1883.

Joachim, Joseph. *Briefe von und an Joseph Joachim.* Edited by Johannes Joachim and Andreas Moser. 3 vols. Berlin: Julius Bard, 1911–13.

Joß, Victor. *Der Musikpädigoge Friedrich Wieck und seine Familie.* Dresden: Oscar Damm, 1902.

Kalbeck, Max. *Johannes Brahms.* 2nd revised ed. 4 vols. Berlin: Deutsche Brahms-Gesellschaft, 1908–22.

Kallberg, Jeffrey. Introduction to *Henri Herz (1803–1888): Selected Works.* Vol. 4 of *Piano Music of the Parisian Virtuosos, 1810–1860.* New York: Garland, 1993.

———. "The Rhetoric of Genre: Chopin's Nocturne in G Minor." *19th Century Music* 11 (1987–88): 238–61.

Kapp, Reinhard. *Studien zum Spätwerk Robert Schumanns.* Tutzing: Hans Schneider, 1984.

Keeling, Geraldine. "Liszt's Appearances in Parisian Concerts, 1824–1844, Part 1: 1824–1833." *Liszt Society Journal* 11 (1986): 22–34.

Kerman, Joseph. *Concerto Conversations.* Cambridge, Mass.: Harvard University Press, 1999.

Kinsky, Georg, and Hans Halm. *Das Werk Beethovens: Thematisch-Bibliographisches Verzeichnis seiner sämtlichen vollendeten Kompositionen.* Munich: Henle, 1955.

Klassen, Janina. *Clara Wieck-Schumann: Die Virtuosin als Komponistin; Studien zu ihrem Werk.* Kassel: Bärenreiter, 1990.

———. Preface to *Konzert für Klavier und Orchester, a-moll, op. 7,* by Clara Schumann. Wiesbaden: Breitkopf and Härtel, [1990].

———. "'Schumann will es nun instrumentieren' - Das Finale aus Clara Wiecks Klavierkonzert op. 7 als frühestes Beispiel einer künstlerischen Zusammenarbeit von Clara und Robert Schumann." In *Schumann-Studien* 3/4, edited by Gerd Nauhaus. Cologne: Dr. Gisela Schewe, 1994.

Koch, Heinrich Christoph. *Versuch einer Anleitung zur Composition.* 3 vols. 1782–93. 2nd reprint, Hildesheim: Georg Olms, 2000.

Köchel, Ludwig Ritter von. *Chronologisch-thematisches Verzeichnis sämtlicher Tonwerke Wolfgang Amadé Mozarts.* 8th ed. Edited by Franz Giegling, Alexander Weinmann, and Gerd Sievers. Wiesbaden: Breitkopf and Härtel, 1983.

Koenigsbeck, Bodo. *Bassoon Bibliography.* Monteux: Musica Rara, 1994.

Kroó, György. "Gemeinsame Formprobleme in den Klavierkonzerten von Schumann und Liszt." In *Robert Schumann: Aus Anlaß seines 100. Todestages,* edited by Hans Joachim Moser and Eberhard Rebling. Leipzig: Breitkopf and Härtel, 1956.

Kropfinger, Klaus. "Klassik-Rezeption in Berlin (1810–30)." In *Studien zur Musikgeschichte Berlins im frühen 19. Jahrhundert,* edited by Carl Dahlhaus. Regensburg: Gustav Bosse, 1980.

Kross, Siegfried. "Aus der Frühgeschichte von Robert Schumanns Neuer Zeitschrift für Musik." *Die Musikforschung* 34 (1981): 423–45.

———. "The Establishment of a Brahms Repertoire 1890–1902." In *Brahms 2: Biographical, Documentary and Analytical Studies,* edited by Michael Musgrave. Cambridge: Cambridge University Press, 1987.

Lara, Adelina de. "Clara Schumann's Teaching." *Music and Letters* 26 (1945): 143–47.

Lawrence, Vera Brodsky. *Strong on Music: The New York Music Scene in the Days of George Templeton Strong, 1836–1875.* 3 vols. New York: Oxford University Press, 1988–99.

Lenneberg, Hans. *Breitkopf und Härtel in Paris: The Letters of their Agent Heinrich Probst between 1833 and 1840.* Stuyvesant, New York: Pendragon, 1990.

Lerdahl, Fred, and Ray Jackendoff. *A Generative Theory of Tonal Music.* Cambridge, Mass.: MIT Press, 1983.

Liszt, Franz. *Sämtliche Schriften.* 5 vols to date. Edited by Detlef Altenburg. Wiesbaden: Breitkopf and Härtel, 1989–2000.

Litzmann, Berthold. *Clara Schumann: Ein Künstlerleben.* 6th-8th eds. 3 vols. 1923–25. Reprint, Hildesheim: Georg Olms, 1971.

Lott, R. Allen. "The American Concert Tours of Leopold de Meyer, Henri Herz, and Sigismond Thalberg." Ph.D. diss., City University of New York, 1986.

———. *From Paris to Peoria: How European Piano Virtuosos Brought Classical Music to the American Heartland.* Oxford: Oxford University Press, 2003.

Macdonald, Claudia. "Critical Perception and the Woman Composer: The Early Reception of Piano Concertos by Clara Wieck Schumann and Amy Beach." *Current Musicology* 55 (1993): 24–55.

———. "'Mit einer eignen außerordentlichen Composition': The Genesis of Schumann's Phantasie in A Minor." *Journal of Musicology* 12 (1995): 240–59.

———. "The Models for Schumann's F-Major Piano Concerto of 1831." *Studi Musicali* 21 (1992: 159–89.

———. "Mozart's Piano Concertos and the Romantic Generation." In *Historical Musicology: Sources, Methods, Interpretations,* edited by Stephen Crist and Roberta Marvin. Rochester: University of Rochester Press, 2004.

———. Review of *Konzertsatz für Klavier und Orchester d-moll,* by Robert Schumann, reconstructed and completed by Jozef De Beenhouwer, edited by Joachim Draheim. *Journal of the American Musicological Society* 45 (1992): 143–53.

———. "Robert Schumann's F-Major Piano Concerto of 1831 as Reconstructed from his First Sketchbook: A History of its Composition and Study of its Musical Background." Ph.D. diss., University of Chicago, 1986.

———. "Schumann's Piano Practice: Technical Mastery and Artistic Ideal." *Journal of Musicology* 19 (2002): 527–63.

Macfarren, George. "Cipriani Potter: His Life and Work." *Proceedings of the Musical Association* 10 (1883–84): 41–56.

Marston, Nicholas. *Schumann: Fantasie, Op. 17.* Cambridge: Cambridge University Press, 1992.

Martin, Uwe. "Ein unbekanntes Schumann-Autograph aus dem Nachlaß Eduard Krügers." *Die Musikforschung* 12 (1959): 405–15.

Mayeda, Akio. *Robert Schumanns Weg zur Symphonie.* Zürich: Atlantis Verlag, 1992.

McCorkle, Margit L. *Robert Schumann: Thematisch-Bibliographisches Werkverzeichnis.* Munich: Henle, 2003.

Mendelssohn Bartholdy, Felix. *Briefe.* 2 vols. Edited by Paul Mendelssohn-Bartholdy and Carl Mendelssohn-Bartholdy. 1861 and 1863. Reprint, Potsdam: Verlag für Berlin-Brandenburg, 1997.

———. *Letters of Felix Mendelssohn to Ignaz and Charlotte Moscheles.* Edited and translated by Felix Moscheles. 1888. Reprint, New York: Benjamin Blom, 1971.

The Mendelssohns on Honeymoon: The 1837 Diary of Felix and Cécile Mendelssohn Bartholdy, together with Letters to their Families. Edited and translated by Peter Ward Jones. Oxford: Clarendon Press, 1997.

Mercer-Taylor, Peter. "Mendelssohn and the Musical Discourse of the German Restoration." Ph.D. diss., University of California at Berkeley, 1995.

Methuen-Campbell, James. *Chopin Playing: From the Composer to the Present Day.* New York: Taplinger, 1981.

Meyer, John A. "The Concerto." In *The Age of Beethoven 1790–1830,* edited by Gerald Abraham. Vol. 8 of *The New Oxford History of Music.* London: Oxford University Press, 1982.

Milligan, Thomas B. *The Concerto and London's Musical Culture in the Late Eighteenth Century.* Ann Arbor: UMI Research Press, 1983.

Moscheles, Charlotte, ed. *Aus Moscheles' Leben: Nach Briefen und Tagebüchern.* 2 vols. Leipzig: Duncker and Humbolt, 1872–73.

Die Musik in Geschichte und Gegenwart. Edited by Friedrich Blume. 16 vols. Kassel: Bärenreiter, 1949–79.

Die Musik in Geschichte und Gegenwart. 2nd. rev. ed. Edited by Ludwig Finscher. 26 vols. projected, in 2 parts. Kassel: Barenreiter, 1994-.

Nauhaus, Gerd. "Schumanns Klaviersonate f-Moll op. 14 und ihre Überlieferung." In *Schumann-Studien* 2, edited by Nauhaus. Zwickau: Rat der Stadt Zwickau, 1989.

Nautsch, Hans. *Friedrich Kalkbrenner: Wirkung und Werk.* Hamburg: Karl Dieter Wagner, 1983.

Neumann, Werner. "Welche Handschriften J. S. Bachscher Werke besaß die Berliner Singakademie?" In *Hans Albrecht in Memoriam,* edited by Wilfried Brennecke and Hans Haase. Kassel: Bärenreiter, 1962.

The New Grove Dictionary of Music and Musicians. Edited by Stanley Sadie. 20 vols. London: Macmillan, 1980.

The New Grove Dictionary of Music and Musicians. 2nd ed. Edited by Stanley Sadie and John Tyrell. 29 vols. London: Macmillan, 2001. Online ed. at http://www.grovemusic.com.

Newcomb, Anthony. "Schumann and the Marketplace: From Butterflies to *Hausmusik.*" In *Nineteenth-Century Piano Music,* edited by R. Larry Todd. New York: Schirmer, 1990.

Niecks, Frederick. *Frederick Chopin as a Man and Musician.* 2 vols. London: Novello, Ewer, 1888.

———. *Robert Schumann.* London and Toronto: J. M. Dent, 1925.

Nieman, Alfred. "The Concertos." In *Robert Schumann: The Man and his Music,* edited by Alan Walker. London: Barrie and Jenkins, 1972.

Nitschkova-Goleminova, Lilia. "Schumann-Moscheles-Paganini: Berichtigungen zur Biographie Robert Schumanns." *Die Musikforschung* 31 (1978): 16–28.

Norris, Jeremy. *The Russian Piano Concerto.* Vol. 1, *The Nineteenth Century.* Bloomington: Indiana University Press, 1994.

Ostwald, Peter F. "Florestan, Eusebius, Clara, and Schumann's Right Hand." *19th Century Music* 4 (1980–81): 17–31.

Parkins, Robert. "Mendelssohn and the Érard Piano." *Piano Quarterly,* no. 125 (spring 1984): 53–58.

Pazdírek, Franz. *Universal-Handbuch der Musikliteratur.* 12 vols. 1904–10. Reprint, Hilversum: F. Knuf, 1967.

Pederson, Sanna. "A. B. Marx, Berlin Concert Life, and German National Identity." *19th Century Music* 18 (1994–95): 87–107.

———. "Enlightened and Romantic German Music Criticism, 1800–1850." Ph.D. diss., University of Pennsylvania, 1995.

Petzoldt, Richard. "Klassik, Romantik und Klassizismus bei Robert Schumann." *Robert Schumann: Aus Anlass seines 100. Todestages.* Edited by Hans Joachim Moser and Eberhard Rebling. Leipzig: Breitkopf and Härtel, 1956.

Piggott, Patrick. "John Field and the Nocturne." *Proceedings of the Royal Musical Association* 95 (1968/69): 55–65.

———. *The Life and Music of John Field, 1782–1837: Creator of the Nocturne.* Berkeley: University of California Press, 1973.

Plantinga, Leon. "The Piano and the Nineteenth Century." In *Nineteenth-Century Piano Music,* edited by R. Larry Todd. New York: Schirmer, 1990.

———. Review of *Robert Schumann: Herald of a "New Poetic Age,"* by John Daverio. *Journal of the American Musicological Society* 51 (1998): 384–92.

———. *Schumann as Critic.* New Haven, Conn.: Yale University Press, 1967.

Ranft, Peter. *Felix Mendelssohn Bartholdy: Eine Lebenschronik.* Leipzig: Deutscher Verlag für Musik, 1972.

Reich, Nancy B. *Clara Schumann: The Artist and the Woman.* Ithaca, N.Y.: Cornell University Press, 1985.

———. *Clara Schumann: The Artist and the Woman.* Rev. ed. Ithaca, N.Y.: Cornell University Press, 2001.

Reynolds, Christopher. "A Choral Symphony by Brahms?" *19th Century Music* 9 (1985–86): 3–25.

Richards, Annette. *The Free Fantasia and the Musical Picturesque.* Cambridge: Cambridge University Press, 2001.

Rink, John. *Chopin: The Piano Concertos.* Cambridge: Cambridge University Press, 1997.

Roeder, Michael Thomas. *A History of the Concerto.* Portland, Ore.: Amadeus Press, 1994.

Roesner, Linda Correll. "Ästhetisches Ideal und sinfonische Gestalt: die d-Moll-Sinfonie um die Jahrhundertmitte." In *Schumann in Düsseldorf: Werke - Texte - Interpretationen,* edited by Bernhard R. Appel. Mainz: Schott, 1993.

———. "The Autograph of Schumann's Piano Sonata in F Minor, Opus 14." *Musical Quarterly* 61 (1975): 98–130.

———. "Schumann's 'Parallel' Forms." *19th Century Music* 14 (1990–91): 265–78.

Rosen, Charles. "Influence: Plagiarism and Inspiration." *19th Century Music* 4 (1980–81): 87–100.

Rosenblatt, Jay Michael. "The Concerto as Crucible: Franz Liszt's Early Works for Piano and Orchestra." Ph.D. diss., University of Chicago, 1995.

Roßner, Johannes. "Clara Wiecks frühe Virtuosenjahre - Repertoiregestaltung zwischen Tradition und persönlichem Anspruch." In *Schumann-Studien* 3/4, edited by Gerd Nauhaus. Cologne: Dr. Gisela Schewe, 1994.

Rothstein, William. *Phrase Rhythm in Tonal Music.* New York: Schirmer Books, 1989.

Sachs, Joel. "Authentic English and French Editions of J. N. Hummel." *Journal of the American Musicological Society* 25 (1972): 203–29.

———. Introduction to *Piano Concerto, Op. 113,* by Johann Nepomuk Hummel. Madison, Wisc.: A-R Editions, 1980.

———. *Kapellmeister Hummel in England and France.* Detroit: Information Coordinators, 1977.

Samson, Jim. *The Music of Chopin.* London: Routledge and Kegan Paul, 1985.

Schachter, Carl. "Rhythm and Linear Analysis." *The Music Forum* 4 (1976): 281–334; 5 (1980): 197–232; 6 (1987): 1–59.

Schering, Arnold. *Geschichte des Instrumentalkonzertes bis auf Gegenwart.* 2nd rev. ed. Reprint, Hildesheim: Georg Olms, 1965.

Schleuning, Peter. *The Fantasia.* Translated by A. C. Howie. 2 vols. Cologne: Arno Volk Verlag, 1971.

Schmid, Manfred Hermann. *Musik als Abbild: Studien zum Werk von Weber, Schumann und Wagner.* Tutzing: Hans Schneider, 1981.

Schoppe, Martin. "Schumanns *Litterarischer Verein.*" In *Robert Schumann und die Dichter: Ein Musiker als Leser,* edited by Bernhard R. Appel und Inge Hermstrüwer. Düsseldorf: Droste, 1991.

Schumann, Clara, and Johannes Brahms. *Clara Schumann - Johannes Brahms, Briefe aus den Jahren 1853–1896.* Edited by Berthold Litzmann. 2 vols. 1927. Reprint, Hildesheim: Georg Olms, 1970.

Schumann, Clara, and Robert Schumann. *Briefwechsel: Kritische Gesamtausgabe.* Edited by Eva Weissweiler. 3 vols. Frankfurt am Main: Sternfeld/Roter Stern, 1984–2001.

———. *The Complete Correspondence of Clara and Robert Schumann.* Edited by Eva Weissweiler. Translated by Hildegard Fritsch, Ronald L. Crawford and Harold P. Fry. 3 vols. New York: Peter Lang, 1994–2001.

Schumann, Eugenie. "Eugenie Schumann über das letzte Werk ihres Vaters Robert Schumann." *Schweizerische Musikzeitung* 78 (1938): 8–10.

———. *Robert Schumann: Ein Lebensbild meines Vaters.* Leipzig: Hase and Koehler, 1931.

Schumann, Robert. *Briefe: Neue Folge.* 2nd ed. Edited by F. Gustav Jansen. Leipzig: Breitkopf and Härtel, 1904.

———. *Gesammelte Schriften über Musik und Musiker.* 5th ed. Edited by Martin Kreisig. 2 vols. 1914. Reprint, Farnsborough, Hants, England: Gregg, 1969.

———. *Jugendbriefe.* 2nd ed. Edited by Clara Schumann. Leipzig: Breitkopf and Härtel, 1886.

———. *Selbstbiographische Notizen - Faksimile.* Edited by Martin Schoppe. Zwickau: Robert-Schumann-Gesellschaft, 1977.

———. *Tagebücher.* Vol. 1, *1827–1838.* 2nd. rev. ed. Edited by Georg Eismann. Leipzig: Deutscher Verlag für Musik, 1971.

———. *Tagebücher.* Vol. 2, *1836–1854.* Edited by Gerd Nauhaus. Leipzig: Deutscher Verlag für Musik, 1987.

———. *Tagebücher.* Vol. 3, *Haushaltbücher.* Parts 1, *1837–1847,* and 2, *1847–56.* Edited by Gerd Nauhaus. Leipzig: Deutscher Verlag für Musik, 1982.

Schumann, Robert, and Clara Schumann. *Briefe und Notizen Robert und Clara Schumanns.* 2nd rev. ed. Edited by Siegfried Kross. Bonn: Bouvier, 1982.

Schwarz, Werner. "Eine Musikerfreundschaft des 19. Jahrhunderts. Unveröffentlichte Briefe von Ferdinand David an Robert Schumann." In *Zum 70. Geburtstag von Joseph Müller-Blattau,* edited by Christoph-Hellmut Mahling. Kassel: Bärenreiter, 1966.

Steinberg, Michael. *The Concerto: A Listener's Guide.* New York: Oxford University Press, 1998.

Stravinsky, Vera, and Robert Craft. *Stravinsky in Pictures and Documents.* New York: Simon and Schuster, 1978.

Struck, Michael. "'Gewichtsverlagerungen' - Robert Schumanns letzte Konzertkompositionen." In *Schumanns Werke - Text und Interpretation,* edited by Akio Mayeda and Klaus Wolfgang Niemöller. Mainz: Schott, 1987.

———. *Die umstrittenen späten Instrumentalwerke Schumanns.* Hamburg: Karl Dieter Wagner, 1984.

Taylor, Ronald. *Robert Schumann: His Life and Work.* London: Granada, 1982; Panther, 1985.

Temperley, Nicholas. "Schumann and Sterndale Bennett." *19th Century Music* 12 (1988–89): 207–220.

Thayer, Alexander Wheelock. *Thayer's Life of Beethoven.* Rev. and edited by Elliot Forbes. Princeton, N.J.: Princeton University Press, 1967.

Todd, Ralph Larry. "The Instrumental Music of Felix Mendelssohn-Bartholdy: Selected Studies Based on Primary Sources." Ph.D. diss., Yale University, 1979.

Tovey, Donald Francis. *Essays in Musical Analysis.* Vol. 3, *Concertos.* London: Oxford University Press, 1936.

———. *Essays in Musical Analysis: Chamber Music.* 1944. Reprint, Oxford: Oxford University Press, 1989.

Turchin, Barbara. "Schumann's Conversion to Vocal Music: A Reconsideration." *Musical Quarterly* 67 (1981): 392–404.

Voss, Egon. "Einführung und Analyse." In *Konzert für Klavier und Orchester a-Moll,* by Robert Schumann. Mainz: Schott, 1979.

Waldbauer, Ivan F. "Riemann's Periodization Revisited and Revised." *Journal of Music Theory* 33 (1989): 333–91.

Walker, Alan. *Franz Liszt.* Vol 1, *The Virtuoso Years.* Rev. ed. Ithaca, N.Y.: Cornell University Press, 1987.

Walker-Hill, Helen. "Neglected Treasure: The Piano Concerto of Clara Wieck Schumann." *Women of Note Quarterly* 1, no. 2 (August 1993): 22–30.

Wasielewski, Wilhelm Joseph von. *Life of Robert Schumann.* Translated by A. L. Alger. Boston: Oliver Ditson, 1871.

———. *Robert Schumann: Eine Biographie.* Dresden: Rudolf Kunze, 1858.

———. *Schumanniana.* Bonn: Emil Strauß, 1883.

Weber, Max Maria von. *Carl Maria von Weber: Ein Lebensbild.* 3 vols. Leipzig: Ernst Keil, 1864–66.

Wendt, Matthias. "Zu Robert Schumanns Skizzenbüchern." In *Schumanns Werke - Text und Interpretation,* edited by Akio Mayeda and Klaus Wolfgang Niemöller. Mainz: Schott, 1987.

Wenke, Corina. "Aspekte zu Robert Schumanns Entwicklung in seiner Kinder- und Jugendzeit in Zwickau. Ergebnisse der Untersuchung und Übertragung von Quellenmaterial aus den Archiv des Robert-Schumann-Hauses in Zwickau." Ph.D. diss., Karl-Marx-Universität, Leipzig, 1987.

Wieck, Friedrich. *Piano and Song (Didactic and Polemical).* 1853. Translated and edited by Henry Pleasants. Stuyvesant: Pendragon, 1988.

Wieck, Marie. *Aus dem Kreise Wieck-Schumann.* Dresden: E. Pierson, 1912.

Winter, Robert. "The 19th-Century: Keyboards." In *Performance Practice,* edited by Howard Mayer Brown and Stanley Sadie. Vol. 2, *Music after 1600.* New York: W. W. Norton, 1989.

———. "Striking It Rich: The Significance of Striking Points in the Evolution of the Romantic Piano." *Journal of Musicology* 6 (1988): 267–92.

Index

Page numbers in italics refer to musical examples, figures and tables.

A

Appel, Bernhard R., 228, 240, 264, 265, 330n. 46
Arnold, Carl, songs, 7
Attwood, Thomas, 86

B

Bach, Carl Philipp Emanuel, 63, 207
Bach-Gesellschaft, 210
Bach, Johann Christian, 207
Bach, Johann Christoph Friedrich, 207
Bach, Johann Sebastian, 206–212
    Art of the Fugue, 211, 327n. 59
    Brandenburg concertos, 217
    Chorale Preludes, 211
    Chromatic Fantasy and Fugue, BWV 903, 211
    Double Keyboard Concerto in C Minor, BWV 1060, 291
    fugues, 207–208, 211, 212, 327n. 34
    keyboard concertos, 75–76, 197, 200, 210, 328n. 84
    keyboard playing, 136
    Mendelssohn and Moscheles, influence on, 136–137
    reception, 1830 to 1840, 208–210
    St. Matthew Passion, 206
    Schumann on, 206–212, 217
    Solo Keyboard Concerto in D Minor, BWV 1052, 200, 209–210, 215–217, 218, *219*
    Sonata for Violin and Keyboard in E Major, BWV 1016, 210
    sonatas and partitas for solo violin, 209, 211, 212
    Suite for Orchestra in D Major, BWV 1068, 210
    Toccata and Fugue in D Minor, BWV 565, 202, 221
    toccatas, 219
    Triple Keyboard Concerto in D Minor, BWV 1063, 208–209, 215–217, *276*, 327n. 44
    violin concertos, 217
    Well-Tempered Clavier, 208, 211
Bach, Wilhelm Friedemann, 207
Bargiel, Marianne Wieck, 77, *78*, 99
Bartók, Béla, *Duke Bluebeard's Castle*, 74
Beale, John, 80
Becker, Carl Ferdinand, 163, 165, 173
Beenhouwer, Jozef De, 212
Beethoven, Ludwig van, 1, 11, 128, 130, 223, 252
    An die ferne Geliebte, Op. 98, 179
    Cello Sonata in C Major, Op. 102, No. 1, 226
    chamber music, 7, 9
    Chopin, influenced by, 68
    Choral Fantasy in C Minor, Op. 80, *279*
    fugues, 211
    Herz's borrowing from, *133*, 141
    Mendelssohn and Moscheles, influenced by, 136–137
    Overture to *Coriolanus*, Op. 62, 200
    piano compositions, 53
    Piano Concerto in C Major, No. 1, Op. 15, 16, 280
    Piano Concerto in C Minor, No. 3, Op. 37, 280
        first movement, first solo, close, 21, *24–25*, 25–26, 267

performed in Leipzig, *79*,
89–90
rondo, 292
rondo, Brahms and, 303, 306
rondo, Moscheles's homage to,
149
Schumann's reception of, 14, 74,
89–90
Piano Concerto in E-flat Major,
Emperor, No. 5, Op. 73
first movement, cadenza, 17
first movement, first tutti, 16, 175
four-hand arrangement, 88
performed by Clara Schumann,
276, 277, *278–280*, 280, 287
performed in Leipzig, *79,* 90, 144,
311n. 2
Schumann's reception of, 14, 74,
89–90
Piano Concerto in G Major, No. 4,
Op. 58
form, 19, 187, 265
Hiller Concerto in F Minor,
compared to, 118
and Mendelssohn, 186, 198, 200
Moscheles's edition, 88, *89*
motivic relationships, 16, 19
performed by Beethoven, 19
performed by Clara Schumann,
276–277, 277, *278–279*, 280
performed in Leipzig, *79*, 88–89
Schumann's reception of, 74,
88–89, 90
piano concertos, 192, 281, 304, 306
cadenzas, 88, 237–238
early editions, 88, 317n. 68
first movement compositional
procedures, 16, 34
first movement close, 28, 34, 184,
235
orchestration, 136
performed in Leipzig, 77, 315n. 12
performance practice, 74, 88–89
Schumann's knowledge of, 1, 11,
14
Schumann's reception of, 14,
73–74, 197
piano four-hand arrangements, 3
piano playing, 112, 136
Piano Sonata in A Major, Op. 101,
179, 226
Piano Sonata in C Major, *Waldstein*,
Op. 53, 287
Piano Sonata in C Minor, Op. 111, 227

Piano Sonata in C-sharp Minor,
Moonlight, Op. 27, No. 2, 226–227
Piano Sonata in E-flat Major, Op. 27,
No. 1, 226
Piano Sonata in E Major, Op. 109, 227
quartets, 3
Schumann on, 75–76, 186, 200, 207,
208
songs, 7
String Quartet in C-sharp Minor,
Op. 131, 226
string quartets, 140
symphonic cycle, 7, 309n. 54
symphonies, 199–200
Herz's borrowing from, *133*
performed in Heidelberg, 9
performed in Leipzig, 7, 76,
309n. 54
symphonies and masses, Schumann's
judgment of, 90
Symphony in A Major, No. 7, Op. 92,
139
Symphony in C Minor, No. 5, Op. 67,
179, 224–225, 226
Symphony in D Minor, Op. 125, 291
Symphony in E-flat Major, *Eroica*,
No. 3, Op. 55, 3
Violin Concerto in D Major, Op. 61,
16, *278–280*, 298
Belcke, Christian Gottlieb, flute concerto, 8,
309n. 55
Belleville, Anna Caroline de, 77, *78*, 121,
161
Bellini, Vincenzo, *La sonnambula*, 194
Bennett, William Sterndale
Caprice, Op. 22, 253, 258, 259–261
lyricism, 260–261, *260*, 265
performed by Bennett, 258, 259
Schumann's review of, 247, 248,
259–260, 265
virtuosic style, 260–261
concertos performed by, 192
friendship with Schumann, 190–191
Piano Concerto in C Minor, No. 3,
Op. 9, 169, *171*, 189–195, 259
Allgemeine musikalische Zeitung
review, 191
Beethoven concertos as model,
190, 192, 194, 195
lyricism, 194
Mendelssohn on, 191
motivic relationships, 189,
193–194, *193*, 215
performed by Bennett, 191–192

Romanze, 189, 191, 194–195
rondo, 191, 195
Schumann's reviews of, 171,
191–195, 215, 260–261
Piano Concerto in F Minor, No. 4,
Op. 19, 258–259
form, 258–259, 269
performed by Bennett, 258
recording, 331n. 27
Schumann's review of, 247, 248,
258–259, 261
piano concertos, *xii*
student of Mendelssohn, 171, 253
student of Potter, 192
Berger, Ludwig, 77, 80, 181
Bergmann, Johann Gottfried, 6
Berlin
Beethoven and Mozart concertos
performed in, 77, 79, 85, 87
Singakademie, 206, 209, 210, 327n. 52
Berlioz, Hector, 80
on Chopin, 107, 125
Bernsdorf, Edward, 281
Blahetka, Léopoldine, 77, *78*, 80, 97, 160
Bloom, Harold, 225, 329n. 10
Bocklet, Carl Maria von, 80–81
Bockmühl, Emil, 288
Boetticher, Wolfgang, 240, 330n. 45
Böhner, August Nathanael, 7
Böhner, Ludwig
chamber music, 7
Piano Concerto in E-flat Major, No. 1,
Op. 7, 4, 14
Boieldieu, Adrien, *Jean de Paris*, 4
Bonds, Mark Evan, 224–225, 226, 232, 237
Botgorscheck, Caroline, 261
Brahms, Johannes, 292, 295, 296,
297–298
Piano Concerto in D Minor, No. 1,
Op. 15, *xiii*, 280, 297–298,
303–306
classical models, 304, 306
compositional process, 303, 304
form, 304–306, *305*
performed by Brahms, 304, 306
program, 304–306
reception, 306
Schumannian ideal, 306
second movement, 303
third movement, 303
Branson, David, 100
Brown, Julie Hedges, 330n. 51
Bruyck, Carl van, 112
Burkholder, Peter, on modeling, 39

C

Carus, Agnes, 3, 7, 8, 38, 223
Carus, Ernst August, 7, 8, 10
Carus, Karl Erdmann, 3
Casals, Pablo, 291
Chaminade, Cécile, 297
Charles-René, 97
Cherubini, Luigi, Overture to *Medea*, 291
Chopin, Fryderyk
Bach Triple Concerto performed by,
208, 327n. 44
Beethoven and Mozart, influenced by,
68, 75
Herz's borrowing from, *133*, 141
on Hiller, Concerto in F Minor, 114
on Kalkbrenner, Herz, Liszt, and
Hiller, 121
Piano Concerto in E Minor, No. 2,
Op. 11, 66–67
difficulty, bizarreness, 105–106
Field-like, 68
first movement, first solo, 43,
313n. 21
first movement, tonal scheme,
106–107
Herz's borrowing from, *133*,
322n. 65
orchestration, 107, 136
performed by Chopin, 68, 105,
106, 275, 314n. 31
performed by Clara Schumann,
105–106
Piano Concerto in F Minor, No. 2,
Op. 21, 52, 66–67, 107–110
first movement, first solo, close,
68–69, *69–70*
form, 45, 116
Larghetto, 108–110, *109*, 119
motivic relationships, 107–108,
108, 111
orchestration, 107, 136
performed by Chopin, 106
performed by Clara Schumann,
106, 275, *276*, 277, *278*, 280
Schumann's F Major Concerto,
compared to, 68–69
piano concertos, *xi*, 91, 94, 104–110,
111, 130, 182, 186, 232
Fink's review of, 69
reception, 92, 104–105, 110, 166
Schumann's review of, 67,
104–105, 107–110, 114,
170–172, *170*

piano playing, 113
reception, Clara Schumann's influence
    on, 105
Schumann, meeting with, 105
Variations on *Là ci darem la mano*,
    Op. 2, 10–11, 275
Clementi, Muzio, 112
Cooper, Jeffrey, 80
Cramer, Johann Baptist
    chamber music, 7
    etudes, 8
    Mozart concerto arrangements, 83, 87
        Concerto in D Minor,
            83, *84*, 316n. 45
    Mozart concertos performed by, 80
Crusell, Bernhard Henrik, clarinet
    concerto, 8
Czerny, Carl, 52, 212, 251, 332n. 46
    Beethoven concerto performed by, 80
    Concertino for Piano and Orchestra in
        C Major, Op. 650, 251–252
        form, 251
        Schumann's review of, 247, 248,
            251
        virtuosic style, 248, 251–252,
            265
    Four-Hand Piano Concerto in C Major,
        Op. 153, 311n. 6
    piano compositions, 53
    piano four-hand works, 3, 7
    School of Practical Composition, 225
    variations, 4
Czerny, Joseph, 160

D

Dahlhaus, Carl, 200, 202, 216, 218, 242
Danzi, Franz, songs, 7
Daverio, John, 143, 200, 222, 225, 286
David, Ferdinand, 201, 209, 211, 287,
    306
David, Louise, *see* Dulcken, Louise David
Della Maria, Dominique, overture, 4–5
Dessauer, Heinrich, 100
Döhler, Theodor, 113, 124, 136, 202
    Italian origins, 118–119
    Piano Concerto in A Major, Op. 7,
        52–53, 111, 118–120
        Adagio, 119, *120*, 187
        Allgemeine musikalische Zeitung
            review, 114
        performed by Döhler, 119–120
        reception, 119–120, 132

Schumann's review of, 114, 115,
    118–120, 139, *170*
title page, 119
study with Czerny, 118
Döhner, Gotthilf Ferdinand, 5
Dörffel, Alfred
    on Beethoven and Mozart symphonies
        and concertos, 76–77
    on Field, Concerto in C Minor, 100
Dorn, Heinrich, 41, 62–63
    Mozart Concerto in D Minor
        performed by, 77, *79*, 86, 90
    Schumann's study with, 208
Dotzauer, Justus Johann Friedrich, 6, 77, *78*
    rondo for cello, 9
Draheim, Joachim, 166, 212, 218, 288, 291
Drouet, Louis, 80
Dulcken, Louise David, 77, *78*, 161,
    315n. 12
Dussek, Jan Ladislav
    chamber music, 7
    piano concertos, 192
    sonata for violin and piano, 4

E

Edler, Arnfried, 306
Eichner, Ernst, *Sinfonie*, 4–5
Ellsworth, Therese, 80
Engel, Hans
    on Bennett, Concerto in C Minor, 192
    on Herz, Concerto in C Minor,
        142–143
    on Hummel, Concerto in F Major, 95
    on Lasekk, Concertino *brillant* in
        C Major, 189
    on Moscheles, Concerto in C Minor,
        160
    on Ries, Concerto in G Minor, 98
    on Schmitt, Aloys, Concerto in E-flat
        Major, 172
    on Schumann, Robert, Concerto in
        A Minor, 264, 270
    on Thalberg, Concerto in F Minor, 138
Ernst, Heinrich Wilhelm, 10
Etudes, piano, 112
Evers, Charles, 97

F

Fantasy concertos, 227–228, 242, 246
Fantasy genre, 224, 225, 226–228
Faulhaber, Christian, 9

Fauré, Gabriel, 297
  Ballade in F-sharp Major for Piano and
    Orchestra, Op. 19, 246
Fétis, François-Joseph
  Chopin, Concerto in E Minor, review
    of, 106
  on Chopin's playing, 113
  Field, Concerto in C Minor, review of,
    100
Field, John
  Chopin, compared to, 68, 75
  piano compositions, 53
  Piano Concerto in A-flat Major, No. 2,
    13, 37, 104
    Chopin's knowledge of, 67
    editions, 100
    form, first movement, 19, 20,
      312n. 12
    orchestration, 21
    performances, 99–100, 275
    reception, 100, 110, 318n. 32
    Schumann on, 100
    Schumann's improvisation on,
      41–42
    Schumann's modeling on, *41*,
      41–42, 62–63
  Piano Concerto in C Minor, No. 7,
    99–104, 134, 196, 232, 267
    Allgemeine musikalische Zeitung
      review, 100
    form, 100–101, *101*, 103–104
    Liszt on, 103
    motivic relationships, 100–101,
      101–102, 107
    orchestration, 136
    performed by Field, 100,
      102–103
    Schumann's review of, 100, 101,
      111, 170, *170*, 173
    slow movement, lack of, 102–103,
      319n. 41
  Piano Concerto in E-flat Major, No. 3,
    102, 319n. 39
  piano concertos, *xii*, 62, 91–92, 94,
    170, 189, 315n. 12
    classical model, 17–18
    modern edition, 312n. 24
    recording, 312n. 24
  playing style, 101
  school of, 41
Fink, Charlotte, 161
Fink, Gottfried Wilhelm, reviews by
  Chopin, concertos, 69, 106–107
  Herz, Concerto in A Major, 140–141

Herz, Concerto in C Minor, 137, 141,
    142
Hummel, Concerto in F Major, 95
Kalkbrenner, Concerto in A Minor,
    312n. 36
Mendelssohn, Concerto in G Minor,
    174–175, 178
Mozart, Concerto in C Major,
    arrangement by Kalkbrenner, 84–85
Ries, Concerto in G Minor, 97–98
Finson, Jon W., 224, 328–329n. 4
Flechsig, Emil, 6
Franck, César, 297
  Symphonic Variations, 246
Fuhrmann, Moritz Adolph, 77, *78*, 215n. 12

G

Glasschord, 5
Gleichauf, Xaver, 88, 317n. 68
Glock, Christian Gottlob, 7, 207
Gluck, Christoph Willibald, *239*
Goethe, Johann Wolfgang von, 207
Gooley, Dana, 180
Grayson, David, 83
Green, Richard David, 212
Grieg, Edvard, Piano Concerto in A Minor,
    Op. 16, 246
Grosheim, Georg Christoph, overture, 5
Guschl, *Demoiselle*, 79

H

Haack, Helmut, 300
Habeneck, François-Antoine, 80
Hallé, Charles, 321n. 49
Handel, George Frederic, 141
  fugues, 211
  keyboard compositions, 86
  keyboard playing, 75, 136
  Mendelssohn and Moscheles,
    influence on, 136–137
Härtel, Hermann, 287
Härtel, Raymund, 202
Hanslick, Eduard, 229, 271
Hartknoch, Carl Eduard, 124
  Hummel Concerto in B Minor
    performed by, 77, *78*
  Piano Concerto in G Minor, Op. 14,
    127–130
    Adagio, 129
    autobiographical reading of,
      129–130

Chopin, influenced by, 130
Hummel Concerto in B Minor,
compared to, 128, *129*
motivic relationships, 128
Schumann's review of, 111, 115,
127–130, *170*
style, 127, 128
study with Hummel, move to Russia,
127
Hauk, Wenceslas, 79, 85–86, 87
Hauser, Franz, 209
Haydn, Franz Joseph, 1, 11
The Creation, 2, 4
keyboard compositions, 86
piano four-hand arrangements, 3
Schumann on, 207
symphonies, 9, 92, 317n. 3
Heidelberg *Museum*, 9
Heine, Heinrich, 115, 320n. 19
Heinze, Wilhelm Heinrich, 309n. 55
Heldt, Gerhard, 290–291
Hensel, Fanny Mendelssohn, 191, 201, 202,
211
Henselt, Adolf
Beethoven concerto performed by,
80–81
Concert Variations, 164
Piano Concerto in F Minor, Op. 16,
276, 277, *278*
playing style, 125, 202
Weber *Concertstück* performed by,
180
Herz, Henri, 115, 130, 212
Beethoven, compared to, 144
Bravura Variations, Op. 20, 3, 275
Chopin on, 121
etudes, 112
Parisian school, 17, 21, 178
piano compositions, 53
Piano Concerto in A Major, No. 1,
Op. 34, 13, 37, 52–53
Fink's review of, 140–41
first movement, first solo, close,
21, 30–34, *31–33*, 45, 124
first movement, recapitulation, 20
Schumann's modeling on, *xi*, 17,
21, 51, 53–61, *54*, *55*, *56*, 63
Piano Concerto in C Minor, No. 2,
Op. 74, 140–145
Beethoven Concerto in C Minor as
model, 144
bravura, 144, *145*, 167
final movement, 144, 187
Fink's review of, 137, 141, 142

form, 135, 137, 142–45, 170, 249,
274
performed by Herz, 130, 141–142
reviews of performances, 141–142,
144
Schumann's review of, 76, 114,
140–141, 142, *170*, 172–173,
249
second movement, 144
Piano Concerto in D Minor, No. 3,
Op. 87, 130–132
Allgemeine musikalische Zeitung
review, 132
bravura, 132, 134
expression marks, 131, *132*, 172
orchestration, 131, 136
pastiche construction, borrowings,
131, *133*, 141, 322n. 65
reception, 132–134
Schumann's review of, 76, 111,
130–132, 141, *171*
piano concertos, *xii*, 170, 297
piano four-hand works, 7
quartets, 3
playing style, technique, 130, 136,
137
reception, 140
reputation, 130, 140
Rondo, Op. 37, 52
upper keyboard register, use of, 113,
114
Variations, Opp. 23 and 76, 275
Hiller, Ferdinand, 287
Bach Triple Concerto performed by,
208, 212, *276*, 327n. 44
Beethoven, compared to, 111, 115,
118
Beethoven Concerto in E-flat Major
performed by, 80
Chopin on, 121
Impromptu, 270
meeting with Schumann, 118
Mozart concertos performed by, *79*, 86
Piano Concerto in F Minor, No. 1,
Op. 5, 115–118
Adagio, 118
Chopin on, 114–116
form, 116
reception, 116, 132
Schumann's review of, 76, 111,
115–118, *170*
style, 116–117, *117*
Piano Concerto in F-sharp Minor,
Op. 69, 116, 118, 320n. 22

romantic, 111, 115
Twenty-Four Etudes, Op. 15, 115
Die Zerstörung Jerusalems, 116, 118
Hoffmann, Julius, 80
Hoffmann, Philipp Carl, 81
Hofmann, Friedrich Joseph, 9
Horak, Václav, 6
Hummel, Johann Nepomuk, 1
  Clavierschule (etudes), 8, 112,
    310n. 59
  Mozart concerto arrangements, 82–83,
    86, 87, 237–238, 316n. 44
    Concerto in C Minor, 85
    Concerto in D Minor, 83, *84*, 85,
      86
  Mozart, influenced by, 68
  Piano Concerto in A-flat Major,
    Op. 113, 95
  Piano Concerto in A Minor, Op. 85,
    13, 37, *78*
    Chopin's knowledge of, 67
    editions, 312n. 24, 318n. 20
    first movement, first solo, close,
      21, 26–30, *27–30*, 31, 34, 61,
      95–96
    form, 19, 187
    orchestration, 21
    performed by Hummel, 77, *78*
    performed by Schumann, *xi,* 4, 7,
      8, 9
    reception, 67, 92–93, 96, 110
    recordings, 312n. 24
    Schumann's modeling on, *xi*,
      44–49, *45*, 51, 61
  Piano Concerto in B Minor, Op. 89,
    13, *78*
    Chopin's knowledge of, 67
    editions, 312n. 24, 318n. 20
    form, 20
    model for Hartknoch, 128, *129*
    orchestration, 21
    performed in Leipzig, *78*
    reception, 67, 95, 110
    recordings, 312n. 24
  Piano Concerto in E Major,
    Les adieux, Op. 110, *78*
  Piano Concerto in F Major, Op. post.,
    94–96
    Fink's review of, 95
    orchestration, 136
    passagework, 95–96, *96*
    performed by Hummel, 94–95,
      318n. 17
    reception, 94–95

  Schumann's review of, 94–96,
    247
  style, 95–96, 98, 104, 107, 111,
    134
  piano concertos, *xii*, 39, 172, 183, 192,
    315n. 12
    classical model, 17–18
    passagework, 62, 184, 189
    Schumann's reviews of, 91–94
  piano four-hand works, 3
  school of, 252
  Schumann's plan to study with, 44, 51,
    70, 94, 111
  Sonata in F-sharp Minor, Op. 81, 94
  tour to England of 1833, 94
Hünten, Franz, 7, 52, 141, 212, 313n. 4

I

International Clara Schumann Piano
  Competition, 166

J

Jean Paul, *see* Richter, Johann Paul
  Friedrich
Jehnichen, 288
Joachim, Johannes, 300
Joachim, Joseph, 292, 298, 304
  Beethoven Violin Concerto performed
    by, *278–280*
  Schumann Violin Concerto performed
    by, 300–301
  Schumann Violin *Phantasie* performed
    by, 298, 300
Jones, Joela, 166
Jüllig, Franz, 271
Jupin, Charles-François, 122

K

Kalbeck, Max, 304
Kalkbrenner, Friedrich, 1, 132
  chamber music, 7
  Chopin on, 121
  Herz's borrowing from, *133*, 141
  etudes, 112
  Mozart concerto arrangements, 82,
    86
    Concerto in C Major, K. 503,
      reviews of, 83–85
  Parisian school, 17, 178
  performance in Leipzig, 121

performance in Strasbourg, 122
Piano Concerto in A-flat Major, No. 4,
  Op. 127, 122–127
  Allgemeine musikalische Zeitung
    review, 122
  expressive extremes, 122–125,
    125, 172, 251
  Kalkbrenner Concerto in D Minor,
    compared to, 122
  orchestration, 136
  performed by Kalkbrenner, 122
  reception, 122, 132–134
  romantic school, 123
  rondo, 127, 321n. 50
  Schumann's review of, 122–124,
    127, 170, *170*, 172–173, 251
  second movement, 123–124
  tempo changes, 125–127, *126*
  tuttis, 122–123, 175
Piano Concerto in A Minor, No. 3,
  Op. 107, 121–122
  Fink's review of, 321n. 36
  performed by Kalkbrenner, 121
Piano Concerto in D Minor, No. 1,
  Op. 61, 13, 127, 170
  Chopin's knowledge of, 67,
    314n. 25
  form, 44–45
  Herz's borrowing from, *133*
  performed by Schumann, *xi*, 2, 3,
    4, 7, 37, 38
  performed in Leipzig, *78*
  reception, 67
  recording, 312n. 24
  style, 20, 41
Piano Concerto in E Minor, Op. 80, *78*,
  111
piano concertos, *xii*, 62, 170, 183–184,
  315n. 12
  projected fifth concerto, 127
piano four-hand works, 7
Rondo brillant, Op. 101, 275
Schumann's meeting with, 115, 121
technical facility, 121, 136, 202,
  321n. 49
Two-Piano Concerto in C Major,
  Op. 127, 321n. 51
upper keyboard register, use of, 113,
  114
Kallberg, Jeffrey, on modeling, 38–39, 49
Kalliwoda, Johannes Wenzeslaus, 8,
  309n. 55, 317n. 3
Kaskel, Carl von (pseud. Carl Lasekk), 169,
  186, 188

Concertino *brillant* in C Major for
  Piano and Orchestra, 188–189, 190
  à la Thalberg passage, 188, 189
  form, 188–189, *190–191*,
    227–228
  orchestration, 188, 189
  Schumann's review of, 169, *170*,
    188–189
Concertino in B Minor for Piano and
  Orchestra, Op. 10, 186–188
  form, 186–187
  Schumann's review of, 151, *170*,
    171, 186–188
  Wieck Concerto in A Minor,
    compared to, 188
Keller, Karl, variations for flute, 9
King, A. Hyatt, 81
Kistner, Carl Friedrich, 210, 298
Klassen, Janina, 161, 166
Klingemann, Karl, 201
Klughist, Julius, 9
Knorr, Julius, 7
Koch, Heinrich Christoph
  concerto, opening ritornello, 311n. 9
  Introductory Essay, 22, 135–136
Köhler, Ernst, 6
Kosciuszko, Tadeusz, 301, 333n. 16
Kreutzer, Conradin
  double concerto for two violins, 9
  piano concertos, 315n. 12
  vocal trio, 4–5
Krogulski, Joseph, 77, *78*, 315n. 14
Kropfinger, Klaus, 79
Kross, Siegfried, 91
Kufferath, Hubert Ferdinand
  Capriccio for Piano and Orchestra in
    C-sharp Minor, Op. 1, 254–258
  form, 255–257, *256*
  lyricism, 255, *255*, 256, 257–258
  Mendelssohn *Capriccio brillant* as
    model, 253, 254–255, 257–258
  orchestration, 255, 256, *256*, 257
  Schumann's reviews of, 247, 248,
    254–255, 256–258
Kummer, Friedrich August, 6
  oboe concertino, 8
Kuntsch, Johann Gottfried, 2, 6, 208

L

Lafont, Charles Philippe, chamber music, 7
Laidlaw, Robena Ann, 97, 161
Lara, Adelina de, 233

Lasekk, Carl, *see* Kaskel, Carl von
Lecourt, Pierre, Piano Concerto in C Major, Op. 1, 5, 14
Leichsenring, E. J., 288
Leipzig Gewandhaus chamber concerts, 211–212
Leipzig Gewandhaus Orchestra concerts
    Bach performed at, 208–210
    Beethoven performed at
        concertos, 77, *79*, 315n. 12
        symphonies, 7, 76, 92, 309n. 54
    concertos (not by Mozart or
        Beethoven) performed at, 7–8, 77, *78*, 92, 309n. 55, 315n. 13
    Mozart performed at
        concertos, 77, *79*, 86–87, 92, 315n. 12, 317n. 3
        symphonies, 77
    symphonies (not by Mozart or
        Beethoven) performed at, 92, 317n. 3
Lemke, J. August, 9
Lenneberg, Hans, 169, 202
Leonhardt, Emil
    Beethoven Concerto in G Major performed by, *79*
    Mozart Concerto in C Minor performed by, *79*, 87
Lidel, Joseph, *239*
Liebenau, Friedrich Christian von, 3
Liebenau, Sussette, 3
Lipinski, Karol, 209, 212
Liszt, Franz
    Après une lecture du Dante, 242
    Bach Triple Concerto performed by, 208, 212, 327n. 44
    Beethoven concerto performed by, 80–81
    Chopin on, 121
    on Field, Concerto in C Minor, 103
    Piano Concerto in A Major, No. 2, 242, *243*, 246, 330n. 56
    Piano Concerto in E-flat Major, No. 1, 136, 242, 246, 330nn. 53, 56
    Piano Concerto in E-flat Major, Op. post. 242, 243–246, *244–245*, 330n. 56
        edition by Rosenblatt, 242, *245*
    piano concertos, *xii*, 166, 224, 242–246, 297, 306
    Piano Sonata in B Minor, 242
    playing style, 125, 202
    on Schumann, *Carnaval*, 71
    Thalberg rivalry, 139

Weber *Concertstück* performed by, 180, 325nn. 22, 23
Loewe, Carl
    piano sonatas, 53, 214
    songs, 7
London, Beethoven and Mozart concertos performed in, 77, 80, 86–87
Lorenz, Gottlieb, 4
Lott, R. Allen, 142
Louis Ferdinand, Prince of Prussia, chamber music, 3, 7

M

MacDowell, Edward, 297
Macfarren, George, 86
Maria Isabelle de Bourbon, 119
Marpurg, Friedrich Wilhelm, *Abhandlung von der Fuge*, 208, 211
Marschner, Heinrich, 8
Marston, Nicholas, 226
Martin, Uwe, 211
Marx, Adolph Bernhard, 79, 80
Mayer, Charles (Carl), 250–251
    Etudes, Op. 55, 250
    nocturne, 4
    Piano Concerto in D Major, Op. 70, 251
        form, 251, 274
        Schumann's review of, 247, 248, 249, 251
        virtuosic style, 248, 251, 331n. 18
    rondo, 3, 4
    Schumann's reviews of, 331n. 14
    toccata, 4
    variations, 4
Mayseder, Joseph
    chamber music, 7
    violin concerto, 8
Mehner, Carl, 228–229, 240
Meißner, Karl Gottlob, 3
Mendelssohn, Fanny, *see* Hensel, Fanny Mendelssohn
Mendelssohn, Felix, 111, 223, 240, 246, 275
    Bach performed by, 200, 201, 206, 208–212, *276*
    Beethoven, compared to, 76
    Beethoven concertos performed by, 77, *79*, 80, 88–89, 176, 200
    Capriccio brillant, Op. 22, 253–254, 255–258, 275, 292
        form, 253–254, *254*
        orchestration, 253

performed by Clara Schumann,
253, 275, *276*, 280–281
reception, 253
Schumann on, 248, 253
concerted works for piano, *xii*, 166,
197, 232, 263, 277, 280
Duo for piano four-hands, *239*
Die Hebriden, 291
influences on, 136–137
Lieder ohne Worte, *239*, 270–271
Mozart concertos performed by, 77,
79, 80, 86–87, 199, 237
Oedipus at Colonus, 287
Piano Concerto in D Minor, No. 2,
Op. 40, 201–206
Baroque homages, 202, *203–204*,
206, 219
bravura (also, lack of), 198, 199,
201–202, 217
compositional process, 198, 200,
201, 202
form, 135, 202–206, *205*, 221
fugue, 202, *203–204*
Mendelssohn Concerto in
G Minor, compared to,
202–203, 205
Moscheles on, 201
opening, 202, *203*, 218–219
orchestration, 217
performed by Clara Schumann,
277, 277, *278*, 280, 281, 295
performed by Mendelssohn, 198,
199, 200, 206, 217
Schumann's review of, 171,
197–198, 201, 206, 217
Piano Concerto in G Minor, No. 1,
Op. 25, 169, 173–180, 181, 190, 233
Beethoven Concerto in G Major as
model, 176, 186
classical (Apollonian) ideal, 174,
178
cyclicism, 179–180
editions, 178
Fink's review of, 174–175, 178
form, 135, 174–180, *177*, 227–228,
325n. 14
improvisatory quality, 176, 196
orchestration, 174–175, 178
performed by Clara Schumann,
276–277, 277, *278*
performed by Mendelssohn, 174,
198, 215
Schumann's knowledge of, 174,
178

Schumann's review of, 170, 174,
179–180, 198, 215
Weber *Concertstück* as model,
178–180
popularity, 198–199
Preludes and Fugues, Op. 35, 211, 212
St. Paul, 201
school of, 143
Serenade und Allegro giojoso, Op. 43,
253, 258, 261–263, 292
compositional process, 261
motivic relationships, 262, *263*
form, 262, 267
performed by Mendelssohn,
261–262
Schumann's review of, 247, 248,
261
Violin Concerto in E Minor, Op. 64, 290
Weber *Concertstück* performed by,
178, 325n. 16
Mendelssohn Bartholdy, Lea, 201
Merrick, Frank, 102
Methuen-Campbell, James, 105
metronomic playing, 125
Meyer, John A.
on Chopin, 67
on Field, 103
Milder-Hauptmann, Pauline Anna, 6
Mitchell, J., 9
Mittermaier, Karl Joseph Anton, 8
Modeling, compositional, 38–39, 49,
see also specific compositions
Molique, Bernhard, Violin Concerto in
D Major, No. 4, Op. 14, *276*
Moscheles, Charlotte, 146, 160, 217
Moscheles, Ignaz, 1
Alexander Variations, 3, 6, 8, 9–10, 41
Bach Triple Concerto performed by,
208, *276*
Beethoven concerto arrangements, 88,
89, 238
creative periods, 146, 147
etudes, 112
Herz's borrowing from, *133*, 141
Hommage à Haendel, Grand Duo for
Two Pianos, Op. 82, 202, *203*,
219–220
influences on, 136–137
Mozart concerto arrangements, 82–83
Piano Concerto in B-flat Major,
Fantastique, No. 6, Op. 90, 146,
147, 150–55
form, 135, 143, 151–152, 154–55,
166, 171, 175, 221

motivic relationships, 152, *153*,
215, 227
orchestration, 154, 166
performed by Moscheles, 136, 137,
146, 150–151, 166, 217
Schumann's review of
(performance), 137, 150–151,
154, 166–167
Schumann's review of (score),
146, 150–151, 154–155,
166–167, *170*, 171, 173, 215
tonal play, 152–154
Piano Concerto in C Major, No. 5,
Op. 87, 145, 146–150
Adagio, 147
center of gravity, 147–150,
269
motivic relationships, 135,
147–150, *148–149*, 167
performed by Moscheles, 77, *78*
rondo, 149–150
Schumann's reviews of, 146–147,
149, 150–151, 170, *170*
virtuosic style, 147, 149, 167
Piano Concerto in C Minor,
Pathétique, No. 7, Op. 93, 146, 150,
155–160, 237
bravura, lack of, 157–158,
159–160, 217
form, 135, 137, 156–160, 166, *157*,
175, 187, 216, 221
motivic relationships, 158–159,
159, 215
orchestration, 136, 156, 159–160,
166, 217
performed by Moscheles, 146, 155,
217
reception, 156, 160
Schumann's reviews of, 146,
155–156, 171, 173, 197–198,
215, 217
Piano Concerto in D Major, *Pastorale*,
No. 8, Op. 96, 146
Piano Concerto in E-flat Major, No. 2,
Op. 56, 13, 145, 146, 275
form, 18, 20, 41, 312n. 12
orchestration, 21
performed in Leipzig, 77, *78*
recording, 312n. 24
Piano Concerto in F Major, No. 1,
Op. 45, 13, 145
form, 20, 187
recording, 312n. 24
Schumann's knowledge of, 41

Schumann's modeling on, *40*,
40–41
Piano Concerto in G Minor, No. 3,
Op. 60, 13, 45, 277, *278*
Chopin's knowledge of, 67
first movement cadenza, 20
form, 187
Herz's borrowing from, *133*
performed in Leipzig, 77, *78*
performed by Moscheles, 146,
276
reception, 146, 156, 160
recordings, 312n. 24
Schumann on, 137, 145–147,
155–156, 170
piano concertos, *xii*, 37, 39, 197, 297,
315n. 12
classical model, 18
recordings, 146, 323nn. 37, 38
romanticism, 146, 147, 155–156,
167
piano four-hand works, 7
Schumann, contact with
Carlsbad encounter, 7
correspondence, 146, 155
Schumann, writings about
Concert sans orchestre, 92
*Introduction und Allegro
appassionato*, 281
style, 178
Moser, Andreas, 303
Möser, Karl, 79, 80
Mozart, Franz Xaver (Wolfgang
Amadeus, Jr.)
Mozart concertos performed by, 81,
82
Piano Concerto in C Major, Op. 14,
82
Mozart, Leopold, 199
Mozart, Wolfgang Amadeus, 1, 11
chamber music, 7
Don Giovanni (Don Juan), 131, 218
Die Entführung aus dem Serail, 5
Hummel, influenced by, 68
Mendelssohn and Moscheles,
influenced by, 136–137
Piano Concerto in A Major, K. 488,
15, 312n. 10
Piano Concerto in C Major, K. 467, 15
performed by Mozart Jr., 82
Piano Concerto in C Major, K. 503, 15,
16, 17
arrangement by Kalkbrenner,
83–85

Piano Concerto in C Minor, K. 491,
15, 280
  arrangement by Hummel, critical
    judgment, 85
  performed in Leipzig, *79*
Piano Concerto in D Minor, K. 466,
15, 198, 280
  arrangement by Hummel, critical
    judgment, 85–86
  arrangements by Cramer and
    Hummel, 83, *84*
  edition by André, 85
  performed by Hiller, 86
  performed by Mendelssohn,
    86–87, 199
  performed by Mozart, 199
  performed in Leipzig, *79*
  Schumann's reception of, 89–90
Piano Concerto in E-flat Major, K.
449, 15, 17, 311n. 2
piano concertos, 182, 192, 281, 304,
306
  arrangements, 82–83, 86, 88, 241
  arrangements, critical judgment,
    83–86
  cadenzas, 237–238, 329n. 36
  elaborations, 81
  first movement compositional
    procedures, 15–16, 21, 34
  first movement close, 28, 34, 184,
    235
  orchestration, 136
  performed in Leipzig, 77,
    315n. 12
  performance practice, 74, 81–87
  Schumann's knowledge of, 1, 11,
    14
  Schumann's reception of, 14,
    73–74, 197
piano four-hand arrangements, 3
piano playing, 112, 136, 198
Piano Quartet in E-flat Major, K. 493, 3
Schumann, influenced by, 136
Schumann on, 75–76, 186, 200, 207,
208
Symphony in C Major, 317n. 3
Symphony in C Major, *Jupiter*, K. 551,
76–77
Symphony in D Major, *Prague*, K.
504, 76–77
Symphony in E-flat Major, K. 543,
76–77
Symphony in G Minor, K. 550, 76–77,
317n. 3

Two-Piano Concerto in E-flat Major,
K. 365, performed in Leipzig, *79*
Mühling, Heinrich Leberecht, vocal trio, 4
Müller, August Eberhard, 87
  *Guide to the Accurate Performance
    of the Mozartean Piano Concertos*,
    81
Müller, Christian Gottlieb, bass trombone
  concerto, 8
Müller, Maria Catharina, 80–81, 87

N

Napoleon Bonaparte, 97
Nautsch, Hans, 121–122
Neate, Charles, 80
Neue Zeitschrift für Musik, purpose of,
  xi–xii, 73
Newcomb, Anthony, 71
Nissen, Henriette, 287
Norris, Jeremy, 246
Nottebohm, Gustav, 271

O

Onslow, George
  chamber music, 7, 9
  piano four-hand works, 7
Ortigue, Joseph d', 101

P

Paganini, Nicolò, 10
Paris, Beethoven and Mozart concertos
  performed in, 77, 80
Parisian school of piano virtuosos, 112, 178,
  194, 195, 250, 271
  concerted works for piano by, 17, 21,
    253
Pechatschek, Frantisek Martin, variations
  for oboe, 9
Pederson, Sanna, 199
Perthaler, Caroline, 77, *78*
Petzoldt, Richard, 63
Phrase construction analysis,
  see Waldbauer-Riemann method
Piano concertinos, 187–188, 249, 252–253,
  274, *see also* Czerny, Carl; Kaskel, Carl
  von; Rosenhain, Jacques; Schumann,
  Clara
Piano concertos
  classical, 15–17
    double exposition, 16, 311n. 9

new forms, 134, 135–137, 169–173,
182–183, 197–201
orchestration, 135–137
virtuoso, 14, 17–21, 34
bravura, 134
changing affects, 93–94, 248
Mozart and Beethoven reception,
influence on, 74, 91
performance conditions, 21, 35
Schumann and, 110, 170–171,
186
Pianos
Erard, 112
early nineteenth-century, 113–114
Pleyel, 113
Piatigorsky, Gregor, 291
Piggott, Patrick, 100
Piltzing, Friedrich August, 3, 5
Pixis, Johann Peter
chamber music, 7
Concert Rondo (*Les trois clochettes,
Grand Rondeau brillant*), Op. 120,
121, 275
Fantasie militaire, Op. 121, 275
Parisian school, 17
Piano Concerto in C Major, Op. 100,
13, 37, 275, 315n. 12
form, 20, 44–45, 187
Variations and Rondo, Op. 20, 275
Plantinga, Leon
on the *Neue Zeitschrift für Musik*, 52
on Schumann, Concerto in A Minor,
269
on Schumann on chamber music,
241
on Schumann on Chopin, 104
on Schumann on Field, 173
on Schumann on Thalberg,
139–140
on Schumann's reviewing style, 67
Pleyel, Camilla
Beethoven C Minor Concerto
performed by, *79*, 90
Weber *Concertstück* and Mendelssohn
G Minor Concerto performed by,
178, 180
Pleyel, Ignaz Joseph, piano four-hand
variations, 2
Pohle, Christian Friedrich, 77, *78*
Pohle, Eduard, 288
Ponti, Michael, 146
Potter, Cipriani, 80, 86, 192
Praetorius, Carl, 4
Probst, Heinrich, 7, 202

Q

Queisser, Carl, 309n. 55

R

Rakemann, Louis, 208, 319n. 51,
327n. 40
Regondi, Giulio, *239*
Reich, Nancy B., 161, 166, 313n. 16
Reichold, Emilie, 8, 161, 311n. 6
Beethoven Concerto in E-flat Major
performed by, 311n. 2, 315n. 12
Ries Concerto in E-flat Major
performed by, 38, 42, 77, *78*,
309n. 55
Reinecke, Carl, 97, 146, 316n. 56,
318n. 20
Reissiger, Karl Gottlieb
chamber music, 7
performance in Leipzig, 77, *78*
piano four-hand works, 7
Rellstab, Ludwig, 83
Repertory formation, 91–92
Reuß-Köstritz, Heinrich II, Graf von, 209
Reynolds, Christopher, 303
Richards, Annette, 227
Richarz, Franz, 273
Richter, Johann Paul Friedrich (pseud. Jean
Paul), 207, 208, 212
Riemann, Hugo
analytical system, 22–23, 233
Stillstand auf der Penultima, 26
Ries, Ferdinand
chamber music, 7
Fantasie, Op. 77, 4
Piano Concerto in A Minor,
Abschiedsconcert von England,
No. 7, Op. 132, *78*
Piano Concerto in C Minor, No. 4,
Op. 115, 13, 21, 187
performed by Ries, 77, *78*, 97
Piano Concerto in C-sharp Minor,
No. 3, Op. 55, 13, 187
editions, 97
performed in Leipzig, *78*, 97
reception, 97, 110
recording, 312n. 24
Schumann on, 96–97
Schumann's possible modeling on,
42, 55, *55*
Piano Concerto in E-flat Major, No. 2,
Op. 42, 8, 13, 41, 42, 309n. 55
form, 42, 187

introduction to finale by Czerny,
332n. 46
orchestration, 21
performed in Leipzig, *78*
Schumann's possible modeling on,
38, 41, 42
Piano Concerto in G Minor, No. 9,
Op. 177, 91–92, 97–99
Fink's review of, 97–98
form, 98
motivic relationships, 94, 98, *99*,
104, 107
reception, 97
Schumann's review of, 97, 98–99,
170, *170*
style, 98–99, 104, 111, 134
piano concertos, *xii*, 37, 39, 62, 172,
184, 311n. 1, 315n. 13
classical model, 17–18, 20
piano four-hand works, 7
Rietz, Julius, 287, 303
Righini, Vincenzo, Overture to *Tigrane*, 4
Rink, John, 107, 108–110
Rode, Pierre
chamber music, 3
violin concerto, 7, 9
Roesner, Linda Correll, 326n. 34
Roitzsch, Ferdinand August, 97
Röller, Eduard, 6, 9
Romberg, Bernhard, *278*
Romberg, Cipriano, 251
Rosen, Charles, 38, 303
Rosen, Gisbert, 8, 9, 10
Rosenblatt, Jay, 242, *245*, 246, 330n. 56
Rosenhain, Jacques, 249–250
Concertino for Piano and Orchestra in
A Minor, Op. 30
form, 249, 274
Schumann's review of, 247, 248,
250
virtuosic style, 248, 250, 265
etudes, 250
Trio for Piano and Strings, Op. 2,
249–250, 330n. 47
Rossini, Gioachino, 52
Roßner, Johannes, 314n. 31
Rothstein, William, 233
hypermeasures, 26, 233
phrase rhythm, 21
Phrase Rhythm in Tonal Music, 22
suffixes, 16, 18, 235
Rubinstein, Anton, piano concertos,
246
Rückner, Carl Heinrich, 309n. 55

Rudorff, Ernst, 146
Rummel, Christian, piano four-hand works, 7

S

Sahr, Heinrich von, 306
Saint-Saëns, Camille, 297
Salaman, Charles, 130
Sallomon, Fanny, 80
Samson, Jim, 106–107
Scarlatti, Domenico, *239*
Schilling, Gustav, 221
Schladebach, Julius, 270
Schlegel, Johann Georg, 3, 4
Schleuning, Peter 227
Schloß, Sophie, *239*
Schmid, Manfred Hermann, 265
Schmidt, J. P., 317n. 68
Schmitt, Aloys, 171, 252
Hummelian school, 252
Piano Concerto in E-flat Major, No. 6,
Op. 76, 169, 171–173, 252
motivic relationships, 172–173,
172, 325n. 6
orchestration, 172–173
review of, 171–173, 252
piano concertos, 315n. 12
Rondeau brillant, Op. 101
Beethoven, compared to, 252
Field-like, 252
Schumann's review of, 247, 248
virtuosic style, 248
Schmitt, Jacques, 252
Piano Concerto, Op. 300
form, 249
Schumann's review of, 247, 248,
249
Schmittbach, Carl Ferdinand, 92
Schneider, Friedrich, 209
concertos performed by, 77, *78*,
315n. 12
Das Weltgericht, 2, 38
Schornstein, E. Hermann, 124
Piano Concerto in F Minor, No. 1,
Op. 1, 93, 317–318n. 8
Schumann's review of, 75, 93, 107,
170, 171, 172
student of Hummel, 75
Schröder-Devrient, Wilhelmine, 287
Schubert, Franz, 1, 11, 223
chamber music, 9
Chopin, compared to, 75
Fantasy in C Major, *Wandererfantasie*,
D. 760, 226, 227, 242

piano compositions, 53
piano four-hand works, 7
Piano Trio in E-flat Major, Op. 100,
  D. 929, 7
Schumann on, 207, 208
songs, 7
Symphony in C Major, *Great*, D. 944,
  100, 224
waltzes, 4
Schüler, Wilhelm, 274
Schultz, Clemens, 146
Schultz, J. R., 82–83
Schumann, Carl, 10
Schumann, Clara, 8, 92, 211, 212, 217, 306
  chamber concerts, 275
  on Mendelssohn, 198–199
  on Mozart performance, 86, 87
  performances
    Bach, fugues, 207–208, 327n. 34
    Bach, Triple Concerto in D Minor,
      208, *276*
    Beethoven, Concerto in C Major,
      280
    Beethoven, Concerto in C Minor,
      280
    Beethoven, Concerto in E-flat
      Major, *276*, 277, *278–280*, 280,
      287
    Beethoven, Concerto in G Major,
      276–277, 277, *278–279*, 280
    Beethoven, Sonata in C Major,
      Op. 53, 287
    Brahms, Concerto in D Minor, 280
    Chopin, Concerto in E Minor, 105,
      275
    Chopin, Concerto in F Minor, 238,
      239, 275, *276*, 277, *278*, 280
    Chopin, Variations, Op. 2, 121,
      275
    Field, Concerto in A-flat Major,
      41, 99–100, 275, 313n. 16
    Henselt, Concerto in F Minor, *276*,
      277, *278*
    Herz, Bravura Variations, Op. 20,
      121, 275
    Herz, Concerto in A Major, 51,
      313n. 1
    Herz, Variations, Op. 23 and 76,
      275
    Kalkbrenner, Concerto in A Minor,
      121, 312n. 36
    Kalkbrenner, *Rondo brillant*, 275
    Mendelssohn, *Capriccio brillant*,
      253, 275, *276*

Mendelssohn, Concerto in
  D Minor, *277*, 277, *278*, 280,
  281, 295
Mendelssohn, Concerto in
  G Minor, *276–277*, 277, *278*,
  280–281
Moscheles, Concerto in E-flat
  Major, 275
Mozart, Concerto in C Minor, 280
Mozart, Concerto in D Minor, 280
Pixis, Concerto in C Major, 275
Pixis, Concert Rondo (*Rondo
  brillant*), 121, 275
Pixis, *Fantasie militaire*, 275
Pixis, Variations and Rondo, 275
Schumann, *Andante* and
  Variations, 264–265, 332n. 42
Schumann, *Concert-Allegro*, xii,
  277–281, *278–279*, 292
Schumann, Concerto in A Minor,
  xii, 241, 266, 273, 280, 330n. 48
Schumann, Concerto in A Minor,
  1845 to 1856, 275, *276–277*,
  277, *278–280*, 280
Schumann, Concerto in A Minor,
  premiere, 270–271
Schumann *Introduction und
  Allegro appasionato*, xii,
  277–281, *278*, 280, 281–282
Schumann, *Papillons*, 71
Schumann, *Phantasie*, 228, 238,
  240
Schumann, Piano Quintet, 241,
  330n. 48
Schumann, Violin Concerto
  (as accompanist), 301
Schumann, Violin *Phantasie*
  (as accompanist), 298, 300
Thalberg, Concerto in F Minor,
  322n. 6
Thalberg, Fantasy on Themes from
  Moses, 238, *239*
Weber, *Concertstück*, 276, *276*,
  277, *278–279*, 280–281, 284,
  294–295
Wieck, Concerto in A Minor, *see
  under* Schumann, Clara, Piano
  Concerto in A Minor, No. 1, Op. 7
Piano Concerto in A Minor, No. 1,
  Op. 7, *xii*, 135, 160–166
  Becker's review of, 163, 165, 171,
    171, 173
  as concertino, 187–188, 249, 274
  editions, 162, 166

form, 137, 143, 162, 165–166, 171,
175, 221, 227, 297
motivic relationships, 163–164,
164
orchestration, 71, 136, 161, 264
performed by Clara Schumann,
136, 161, 164–165, 188, 215, 275
recordings, 166, 324n. 84
Schumann's reviews of, 161–162,
170, 188, 215
tonality, 162, 163
playing style, 125, 238, 265
programs with Robert Schumann, 273,
275–281, 282
on Schumann, 232–233
Schumann, Robert, relationship to
1840, 161, 162–163, 164–165, 188,
221, 223
songs, *239*
and Thalberg, 139
tours
to Berlin, 164, 275
to Paris, 71, 105, 113, 275
to Russia, 275
to Vienna, 165, 271, 275
as woman composer, 160–161, 163,
165, 166
Schumann, Eduard, 221
Schumann, Emilie, 3
Schumann, Eugenie, 300
Schumann, Friedrich August, 2, 4, 5, 6, 207
*Bildnisse der berühmtesten Menschen
aller Völker und Zeiten*, 6, 207
Schumann, Johanne Christiane, 2, 8, 10,
121
Schumann, Julius, 3–4
Schumann, Robert
Abegg Variations, Op. 1, 10
Allegro in B Minor, Op. 8, *239*
Allegro in C Minor, 221
"Älteste musikalische Erinnerungen,"
207
Andante and Variations for Two
Pianos, Op. 46, 264–265
Arabeske, Op. 18, 212
Bach reception, 200, 201, 206,
207–212, 217
on Beethoven, 75–76, 207, 208
Beethoven concertos
critical judgment, 88–90
exposure to, *xii*, 73–74
"Blätter und Blümchen aus der
goldenen Aue," 5, 207
Blumenstück, Op. 19, 212

Carnaval, Op. 9, 214, 328n. 75
Cello Concerto in A Minor, Op. 129,
xiii, 274, 288–291, 297
bravura, lack of, 290–291
cadenza, 291
chamber quality, 289, 291
form, 289–290, *290*
Neue Berliner Musikzeitung
review, 290
premiere, 288, 291
publication, 289
on chamber music, 241
"Das Clavier-Concert," *see under*
Schumann, Robert, piano concerto
review series
compositional models, 38–39
Concert-Allegro mit Introduction in
D Minor, Op. 134, *xii–xiii*, 273,
291–296, 297, *298*
bravura, *xiii*, 274, 294
cadenza, 293–294
dedication to Brahms, 295
Durchbruch, 294
form, 273–274, 292–293
inwardness, 296
motivic relationships, 274, 293,
293
orchestration, 274, 294, 296
performed by Clara Schumann, *xii*,
277–281, *278–279*, 292
publication, 292
reception, 273, 274, 292, 294,
296
references, 294–295, *295*, 296
Concert sans orchestre, Op. 14, 92
Concertsatz in D Minor, *xii*, 195–196,
197–198, 201, 202, 206–207,
212–222
Animato close, 213, 218,
219–220
Bach keyboard concertos as model,
200, 215–217, 218, *219–220*
bravura, lack of, 216–217, 222,
224, 329n. 7
compositional process, 212, 217,
221
form, 213, 221, 218, 222
intimacy (chamber music quality),
199, 217, 222
introduction, 220–221, *220*, 222
Mendelssohn D Minor Concerto as
model, 215
Moscheles *Pathétique* Concerto as
model, 215–216

motivic relationships, 213, *213*,
214–215, 222
orchestration, 217
phrase syntax (flow), 213–214,
214, 215, *216*, 218, 222,
328n. 81
scherzo, 221
Concertstück in F Major for Four
Horns, Op. 86, *xiii*, 274, 287–288,
297
compositional process, 287
difficulty, 288, 332–333n. 20
form, 287–288
orchestration, 287
premiere, 287–288
valve horns, 288
early literary endeavors, 5–6
early musical programs, 4–5
early public piano performances, 8,
9–10
as Eusebius, 161, 174
Fantasie, Op. 17, 214, 224,
226–227
Faschungsschwank aus Wien, Op. 26,
212
finger injury, *xi*, 71
as Florestan, 20, 331n. 18
Genoveva, 287
Grieg, influence on, 246
Humoreske, Op. 20, 212
improvisation, 3, 4, 7, 9, 10
institutionalization, 273, 277, 280,
292, 294, 300, 303
Introduction und Allegro appassionato
in G Major for Piano and Orchestra,
Op. 92, *xii–xiii*, 273, 281–286
bravura, lack of, 274, 281, 282,
286
form, 273–274, 283–286, *283*
motivic relationships, 282,
283–286, *284*
orchestration, 281–282, 283–286,
285
performed by Clara Schumann, *xii*,
277–281, *278*, *280*, 281–282
reception, 273, 274, 281–282, 286
symphonic nature, *xiii*, 282, 286,
297
tonality, 282–283, *283*, 285–286
Kinderszenen, Op. 15, 206, *206*, 213
Kreisleriana, Op. 16, 71
law study in Heidelberg, 8–9
"Leipziger Konzertnotizen von 1833,"
181–182

Litterarischer Verein, 5
Moscheles, plan to study with, 10, 41,
44
on Mozart, 75–76, 207, 208
Mozart concertos
critical judgment, 87–88, 90
exposure to, 73–74
music director in Düsseldorf, 298
Nachtstücke, Op. 23, 212
opera and overture beginnings, 38
Overture, Scherzo and Finale, Op. 52,
212, 223, 224, *276*, 328nn. 4, 73
Papillons, Op. 2, 71
performance on *Gymnasium* programs,
2–3, 4, 6, 307n. 6
Phantasie in A Minor for Piano and
Orchestra, *xi*, *xii*, 212, 222, 223–224,
228–242
cadenza, 224, 238
as chamber music, 241–242
compositional process, 224,
228–229, 248, 329n. 5
form, 151, 197, 229, 235–237,
329nn. 28, 30, 34
Liszt's concertos, compared to,
242–246
lyricism, 224, 232–33, 237, 238
motivic relationships, 224,
229–232, *230–231*, 329n. 32
orchestration, 224, 238–241, 246,
264
performed by Clara Schumann,
228, 238, 240, 247
phrase structure, 233–235, *234*,
236
publication attempts, 228,
247–248
relation to Schumann, Concerto in
A Minor, first movement,
228–229, 246, 264
and Schumann's D Minor
Symphony, 225
Phantasie in C Major for Violin and
Orchestra, Op. 131, *xiii*, 280, 295,
297, 298–300
form, 299–300
motivic relationships, 299, *299*
performances, 298
reception, 298
virtuosity, 300
Piano Concerto in A Minor, Op. 54
bravura, 270
compositional process, 248,
270

first movement, *xi, xii*, 196, 224,
see also Schumann, Robert,
Phantasie in A Minor for Piano
and Orchestra
form, 263
motivic relationships, 138
orchestration, 136, 242, 246, 297
performed by Clara Schumann,
see under Schumann, Clara,
performances
reception, 270–271, 281–282
reviews, 270–271
tribute to Hummel, 44
Piano Concerto in A Minor, Op. 54,
Intermezzo, *xii*, 263–267
bridge to finale, 265–267, *266*
compositional process, 264
form, 264
lyricism, 264–265
orchestration, 264
Piano Concerto in A Minor, Op. 54,
Rondo, *xii*, 263–264, 267–269
center of gravity, 267–268, 269
compositional process, 264
form, dramatic build, 248–249,
267–269
motives, 267, *268*
orchestration, 267
Piano Concerto in E-flat Major, 38
Piano Concerto in E Minor, 38
Piano Concerto in F Major, *xi*, 1, 10,
13–14, 35, 223, 232, 297
Chopin Concerto in F Minor,
compared to, 68
dedication, 44, 70, 313n. 24
Field Concerto in A-flat Major as
model, *41*, 41–42
Herz Concerto in A Major as model,
xi, 51, 53–61, *54, 55, 56*, 63
Hiller Concerto in F Minor,
compared to, 117–118
Hummel Concerto in A Minor as
model, *xi*, 44–49
last movement, 70–71
Moscheles Concerto in F Major as
model, *40*, 40–41, 49
performed by Schumann, 37, 51,
61, 62–63, 70
romantic style, 51–52, 61–63, 69
Piano Concerto in F Major, first
movement
development, 63
exposition, first version, 37–38,
39–43, *40, 41*, 49

exposition, second version, 37–38,
39–40, 41, 43–49, *45, 46–48*,
313n. 15
exposition, second version revised,
53–60, *54, 55, 56, 56–59*, 61,
314nn. 12, 13
recapitulation, 63–66, *64–66*, 267,
314n. 21
tutti, final, 66, *66*
tutti, first, 40–41, *40*, 62, 229
tutti, second, 43, 62
tuttis, 53, *54, 56*, 57, 61, 63, 123,
175
piano concerto review series, *xi–xii*, 91,
169–171, *170, 171*, 173, 247, 317n. 1
1837, 163, 188
1839 ("Das Clavier-Concert"),
135, 171, 197, 215, 217, 238–239
1840, 247
1843, 247, 249
piano concertos
armchair critic of, 111, 114–115,
118
features advocated, 195–196, 197
standards for, 139–140
piano four-hand works (early), 7, 38
piano practice, 8, 9–10, 112
Piano Quartet in C Minor, Op. V, 7,
38, 223
Piano Quintet in E-flat Major, Op. 44,
222, 223, 224, 241–242
programs with Clara Schumann, 273,
275–281, 282
Psalm No. 150, 4, 38
Quartett- and *Terzettabende*, 7,
309n. 49
Rubinstein, influence on, 246
Scenen aus Goethes Faust, 287
on Schubert, 207, 208
Schwärmbriefe, 170, 174, 208
"Selbstbiographische Notizen," 207,
307n. 2
Sketchbook I
charts, 53–57, *54, 55, 56*, 314n. 12
Concerto in F Major, first solo, 37,
43, *45*, 51
Concerto in F Major, first solo,
close, 57, *46–48*, 58–59,
314n. 13
Concerto in F Major,
recapitulation, *64–66*, 314n. 21
Sketchbook III, 327n. 37
F Major Concerto, exposition, 37,
40, 41, 43, 55, 57, 313n. 15

songs, 7, 38, 223, *239*, 328n. 1
string quartets, 223
student years in Leipzig, 7–8
study with Dorn, 208, 327nn. 37, 38
study with Wieck, 8, 10, 53, 112, 166
Symphonic Etudes, Op. 13, 71
symphonies, 223, 328n. 1
Symphony in B-flat Major, *Spring*,
No. 1, Op. 38, 212, 223, 224,
328n. 73, 328n. 3
performances, 238, *239*, 271,
276–277, 278
Symphony in C Major, No. 2, Op. 61,
277, 278, 280, 292
Symphony in D Minor, No. 4, Op. 120,
223, 224–225, 226, 232, 237,
328n. 3
first version, 212, 224,
328–329n. 4, 329n. 14
performances, *276, 278–280*
Symphony in E-flat Major, *Rhenish*,
No. 3, Op. 97, *278*, 292, 294
Symphony in G Minor, 71, 223
Toccata in C Major, Op. 7, 10
in Vienna, 212, 215, 221, 258, 271
Violin Concerto in D Minor, 297,
300–303
form, 301–302, *302*
performances, 300–301, 302
publication, 300
reception, 300–301
viability, 302–303
Von Pagen und der Königstochter, 278
Wieck, Clara, relationship to 1840,
161, 162–163, 164–165, 188, 221,
223
youth in Zwickau, *xi*, 1–7
Schumann, Therese, 114
Schuncke, Ludwig, Beethoven Concerto in
E-flat Major performed by, 77, *79*, 90,
144
Sedlak, Nina, 80
Shostakovich, Dmitry, 291
Siebeck, Karl Christian, 2, 3
Sobieski, Jan, 301, 333n. 16
Spohr Louis
chamber music, 9
Herz's borrowing from, *133*, 141
songs, 3, 7
Symphony in C Minor, No. 3, Op. 78,
317n. 3
violin concerto, 7
Stamaty, Camille, 136
friendship with Schumann, 114, 209

Piano Concerto in A Minor, Op. 2, *171*
performed by Stamaty, 114, 115
Schumann's review of, 112,
114–115
study with Mendelssohn and
Kalkbrenner, 114
Starker, Janos, 291
Steibelt, Daniel, 112
Steinberg, Michael, 291
Strackerjan, August, 298
Stradella, Alessandro, aria, 287
Strauss, Richard, *Tod und Verklärung*, 294
Strauss waltzes, 270
Stravinsky, Igor, *Petrushka*, 92
Strong, George Templeton, 142, 143
Struck, Michael, 294, 298, 302
Swoboda (harpist), 6

T

Täglichbeck, Johann Friedrich, 7
Taubert, Wilhelm,
Beethoven Concerto in C Minor
performed by, 77, *79*, 89–90
Concerto in E Major, Op. 18, 169, *170*,
173–174, 181–186, 325n. 25
Beethoven concertos as model,
181–182, 183, 186
cyclicism, 185–186
first movement, first solo, close,
183–185, *184*
form, 181, 182–183, 185–186,
227–228
Mendelssohn Concerto in G Minor
as model, 181, 183–184,
185–186
orchestration, 181, 183, 186
Schumann's reviews of, 75,
181–185
Tedesco, Ignaz, *79*, 81, 87
Thalberg, Sigismond, 124, 132, 197
Beethoven concerto performed by, 80
Fantasy on Themes from Rossini's
Moses, Op. 33, 238, *239*
friendship with Schumann, 139–140,
197
Herz's borrowing from, *133*, 141
Liszt rivalry, 139
Piano Concerto in F Minor, Op. 5, *xii*,
137–140, *170*, 197
form, 137–138, 170
motivic relationships, 135, 136,
137–138, *138*, 167, 215

orchestration, 136
    Schumann's review of, 138, 170,
        173, 215
    playing style, technique, 125, 136,
        137, 139–140, 202
    Schumann's reviews of various piano
        works, 139–140
Thibaut, Anton Friedrich Justus, 8, 207
Todd, R. Larry, 178–179
Töpken, Theodor, 9
Tovey, Donald Francis
    on Beethoven, Concerto in C Minor,
        303
    on Chopin concertos, 106–107,
        108
    on concertos, 136
        double exposition, 311n. 9
    purple patch, 33
    on Schumann, Cello Concerto, 289,
        291
    on Schumann, Concerto in A Minor,
        269
    on Schumann, *Introduction und
        Allegro appassionato*, 286
    on Schumann, Quintet, 241

V

Verhulst, Johann, 209
Vienna, Beethoven and Mozart concertos
    performed in, 77, 80–81
Vieuxtemps, Henri, *279*
Vogler, Georg Joseph (Abt), 317n. 3
Voigt, Henriette, 200, 209, 212
Vollaert, August, 2–3

W

Wagner, Richard, *Tannhäuser*,
    111–112
Waldbauer, Ivan F.,"Riemann's
    Periodization Revisited and
    Revised," 22
Waldbauer-Riemann method, 22, 22–25
    analyses
        Beethoven, Concerto in C Minor,
            24–26, *24–25*
        Chopin, Concerto in F Minor, 68,
            69–70, 109, 110
        Döhler, Concert in A Major, 119,
            120
        Field, Concerto in C Minor, 104

Herz, Concerto in A Major, 30–34,
    31–33
Hummel, Concerto in A Minor,
    26–28, *27–30*
Lasekk, Concertino *brillant* in
    C Major, 189, *190–191*
Schumann, Concerto in F Major,
    58–59, *58–59*
Walther, Hermann, 6
Watson, Henry Cood, 130, 142
Weber, Bernhard Anselm, *Der Gang nach
    dem Eisenhammer*, 3, 307n. 14
Weber, Carl Maria von, 1, 210
    Aufforderung zum Tanz, 2, 4
    chamber music, 7
    Concertino for Clarinet, 7–8
    Concertstück in F Minor for Piano
        and Orchestra, Op. 79, 173,
        294
        form, 135, 179
        performed by Clara Schumann,
            275, *276*, 277, *278–279*,
            280–281, 294–295
        performed by Liszt, Thalberg,
            Henselt, 180, 325nn. 22, 23
        performed by Weber,
            325n. 22
        program, 180
        Schumann's review of, 178
    Herz's borrowing from, *133*, 141
    piano concertos, 315n. 12
    piano four-hand works, 3
    Preciosa, incidental music, 4
    Schumann's plan to study with, 6
    Variations for Piano and Clarinet,
        Op. 33, 4–5
Weber, Friedrich, 9
Weber, Gottfried, 85, 87
Wendt, Matthias, 312n. 1
Wenke, Corina, 207
White, Richard Grant, 142
Wieck, Clara, *see* Schumann, Clara
Wieck, Friedrich, 9, 14, 41, 62–63, 77, 100,
    161
    on Chopin, 68, 105
    opposition to Clara and Robert, 162,
        165, 188, 221
    on performance of early piano music,
        86, 87
    Schumann's study with, 8, 10, 53, 112,
        166
    tour to Paris, 71
Wieck, Marianne, *see* Bargiel, Marianne
    Wieck

Wieck, Marie, 282, 330n. 53
Wiedebein, Gottlob, songs, 3, 9
Wild, Earl, 242
Wilke, C., 288
Wilms, Jan Willem, variations for flute and
   piano, 4–5
Winter, Robert, 113
Wolff, Hermann, 9

Wolfram, Joseph, 6
Wörlitzer, Friedrich, 8, 77, *78*, 309n. 55
Wüstenfeld, A., 9

Z

Zelter, Carl Friedrich, 206, 210, 327n. 52

MAV